# GRAPHICS PRIMER FOR THE IBM® PC

Mitchell Waite
Christopher L. Morgan

Osborne/McGraw-Hill
Berkeley, California

Published by
Osborne/McGraw-Hill
2600 Tenth Street
Berkeley, California 94710
U.S.A.

For information on translations and book distributors outside of the U.S.A., please write to Osborne/McGraw-Hill at
the above address.

Apple is a registered trademark of Apple Computer, Inc.
Atari is a registered trademark of Atari, Inc.
Cromemco is a registered trademark of Cromemco, Inc.
Microsoft is a trademark of Microsoft Corporation.
North Star is a trademark of North Star Computers, Inc.
Ping-Pong is a registered trademark of Harvard Table
    Tennis, Inc.
TI is a trademark of Texas Instruments, Inc.
TRS-80 is a trademark of Tandy Corporation.
VisiCalc is a registered trademark of Personal Software.
WordStar is a trademark of MicroPro International
    Corporation.

**GRAPHICS PRIMER FOR THE IBM® PC**

1234567890 DODO 89876543

ISBN 0-931988-99-3

Mary Borchers, Acquisitions Editor
Paul Hoffman, Technical Editor
Ted Gartner, Copy Editor
Nancy Benedict, Text Design
Yashi Okita, Cover Design
Irene Imfeld, Technical Illustrator

# CONTENTS

| | | |
|---|---|---|
| | Preface | v |
| **1** | IBM PC Graphics—A Quick Look | 1 |
| **2** | Graphics and Text Modes | 29 |
| **3** | Plotting and Line Drawing | 55 |
| **4** | Graphics Definition Language | 161 |
| **5** | Area Filling | 207 |
| **6** | Image Array Plotting | 257 |
| **7** | Custom and Graphics Characters | 299 |
| **8** | Special Programming on the Color/Graphics Adapter | 337 |
| **9** | Graphics on the Monochrome Display | 369 |

## Appendices

| | | |
|---|---|---|
| **A** | 3-D Rotations | 417 |
| **B** | ASCII Characters and Secondary Codes | 421 |
| **C** | Bibliography | 429 |
| **D** | Glossary | 431 |

## Index

438

# PREFACE

The IBM PC, with its extremely high-resolution screen and friendly, forgiving software, represents an entirely new breed of drawing machine. Unlike its predecessors, such as the Atari and the Apple computers, the IBM PC can control 128,000 independent pixels. This is twice the resolution of earlier machines, making the PC more than adequate for business and especially useful for engineering and scientific graphics. Compared to the six colors of the Apple II, the IBM excels in its color complement, allowing 16 *different* colors on the screen at one time.

To ease the programmer's efforts, the PC has a powerful yet easy-to-use graphics language that turns fledgling artists into modern Michelangelos and Rembrandts with the mere "stroke" of a few keys. At the same time, for the three-piece-suit, asphalt-jungle business world, the IBM PC excels in outputting forms, pie charts, bar graphs, and similar business graphics with a few keystrokes. The IBM PC can produce sophisticated computer aided design (CAD)—detailed schematics, floor plans, and engineering drawings—realistically on the screen.

The IBM PC is particularly suited for business graphics because of its wide variety of graphics characters (plus the ability to define your own custom characters), page flipping, line drawings, and its PAINT command.

This is the first book to explain all the concepts you need to create useful and effective graphics on the IBM PC. Using the popular *primer* format, the book is designed for beginners and professionals alike. In these pages, you will see how to create forms, drawings, charts, maps, animations, two-dimensional (2-D) scenes, and even three-dimensional (3-D) graphs which can be used in business, engineering, education, and recreation. As an extra bonus, this book reveals little-known secrets of graphics such as animation techniques, alternate hidden graphics modes, character graphics editing, "getting" and "putting" images, and the IBM graphics definition language.

Chapter 1 presents an overview of the graphics hardware and software of the IBM PC and concludes with a quick tour of some of the graphics statements (using a limited set of options on a limited set of commands). Chapter 2 provides detailed explanations of the text and graphics modes and shows you how to get into and out of each mode. Chapter 3 introduces your first drawing commands, explaining how to plot (PSET), erase (PRESET), construct lines, and use the flexible CIRCLE command. You will learn how to construct all kinds of bar and pie charts, as well as use 2-D and 3-D graphics techniques. The approach in this chapter, as well as in subsequent chapters, is to start small and grow more advanced within a constant format.

Chapter 4 explores the new IBM PC graphics definition language, or *GDL*. This is a feature containing commands for drawing on the screen with an imaginary cursor that you control. You can set the cursor's direction, heading, distance to move, rotation, scale, and so on. The GDL is similar in many ways to the popular *turtle graphics* found in languages such as LOGO.

Painting, filling, and flooding are the subjects covered in Chapter 5; Chapter 6 explores image array plotting with IBM's GET and PUT commands. In addition, you learn to do animation in this chapter. Chapter 7 covers custom and graphics characters. You learn how to write computer games in this mode, as well as develop business forms and even your own custom fonts. Chapter 8 covers special programming. It explores the inner world of the Color/Graphics Adapter and shows you how to define your own graphics modes. Chapter 9 explains the Monochrome Adapter.

This book is full-color to help you understand how the PC "works" its screen and to show you the color capability of this remarkable personal computer.

For each graphics command plenty of examples are provided to show you the syntax of the command and how to use each command to produce effective graphics on the IBM PC. In addition to short examples that emphasize the syntax of individual commands, there are longer examples that show you how to combine various graphics commands with each other and with nongraphics commands to produce useful results.

# IBM PC GRAPHICS — A QUICK LOOK

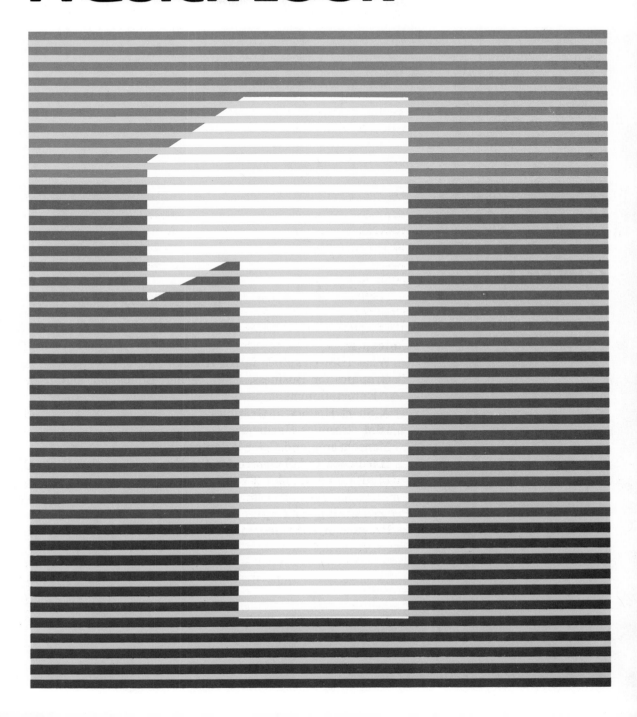

# CONCEPTS

**Concepts**
  What IBM Graphics Is All About
  Graphics for Business, Engineering, Education, and
    Entertainment
  A Short History of Graphics
  IBM Graphics Hardware
  Monochrome and Color Adapters
  Hardware and Software for the Examples in this Book
  Limitations of Color TV

**Programming Examples**
  Preview of IBM Graphics Commands

# INTRODUCTION

This chapter is an introduction to computer graphics in general and to IBM PC graphics in particular. It explains why computer graphics is so vital to today's personal and professional needs and how computer graphics relates to all major application areas of computing. More importantly, this chapter also provides an overview of the workings of the graphics hardware and software of the IBM PC. It discusses the features of the Color/Graphics and Monochrome Adapters, the basic concepts and limitations of color video, and the advantages of using an interactive high-level language such as IBM PC Advanced BASIC to create and control graphics output.

The chapter concludes with a preview of some of the most basic graphics commands in the IBM 640×200 high-resolution graphics mode. You will be shown a reasonably short and simple program that will help "bootstrap" your understanding of the PC's outstanding capability. This program is presented to let you get into the PC fast, without having to wade through lots of introductory lessons.

We begin with a discussion of the development and significance of computer graphics, giving a bit of the historical developments that led up to the IBM PC and its Color/Graphics Adapter.

**What's In a Name**

The name *computer graphics* conjures up images of two quite diverse fields. *Graphics* is the name that has been designated for the production of synthetic (designed and artificially produced) pictures for such fields as entertainment, advertising, business, medicine, education, scientific research, and engineering. The resulting pictures are also called graphics, and when good quality graphics are required, people called *graphic artists* are often called in. Using such specialists for every such picture is both expensive and time-consuming. A cost-effective alternative is to employ a *computer*—the other part of the name.

There is a definite need to automate the picture-making process, especially pictures that can be generated using a set of rules. But in many applications of computer graphics, businesses are using computers in numerous other ways, such as accounting and general scientific computing. These areas require general-purpose computers.

Now, if you were to design an ideal machine to generate graphics automatically, you would soon realize you were designing a rather general-purpose computer system with, of course, some extra bells and whistles such as a color TV monitor and a color printer.

Thus, it is clear that the name computer graphics quite adequately describes the important and useful process of the automated production of synthetic pictures.

It should be mentioned that automating graphics does not dehumanize it, nor does it make the production of graphics trivial. The computer can really only act as a powerful tool that extends our abilities, rather than cutting them off. With a computer's assistance, we are able to specify pictures of our own choosing, letting the computer execute these specifications at our will. The computer will repeatedly, without tiring or complaining, execute draft after draft of the picture. We can explore different placements, different perspectives, different colors, and the like until we are satisfied with the results.

A large number of people are directly involved in fields which require graphics, and nearly everyone is affected by the results. As computer graphics continues its phenomenal growth, more and more people will be affected, many in ways that they never dreamed of. The advent of the inexpensive personal computer is making most of this growth possible.

Computer graphics is becoming popular for less business-like pursuits as well. The movie *TRON* and the "Genesis" scene from *Star Trek II* are examples of how computer graphics has been used in the film industry. And Lucasfilms, the people who brought us *Star Wars*, has brought together some of the most talented people in computer graphics to work on new approaches to cinematography. Video arcades have led the way in bringing computer graphics technology to the public. Other examples of computer graphics in entertainment are the scoreboards at sports stadiums and portable video games that can be held in your hand (or even strapped to your wrist).

## OUR INTERESTED READER

This book is for the person who has had little or no prior experience with computer graphics or with graphics on the IBM PC. Although knowledge of the BASIC programming language is helpful when using the book, it is not necessary to understand BASIC to learn from the examples. The dozens of graphics examples are short enough to be typed into your own PC and run on the spot. You should have the PC-DOS booted up and BASICA loaded in drive A. Each example has a problem statement, a solution in the form of a program, a listing solution, and a color photograph showing the output on the screen when the program is run. By looking at our examples and studying the accompanying listings and photographs, it is quite possible to learn graphics away from the PC.

**Note:** We expect you to be aware of things like CPU and memory, and if you have had a course in high school algebra or trigonometry, some of the more advanced material will be easier to understand. Our goal is to make graphics fun to learn; consequently, we have designed the book to be easy to read sequentially from Chapter 1 to Chapter 9. Each chapter builds on the previous one's examples. The more advanced reader can, however, jump from chapter to chapter at will, choosing to learn the graphics concepts and commands of the IBM PC in any desired order.

## Examples of Computer Graphics

Examples of computer graphics abound. They range from playfields for video games to bar charts showing profits and losses, to elaborate models of DNA molecules. In this book we will show many more examples, including pie charts, two-and three-dimensional function plotting, 3-D figures with hidden lines removed, electronic symbols, figures for games, a computerized lesson, and two types of graphics editors.

## A Short History of Computer Graphics

Until fairly recently the practice of computer graphics has been restricted to special research laboratories and large scientific computing facilities. This was because the necessary equipment was quite expensive and somewhat old-fashioned. It was possible to find Tektronix storage tube machines at certain universities and industrial sites by the early 1970s, but they were often zealously guarded because they cost as much as a very expensive car (but unfortunately without equivalent performance). Then in the mid-1970s a hint of what was to come appeared in the flashing lights of the video arcades and in inexpensive, home video games. However, computer graphics did not become available to ordinary mortals until personal computers came on the market a couple of agonizing years later.

The Apple computer marked the turning point. It was perhaps the first computer that you could expect to operate with a minimum of fuss—just like an appliance. On top of that, it had several types of color graphics.

Apple computers spread through the land, along with other machines such as the TRS-80, the PET, and lesser-known varieties with names like IMSAI, SOL-20, Digital Group, North Star, Heathkit, Vector Graphics, Cromemco, and the like. Graphics components that you could add on to an existing system flourished too, such as CAT-100, Microangelo, SDI, HP, Bit Pad, and HPLOT. To put many of these systems together required either a large budget or a lot of tinkering, and even then many never functioned properly.

Although many people scoffed at these machines, calling them toy or hobby computers, others were putting a great deal of effort into making these computers workhorses of ordinary life. Many of these computers ended up gathering dust, many ended up gulping in tedious strings of numbers and spitting out columns of numbers in return, and many ended up as monuments to their owners' tenacity and skills in electronics. Others, however, were destined for greater things, such as writing books, generating educational displays, and teaching children the joys of computing.

In the late 1970s, new waves hit the beach, including those of ATARI and Texas Instruments. These machines could do fancier graphics than the Apple. The newer computers employed such techniques as sprites, players, missiles, and the like, which allowed a programmer to move shapes and figures independently over a fixed background. These computers straddled the fence between game playing and more serious pursuits. The "small is better" approach flourished with the introduction of the Osborne OS-1 and its imitators, as well as with the pocket-sized machines.

On the other hand, microcomputer companies like Altos, CompuPro, and Cromemco, which were growing larger and more powerful, thus began to challenge the midsized machines (minicomputers). Amazingly, all these types of personal computing machines that were being produced tended to do their jobs very well, finding their own niche in the ever growing and ever demanding marketplace.

As the hardware situation matured, software (that is, computer programs) began to take on the importance it deserved. Numerous word processing programs were developed, and new ideas about how to enter data into computers were developed with the advent of software products such as VisiCalc, a program that allows you to work with numbers in the setting of spread sheets. People started to buy computers because the software to do what they wanted was becoming available. Many of these people started to write useful programs, which then sold even more computers.

Into this raging billion-dollar war stepped IBM, the largest computer firm in the world. IBM introduced its machine, the IBM PC, in the summer of 1981. People expected the IBM PC to be old-fashioned and rigid. However, IBM's choice of the Microsoft team to supply much of the software and their choice of microprocessor and disks supplied by other manufacturers made it a young and exciting machine. For a product by such a large and well-established company, it was surprisingly compatible with the existing hardware and software in this so-called hobby market.

As its middle name implies, IBM built its machine to do useful work. And in addition, it had *color* graphics with its Color/Graphics Adapter, a special board installed in the machine and connected to a color TV or monitor. With this adapter came the possibility of a friendlier hardware environment for entry of data, and a much more expressive way to display the results of computations based upon that data.

A new era in *human factors* in computing is now opening up. Programs like spread sheets now have a colorful hardware environment in which they can work their magic. Much of the old software that worked on other machines has quickly been adapted to work on the IBM PC. Programs like Word-Star and VisiCalc and languages like Pascal, FORTRAN, and COBOL have appeared.

As you can see, computer graphics is a very large field. The IBM PC is uniquely designed to accommodate the high-resolution graphics described in this book. It can also use other graphics devices such as light pens, x-y plotters, graphics tablets, and joysticks to produce dynamic interactive graphics. The uses of these devices are beyond the scope of this book, but the interested reader can read about them in magazines that write about the IBM PC.

This book concentrates on just one language, IBM Advanced BASIC, or BASICA (pronounced BASIC-A). With this language you will easily be able to create a wide variety of pictures for whatever application you might have in mind.

# OVERVIEW OF PC
# HARDWARE AND SOFTWARE

Let's look at the IBM PC in terms of what you need to use this book effectively. We will discuss the configuration of the IBM PC that we used to develop our examples, and we will explain alternatives and variations.

To use this book you will need to have the Color/Graphics Adapter, but not necessarily the Monochrome Adapter.

This book explains the "softcopy" video displays—not pictures produced with plotters and other hardcopy devices. We will explain the Color/Graphics Adapter in Chapters 2 through 8, and the Monochrome Adapter in Chapter 9.

Both of these adapters consist of printed circuit boards you plug into the IBM PC. They connect to a video monitor, and both can be used to produce the main output for listing programs and displaying output data. The Monochrome Adapter requires a special nonstandard display monitor called the Monochrome Display Unit. The Color/Graphics Adapter can be connected to a variety of video monitors and TVs. The Color/Graphics Adapter produces a multicolor TV signal and the Monochrome Adapter produces a single color signal. We will explore other similarities and differences between these two adapters throughout the rest of this book.

It is possible to run the machine with either adapter or both adapters. You plug the adapters into slots on the main circuit board and set certain switches to let your machine know what it is carrying. These switches are inside the chassis. There is even a switch setting described in the IBM manual for the case of *no* adapters, but it is hard to see how that particular "combination" would be useful. How good is a general-purpose computer without any main output?

If you only have the Color/Graphics Adapter and you set the switches properly, your machine will show output on your color monitor. If you only have the Monochrome Adapter or if you have both adapters, the machine will output to the Monochrome Display Unit. (This is connected to the Monochrome Adapter.)

If you have both adapters installed, you will need to switch back and forth between them. With DOS 2 there is a simple way to do this using the DOS MODE command. If you are in DOS (not BASIC), then

MODE CO40

will switch the output to the Color/Graphics Adapter in the 40-column text mode, and

MODE MONO

will switch the output to the Monochrome Adapter. There are other possibilities with the MODE command such as CO80 for the Color/Graphics Adapter in the 80-column mode and BW40 and BW80 for the Color/Graphics Adapter in these two modes with the color disabled. In Chapter 9, we discuss a way to switch back and forth between the adapters while you are in BASIC.

When you turn on a machine that has this configuration, you should initialize both units. To do this, immediately switch over to the Color/Graphics Adapter. If you plan to work with the Monochrome Adapter, then you can switch right back. The reason it is a good idea to initialize both devices is that they both contain various circuits that are designed to oscillate at certain predictable frequencies. If they are not initialized, they will oscillate wildly, generating extra heat that could build up and damage some of the components on the adapters. These uninitialized signals can also damage the monitor attached to the adapter.

Although the basic model IBM PC doesn't include disk drives, this book was written for a machine that does have them. Either the single-density or double-density drives will do. We need the drives to support IBM Advanced BASIC. This BASIC takes up more memory, but is well worth it because of extra features such as CIRCLE, PUT, GET, PAINT, and DRAW, which are the subject matter of several chapters of this book. You will definitely need Advanced BASIC to enjoy and make proper use of this book.

Every example in this book was developed with 64K memory, so you will not need to purchase any extra memory to get the examples to work. There is no harm in having more memory, but there is no need for it to use this book.

To sum up, the minimum PC configuration needed to use this book consists of

- The Color/Graphics Adapter
- One single-density, floppy disk drive

- 64K of memory
- PC-DOS Operating System
- IBM Advanced BASIC.

**The Two Video Adapters**

Now let's look more closely at the two video adapters. We start with the Monochrome Adapter.

*Monochrome Adapter.* The Monochrome Adapter is a board that is installed inside the main computer enclosure. It works in conjunction with the Monochrome Display Unit, a special 12-inch TV monitor that has a long-persistence, green phosphor CRT, which gives a green color to the letters. The reason for the long-persistence phosphor is to reduce flicker, an annoying effect caused by visible oscillation of the intensity level of the image. The Monochrome Adapter produces a video signal with a slower scan rate than that of a standard TV. The IBM Monochrome Adapter scans at about 50 times per second through the picture, while the American TV standard is about 60 times per second. At this slower frequency, an image displayed using regular white phosphor will fade noticeably in between scans, and thus the image will appear to flicker. The green phosphor retains the light longer than a white phosphor and thus compensates for this slower scan rate.

In addition to the scan rate, there are other differences that make the IBM Monochrome Adapter incompatible with standard TV monitors. These include the fact that the horizontal and vertical synchronization signals are carried over separate wires instead of being combined with the main video signal.

The Monochrome Adapter produces a textual display of 80 characters horizontally and 25 characters vertically. It has only one mode. This Monochrome Display produces an excellent quality image, as shown in Figure 1-1. Each character is formed within a dot matrix which is 9 dots wide by 14 dots tall. Because of this, the Monochrome Adapter is better suited for word processing and extensive data entry applications.

*Color/Graphics Adapter.* The Color/Graphics Adapter produces a standard video signal. It can be hooked up to a TV or monitor in three different ways.

1. You can use an ordinary TV through an RF NTSC modulator which you can buy (these terms are defined

**Figure 1-1**

Single Character on the Monochrome Adapter

in the section "Limitations of Color Video"). This provides the poorest image.

2.  You can use an output from an RCA-type phono plug to directly drive the video input of an NTSC color or black-and-white video monitor. This gives a better image.

3.  You can connect an output from a 9-pin "D" shell connector to a special TTL RGB color monitor. This gives the best image.

In addition to being listed in order of excellence of image, these three methods are listed in increasing order of expense. We will discuss some of the subtleties involved in this video magic later in this chapter.

The Color/Graphics Adapter has two supported text modes and two supported graphics modes. It is possible to print text in all four modes, although the machine carries this out by quite different methods, as we shall see in Chapter 7. Of the text modes, there is a lower-resolution and a higher-resolution mode, and the same is true for the graphics modes. The lower-resolution modes for both text and graphics have 40 characters horizontally, and the higher-resolution modes for both text and graphics have 80 characters across the screen. The number of characters horizontally across the screen is related to the horizontal size of the characters and is a good measure of the resolution of the particular mode. See Table 1-1 for a list of these modes.

The lower-resolution modes (text and graphics) are designed for use with a color TV using the RF modulator or

**Table 1-1**

Supported Modes of the Color/Graphics Adapter

| Mode | Text/Graphics | Horizontal Resolution | Vertical Resolution | Characters per row | Number of rows of characters | Number of pixels | Color |
|---|---|---|---|---|---|---|---|
| Low-resolution text | Text | 40 | 25 | 40 | 25 | | 16 foreground<br>8 background<br>16 border |
| High-resolution text | Text | 80 | 25 | 80 | 25 | | 16 foreground<br>8 background<br>16 border |
| Medium-resolution text | Graphics | 320 | 200 | 40 | 25 | 64,000 | 3 foreground<br>16 background |
| High-resolution | Graphics | 640 | 200 | 80 | 25 | 128,000 | Black-and-white |

NTSC color monitor. In both of these cases, the electronics are just not good enough to support much more resolution; but by restricting the display to 40 characters across, we get a very readable display. Almost all the examples in the book (except for those which especially illustrate the high-resolution modes) are kept to this shorter line length.

Both text modes allow you to color each character on the display separately. In fact, the foreground of each character can be given one of 16 different colors and the background one of eight colors. In addition, the characters can be individually put into blinking or nonblinking modes. The "secret" lies in the fact that each character position is assigned a special 8-bit number to control the color and blinking "attributes" of the character in that position. We will look at this more carefully in Chapter 7.

The lower-resolution graphics mode (usually called the medium-resolution graphics mode) is the main mode used in this book. Although we call the resolution low or medium, it has 320 dots (pixels) horizontally by 200 dots vertically, giving a total of 64,000 individually controllable dots on the screen. Each dot on the screen can be assigned one of four different colors. For this reason we sometimes refer to this mode as the colorful mode. In Chapter 2 we will give it a more detailed discussion.

The higher-resolution modes (both called high-resolution) produce a display that is quite readable if a black-and-white

TV monitor is used instead of a color monitor. The NTSC output (either through the RF modulator or direct video) for both the text and the graphics high-resolution modes is black-and-white signals.

The higher-resolution graphics mode has a nice horizontal resolution of 640 dots and a respectable vertical resolution of 200 dots. That is 640×200, or 128,000 dots altogether on the screen. However, there are only two "colors" for each dot: black or brightly lit. This is all that can be done with a total of 16K of memory for the screen.

For all four modes, there are 25 characters vertically. Given this same vertical packing, it is interesting to see how much the horizontal squeezing and unsqueezing of characters dominates the readability of the characters.

## Limitations of Color Video

What makes color video tick? In particular, why can't you get more resolution out of a color TV than the IBM PC does? You must remember that black-and-white TV came first and then color was added. Because of this, there had to be special adjustments to make sure that black-and-white TVs would still work the same.

Let's start by looking at how the picture is produced on a TV or video monitor (see Figure 1-2). For standard broadcast TV, an electron beam constantly sweeps across the face of the picture tube in a *raster scan* pattern. In this pattern, the

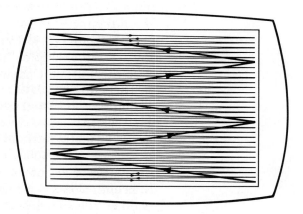

**Figure 1-2**

Raster Scan

beam begins at the upper left corner of the tube (or top center), sweeping horizontally across the tube toward the right. During this left-to-right motion, it makes one *scan line* of the picture by shooting out electrons that light up the phosphor on the face of the tube.

When the beam reaches the right side of the tube, it reverses its direction and travels back to the left side of the picture tube. During the right-to-left return trip, the electron beam shoots out only a few electrons, and it travels at a much faster rate of speed. This is called *horizontal retrace*. As the beam sweeps back and forth, it gradually moves down. Thus, each scan line it produces is slightly lower than the previous scan line. The beam travels more than 200 scan lines in this manner before it reaches the bottom of the picture tube. When it reaches the bottom, it quickly moves to the top again, to begin the whole trip over. This quick bottom-to-top return trip is called *vertical retrace*.

On a standard TV, every second trip through the raster scan pattern is slightly different from the first in that it produces scan lines in between those of the first trip, thus achieving what is called an *interlaced* pattern. Each trip through the raster is called a *field*. With an interlaced display, two fields form a *frame* to make a complete picture. Standard TV presents us with two slightly different pictures of two interlaced fields that form a complete picture. The interlacing produces twice the resolution possible with just one field per frame. However, most computer-generated frames do not take advantage of the extra resolution brought about by interlacing, but rather give the same picture for the two different fields.

The reason for the difference in interlacing between standard TV and computer-generated displays is that computer-generated pictures have a high degree of contrast from one point to another, while ordinary broadcast pictures usually blend smoothly from one point to another. In a normal interlaced display, the fields of a picture are drawn at a rate of about 60 per second. But since it takes two fields to complete a picture, any particular dot on the screen is redrawn only about 30 times a second. If the dot is brightly lit and the adjoining dots are not, it will most likely appear to flicker. If a pixel contains a pair of dots, one in each field, it will be redrawn twice as often and have considerably less flicker. In other words, since there is so much contrast in a computer-generated picture, interlacing would cause flickering. Hence, it is not normally used to gain increased vertical resolution. We have already discussed how the choice of a long-persistence green phosphor for the Monochrome Display Unit helps reduce flicker. Long-persistence phosphors for color monitors are now available.

It should be noted that most TVs overscan the picture; that is, the scan lines extend both to the left and to the right of the visible part of the picture tube. Thus, you never see all of what is being sent to the TV receiver. Overscan is acceptable for ordinary TV pictures, but not for most computer-generated displays. The reason that broadcast TV overscans is because the picture may tend to shrink as the components in a TV age. If the picture was not originally larger than the screen (that is, overscanning it), the picture could shrink enough to cause ugly borders to appear.

## Broadcast Video Signals

Now let's look at the broadcast video signals that drive such displays. We start with black-and-white broadcast TV. The black-and-white TV signal consists of several components: the *horizontal synchronization signal*, the *vertical synchronization signal*, and the *luminance signal*, which carries information on the proper intensity for the beam as it scans the dots on the screen. The TV receiver uses the synchronization signals to set up its *raster scan* pattern on the face of the picture tube. The horizontal and vertical synchronization signals separately coordinate the horizontal and vertical motion of the beam to achieve the proper pattern. The intensity signal is also carefully synchronized with the synchronization signals to make the dots appear precisely where they should on the screen.

There is a standard called *RS-170* for combining these synchronization and intensity signals into one signal for black-and-white TV. With this standard, there are exactly 525 lines displayed on the screen in an interlaced pattern. Because of the vertical retrace, only about 480 lines are available for display. This is the effective limit on the vertical resolution of the picture, although, because of flicker, you normally have to settle for half of this, or 240 lines.

To add color, another signal is needed. This signal is called the *chrominance*. It actually carries two kinds of color information: *hue* and *saturation*. Hue is what you usually call "color," such as blue, red, green, and so on; while saturation is the "degree" of color, that is, the brilliance of the color. If you add white to a "pure" color, it will appear less saturated. Most color TVs have a hue control knob to adjust the hue and a color control knob which adjusts the saturation. If you turn the color control all the way down, you get a black-and-white picture, and if you turn it all the way up, the picture appears garish. The chrominance signal is assigned a special frequency of 3.579 million cycles per second within the total TV signal channel. This is called the color *subcarrier frequency*. Incidentally, fractional multiples of this frequency are used within the IBM PC to synchronize the clocks that control its CPU and memory activity.

Before the beginning of each line on the screen, there is a special alignment time period in which the color subcarrier is produced. This is called the *color burst*. The color of the dots on the following line is determined by comparing the chrominance signal against the standard frequency set up by this color burst. A phase shift (a slipping ahead or behind) causes a change in hue and a change in amplitude causes a change in saturation. Because the phase shift is so hard to control, the hue varies widely from one TV to another and needs to be carefully adjusted.

The standard for sending color video signals in the United States is called NTSC, which stands for National Television Standards Committee. Because of the difficulties in getting the hue just right, some people refer to this standard as Never Twice the Same Color.

Now let's look at a definite limitation of the NTSC standard when it sends pictures generated by a computer. This limitation is caused by the frequency of the subcarrier. Changes in color cannot effectively be made faster than the frequency of this subcarrier. This is a real limitation. A careful computation will show that there are exactly 227.5 cycles of the color subcarrier for each line of the display. Thus, the horizontal color resolution cannot be greater than this number. However, only some of these cycles are available in the display itself because some of these cycles occur during times when the beam is not active, such as while it is "retracing" (moving back from the right side of the screen to the left in preparation for the next line).

With the IBM PC there are exactly 160 cycles of this color subcarrier that occur while the beam is actively scanning a line. Since you cannot change information faster than its carrier frequency, you are limited to 160 valid color changes per line of the screen. We say that we have 160 *color clocks* per line. The horizontal resolution in the medium-resolution color graphics mode is twice that, namely 320. Thus, we have a dot resolution that is *twice* the color resolution. This leads to some very interesting effects which we will explore in Chapter 8.

This discussion of the limitations of color video has shown how NTSC color transmission restricts the amount of information a computer can put on an NTSC color screen. The IBM PC also supports RGB transmission, which eliminates most of these restrictions. However, since IBM decided to support *both* types of transmission, the NTSC restrictions are the dominant factor in limiting the graphics resolution on the IBM PC.

## Advantages of Using BASICA

As noted earlier, all our examples and detailed discussions use IBM Advanced BASIC (or BASICA as it's called in the directory). Let's explore why this is such a good choice for graphics.

The history of BASIC is well known. It was invented at Dartmouth College to be a computer language that was easy to learn and easy to work with. It is normally implemented as an *interpreter;* that is, you can edit and run programs within the same working environment. Thus, it presents a very friendly system to work with.

The IBM BASICs, including BASICA, were developed by Microsoft, Inc. Microsoft has supplied BASICs for a number of other machines. For example, it developed Applesoft for the Apple computer. All of these Microsoft BASICs have certain standard extensions to the minimal BASIC which was originally developed at Dartmouth. Thus, BASICA represents a standard.

Once you have graphics hardware such as the IBM Color/ Graphics Adapter, you need to be able to make that hardware perform. The first task is to make it plot points. You could write a BASIC subroutine to do this, but that would have several disadvantages: the performance would be poor, extra code would be needed, extra variables would be used, and your main program would be much less readable.

Fortunately, Microsoft has incorporated the point plotting commands, PSET and PRESET, into BASICA. These commands are encoded in machine language for increased efficiency and they are easy to use—just write the command in one line of code with some numbers and the point will appear on the screen whenever that code is executed.

| | |
|---|---|
| CIRCLE | PAINT |
| CLS | PRESET |
| COLOR | PSET |
| DRAW | PUT |
| GET | SCREEN |
| LINE | WIDTH |
| LOCATE | |

**Figure 1-3**

BASICA Graphics Commands

Once you can plot points, you need to draw lines. This is surprisingly difficult to do in BASIC if you want any reasonable speed. Again, line drawing was built into BASICA by Microsoft. Next, you would want to be able to plot characters. Fortunately, the PRINT statement works in all modes, so you can label your drawings. Thus, BASICA has the most essential graphics commands already built into its command structure.

Using just points, lines, and text, you can draw almost any picture, at least in wire frame or outline form. To fill in areas of color it would be nice to have a paint command. Again, this has been supplied by Microsoft. In fact, as we shall see as we explore the pages of this book, Microsoft has added a complete set of graphics commands that allows you to bring about extensive, useful graphics activity in response to a few simple commands. (These commands are listed in Figure 1-3.)

It is important to realize what power these graphics commands bring you. Very simply, if it is hard to do something (such as filling an area or drawing a circle), then it will be done infrequently. If a particular task is made ten times easier, it probably will be done ten times more often, thus increasing productivity by that much. This is one of the key principles behind the computer revolution.

## Saving BASICA Programs

To develop and run your programs on the IBM PC, you must first enter the IBM PC's Advanced BASIC. The easiest way to do this is to make sure you are in DOS and that you have the file BASICA.COM on the disk in drive A. Then type

BASICA

and the Advanced BASIC will sign on. To add a line to your program (this goes for the first line of your program as well), just type it in with its line number. BASICA will insert it where it belongs in your program. To delete a line, just type its line number and the line will disappear from your program. You should read the *IBM PC BASIC* manual to learn how to use the INSERT, DELETE, and cursor keys to edit your program efficiently. To save your program type

SAVE "filename"

where *filename* is a name that you want to give your program as it is stored on the disk. You should back up your program by saving it on a second disk as well. If you have a second drive (drive B), make sure there is a formatted disk in it and type

SAVE "B:filename"

using the same *filename* as before. Whenever you need the program again, type (from BASICA)

LOAD "filename"

The example programs in the beginning of Chapters 3 through 6 are written to be parts of longer programs. More explicitly, for each of these chapters, the first few examples are called lesson examples because they deal with the syntax of the commands. They are meant to be part of a program called CnLESSON, where *n* is the chapter number. Before you start with the lesson examples for a given chapter you must type in a few beginning lines and a couple of common subroutines. Nonoverlapping line numbers allow you to enter all the lesson examples for a given chapter one by one without destroying any previous line. At any time, you can save what you have entered so far by typing

SAVE "CnLESSON"

where *n* is the chapter number (3 through 6). Don't forget to back it up on a second disk. When you have finished entering in all the lesson example programs for that chapter, you will have a program that allows you to quickly flip through the lessons for that particular chapter. This method saves disk space (the bytes are more tightly packed on the disk) and time (fewer disk accesses).

## Advanced BASIC Version 2

With DOS 2 has come an improved version of Advanced BASIC that we will call BASICA 2. This new version of Advanced BASIC is supplied on one of the floppy disks that you receive when you buy DOS 2.

BASICA 2 has a number of distinct advantages over previous versions (BASICA 1.0 and 1.1, or BASICA 1 for short) for drawing graphics. In particular, there are two new commands, WINDOW and VIEW, to help you "size up" your picture to the screen. These commands make it very easy for you to "zoom" and "pan" a picture as well as put several pictures on the screen at once. (We will discuss how this is done in Chapter 3.) The LINE command allows you to plot dashed or dotted lines, as well as other styles. There are also two new options to the DRAW command, providing you with better ability to "drive around the screen" by turning at any angle and to "paint" as you "drive." The PAINT command itself now has the ability to "tile" or paint with a texture.

This book is designed to work for both BASICA 2 and BASICA 1 in that the majority of example programs will work for both versions. There are two exceptions. The first is programs that explicitly illustrate the new options of LINE, DRAW, and PAINT. These programs cannot be modified to work under BASICA 1. A second exception is the programs in the second half of Chapter 3 that use the new WINDOW and VIEW commands, programs in Chapter 5 that paint the pictures developed in Chapter 3, and programs that use "bugs." However, all programs of the second type can be modified (as we will indicate) to work with BASICA 1. In fact, we originally developed these programs under BASICA 1 without the benefit of the nice new commands and options of the new version of BASICA.

One thing that this book does not cover is the use of assembly language to do graphics. There are at least two reasons for this. First, IBM has supplied a very rich graphics structure within its Advanced BASIC, allowing the user to easily do many of the things that in the past have required assembly language. Second, we have tried to keep this book at the primer level, aiming for those whose training and inclinations do not necessarily include assembly language. Nevertheless, it is possible to use assembly language routines to do graphics on the IBM PC and it is possible to "call" such routines from BASICA by using the CALL and USR commands in BASICA.

# PREVIEW OF
# THE GRAPHICS COMMANDS

Now let's have a quick preview of some of the most basic graphics commands in the IBM black-and-white 640 × 200 high-resolution graphics mode. We will look at a short and simple program that will help "bootstrap" your understanding of the PC's outstanding capabilities. This program is presented to let you get into the PC quickly.

We will use the commands SCREEN, KEY OFF, CLS, PSET, and LINE. We will give a quick explanation of what each does and then look at a simple program that uses the commands to produce a mandala pattern with a title in large letters in the center.

We start with the SCREEN command. Its simplest syntax is

SCREEN mode

where *mode* is an expression whose value is 0, 1, or 2. In this form, this command selects the mode. The two text modes are both designated by 0 (you will have to use the WIDTH command to go between them); the medium-resolution graphics mode is indicated by 1; and the high-resolution graphics mode is indicated by 2. In our first example, we want the high-resolution mode (mode 2). The syntax for this command is

SCREEN 2

When this command is executed, the screen will configure itself into the high-resolution mode.

The KEY OFF command is used to remove the special function key display at the bottom of the screen. Our pictures will look a lot nicer without this function key display. The syntax for this command is simply

KEY OFF

There is a command to turn the function key back on. As you might have guessed, it is KEY ON. When the KEY OFF command is executed, the display immediately disappears.

The next command is CLS. This stands for clear screen, and that is what it does. If the SCREEN command actually caused us to *change* modes, the screen would be cleared automatically. However, if we were already in high-resolution mode and the SCREEN 2 command were executed to put us in high-resolution mode, the screen would not be cleared. Thus, we need the CLS to clear the screen. The syntax is simply

CLS

When this is executed, the screen will be set to the background color. (See Chapter 2 for a discussion of background and foreground colors.)

Now we get to the commands that actually draw things.

The PSET command is used to draw points, and the LINE command is used to draw lines (actually line segments). As we will use it in this chapter, the PSET command has the following syntax:

PSET (x,y)

where $x$ and $y$ are BASIC expressions that specify the $x$ and $y$ coordinates of the point to be plotted. In the high-resolution mode, the possible values for $x$ range from 0 to 639 and the possible values of $y$ range from 0 to 199 with the point (0,0) in the upper-left corner of the screen. This gives us access to any point in the 640 horizontal by 200 vertical screen.

We will use two forms of the LINE command in this chapter. The first one

LINE (x1,y1)—(x2,y2)

draws a line from the point $(x1,y1)$ to the point $(x2,y2)$. The second form

LINE —(x2,y2)

draws a line from the *current position* (last point plotted) to the point $(x2,y2)$. In either case, the quantities $x1$, $x2$, $y1$, and $y2$ are expressions in BASIC. The second form is very handy when we want to draw a path consisting of several line segments.

Now let's look at an example which shows how to use these commands to make a design.

EXAMPLE 1-1

## MANDALA

Draw a mandala with the title "IBM PC" in the center in
large letters. There should be a dotted border around this
title. Use just a few commands including the simplest
forms of the LINE and PSET commands. The output of
this program is shown in Figure 1-4.

## Solution

```
100 ' MANDALA
110 '
120 ' This program draws a mandala
130 ' and then prints the title
140 ' "IBM PC" in the center with
150 ' large letters.
160 '
170     SCREEN 2 ' high res graphics
180     KEY OFF
190     CLS
200 '
210     FOR I = 0 TO 20
220       X1 = 32*I
230       X2 = 640 - 32*I
240       Y1 = 10*I
250       Y2 = 200 - 10*I
260       LINE (X1,0)-(640,Y1)
270       LINE (X1,200)-(640,Y2)
280       LINE (X2,0)-(0,Y1)
290       LINE (X2,200)-(0,Y2)
300     NEXT I
310 '
320 ' border of points
330     FOR X = 160 TO 480 STEP 8
340       PSET (X,70)
350       PSET (X,130)
360     NEXT X
370 '
380     FOR Y = 70 TO 130 STEP 4
390       PSET (160,Y)
400       PSET (480,Y)
410     NEXT Y
420 ' the letter I
430     LINE (200,80)-(200,120)
440     LINE (192,80)-(208,80)
450     LINE (192,120)-(208,120)
460 '
470 ' the letter B
480     PSET (248,100)
490     LINE -(256,104)
500     LINE -(256,116)
510     LINE -(248,120)
520     LINE -(224,120)
530     LINE -(224,80)
540     LINE -(248,80)
550     LINE -(256,84)
560     LINE -(256,96)
570     LINE -(248,100)
580     LINE -(224,100)
590 '
600 ' the letter M
610     PSET (280,120)
620     LINE -(280,80)
630     LINE -(296,88)
640     LINE -(304,88)
650     LINE -(320,80)
660     LINE -(320,120)
670 '
680 ' the letter P
690     PSET (360,120)
```

▶

# Example 1-1

## Solution, Continued.

```
700    LINE -(360,80)            830    LINE -(424,80)
710    LINE -(384,80)            840    LINE -(440,80)
720    LINE -(392,84)            850    LINE -(448,84)
730    LINE -(392,96)
740    LINE -(384,100)
750    LINE -(360,100)
760    '
770    ' the letter C
780    PSET (448,116)
790    LINE -(440,120)
800    LINE -(424,120)
810    LINE -(416,116)
820    LINE -(416,84)
```

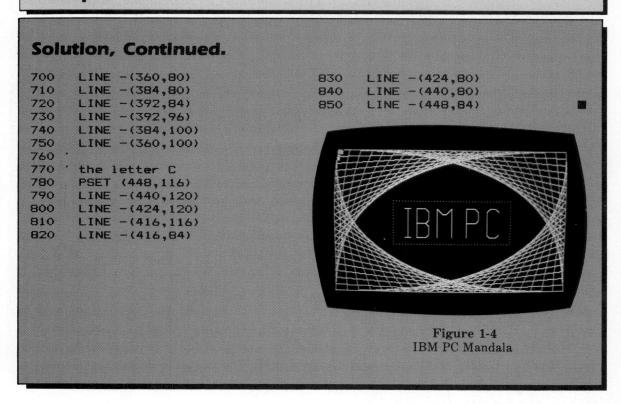

Figure 1-4
IBM PC Mandala

In lines 170-190, we use the SCREEN, KEY OFF, and CLS commands to make sure that the screen is initialized (that is, it is in the right mode and is erased). Then we use a combination of the PSET and LINE commands to draw our picture.

The most intricate part of the picture is a mandala effect around the outside of the screen. However, it turns out that this is very easy to do and is one of the smallest sections of the program. The mandala is achieved with the first form of the LINE command. We just march the end points of the line around the boundary of the screen. The FOR loop in lines 210-300 controls this.

Lines 320-410 show what you can do with the PSET command. Here we use it to make a dotted border around a title which will soon appear. Two FOR loops are needed here, one for the horizontal sides of the border, and one for its vertical sides.

The last section, lines 420-850, draws the title. This is the longest section because each stroke of each letter is individually encoded with a separate LINE command. Notice how the PSET command is used to set the current position before a series of LINE commands (in the second form) is used to trace out the letter. The current position is a hidden graphics cursor, secretly pointing to where you are as you draw. Each command in this section advances this cursor to a new current position. The PSET commands advance it without drawing, and the LINE command advances it, drawing at the same time.

This section of the program points out what happens when you don't have a certain advanced graphics capability. In this case the IBM PC does not have variable-sized lettering. If it did, the whole section could be done in three easy statements: one to define the size of the lettering, a second to specify the position of the lettering, and a third to specify the string of characters to be printed and initiate the printing. This would be a considerable savings in programming effort and would make the program much more compact.

Although the IBM PC does not have this particular graphics capability, the many graphics commands and capabilities that it does have will definitely give you the kind of savings we have indicated here. Also, someone could write a package of assembly language routines to do variable-sized lettering.

# CONCLUSION

In this chapter we have begun our journey through the world of IBM PC graphics. We have seen how computer graphics has its roots in both the graphic arts and the personal computer revolution, and we have seen how the IBM PC represents part of a natural development in the midst of the personal computer revolution. Indeed, it represents a very fortunate step toward bringing colorful graphics within the grasp of the average person.

We have also presented a quick overview of the hardware and software you need to enjoy and make the most of this book. In particular, we discussed the Color/Graphics Adapter on the hardware side and IBM Advanced BASIC on the software side. These are the two most important tools to take us through most of the rest of our journey.

In Chapter 2, we will discuss the technical details of the various text and graphics modes. In Chapter 3, we will explore the various point plotting, line drawing, and circle drawing commands. In Chapter 4, we will explore the DRAW command, which is used for drawing various shapes. In Chapter 5, we will explore painting areas of the screen. In Chapter 6, we show how to save parts of the screen into arrays and then PUT these images wherever we want on the screen. In Chapter 7, we will explore the production and use of text in graphics both in the text and graphics modes. In Chapter 8, we will delve into the depths of the Color/Graphics Adapter and its video controller chip. Finally, in Chapter 9, we will take a close look at the Monochrome Adapter and what can be done with it.

# GRAPHICS AND TEXT MODES

# CONCEPTS

**Concepts**
　Text and Graphics Modes
　Memory Mapping
　Extended ASCII Code
　Attributes
　Foreground, Background, and Border Colors

**Commands**
　SCREEN
　CLS
　WIDTH
　COLOR

# INTRODUCTION

This chapter explores the various text and graphics modes on the Color/Graphics Adapter card. The low-resolution and high-resolution text modes and the high-resolution and medium-resolution graphics modes are introduced and explained. The BASIC commands SCREEN, CLS, WIDTH, and COLOR are introduced and thoroughly explained. With these commands you will be able to obtain each mode and the various features within it.

# TEXT MODES

As we briefly discussed in Chapter 1, there are two text modes: a low-resolution text mode with 40 characters horizontally and 25 characters vertically, and a high-resolution text mode with 80 characters horizontally and 25 characters vertically. Both have the same vertical resolution, but the high-resolution text mode has twice the horizontal resolution. Since text is arranged in rows and columns, we can refer to these modes by the maximum number of rows and columns they hold, instead of the total number of horizontal and vertical character positions. We will not mention the number of rows, however, since both modes have the same number. Thus, we will often refer to the low-resolution text mode as the *40-column text mode* and the high-resolution text mode as the *80-column text mode*.

The 40-column low-resolution mode is designed for a color display, while the 80-column high-resolution mode is designed for a black-and-white display. However, both modes have the same provisions for producing individually colored letters. Later, we will see how to turn the color on and off as we please in both modes, but first let's see how to get into the text modes.

## SCREEN Command

The SCREEN command will allow us to select the mode (text in our example). The full syntax for this command is

SCREEN [mode] [,burst] [,[apage] [,[vpage]]]

Square brackets around a quantity indicate that the quantity is optional. Any parameter that is omitted will retain its previous value. For this command, it seems that all quantities are optional. This is not actually true, for if you type in just the key word SCREEN, the machine will respond with the error message "Missing operand."

In the syntax of the command, *mode* indicates the mapping mode according to the following:

0 = Text mode
1 = Medium-resolution graphics mode
2 = High-resolution graphics mode

We use mode 0 (text) in our first example. Notice that both the 40-column and 80-column text modes are assigned this same mode numerical code. That is why we will need the WIDTH command to select which of the two text modes we want.

The next parameter, *burst*, indicates whether or not the color is turned on. Sometimes you may want to turn off the color to improve the readability of the display. A value of 0 specifies black-and-white only, while a value of 1 specifies the presence of color. The word "burst" refers to a special alignment burst at the beginning of each horizontal line of the picture. Without that burst, there can be no color.

We will not discuss the parameters *apage* and *vpage* in this chapter. They will play an important role in Chapter 7 when we use them for page flipping. As a result, the simplified syntax of the SCREEN command is

SCREEN [mode] [,burst]

Try typing this command with various combinations of parameters.

## WIDTH Command

The WIDTH command lets us select between the two text modes. It can also be used to set the line widths for output to floppy disk files or to other output devices. For us, the output device will be the screen, and we will use it to differentiate between the two text modes with their different line lengths. It will also switch between the medium- and high-resolution graphics modes because they have different resolutions and, hence, different line lengths for the text they produce.

The full syntax for the WIDTH command is

WIDTH value

where *value* is an expression which is equal to 40 or 80. If we are in mode 0 (text), entering a value of 40 puts us in the low-resolution text mode, and 80 puts us in the high-resolution text mode. In a graphics mode, using 40 puts us in medium-resolution mode, and 80 puts us in high-resolution mode. Any time that the width is changed, the screen will be cleared, but if you use the WIDTH command to set the width to what it already was, the screen will not be cleared.

In the upcoming examples we use 40 to ensure that we are in the low-resolution text mode, but you can type WIDTH 40 and WIDTH 80 directly to see their effect on the display.

## CLS Command

The CLS command is used to clear the screen. For this command, the syntax is just

CLS

Now that we know how to get in and out of the text modes, let's see what is there and how to color it.

## COLOR Command

The COLOR command allows us to select the foreground and background colors for letters on the screen. For the

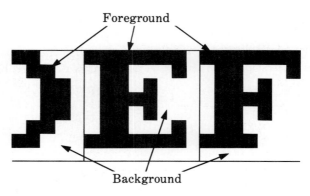

Foreground

Background

**Figure 2-1**

Foreground and
Background of Characters

COLOR command in the text mode, the syntax is

COLOR [foreground] [, background] [, border]]

where *foreground* is an integer expression that indicates the foreground color and the blinking attribute of subsequent characters; *background* is an expression that indicates the background color of subsequent characters; and *border* is an expression that indicates the color of the border of the screen. Figure 2-1 illustrates the foreground and background of characters.

The syntax for this command in the *graphics* modes is different and will be discussed later in this chapter.

It is important to understand that the COLOR statement does not change the foreground or background colors and the blinking characters already on the screen. Instead, the COLOR statement affects the coloring of only those characters printed on the screen after it is executed. In contrast, the border color changes immediately upon execution of any COLOR command that specifies a new border color.

The foreground, background, and border colors and blinking are specified using the numerical codes indicated in Table 2-1. As this table indicates, any value between 0 and 31 is valid for this combined blinking or foreground parameter.

Notice that in contrast to the wide selection of foreground colors, there are only eight background colors. This is because there are just not enough bits available to provide more. Background color values lie between 0 and 7. In fact, the

**Table 2-1**

Foreground, Background, and Border Colors

| Code | | Color/Effect | | |
|---|---|---|---|---|
| Decimal | Binary | Foreground | Background | Border |
| 0 | 00000 | Black | Black | Black |
| 1 | 00001 | Blue | Blue | Blue |
| 2 | 00010 | Green | Green | Green |
| 3 | 00011 | Cyan (greenish blue) | Cyan | Cyan |
| 4 | 00100 | Red | Red | Red |
| 5 | 00101 | Magenta (purplish) | Magenta | Magenta |
| 6 | 00110 | Brown | Brown | Brown |
| 7 | 00111 | White | White | White |
| 8 | 01000 | Gray | | Gray |
| 9 | 01001 | Light blue | | Light blue |
| 10 | 01010 | Light green | | Light green |
| 11 | 01011 | Light cyan | | Light cyan |
| 12 | 01100 | Light red | | Light red |
| 13 | 01101 | Light magenta | | Light magenta |
| 14 | 01110 | Yellow | | Yellow |
| 15 | 01111 | Bright white | | Bright white |
| Bit 7 ON | | | | |
| 16 | 10000 | Black | | |
| 17 | 10001 | Blinking blue | | |
| 18 | 10010 | Blinking green | | |
| 19 | 10011 | Blinking cyan (greenish blue) | | |
| 20 | 10100 | Blinking red | | |
| 21 | 10101 | Blinking magenta (purplish) | | |
| 22 | 10110 | Blinking brown | | |
| 23 | 10111 | Blinking white | | |
| 24 | 11000 | Blinking gray | | |
| 25 | 11001 | Blinking light blue | | |
| 26 | 11010 | Blinking light green | | |
| 27 | 11011 | Blinking light cyan | | |
| 28 | 11100 | Blinking light red | | |
| 29 | 11101 | Blinking light magenta | | |
| 30 | 11110 | Blinking yellow | | |
| 31 | 11111 | Blinking bright white | | |

table for the background colors consists of the first eight rows of Table 2-1.

There are 16 colors possible for the *border*. They are given in the first 16 rows of Table 2-1. The border is that part of the screen that does not correspond to character positions or to graphic dots. As its name implies, it runs around the outside of the screen. Figure 2-2 illustrates its placement on the screen. One reason computers such as the IBM PC have a border is that they are meant to work with ordinary color TVs that overscan.

In the following example, we will make a blue border by selecting the value 1 for this parameter. Our example will simply put the letter A across the screen in the various color combinations described in Table 2-1. We choose to display many copies of just one letter so that you can clearly see the effects of the coloring schemes.

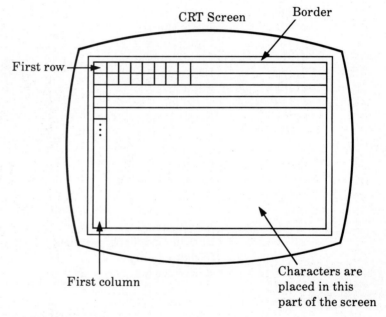

**Figure 2-2**

Parts of a Screen

EXAMPLE 2-1

## COLORFUL TEXT

Display the letter A in all possible color combinations.
Show your results as a block of A's with the 32 foreground
color combinations corresponding to the 32 columns of
the display and the 8 background color combinations
corresponding to the 8 rows of the display. The result is
shown in Figure 2-3.

## Solution

```
100 ' TEXT                              210    PRINT:PRINT:PRINT
110 '                                   220    FOR I = 0 TO 7
120 ' Displays text characters in       230     FOR J = 0 TO 31
130 ' various colors.                   240       COLOR J, I, 1
140 '                                   250       PRINT "A";
150    SCREEN 0,1                       260     NEXT J
160    WIDTH 40                         270     PRINT
170    CLS                              280    NEXT I
180 '                                   290
190    PRINT TAB(18);"TEXT"             300    COLOR 15,0, 1
200 '
```

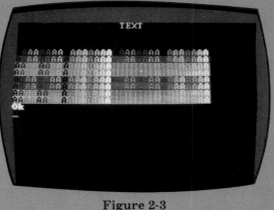

Figure 2-3
Colorful Text

In this program, you see how the various commands such
as SCREEN, WIDTH, and CLS are being used to set up the
mode and the screen properly. Then you see a title being

printed. After the title, three PRINT commands skip some lines to separate the title from the display. Next, a double FOR loop controls the COLOR and PRINT statements to make the display. Here we see how the 8 rows of 32 columns are made.

If you want to see what characters look like in the 80-column text mode, change the width to 80 in line 160. If you are using an NTSC TV or monitor, the letters will be very hard to read in this higher resolution. If you turn off the color by changing line 150 to

150 SCREEN 0,0

the characters will be a lot more readable.

In the next section we show why and how these commands work. To do this, we will introduce the idea of *video mapping*.

## Mapping

In either text mode, each character position on the entire screen is assigned two bytes in a special area of the system's main memory. This area is called the *video RAM*. The chips that contain this memory are actually on the Color/Graphics Adapter, and in this sense, the Color/Graphics Adapter acts like a 16K-byte extension to your system's main memory. Video memory starts at the absolute address B8000 hexadecimal (or 753,664 in decimal), which is a very high address, so that it is out of the way of ordinary memory. The video memory is special in that it is constantly being scanned by special video circuitry. This circuitry puts out video signals that depend upon what is stored in the various locations of the video memory and upon the particular mode that you are in. We say that this circuitry "maps" the video memory to the video screen.

In the two text modes, the mapping assigns pairs of bytes in the video RAM in a straightforward *raster pattern*. (See Figure 2-4.) In this pattern, the first two bytes of video RAM are mapped to the upper-left corner of the screen (the first character position), the next two bytes to the next character position—just to the right of the first character position—and so on across the first row of characters. After that, the next two bytes "map" to the leftmost character position in the second row, and so on from left to right across that row. The pattern continues row by row until the bottom of the screen. For the low-resolution text mode, there are $40 \times 25$, or 1000 characters. With two bytes per character, this gives $2 \times 1000$,

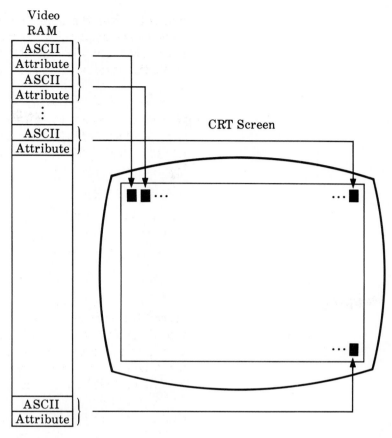

**Figure 2-4**

Memory Mapped Screen

or 2000 bytes of video memory. For the high-resolution text mode we need $2 \times 80 \times 25$, or 4000 bytes of video memory.

For any given character position, we can use the following formulas to compute the position of the corresponding bytes in the screen memory:

ASCII:  First byte $= 80 \times (row-1) + 2 \times (column-1)$

Attributes:  Second byte $= First\ byte + 1$

For example, the character in the first column, first row is stored in bytes 0 and 1 of the screen memory, and the character in the second row, first column is stored in bytes 80 and 81 of the screen memory.

For the 80-column mode, just replace the 80 in the first formula with 160.

Here we must use the IBM convention that rows and columns start counting with 1 rather than 0. The formulas we use give *memory offsets*. These are the number of bytes from the beginning of a *segment* of memory. It is the usual practice to define the screen memory to be such a segment. On the IBM PC, the following BASIC statement will set this segment for you:

DEF SEG = &HB800

This tells BASIC that you want to access *memory data* (perhaps using PEEK and POKE) whose segment number is B800 hexadecimal (base 16). The actual starting address in memory for this segment is 16 times this number, or B8000 hexadecimal.

Once the DEF SEG sequence is invoked, we can call the PEEK and POKE commands using the memory offsets given by the previous formulas.

Now that we have looked at the mapping in detail, let's examine the encoding of the characters and their coloring. The two bytes that map to each character position are used in the following manner. The first byte (at an even address in the video RAM) specifies the extended ASCII code for the character, and the second byte (with an odd address) determines the coloring scheme.

Tables showing the extended ASCII code are contained in the *IBM BASIC* manual, the *IBM Technical Reference* manual, and in Appendix B. Each number from 0 to 255 is assigned a certain meaning and a certain symbol. By putting the numbers into the right spots (even-numbered locations) of video memory, we can make the corresponding symbols appear on the screen.

The usual ASCII code only includes the numbers from 0 to 127, but this *extended code* goes from 0 to 255 (twice as large). The exact form of the symbols is not standard, nor is the choice of symbols for codes other than those for letters, punctuation, and digits. Among the nonstandard symbols for the IBM PC are various graphics shapes, all sorts of lines and corners, and some Greek and German letters.

Now let's look at the second byte, the one that determines the coloring scheme. It is often called the *attribute byte*. To see what it does, recall that each character symbol consists of the character itself (called the foreground) and the rectangular area immediately surrounding it (called the background).

Attribute Byte

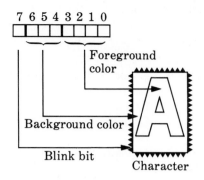

**Figure 2-5**

How the Attribute Byte Works

**Table 2-2**

Encoding for Primary Colors

| Decimal | Binary | Color |
|---------|--------|-------|
| 1 | 0001 | Blue |
| 2 | 0010 | Green |
| 4 | 0100 | Red |
| 8 | 1000 | Gray |

(See Figure 2-5, where this is illustrated.) The lower four bits (bits 3, 2, 1, and 0) of the attribute byte determine the foreground color of the symbol; bits 6, 5, and 4 determine the background color; and bit 7 determines whether or not the letter blinks. By executing a special command (to be discussed in Chapter 8) it is possible to make the "blink" bit (bit number 7) assume partial control of the background color instead.

It is interesting to note that bit number 7 (the blink bit) is grouped with bits 3, 2, 1, and 0 to form a 5-bit number that is the *foreground* parameter of the COLOR command. Bits 6, 5, and 4 form a 3-bit number that is the *background* parameter of the COLOR command.

When the COLOR command is executed, the integer parameter *border* sets some bits in the machine memory that determine the color of the border, and the integer parameters *foreground* and *background* are converted into bits of a "model" or "master copy" attribute byte. This master copy is copied into the attribute byte for each subsequent character printed on the screen until the next COLOR command is executed.

The individual bits in this attribute byte actually control individual colors which are then mixed together by the video circuitry to make the foreground or background color. It must be understood that TV colors are combined in an *additive* manner. This means when colors are combined, you get more light instead of less light, as is the case with pigments or filters that use a *subtractive* color scheme. This often gives results which seem strange to people who are accustomed to a subtractive color scheme.

With the additive color system, we can start with red, green, and blue. In the color code used in the IBM PC, we have the "primaries" coded, as shown in Table 2-2. Just one bit is "on" (equal to 1) in each of these code numbers. Every other color produced by the Color/Graphics Adapter is obtained by adding combinations of these primaries. Bit 0 controls whether or not blue is to be added, bit 1 controls whether or not green is to be added, and bit 2 controls whether or not red is to be added. The fourth bit (bit number 3) controls whether or not an additional amount of white (or gray) is to be added in. Table 2-3 lists all the colors and their codes.

In this table the numbers 1, 2, and 4 correspond to the binary numbers 0001, 0010, and 0100, each of which specifies

**Table 2-3**

Basic Color Codes

| Decimal code | Binary code | Color/effect |
|:---:|:---:|:---|
| 0 | 0000 | Black |
| 1 | 0001 | Blue |
| 2 | 0010 | Green |
| 3 | 0011 | Cyan (greenish blue) |
| 4 | 0100 | Red |
| 5 | 0101 | Magenta (purplish) |
| 6 | 0110 | Brown |
| 7 | 0111 | White |
| 8 | 1000 | Gray |
| 9 | 1001 | Light blue |
| 10 | 1010 | Light green |
| 11 | 1011 | Light cyan |
| 12 | 1100 | Light red |
| 13 | 1101 | Light magenta |
| 14 | 1110 | Yellow |
| 15 | 1111 | Bright white |

just one of the "primary" colors blue, green, or red. In addition, 8 (1000 in binary) is gray.

Observe that adding primary colors corresponds to adding their codes. For example, cyan is a mixture of blue and green, and thus has the binary code

0001 (blue) + 0010 (green) = 0011

which is the decimal number 3. Table 2-4 shows the results for all combinations.

Since four bits are allotted to the foreground color, 16 different numbers (0 through 15) can be represented. Thus, 16 colors are possible for the displayed letter itself. However, since only three bits are allotted to the background color, only eight colors can be represented (0 through 7) in the background of a character in text mode. Thus, only the first eight colors are possible for the rectangle surrounding a character in text mode. Because of the way the bits are arranged, the following formula can be used to compute the color code number for a character position:

Color code = 128 * *blink* + 16 * (*background color*) + *foreground color*

**Table 2-4**

Encoding for Secondary Colors

| Decimal | Binary | Color |
|---------|--------|-------|
| 3 | 0011 | Cyan = green + blue |
| 5 | 0101 | Magenta = red + blue |
| 6 | 0110 | Brown = red + green |
| 7 | 0111 | White = red + green + blue |
| 9 | 1001 | Light blue = gray + blue |
| 10 | 1010 | Light green = gray + green |
| 11 | 1011 | Light cyan = gray + green + blue |
| 12 | 1100 | Light red = gray + red |
| 13 | 1101 | Light magenta = gray + red + blue |
| 14 | 1110 | Yellow = gray + red + green |
| 15 | 1111 | High intensity white = gray + red + green + blue |

The following example demonstrates how all this can be done directly using the POKE command in BASIC.

## EXAMPLE 2-2

## CHARACTER PLOTTER

Use the POKE statement to place any character on the
screen with a given ASCII code, in a given row and
column, with a given color combination. Use the PEEK
command to get the character's dot pattern from where it
is stored in memory. The output is shown in Figure 2-6.

## Solution

```
100 ' CHARACTER PLOTTER
110 '
120    SCREEN 0,1
130    WIDTH 40
140    KEY OFF
150 '
160    CLS
170 '
180    INPUT "Row (1-24)"; ROW
190    INPUT "Column (1-40)"; COLUMN
200    INPUT "ASCII Code (0-255)";ACODE
210    INPUT "Foreground (0-15)"; FCOLOR
220    INPUT "Background (0-7)"; BCOLOR
230    INPUT "Blink (0 or 1)"; BLINK
240 '
250    FBYTE = 80*(ROW-1)+2*(COLUMN-1)
260    CN = 128*BLINK+16*BCOLOR+FCOLOR
270 '
280    CLS
290    DEF SEG = &HB800
300    POKE FBYTE,ACODE
310    POKE FBYTE+1,CN
320 '
330    A$=INPUT$(1)
340    GOTO 160
```

EXAMPLE 2-2

**Solution, continued.**

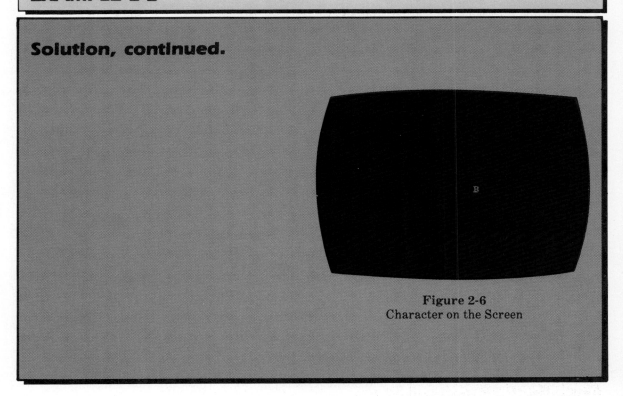

Figure 2-6
Character on the Screen

Let's look at this program carefully. First, the 40-column text mode is invoked, the function keys are turned off, and the screen is cleared. Next, the user is asked to supply all the necessary information. The offset of the first byte is computed and stored in the variable FBYTE. The color code is also computed and stored in the variable CN. Next, the screen is cleared. The screen is then defined as a data segment in memory. Finally, both the ASCII code and the color code are placed into memory with the POKE command. You should see the character at this point. The INPUT$ function in line 330 allows you to pause without clearing the screen. If you press a key, you will go back to make another character.

CLOSE-UP
OF
PIXEL

# GRAPHICS MODES

As we saw in Chapter 1, there are two fully supported graphics modes in the IBM PC: a medium-resolution mode and a high-resolution mode. Like the text modes, the low-resolution mode is designed for color TVs or monitors, and the high-resolution mode is designed for black-and-white images. In this case, the high resolution is not even designed to produce any color. However, in Chapter 8 we will see how to make color with it.

In these graphics modes, each dot that we can control on the screen as a logical unit is called a *pixel*. This stands for picture element. We will use this term rather than "dot" because it is more precise. The problem with the word dot is that there are lots of *physical* dots (made out of phosphor) that make up the entire screen. Often, several physical dots are needed to make up one *logical* dot, or pixel, of our picture. Another problem is that pixels, especially in low-resolution modes, often appear rectangular and not "dot-like."

The medium-resolution mode has 320 pixels horizontally and 200 pixels vertically with four possible colors for each pixel. In Chapter 1, we saw that the horizontal pixel resolution of this mode is twice that of the color resolution of an ordinary (NTSC) color TV signal. This 320-pixel-across mode allows a selection of one of four colors for each point. However, this coloring is true only over a larger area (at least two pixels wide—and more are needed to really see it).

To illustrate this mode we will present an example that shows off the colors. It will use some of the same graphics commands already discussed for the last example. However, in the graphics modes, the COLOR statement has a slightly different syntax. In particular, it is only valid in the medium-resolution graphics mode and, in fact, leads to an error message when it is used in the high-resolution graphics mode.

The full syntax for the COLOR command in the medium-resolution graphics mode is

COLOR [background] [,palette]

Here *background* is any one of 16 colors as specified in Table 2-1. The background color also controls the color of the border (see Figure 2-2). The second quantity, *palette*, gives you a choice between two sets of colors that subsequent graphics commands will work with. In the medium-resolution graphics mode, each pixel on the screen is assigned a number from 0 to 3. Table 2-5 shows how these numerical codes correspond to colors on the screen in these two different palettes.

From this table, you can see that color number 0 is determined by whatever the background color happens to be, but each other number has two possibilities according to the choice of palette.

In the following example, we use a special form of the LINE command to draw solid boxes of color. This "box-fill" form of the LINE command will be thoroughly explored and explained in Chapter 3. For now, we will just use it with a minimum of explanation. The syntax we will use is

LINE (x1,y1)−(x2,y2), color, BF

This command causes a box to be drawn whose corners are $(x1,y1)$, $(x1,y2)$, $(x2,y1)$, and $(x2,y2)$. The entire inside and boundary of the box will be drawn in the color *color*, which is chosen from the current palette.

**Table 2-5**

Palettes for Medium-Resolution Graphics Mode

| Numerical code | Palette #0 | Palette #1 |
|---|---|---|
| 0 | Background (1 of 16) | Background (1 of 16) |
| 1 | Green | Cyan |
| 2 | Red | Magenta |
| 3 | Brown (yellow) | White |

**EXAMPLE 2-3**

## COLORS IN MEDIUM-RESOLUTION GRAPHICS MODE

In the medium-resolution graphics mode draw four boxes, one for each one of the available colors for that mode. Then slowly cycle through all possible choices of background color and palette. A sample of the output is given in Figure 2-7.

## Solution

```
100 ' MEDIUM
110 '
120 ' In this example we draw four
130 ' boxes, one for each of the four
140 ' available colors.  At the end
150 ' we cycle through the various
160 ' background colors and palettes.
170 '
180    SCREEN 1
190    CLS
200 '
210    PRINT TAB(12);
220    PRINT "Medium Resolution"
230 '
240 ' make the boxes
250    LINE ( 40, 40)-(160,100),0,BF
260    LINE (160, 40)-(280,100),1,BF
270    LINE ( 40,100)-(160,160),2,BF
280    LINE (160,100)-(280,160),3,BF
290 '
300 ' now cycle through the
310 ' background colors and palettes
320    FOR I = 0 TO 15 ' foreground
330      COLOR I,0   ' palette 0
340      FOR J= 1 TO 1000:NEXT J ' wait
350      COLOR I,1   ' palette 1
360      FOR J= 1 TO 1000:NEXT J ' wait
370    NEXT I
380
390    COLOR 0,1
```

## EXAMPLE 2-3

## Solution, continued.

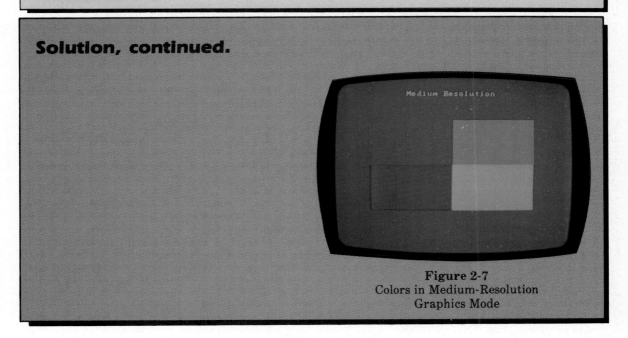

**Figure 2-7**
Colors in Medium-Resolution
Graphics Mode

Let's look at this example in detail. The SCREEN and the CLS commands make sure that we are in medium-resolution graphics mode with a clear screen. The two PRINT statements put a title "Medium Resolution" at the top of the screen. Next, the four LINE statements place the colored boxes on the screen. Notice that we have not let the boxes fill up the entire screen. This is because on some TVs filling the entire screen with strong colors makes the image look as though you had painted the picture on paper and then crumpled the paper.

Notice that each of the four boxes has a different value for the *color* parameter. When the boxes are displayed you will not see one of them, the one which has color code 0. It is not seen because it is the same color as the surrounding background and border. The box with color code 3 is colored with what is called the *foreground color* (white or yellow, depending upon the palette). We will explore the concept of foreground color more in Chapter 3.

The last part of the program cycles through all possible palettes and background colors. This is done in a FOR loop whose index I goes through all 16 background colors. Within the FOR loop, we set the palette to 0 (with background color I) and then wait for a count of 1000 with an empty FOR loop indexed by J. Then we set the palette to 1 (still with background color I) and wait again, using another empty FOR loop indexed by J.

In the graphics modes, the bits in the bytes of the video RAM map directly to the pixels on the screen. In both modes, the video RAM begins at the same address as it does in the text modes. Again, the BASIC statement

DEF SEG = &HB800

will make the video RAM the current data segment for PEEKs and POKEs from BASIC.

In the medium-resolution graphics mode, there are two bits per pixel. This means that each pixel on the screen is controlled by a separate 2-bit number that is stored in one of the bytes of the video RAM. A total of four such 2-bit numbers can fit into each byte of the screen memory. The corresponding pixels line up in a row with the higher numbered bits mapping to pixels toward the left and the lower numbered bits mapping to pixels toward the right (see Figure 2-8). The very first byte of video memory maps to four pixels on the top row of one screen, starting on the left side. The next byte maps to four pixels just to the right of the first four, and so on across the top row for a total of 320 pixels, or 80 bytes. The next row of the screen does not come from the next 80 bytes of video RAM, but rather from 80 bytes of video RAM starting at address BA000 (hexadecimal). This is in the second 8K of the video RAM. The rows on the screen alternately come from the first and second 8K bytes of the video RAM.

Each 2-bit number corresponding to a pixel can store an integer with values 0, 1, 2, or 3, which correspond to the four color numbers that can be assigned to that pixel in the medium-resolution graphics mode. In Chapter 3, we will see how the point, line, and circle plotting commands assign color numbers to pixels.

**High-Resolution Graphics Mode**

Now let's take a quick look at the high-resolution mode. It is definitely less colorful, but it does have excellent horizontal resolution with 640 pixels per line. This is twice as many pixels per line as the medium-resolution graphics mode, and so the pixels are half as long in the horizontal direction. This

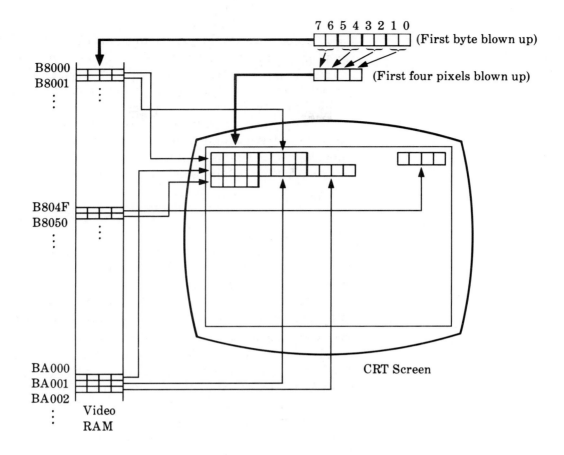

**Figure 2-8**

Mapping in Medium-Resolution
Graphics Mode

will allow finer detail in your pictures and smaller text, an important feature when making labeled diagrams.

The vertical resolution, 200 pixels, is the same as the medium-resolution graphics mode. Each pixel can only be one of two colors: black (off) or brightly lit (on). A color code of 0 indicates black. This is called the *background color* for this mode. A color code of 1 indicates brightly lit. This is called the *foreground color* for this mode. You are allowed to specify color codes 2 and 3, but 2 will be stored as a 0 and 3 will be stored as a 1; that is, the machine can only store the rightmost bit of any numerical color code because there is only one bit per pixel.

The horizontal resolution for the high-resolution graphics mode is four times that of the NTSC color system. But since the color is "turned off" in this mode, the resulting unusual color effects are not a problem. For an example of this mode, see the mandala program in Chapter 1.

In the high-resolution graphics mode there is one bit per pixel. This means that one byte will now map into eight pixels on the screen. The corresponding pixels line up in a row with the higher numbered bits mapping to pixels toward the left and the lower numbered bits mapping to pixels toward the right (see Figure 2-9). Again, the very first byte of video memory maps to pixels on the top row of the screen, starting

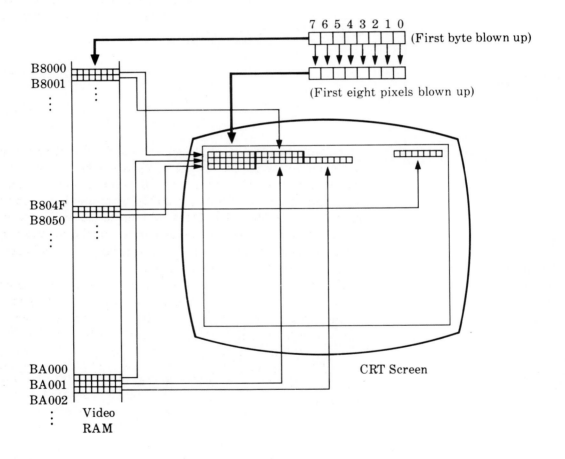

**Figure 2-9**

Mapping in High-Resolution Graphics
Mode

on the left side. The next byte maps to eight pixels just to the right of the first eight, and so on across the top row for a total of 640 pixels, or 80 bytes. The next row of the screen does not come from the next 80 bytes of video RAM, but rather from 80 bytes of video RAM starting at address BA000 (hexadecimal), which is the beginning of the second 8K of the video RAM. Again, the rows on the screen alternately come from the first and second 8K bytes of the video RAM.

In the case of the high-resolution graphics mode, each 1-bit number corresponding to a pixel can store an integer with values 0 or 1, which correspond to the two color numbers that can be assigned to that pixel in this mode. Chapter 3 contains an explanation of how to use the point, line, and circle plotting commands to assign color numbers to pixels on the screen.

## CONCLUSION

In this chapter we explored the standard text and graphics modes of the IBM PC Color/Graphics Adapter. We saw the two text modes, 40-column and 80-column; and we saw the two graphics modes, the $320 \times 200$ colorful medium-resolution mode and the $640 \times 200$ black-and-white mode. We explored the coloring terminology and schemes and the memory mapping involved in each mode. This will lay the foundation for discussions in the rest of the book.

In the next chapters we explain in detail how to draw interesting and useful shapes in the two standard graphics modes using BASICA commands. In Chapter 7 we will explain how to make effective use of the text modes on the Color/Graphics Adapter, and in Chapter 8 we show you how to make new modes. In Chapter 9, we will apply what we've learned about the Color/Graphics Adapter to the Monochrome Adapter.

# PLOTTING AND
# LINE DRAWING

# CONCEPTS

**Concepts**
    Point, Line, and Circle Drawing
    2-D and 3-D Viewing Concepts
    Using Data to Define a Picture

**Commands**
    PSET
    PRESET
    LINE
    CIRCLE

**Applications**
    Pie Charts
    Bar Charts
    2-D and 3-D Function Plotting
    Drawing 3-D Objects with Hidden Lines

# INTRODUCTION

This chapter describes how to use the point, line, and circle plotting commands PSET, PRESET, LINE, and CIRCLE and how to use them in simple and sophisticated applications. These commands were introduced in Chapter 1 in black and white in their simplest forms; this chapter presents these commands in full color with all their available options. Although the syntax (format) of these four statements is simple, their uses in applications are enormous. We start with some simple examples and build toward more complex applications.

Once you have a firm understanding of these ideas, we accelerate to more advanced uses of PSET, LINE, and CIRCLE, concluding with pie and bar charts and two- and three-dimensional graphs. As a conclusion, we present a program that draws a three-dimensional view of an object using data statements to define the picture. The program even hides those lines that should be hidden. We have chosen to display a house, but you can use this same program to display many other 3-D objects with hidden lines. You will only have to change the data. In Chapter 5, we see how to paint this house.

Part of our discussion about computer graphics programs includes some mathematics. This mathematics is not designed to whisk you off to an ivory tower, but rather it is presented to help you produce pictures more efficiently—and not by a series of accidents. You do not need to have a college degree to understand it, but some knowledge of high school mathematics will be helpful.

## Programming Notes

As we explain the graphics commands we will show a series of "stand-alone" program segments. "Stand-alone" means that, although all of these examples are part of one large program, each segment can be run by itself provided your machine is properly initialized.

As we come to each example, we give a small section of BASIC statements for you to type in. You should add these statements to those you have already typed in from previous examples in this chapter. Do not change any of the line numbers since each section of the example "program" has been designed so it will not overlap with any other. As you work your way through the examples you will make a longer and longer program. If you wish to see the results from the beginning of the chapter up through the point where you now are, just type RUN. However, if you wish to see only what you are now working on, type GOTO followed by the line number at the beginning of that example. This method will start the computer at the beginning of that particular example.

When you finish this chapter and have entered all the examples, you will be able to run the program from start to end (by typing RUN) and see the results of all the examples in a kind of "flash card" review.

Our first example is a program that you use to set up your machine for the examples in this section. It will also be used for the same purpose in many of the chapters that follow. This short initialization program will form the first few lines of our program.

After typing in this program, you should see a blank light red screen.

Our next example is used to connect the numerous example program sections together. It consists of two subroutines. The first subroutine stops and asks you to press the **ENTER** key if you wish to continue. This subroutine also calls another subroutine that puts a centered title on the top of the screen.

EXAMPLE 3-1

## INITIALIZING THE PROGRAM

Write a short program that puts the IBM PC in the
medium-resolution color mode, sets the background color to
light red, and selects palette 1. It should also turn off the
function key display at the bottom of the screen and make
sure the screen is cleared. The blank red screen is shown in
Figure 3-1.

## Solution

```
100 ' INTRODUCTORY PROGRAMS - CHAPTER 3
110 '
120 ' INITIALIZATION
130 '
140 ' Put the IBM in medium
150 ' resolution with color.
160 '
170 ' The background color is
180 ' light red and the
190 ' foreground colors are
200 ' chosen from palette 1.
210 '
220    SCREEN 1
230    COLOR 12, 1
240 '
250 ' Clear the screen with keys off.
260 '
270    KEY OFF
280    CLS
290 '
```

Figure 3-1
Initializing the Program

EXAMPLE 3-2

## PAUSE AND TITLE SUBROUTINES

Write a subroutine that stops and asks the user to press
the ENTER key to continue. When it starts again, it should
put a centered title at the top of the screen. Use the
LOCATE statement to position the title. The procedure to
put the centered title on the screen should be in a separate
subroutine that can be called either by the main program
or by the main subroutine in this example.

You should put some steps in your main program that
call the centered title routine to put the title "RED BACK-
GROUND" on the screen. The example output is shown in
Figure 3-2.

## Solution

```
5000  ' SUBROUTINE - PAUSE & TITLE PAGE
5010  '
5020     LOCATE 25,1
5030     INPUT"Press ENTER to continue";A
5040     CLS
5050     GOSUB 5080 ' CENTERED TITLE
5060     RETURN
5070  '
5080  ' SUBROUTINE - CENTERED TITLE
5090  '
5100     LOCATE 1,(40-LEN(T$))/2+1
5110     PRINT T$;
5120  '
5130     RETURN
5140  '



300    T$ = "RED BACKGROUND"
310    GOSUB 5080 ' centered title
320  '
```

## Example 3-2

**Solution, continued.**

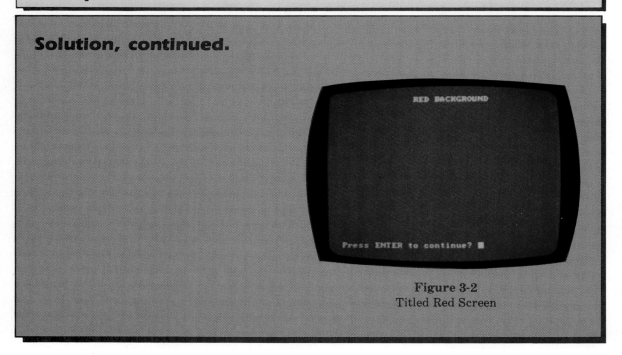

Figure 3-2
Titled Red Screen

Type all of this in now. Do not remove the statements you already typed in Example 3-1.

Now run the program. You should get a red screen titled "RED BACKGROUND" as shown in the photograph.

Notice that the LOCATE command is used several times. Although it is, strictly speaking, not a graphics command, it is extremely useful in graphics. This command positions an unseen "text cursor" to a specified row and column. The cursor allows us to start printing our text anywhere on the screen. Contrary to the usual graphics layout, *row* (y-position) comes first and then *column* (x-position) in this command. This layout is more natural for text (line, column = y,x). Notice that the first LOCATE is used to put the message "Press ENTER to continue" on the 25th row (line) of text. For this to work, the display of function keys on the 25th line must have been turned off with the KEY OFF command as we did in line 270 of our program. The second use of the LOCATE command centers a title contained in the string T$. Here the correct column in which to begin printing is computed using the length of the string T$ containing the message. This computation is located within the LOCATE statement; that is, you can use an expression for the row or column.

You might wonder why we have chosen to divide such simple work into two subroutines when one could do both functions. With Fortran programming, there would have been one subroutine with two entry points—the second would have been used if you wanted only the centered title. This practice is frowned upon in modern approaches to structured programming. Such languages as Pascal and Ada demand neat packaging—no double entry points for these languages. In the long run this is easier for developing and maintaining programs, even though the resulting programs may run more slowly because of the extra "calls" (GOSUB statements). GOSUB statements take time to execute, and more of them make a program run slightly longer. However, this loss of performance is worth the gains in speed of development and ease of program maintenance. In light of this, we will try to "structure" our programs even in the "anything goes" BASIC language.

# THE COMMANDS

Let's start our discussion of the graphics commands with the commands for plotting points.

## PSET and PRESET Commands

The PSET and PRESET commands are used to plot points. Since every picture is made up of points, it is possible to create graphics with only these two commands.

The syntax of the PSET and PRESET commands is as follows:

PSET (x,y) [,color]

PRESET (x,y) [,color]

where (*x,y*) indicates the coordinates of the point and *color* specifies the color.

If the color is not specified (default color mode), PSET plots a point whose color is the *foreground* color and PRESET plots a point whose color is the *background* color. On a clear screen (background color screen), you use PSET to plot points and PRESET to erase points.

The square brackets indicate that the *color* is optional; that is, you do not have to type it in. In fact, if the color is specified, these two commands perform identically. They both plot a point of the indicated color. Note that the square brackets include the comma that normally separates the color specification from the rest of the command. If you do not specify the color, then you should *not* type in this comma.

In the 320 × 200 medium-resolution mode, there are four colors available at one time, indicated by the numbers 0, 1, 2, and 3. These are what are called *logical* colors. How they "map" to actual colors depends upon the COLOR command.

In the PSET and PRESET statements' color option, the number 0 indicates the background color and the number 3 indicates the foreground color. The background color can be one of 16 colors and there are two "palettes" for colors 1, 2, and 3. In our examples we will use the COLOR statement to obtain different background and palette colors in the medium-resolution mode. PSET's *color* option is then used to select one of three colors from the enabled palette.

In the 640 × 200 high-resolution mode, there are two colors. They are specified by the numbers 0 and 1. The number 0 indicates the background color, which is always black, and the number 1 indicates the foreground color, which is white. (If you use a monochromatic green phosphor screen, the foreground color will appear green.) In the high-resolution mode the color number 2 will act the same as a 0, and a 3 will act the same as a 1. Thus, in this mode the background color is produced by both 0 and 2 and the foreground color by both 1 and 3.

All of this means that if the color is not specified, the PSET and PRESET commands will behave according to a default color scheme. This scheme is shown in Table 3-1.

In either graphics mode, a number specified for the color that is not an integer will automatically be converted to an integer by rounding. When we worked with these commands on our machine, if we specified too small a number for color (negative number), we received an "Illegal function number" message, and if we specified a number too large, nothing happened except an "Ok" acknowledging our command.

Coordinates are used to specify the location of points on the screen. The point (0,0) is at the top-left corner. The x-values

**Table 3-1**

Default Colors for PSET and PRESET

| Resolution | Command with Color NOT Specified | Equivalent Commands when Color is Specified |
|---|---|---|
| Medium | PRESET (x,y) | PSET (x,y),0 or PRESET (x,y),0 |
| Medium | PSET (x,y) | PSET (x,y),3 or PRESET (x,y),3 |
| High | PRESET (x,y) | PSET (x,y),0 or PRESET (x,y),0 |
| High | PSET (x,y) | PSET (x,y),1 or PRESET (x,y),1 |

range from 0 to 319 or from 0 to 639, depending upon the resolution, and the y-values range from 0 to 199.

Coordinates can be specified in two different ways: *absolute* and *relative*. With absolute mode you give the actual screen coordinates of the point to be plotted. But with relative coordinates you give a *change* in coordinates. In case you are wondering "change from what," remember that BASIC keeps track of an unseen "graphic cursor" called the *current position*. Each time a PSET, PRESET, LINE, or CIRCLE command is used, the current position is updated with the new position. With the PSET or PRESET commands, the current position is updated to the point that you are plotting.

More precisely, with a PSET or PRESET command, coordinates in *absolute* mode *become* the coordinates of the new current position, and a point is then plotted there. In contrast, coordinates in *relative* mode are *added* to the current position, giving the new current position, which is then plotted.

You can recognize the difference between absolute and relative coordinates in a BASIC statement by looking for the key word "STEP" just before the coordinates in the command line. If it is there, you are using *relative* coordinates; otherwise you are using *absolute* coordinates. For example, "PSET (12,10)" uses absolute coordinates, and "PSET STEP(5,5)" uses relative coordinates.

Both the PSET and PRESET commands will plot a point. Whether this point is seen or not depends upon its color and the color of the surrounding points. It is interesting to note that there is no simple command (like MOVE) that updates the current position. In Chapter 4, we will see how to use the DRAW command to do this.

EXAMPLE 3-3

## POINT PLOTTING

Write a short program that plots a cross of points in
the center of the screen. Use both absolute and relative
coordinates and both the PSET and PRESET commands.
The plotted points are shown in Figure 3-3.

## Solution

```
330 ' POINTS ON THE SCREEN        460    NEXT I
340 '                             470 '
350    T$ = "POINTS ON THE SCREEN" 480    PRESET (159,100)
360    GOSUB 5000 ' pause & title  490    FOR I = 1 TO 10
370 '                             500       PSET STEP(0,4)
380    PRESET (159,100)            510    NEXT I
390    FOR I = 1 TO 10             520 '
400       PSET STEP(4,0)           530    PRESET (159,100)
410    NEXT I                      540    FOR I = 1 TO 10
420 '                             550       PSET STEP(0,-4)
430    PRESET (159,100)            560    NEXT I
440    FOR I = 1 TO 10             570 '
450       PSET STEP(-4,0)          580 '
```

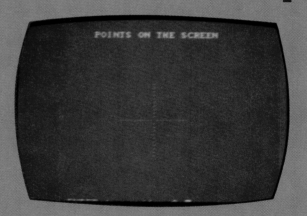

Figure 3-3
Points on the Screen

When this example runs, you will see a number of points
plotted forming a cross pattern. You cannot see the center

point of the cross because it is the same color as the background.

Notice how we invoke our "pause & title" subroutine at the beginning of the program segment. You can see that the line which defines T$ (line 350) can, in fact, serve as documentation for this segment.

Now let's look at the graphics commands. The first command is a PRESET (line 380). Since there is no STEP, the coordinates are in absolute mode. Thus, it will plot a point at (159,100), that is, a point whose x-coordinate is 159 and whose y-coordinate is 100 (x-coordinate is always first in graphics commands). Since the PRESET command plots a point whose color is the background color and since the point (159,100) is already the background color, you will not see this point. Thus, the main purpose of this command is to set the current position. The IBM PC default value for the current position is (160,100), but you should not normally rely on this default position; it is only good immediately after you have cleared the screen.

We see that after the first graphics command, the current position is (159,100). Next we have a FOR loop that repeats the PSET command ten times. This PSET (line 400) has a STEP before the coordinates and is thus in relative mode. Adding its coordinates (4,0) to the current position (159,100) gives a new current position of (163,100). Since this is the foreground-producing PSET command, we see the point as a white dot on the screen. It appears white because we have chosen palette 1 in the COLOR statement (foreground is white). Each time around the FOR loop, the PSET commands move the point by the same amount. We see a total of ten dots equally spaced to the right of the center point of the screen. They are all white because we use the same PSET command each time. Following this FOR loop are three more FOR loops that draw the other arms of the cross.

It is interesting to note that if the default position of (160,100) were used instead of our PRESET position (159,100), the "white" dots would be very hard to see on an NTSC color TV. The production of color was discussed in detail in Chapter 1. As a result of the theory discussed there, we realize that with a red background, white dots should be drawn only on odd-numbered x-coordinates. That is why we start with an odd number, 159, and increment or decrement by an even number, 4. This way we get x-coordinates 159, 163, 167, and so on (moving to the right) or 159, 155, 151 (moving to the left).

Relative coordinates are handy if you have a certain shape such as a marker, icon, or machine part that you wish to place at various spots on the screen, or if you want to "vector" along the boundary of a figure. For example, if you are drawing a room, it is often easier to handle the length and direction of each wall than to handle their absolute coordinates since the "algorithm" for actually measuring a room consists of measuring the length of each wall and noting its direction.

In the next section we extend our graphics capabilities to draw lines. Commands to draw lines are more plentiful in graphics programs than commands to plot points. While we discuss lines we will also see more examples of the various forms of the point plotting commands.

## The LINE Command

The LINE command is used to draw lines, but it is useful for more than drawing lines. In this section we show how to use it to draw unfilled and filled boxes as well. We will continue to use our short "stand alone" program sections.

The full syntax for the LINE command is

LINE [(x1,y1)] − (x2,y2) [,[color] [,B[F]] [, style]]

You could become overwhelmed by the number of parameters for the LINE command. They all indicate various levels of options. Let's start with one of the simplest cases.

LINE (x1,y1) − (x2,y2)

Here $(x1,y1)$ are the coordinates of the beginning point of the line, and $(x2,y2)$ are the coordinates of the end point of the line. This command will cause a line to be drawn from $(x1,y1)$ to $(x2,y2)$.

The color is not specified. In this case we will use the foreground color as described for the PSET command. We will see color 3 if we are in medium-resolution mode and color 1 in high-resolution mode. In the medium-resolution mode, color 3 can be either white or yellow depending upon the palette number that is set in the COLOR command.

Both sets of coordinates for LINE can be in absolute or relative (STEP) mode.

The next example illustrates this simple form of the LINE command. Notice that this example sizes up the screen by using the full range of values for x and y in the medium-resolution mode.

## EXAMPLE 3-4

# DRAWING LINES ACROSS THE SCREEN

Write a short program that draws diagonal lines across the
screen. Use the simple form of the LINE command in
which both end points are specified. The lines that are
drawn are shown in Figure 3-4.

## Solution

```
590  ' LINES ACROSS THE SCREEN
600  '
610    T$ = "LINES ACROSS THE SCREEN"
620    GOSUB 5000 ' pause & title
630  '
640  ' Draw some lines across the screen
650  '
660    LINE (0,0)   -(319,199)
670    LINE (0,199)-(319,0)
680    LINE (0,100)-(319,100)
690    LINE (160,0)-(160,199)
700  '
710  '
```

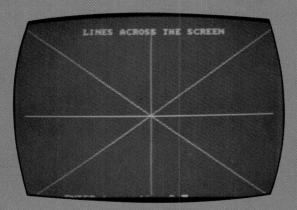

Figure 3-4
Lines Across the Screen

When you run this example you will see four lines that go all the way across the screen in different directions: two diagonally, one horizontally, and one vertically. If you are using an NTSC monitor or TV you may have difficulty seeing the vertical line because its color is white and it lies entirely on even numbered pixels.

The next three examples of the LINE command do not have any pauses between them. They will all appear in one picture (Figure 3-5).

First let's add some color to the syntax for the LINE command.

LINE (x1,y1) — (x2,y2), color

Here *color* can be a number from 0 to 3 following the rules described for the PSET (and PRESET) commands. It is better to relate the LINE command to the PSET command because both the LINE and PSET commands have the same default behavior with regard to color. The next example shows how to draw a rectangle with this form of the LINE command.

EXAMPLE 3-5

# DRAWING A RECTANGLE THE HARD WAY

Write a short program that draws a rectangle. Make each
side of the rectangle a different color. Use the LINE
command to draw the sides of the rectangle. The rectangle
is shown on the left side of Figure 3-5.

## Solution

```
720 ' RECTANGLES
730 '
740    T$ = "RECTANGLES"
750    GOSUB 5000 ' pause & title
760 '
770 ' FIRST THE HARD WAY
780 '
790 ' This is a sequence of four lines.
800 '
810    LINE (51,50)   - (101,50) , 0
820    LINE (101,50)  - (101,150), 1
830    LINE (101,150) - (51,150) , 2
840    LINE (51,150)  - (51,50)  , 3
850 '
```

Figure 3-5
Three Rectangles

When you run this program you will see a rectangle appear on the left third of your screen. Each side of the rectangle is a different color. Notice that the first side is not visible because it is the same color as the background. Absolute coordinates are used each time the LINE command is used.

Now let's explore how to use the LINE command with only the second set of coordinates specified. We will use the *current position*, which was introduced in the discussion of PSET and PRESET. The syntax for this form is

LINE − (x2,y2) [,color]

As you can see, *color* is still optional. This command causes a line to be drawn from the current position to the point specified by the coordinates $(x2,y2)$. The current position is updated to the end of the line (coordinates $(x2,y2)$). The current position is always updated in this way with whatever form of the LINE command is used.

Either absolute or relative coordinates can be used. In the next two examples, we continue to use absolute coordinates, but later we will use relative coordinates. Again, the difference between these modes is indicated by the presence or absence of the key word STEP. In the following example, we march around the rectangle using absolute coordinates (no STEP), providing only the new current position each time. Notice that the PSET command is used to set the current position before the LINE commands start drawing the sides.

EXAMPLE 3-6

## DRAWING A RECTANGLE A LITTLE MORE EASILY

Write a short program that draws a rectangle using the current position. Use the form of the LINE command in which the first pair of coordinates is omitted. The rectangle is shown in the middle of Figure 3-5.

## Solution

```
860 ' NOW A LITTLE EASIER WAY
870 '
880 ' This is a sequence of four lines
890 ' using the current position.
900 '
910    PSET    (151,50)
920    LINE - (201,50),   1
930    LINE - (201,150),  2
940    LINE - (151,150),  3
950    LINE - (151,50),   2
960 '
```

Now let's see how to draw a rectangle with only one graphics command. This example uses the "Box" option of the LINE command. The syntax is

LINE [(x1,y1)] − (x2,y2),[color],B

This command draws a rectangle whose sides are parallel to the sides of the screen and whose x-values are between the x-coordinates $x1$ and $x2$ and whose y-values are between the y-coordinates $y1$ and $y2$. The first coordinate and the color are optional—they are in brackets. If the first coordinates are not specified, the current position will be used instead. If the color is not specified, the foreground color will be used.

Let's look at the coordinates more closely. As we just saw, a rectangle whose sides are parallel to the sides of the screen can be described as a set of points (x,y) such that x is between values x1 and x2 and y is between values y1 and y2. These points are shown in Figure 3-6. Actually, this describes a solid *box*. Using a two-dimensional notion of "between," we could say that this box is the set of all points (x,y) that are between points (x1,y1) and (y1,y2). The rectangle is the boundary of the box, and the points (x1,y1) and (x2,y2) form a pair of opposite corners for the rectangle.

In the next example, we show how to draw such a rectangle in one graphics statement. Notice that both pairs of coordinates are specified, the color is not specified (a place is held for it by the commas), and B is used to specify "Box." Thus, a rectangle is drawn in the foreground color.

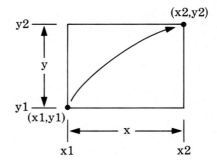

**Figure 3-6**

Rectangle Described by
a Pair of Opposite Corners

## EXAMPLE 3-7

## DRAWING A RECTANGLE THE EASIEST WAY

Write a short program that draws a rectangle in one graphics command. Use the "Box" option of the LINE command. The rectangle is shown on the right side of Figure 3-5.

## Solution

```
870  '
880  ' This is a sequence of four lines
890  ' using the current position.
900  '
910    PSET    (151,50)
920    LINE - (201,50),  1
930    LINE - (201,150), 2
940    LINE - (151,150), 3
950    LINE - (151,50),  2
960  '
970  ' NEXT IN JUST ONE STATEMENT
980  '
990  ' However, there is only one color.
1000 '
1010   LINE (251,50) - (301,150),, B
1020 '
1030 '
```

The next example shows how to use the LINE command to quickly draw many random rectangles. The RND function is used to generate random numbers. The RND function in BASIC generates "pseudo-random" numbers between 0 and 1; that is, it produces a sequence of numbers between 0 and 1 that "behaves" like a sequence of random numbers—even though the computer has a very definite set of rules for producing this sequence.

# EXAMPLE 3-8

## RANDOMLY DRAWN RECTANGLES

Write a short program that draws many rectangles
randomly positioned, randomly sized, and randomly
colored. The rectangles are shown in Figure 3-7.

## Solution

```
1040 ' SEVERAL COLORED BOXES
1050 '
1060    T$ = "COLORED BOXES"
1070    GOSUB 5000 ' pause & title
1080 '
1090 ' Here we use relative
1100 ' coordinates and random numbers.
1110 '
1120    COLOR 0,0
1130 '
1140    FOR I = 1 TO 50
1150       X = 250*RND : Y = 10+110*RND
1160       U = 70*RND  : V = 50*RND
1170       C = 3*RND + 1
1180       LINE (X,Y)-STEP(U,V), C, B
1190    NEXT I
1200 '
```

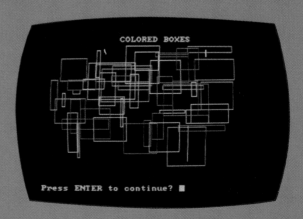

Figure 3-7
Random Colored Rectangles

Each parameter of the LINE statement (line 1180 of our program) is controlled by a separate variable that is randomly generated. Notice that relative mode is used for the second coordinates (x2,y2). This has the effect of controlling the width and height, and hence the size of the rectangle. The variable U controls the width and the variable V controls the height. How U and V are generated with the RND function guarantees that the width will not be any greater than 70 and the height will not be greater than 50. These limits make sure none of the rectangles extends beyond the boundaries of the screen. The variables X and Y control the position of the rectangle (actually the upper-left corner of the rectangle). X must be between 0 and 250 and Y must be between 10 and 120. Each rectangle goes from (X,Y) to (X+U,Y+V). This means that the rectangles fit within an area on the screen whose x-coordinates range between 0 and 250 + 70, or 320, and whose y-coordinates range between 10 and 120 + 50, or 170. Thus, the full width of the screen can be filled, but the height is restricted to allow messages at the top and bottom of the screen. Notice that even the color of the rectangle is randomly generated. We have set the background to black and selected palette 0. This makes the foreground color brown.

It is possible to use the LINE command to *fill* rectangles too. The syntax is

LINE [(x1,y1)] − (x2,y2),[color],BF

Here the letters *BF* at the end stand for *Box Fill*. Let's modify the previous example so that the boxes are filled in. LIST the previous example on the screen and use the screen editing facilities of IBM BASIC to change all the line numbers so that they match those in the next listing. Now add an F at the end of line 1340 so it reads BF, change the remark statements, and add line 1280.

Don't forget to type ENTER on each line after editing it; otherwise it will not be entered into your BASIC program.

## EXAMPLE 3-9

# FILLED RECTANGLES

Modify the previous program so that the rectangles are
filled with color. The filled rectangles are shown in Figure
3-8.

## Solution

```
1210 '  SEVERAL FILLED COLORED BOXES
1220 '
1230    T$ = "FILLED COLORED BOXES"
1240    GOSUB 5000 ' pause & title
1250 '
1260 ' Here we use relative
1270 ' coordinates, random numbers,
1280 ' and fill the boxes.
1290 '
1300    FOR I = 1 TO 100
1310       X = 250*RND : Y = 10+110*RND
1320       U = 70*RND  : V = 50*RND
1330       C = 3*RND + 1
1340       LINE (X,Y)-STEP(U,V), C, BF
1350 '
1360    NEXT I
1370 '
1380 '
```

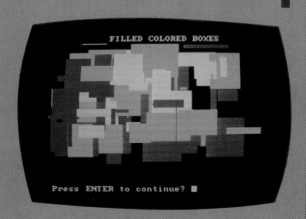

Figure 3-8
Filled Colored Boxes

When this program runs, you will see the rectangles from the last example fill with color.

Version 2 of Advanced BASIC has an additional line-drawing feature called *line style*. This feature allows you to draw dotted or dashed lines. In fact, there are 65,536 different line styles available. The parameter that controls line style is the last parameter of the LINE command. It is an expression whose 16-bit binary value forms a pattern for filling in the pixels along the line. The bits of this number are read from left to right and matched to the pixels along the line. A bit value of 1 indicates that a pixel is to be drawn and a bit value of 0 indicates that it should not be drawn. For example, a binary value 1010101010101010 in the style parameter draws a dotted line. It is important to realize that the 0 bits cause nothing to be drawn; that is, a bit value of 1 will cause a pixel to be plotted that is the color of the line, but a 0 does *not* erase the pixel beneath it.

The mapping from bits to pixels is almost straightforward. The only tricky part is determining where the mapping starts. Usually, mapping from bits to pixels starts with the leftmost bit, mapping it to the pixel on the line with the smallest y-coordinate (the topmost pixel of the line) or, if the line is horizontal, to the pixel on that line with the smallest x-coordinate (the leftmost pixel of the line). In the next example, we illustrate what this looks like.

As the bits get mapped to the pixels along the line, the pattern is used over and over again, repeating itself every 16 pixels. The style 1111111111110000 (in binary) produces a line with long dashes, and the style 1111111100010000 (in binary) produces a dash-dot pattern. For example, if the line drawn is 26 pixels long and the style is 1111000000001111, the pattern drawn is 11110000000011111111000000.

To save space in the program, we often express the style numbers in hexadecimal notation rather than in binary notation. For example, we would write the number AAAA (hex) instead of 1010101010101010 (binary) and FFF0 (hex) instead of 1111111111110000 (binary).

The next example demonstrates a variety of line styles for LINE with and without the Box option. Note that the style parameter cannot be used with the BF (Box Fill) option.

**EXAMPLE 3-10**

## LINE STYLE

Write a program that draws a series of boxes and lines
with different line styles. The boxes should surround each
other starting from the center of the screen. The lines
should slant across the screen, each with a different style
and different slope. The resulting pattern is shown in
Figure 3-9.

## Solution

```
1390 ' LINE STYLES
1400 '
1410    T$ = "LINE STYLES"
1420    GOSUB 5000 ' pause & title
1430 '
1440 ' Boxes with style
1450    FOR I = 0 TO 90 STEP 4
1460     X1 = 160-I : Y1 = 100-I
1470     X2 = 160+I : Y2 = 100+I
1480     LINE(X1,Y1)-(X2,Y2),,B,&HFFFF-I
1490    NEXT I
1500 '
1510 ' Slanted lines with style
1520    FOR I = 0 TO 180 STEP 4
1530     X1 =   0   : Y1 -   10+I
1540     X2 = 319   : Y2 = 200-I
1550     LINE(X1,Y1)-(X2,Y2),2,,&HFFFF-I
1560    NEXT I
1570 '
1580 '
```

**Example 3-10**

**Solution, continued.**

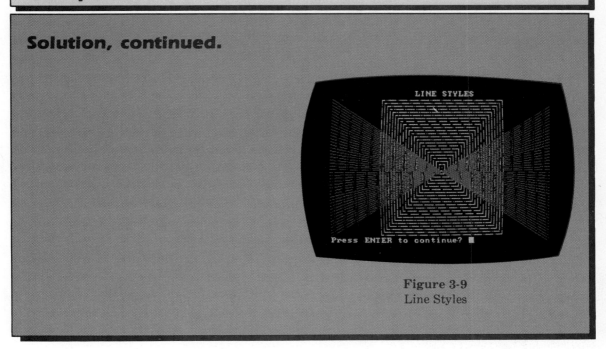

**Figure 3-9**
Line Styles

When this program runs you will first see boxes drawn in yellow (the foreground color), starting with a small box in the center of the screen and working outward with larger and larger boxes. Each box has a slightly different line style. Next you will see a series of red lines slant across the screen, each with a different line style.

In the program for this example, there are two FOR loops. The first (lines 1450-1490) draws the boxes, and the second (lines 1520-1560) draws the slanted lines. In each loop, the index is I and the step size is 4.

Each loop contains just one LINE command. The style parameter is the last parameter. We have used the expression "&HFFFF−I" because, for the small values of I used (less than 200), the style patterns will mostly consist of binary 1s. Thus, the individual lines in the picture will be reasonably solid and distinguishable even if they are densely packed on the screen.

For the lines drawn in the first loop, the Box option is used, producing styled rectangles on the screen with a minimum of fuss. For the lines drawn in the second loop, the Box option is not used, but instead the color option selects a different color for these lines. Using both color and line style provides a very large set of very different lines. This is important in many applications, such as map making.

In the next example, we show how the style bits are mapped to the pixels on the screen. We will use a constant line style pattern, namely 7FFF (hex), throughout this example so that you can easily see how a given pattern is mapped to the screen for a whole series of lines in different positions. We have chosen to arrange the lines as radii of a large circle or disk centered in the middle of the screen. In this way, the entire set of lines has the same starting point, the center of the screen, but the slope ranges throughout all possible values. The effect is quite interesting.

## EXAMPLE 3-11

## MAPPING THE STYLE TO THE SCREEN

Draw a family of lines, all with the style 7FFF; all
starting in the center of the screen; all of the same length,
namely 90; but each of a different angle. The angles should
vary from 0 to 360 degrees and step every 2 degrees. The
lines should be drawn in the foreground color. Before each
line is drawn, its end point should be plotted in a different
color. The resulting picture is shown in Figure 3-10.

## Solution

```
1590 ' STYLED DISK
1600 '
1610   T$ = "STYLED DISK"
1620   GOSUB 5000 ' pause & title
1630 '
1640   STYLE=&H7FFF
1650   PI = 3.1415926535#
1660   XO = 160 : YO = 100 : R = 90
1670 '
1680   FOR T = 0 TO 360 STEP 2
1690    X = XO+R*COS(PI*T/180)
1700    Y = YO+R*SIN(PI*T/180)
1710    PSET (X,Y),2
1720    LINE (XO,YO)-(X,Y),,,STYLE
1730   NEXT T
1740 '
1750 '
```

EXAMPLE 3-11

## Solution, continued.

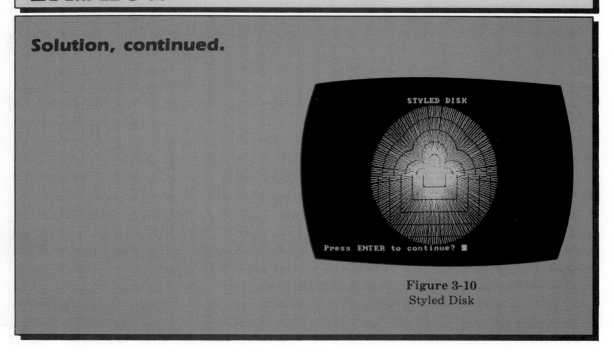

**Figure 3-10**
Styled Disk

When you run this program, you will see the individual radial lines emanate from the center of the screen and terminate on a circle whose radius is 90 units. They are drawn in every 2 degrees, all the way around the circle.

As the lines are drawn you will see gaps every 16 pixels along the lines. This is caused by the style we have chosen, which is 7FFF (hexadecimal). The gaps form interesting patterns in the entire figure. The lower half of the circle contains one pattern and the upper half a different one.

The pattern in the bottom half is rectangular, but the one in the upper half consists of a series of arcs. The reason for this difference is that the style bits start their mapping at the topmost pixel of each line. The topmost pixel of the lines in the bottom of the circle is the center of the circle; thus, the pattern starts in the same place for all of these lines. You can see rectangular gaps in this case. The reason you see this rather than circular gaps is because the pixels are laid out in a rectangular grid, as illustrated in Figure 3-11.

For the lines in the upper half of the circle, the situation is

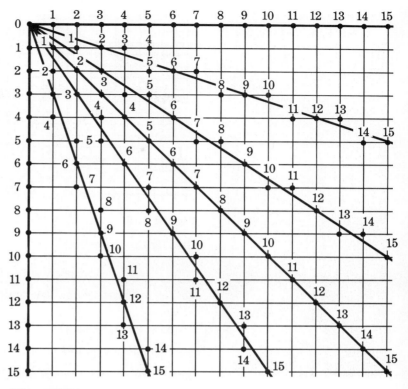

**Figure 3-11**

Rectangular Patterns
on a Grid

quite different. Here the topmost point of each line lies on the
circle; thus, the style mapping starts here. The arcs that you
see reflect this, but the nature of the rectangular grid of pixels distorts these arcs from being true circular arcs. This is
shown in Figure 3-12.

Now let's look at the program for Example 3-11. Notice
that we have defined the variable PI in line 1650. The "#"
indicates double precision. This much precision is entirely
unnecessary, but fun. Actually, pi is a number that can never
be accurately specified by a decimal (or binary) number no
matter how long.

The loop for drawing the lines extends from 1680 to 1730.
On lines 1690 and 1700 we use some trigonometric functions.
If you are unfamiliar with such functions this is a good way

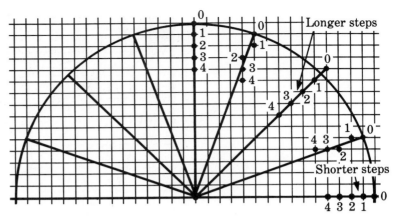

**Figure 3-12**

Grid for the Upper Half

to get to know them. The underlying formulas

$$x = x0 + r*cos(a)$$
$$y = y0 + r*sin(a)$$

are quite useful. If $(x,y)$ are Cartesian coordinates of a point on a circle whose center is at $(x0,y0)$, these formulas give $x$ and $y$ in terms of the radius $r$ and the angle $a$, as shown in Figure 3-13.

In our case, the center $(x0,y0)$ is (X0,Y0), the radius $r$ is R, and the angle $a$ is PI×T/180. The reason for the formula for the angle is to transform degrees to radians, which are required by the trigonometric functions built into BASICA. The angle 2×PI in radians is a complete 360 degrees around the circle, so the angle PI in radians is 180 degrees; thus, to convert from degrees to radians, we must multiply by PI and divide by 180.

Before we draw the line, we plot its endpoint (X,Y) in red. We then draw the line from (X0,Y0) to (X,Y) with the foreground color (yellow) and with style. This provides a test of our understanding of the mapping. You can see the red dots along the top half of the circle, but not along the bottom. On the top half, the mapping begins on the circle and the style 0111111111111111 says to skip the first point, so the red point shows through a gap indicated by a zero. On the bottom half, however, the mapping does not start on the circle itself, so the gap rarely coincides with the circle.

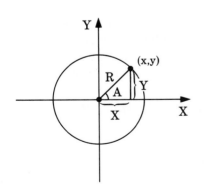

**Figure 3-13**

Cartesian Coordinates
and Circles

Now let's change pace and change the color to light blue. First we draw a single triangle. Here the number of colors matches the number of sides—three colors for three sides. We use absolute coordinates (no STEP). This "fixes" the position of the triangle. In the next example, we will use relative coordinates that will allow us to place the triangle anywhere on the screen.

EXAMPLE 3-12

# A RIGHT TRIANGLE

Write a short program that draws a single right triangle.
Use absolute coordinates. The triangle is shown in the
upper-left corner of Figure 3-14.

## Solution

```
1760 ' RIGHT TRIANGLES
1770 '
1780     T$ = "RIGHT TRIANGLES"
1790     GOSUB 5000 ' pause & title
1800     COLOR 9, 1 ' change color
1810 '
1820 ' Here we use absolute coordinates
1830 '
1840     LINE (21,100) - (71,0), 1
1850     LINE - (71,100), 2
1860     LINE - (21,100), 3
1870 '
```

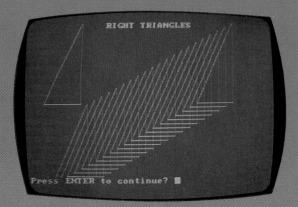

Figure 3-14
Triangles

On the same screen let's use relative coordinates to draw 20 triangles in a diagonal line. In the next example, notice that the (absolute) coordinates in the PSET command are given by *expressions*. This is perfectly legal and a very powerful technique. Notice that relative coordinates are used for the three LINE statements that draw the sides of the triangle. Because only constants are used in these line statements, the triangles all have the same size and shape.

EXAMPLE 3-13

## 20 TRIANGLES IN A LINE

Write a short program that draws 20 triangles along a
diagonal line. Use relative coordinates to allow the triangles
to be easily placed in different spots on the screen. The
triangles are shown in Figure 3-14.

## Solution

```
1880 ' Now we use relative coordinates
1890 ' and make lots of them.
1900 '
1910    FOR T=0 TO 100 STEP 5
1920       PSET (30+2*T,200-T)
1930       LINE - STEP(50,-100), 1
1940       LINE - STEP(0,100), 2
1950       LINE - STEP(-50,0), 3
1960    NEXT T
1970 '
1980 '
```

Now let's make some regular figures which eventually
will lead us to some circles. Since this is a different topic we
also change the background color. This time we call for a yellow background.

EXAMPLE 3-14

# DRAWING A PENTAGON

Write a short program that draws a regular pentagon. The
pentagon is shown in the left of Figure 3-15.

## Solution

```
1990 ' REGULAR POLYGONS
2000 '
2010   T$ = "REGULAR POLYGONS"
2020   GOSUB 5000 ' pause & title
2030   COLOR  5, 1 ' change color
2040 '
2050 ' PENTAGON
2060 '
2070   PI = 3.141592653589793#
2080   AO = 2*PI/5
2090   R = 45
2100 '
2110   PRESET (60+R,100)
2120 '
2130   FOR A = 0 TO 2*PI STEP AO
2140      X=R*COS(A):Y=R*SIN(A)
2150      LINE - (60+X,100+Y)
2160   NEXT A
2170 '
```

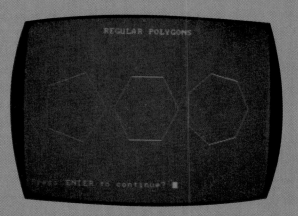

**Figure 3-15**
Regular Polygons

The program is very general, and with only one change (line 2080) will draw a regular polygon of any given number of sides. A polygon is a closed figure made up of line segments. Triangles, squares, rectangles, trapezoids, pentagons, and hexagons are all examples of polygons.

The variable A0 (defined in line 2080) is the STEP size for the FOR loop that draws the figure. By changing this STEP size, you can change the number of sides of the figure. Notice that the STEP in the FOR loop is used differently from the key word STEP that is used to indicate relative coordinates. In line 2090, a radius R is defined. This is the radius of a circumscribing (surrounding) circle around the polygon.

The first plotted point of the figure is set with the PRESET command on line 2110. If you do not do this, you will get an ugly line across the screen.

The FOR loop starts on line 2130. The index of the loop is A which stands for angle. We are using radian measure, so the angle 0 is the beginning of the circle and the angle 2×PI is a complete 360 degrees around the circle. The step size has already been discussed—it determines the number of sides.

To draw the polygon's sides we use the LINE command (line 2150) in absolute coordinates with current position. Notice that the coordinates are simple expressions of the X and Y variables. These expressions help place the figure in the correct spot on the screen. Later we will discuss the topic of positioning or "mapping to the screen" in more detail. The FOR loop ends on line 2160.

The next example is almost identical to the previous one. Only lines 2050, 2080, 2110, and 2150 are different. LIST lines 2050 to 2170 on the screen and change the line numbers so they range from 2180 to 2300. Then change your new lines as indicated in Example 3-15. This will cause a new figure to be drawn with six sides and in the center of the screen. Figure 3-15 shows both polygons as well as a third seven-sided figure called the regular septagon.

**EXAMPLE 3-15**

## DRAWING A HEXAGON

Write a short program that draws a regular hexagon. The
hexagon is shown in the middle of Figure 3-15.

## Solution

```
2180 ' HEXAGON
2190 '
2200    PI = 3.1415926535#
2210    A0 = 2*PI/6
2220    R = 45
2230 '
2240    PRESET (160+R,100)
2250 '
2260    FOR A = 0 TO 2*PI STEP A0
2270       X=R*COS(A):Y=R*SIN(A)
2280       LINE - (160+X,100+Y)
2290    NEXT A
2300 '
```

To get the third figure, edit your previous program and
change the appropriate lines (see Example 3-16). Now it is
easy to generate all of these nearly identical program segments. Many programs are "grown" in a similar way; that is,
a programmer will often start with an old program and modify it so that it performs new tasks. This approach saves a lot
of time. Of course, the resulting programs usually end up
looking quite different from their ancestor programs.

EXAMPLE 3-16

# DRAWING A HEPTAGON

Write a short program that draws a regular heptagon. The
heptagon is shown in the right of Figure 3-15.

## Solution

```
2310 ' HEPTAGON
2320 '
2330   PI = 3.1415926535#
2340   AO = 2*PI/7
2350   R = 45
2360 '
2370   PRESET (260+R,100)
2380 '
2390   FOR A = 0 TO 2*PI STEP AO
2400       X=R*COS(A):Y=R*SIN(A)
2410       LINE - (260+X,100+Y)
2420   NEXT A
2430 '
2440 '
```

Now that we know how to "clone" programs, let's take the
previous idea and make it fancier. We will also introduce
some new ideas that will give our graphics programs more
power and speed.

**Advanced LINE
Command**

In this section we introduce advanced line-drawing concepts such as *positioner functions* and *matrix methods*. These
are methods used in large professional graphics programs.
We will show how scaled down versions of these techniques
can work on small sample graphics programs on the IBM PC.

In our first example we will draw a series of polygons in
different positions and different colors. The color will not look
quite right on an NTSC TV or monitor, so in our second example we will go through the entire picture, enhancing the color.

We are going to compare the performance of this program

with the one following it, so we are asking the computer to time how long it takes to execute this program. We will then be able to tell how much better or worse one is. Often program size, readability, or complexity has to be sacrificed to improve the speed. If we have exact figures for these quantities, we can make more intelligent decisions as to which method to choose.

**EXAMPLE 3-17**

## ADVANCED POLYGONS I

Write a short program that draws a series of polygons,
each one larger and with more sides than the previous one.
Cycle through the colors as you draw successive polygons.
Use trigonometric functions to compute the coordinates of
the polygons. The polygons are shown in Figure 3-16.

## Solution

```
2450 ' ADVANCED POLYGONS I
2460 '
2470    T$ = "MORE POLYGONS"
2480    GOSUB 5000 ' pause & title
2490    COLOR 0,1
2500 '
2510 ' We use trigonometric functions
2520 '
2530    TIME$ = "00:00:00"
2540 '
2550 ' POSITIONING FUNCTIONS
2560    DEF FNX(X)=12*N+X
2570    DEF FNY(Y)=100+Y
2580 '
2590    FOR N = 3 TO 20
2600 '
2610       PI = 3.1415926535#
2620       AO = 2*PI/N
2630       R  = 3*N
2640       C = (N MOD 3) + 1
2650 '
2660       PRESET (FNX(R),FNY(O))
2670 '
2680       FOR A = 0 TO 2*PI+.01 STEP AO
2690          X=R*COS(A):Y=R*SIN(A)
2700          LINE - (FNX(X),FNY(Y)),C
2710       NEXT A
2720 '
2730    NEXT N
2740    LOCATE 3,1
2750    PRINT "time elapsed: ";TIME$
2760 '
2770 '
```

■

**Example 3-17**

## Solution, continued.

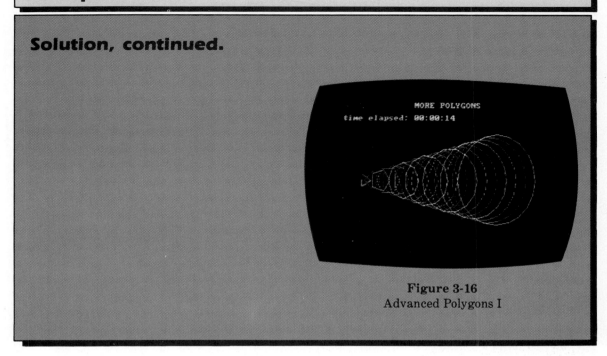

**Figure 3-16**
Advanced Polygons I

Now let's look at the program. On line 2530 we set the time equal to zero, and on line 2750 we print the resulting elapsed time. In this program the positions, the number of sides, the radii, and the colors of the polygons are all computed at various places in the program.

*Positioner functions* are defined on lines 2180-2200. These functions allow you to work with your own x,y-coordinates rather than the screen coordinates. The positioner functions in this program transform coordinates from our model of the figure (using x- and y-positions related to the figure itself) to the actual screen coordinates. The screen coordinates have their origin (the point (0,0)) at the upper-left corner of the screen, whereas in our picture, the origin is set at the center of each polygon as it is being drawn.

The coordinates used to describe the figure are called *user coordinates*. To draw the picture on the screen you must transform or "map" them to the coordinate system of the screen (see Figure 3-17). This transformation is called the *viewing transformation*. These functions help conceal the "ugly" details of the viewing transformation.

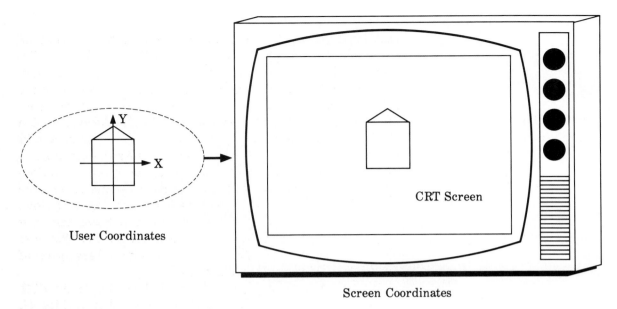

User Coordinates

Screen Coordinates

**Figure 3-17**

Mapping from User
to Screen Coordinates

Almost all professional graphics applications programs work with their own coordinate system and must use a viewing transformation to go from the user's coordinates to the screen coordinates. Effective control of this process is the key to writing programs that draw pictures of all sorts of objects on all sorts of graphics devices with a minimum of fuss. Professional graphics systems normally have these viewing transformations built into the system itself rather than cluttering up the applications program. This makes the applications programs easier to read, write, and understand, as well as less expensive to develop.

Fortunately, the IBM PC also has built-in viewing transformations. Its WINDOW and VIEW commands allow the user to control these transformations in a natural and professional manner. Later in this chapter we give a careful introduction to these commands and discuss how they work. However, in this example, we will do this transformation explicitly so that you can begin to see what is to come.

If you do not use the built-in viewing transformations, you can still use these functions to gain an important advantage;

that is, if you wish to change the viewing transformation, there is only one spot in the program that you have to fix. There is, however, a disadvantage—time. Using these functions instead of direct formulas adds about two seconds to the elapsed time for running this program. On the other hand, using built-in viewing transformations (with BASICA version 2) should not greatly affect the speed because they are in machine language and they are performed automatically.

With graphics there is a constant battle between development time and execution time. As machines get faster, the trend is to do those things that help the development time; that is, it is becoming more important to save the programmer's time than to save the machine's time. The only possible exceptions are animation programs, where speed of execution is of primary importance.

In our polygon program (Example 3-17), the main FOR loop extends from lines 2590 to 2710. The number of sides, N, is the index for this main FOR loop. The step size for the side is now computed in a formula depending upon N (line 2620). The radius is also a function of N (line 2630), and the color uses the MOD function to cycle through the values 1, 2, 3, 1, 2, 3, and so on (see line 2640). Recall that ($x$ MOD $y$) is the remainder when $x$ is divided by $y$.

The positioner functions are invoked on two different lines, the PRESET command (line 2660) and the LINE command (line 2700). You can read these lines more easily with the positioner functions.

If you run this program on a standard TV (or NTSC monitor), you will notice that the polygons seem to be missing pieces or changing colors in unusual ways. This is because the horizontal resolution of the picture is twice that of the color encoding.

Our next example fixes this picture by drawing the same figures one position to the right of what was just drawn. Thus, every point is doubled horizontally. This is essentially one of the $160 \times 200$ color modes which will be described in Chapter 8.

EXAMPLE 3-18

## ADVANCED POLYGONS II

Write a short program that draws a series of polygons
immediately next to the previous ones to improve the color.
Use the matrix method to increase the execution speed of
the program. The polygons are shown in Figure 3-18.

## Solution

```
2780 ' ADVANCED POLYGONS II
2790 '
2800 ' This time we use a matrix
2810 ' method.  We fill in the
2820 ' figure just drawn to give
2830 ' truer color for NTSC.
2840 '
2850    TIME$ = "00:00:00"
2860 '
2870 ' POSITIONING FUNCTIONS
2880    DEF FNX(X)=1+12*N+X
2890    DEF FNY(Y)=100+Y
2900 '
2910    FOR N = 3 TO 20
2920 '
2930       PI = 3.1415926535#
2940       AO = 2*PI/N
2950       R  = 3*N
2960       CO = COS(AO)
2970       SO = SIN(AO)
2980       X  = R       : Y  = O
2990       C = (N MOD 3) + 1
3000 '
3010       PRESET (FNX(R),FNY(O))
3020 '
3030       FOR A = O TO 2*PI+.01 STEP AO
3040          LINE  -(FNX(X),FNY(Y)), C
3050          XO=X:YO=Y
3060          X=XO*CO - YO*SO
3070          Y=XO*SO + YO*CO
3080       NEXT A
3090 '
3100    NEXT N
3110    LOCATE 3,1
3120    PRINT "time elapsed: ";TIME$
3130 '
3140 '
```

## Example 3-18

**Solution, continued.**

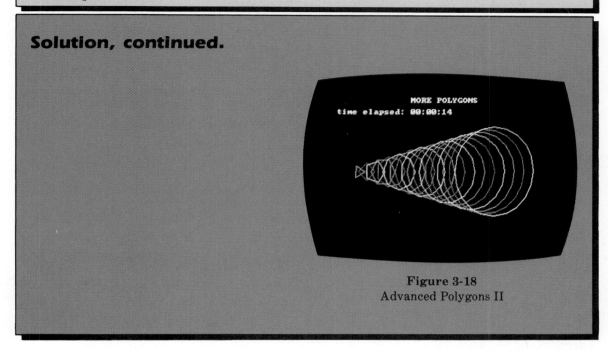

**Figure 3-18**
Advanced Polygons II

The method for computing the points of the figures is speeded up in this example. This time we do not use the trigonometric functions COS and SIN. Instead we use what is called a *matrix method*, which is faster. You will see that even in this method you have to use trigonometric functions to "prime the pump" (that is, compute certain constants initially), but once you get started, no trigonometric functions need to be computed.

The matrix method for drawing polygons might also be called the *addition formula method* because it takes advantage of the addition formulas for the COS and SIN.

The method depends on trigonometry, but it produces an algorithm that does not require computation of any trigonometric functions once the plotting has started.

Start with the addition formulas

$$COS(A+B) = COS(A)*COS(B) - SIN(A)*SIN(B)$$
$$SIN(A+B) = SIN(A)*COS(B) - COS(A)*SIN(B)$$

This tells you how to use just the operations of multiplication

**Plotting and Line Drawing**     **101**

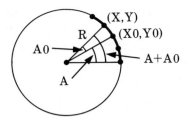

**Figure 3-19**

Stepping Around the Circle

and addition to compute the cosine and sine of (A+B) if you already know the cosine and sine of the angles A and B. In our case, we want the cosine and sine of the new angle (A+A0) in terms of the cosine and sine of the current angle A and the step size, as shown in Figure 3-19.

Multiplying each side of the equations by the radius R and letting the step size A0 replace B, we get

$$R*COS(A+A0) = R*COS(A)*COS(A0) - R*SIN(A)*SIN(A0)$$

$$R*SIN(A+A0) = R*SIN(A)*COS(A0) - R*COS(A)*SIN(A0)$$

In the example program, in lines 2960-2970 we define constant variables C0 and S0 to be COS(A0) and SIN(A0), respectively. Now substitute this into the formulas:

$$R*COS(A+A0) = R*COS(A)*C0 - R*SIN(A)*S0$$

$$R*SIN(A+A0) = R*SIN(A)*C0 - R*COS(A)*S0$$

In line 3050 the current X and Y are saved as X0 and Y0. These are equal to R*COS(A) and R*SIN(A), respectively. Thus, the new coordinates are given by substituting this in the previous pair of formulas, giving

$$R*COS(A+A0) = X0*C0 - Y0*S0$$

$$R*SIN(A+A0) = Y0*C0 + X0*S0$$

A slight rearrangement in order gives the formulas in lines 3060-3070.

$$X = X0*C0 - Y0*S0$$

$$Y = X0*S0 + Y0*C0$$

This can be viewed as, and is equivalent to, the following matrix multiplication:

$$\begin{pmatrix} X \\ Y \end{pmatrix} = \begin{pmatrix} C0 & -S0 \\ S0 & +C0 \end{pmatrix} \begin{pmatrix} X0 \\ Y0 \end{pmatrix}$$

We have just seen how lines can be used to draw all sorts of shapes, including some that look very much like circles. However, considerable effort and mathematical expertise is needed to draw them at a reasonable rate of speed. In the next section, we will study a command to make circles. Since the CIRCLE command is in machine language (as part of BASICA), it will run faster, and since it is invoked as a single command, it is easier to use.

## The CIRCLE Command

The CIRCLE command does much more than its name implies. It also draws arcs and ellipses, providing a fast way to construct curved shapes. This allows you to construct complicated pictures with less effort.

The full syntax for the CIRCLE command is

CIRCLE (xcenter,ycenter),radius[,color[,start,end [,aspect]]]

Here is another place where there are many optional parameters. But let's begin by drawing a plain circle. The syntax for this simple case is

CIRCLE (xcenter,ycenter),radius

where *xcenter* and *ycenter* are the x- and y-coordinates of the center of the circle and *radius* is the radius of the circle. Here we can see that the x- and y-coordinates of the center and the radius are all specified. The quantities *xcenter*, *ycenter*, and *radius* can all be expressions. Either absolute or relative coordinates can be used for the center.

The following example illustrates this simpler form of the command. The coordinates of the center and the radius are all constants in this example. In later examples we will use more complicated expressions.

**EXAMPLE 3-19**

## DRAWING A CIRCLE

Write a short program that draws a circle in the center of
the screen. Use the CIRCLE command. The circle is shown
in Figure 3-20.

## Solution

```
3150 ' CIRCLE
3160 '
3170    T$ = "CIRCLE — THE EASY WAY"
3180    GOSUB 5000 ' pause & title
3190 '
3200 ' Here is the easy way to make
3210 ' a circle.
3220 '
3230    CIRCLE (160,100), 60
3240 '
3250 '
```

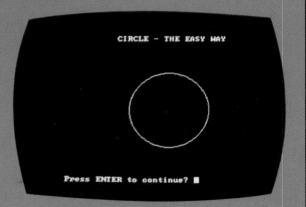

Figure 3-20
Circle

When this program runs it produces a circle in the center
of the screen. The circle is somewhat flattened. The amount of

flattening varies from screen to screen. We will see how to fix this soon.

We should note that in all forms of the CIRCLE command, the *current position* is always updated to be the center of the circle, not the last point drawn on the figure.

If you look closely while the circle is being drawn, you will see that it starts at four points and "grows" in eight different places on the circle at once. There is an algorithm for drawing circles in this way. This algorithm is locked up and hidden in machine language so that it will run very fast.

Now let's explore arcs. As you might suspect, an arc is really part of a circle. Many graphics systems do not have a CIRCLE statement, let alone an ARC statement. In those systems, you would have to do things the hard way. That is what we will do in the next example. Once you see this, you will appreciate the power of the CIRCLE command.

The next example uses trigonometric functions in a very similar way to what was done in drawing polygons. Instead of drawing arcs, it draws spanning sections of 30-sided polygons. With the medium-resolution screen, you cannot tell the difference between this and a true circular arc. In our program we have again included a timer so that you can compare this method with a much easier and faster method that will follow.

This program draws ten arcs that all start at the center of the screen, but belong to different circles. Look at Figure 3-21 to see how they are arranged. We will not explain the decisions we made to get this program working in as few steps as possible, but you are welcome to study the listing yourself.

EXAMPLE 3-20

# MAKING ARCS THE HARD WAY

Write a short program that draws ten arcs which all start
at the center of the screen, but belong to different circles.
Use trigonometric functions and the LINE command to
draw the figure. Use the computer's clock to time the
program. The arcs are pictured in Figure 3-21.

---

## Solution

```
3260 ' MAKING ARCS - THE HARD WAY
3270 '
3280    T$ = "ARCS - THE HARD WAY"
3290    GOSUB 5000 ' pause & title
3300 '
3310 ' This uses trigonometric
3320 ' functions.
3330 '
3340    PI = 3.1415926535#
3350    A0 = 2*PI/30
3360    R  = 40
3370    FUDGE=.01
3380 '
3390    TIME$="00:00:00"
3400    FOR E0=0 TO 2*PI+FUDGE STEP PI/5
3410 '
3420      PRESET (160,80)
3430 '
3440      FOR A = E0 TO -FUDGE STEP -A0
3450          X=R*COS(A)-R*COS(E0)
3460          Y=R*SIN(A)-R*SIN(E0)
3470          LINE - (160+X,80+Y)
3480      NEXT A
3490 '
3500    NEXT E0
3510 '
3520    LOCATE 3,1
3530    PRINT "time elapsed: ";TIME$
3540 '
3550 '
```

**Example 3-20**

**Solution, continued.**

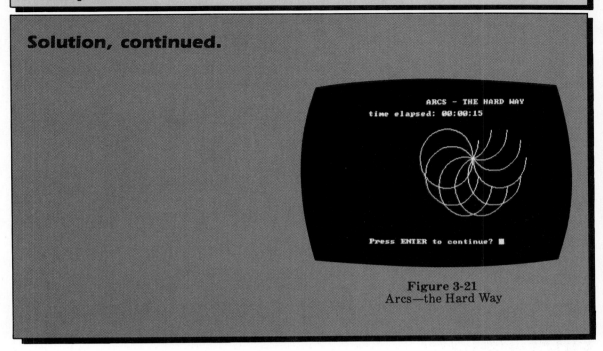

**Figure 3-21**
Arcs—the Hard Way

Notice that this program has a very important ingredient: FUDGE. Because of rounding errors, FOR loops with real indices do not always execute the very last case. What happens is that because of rounding errors, the value of the index the last time through is slightly larger than the correct stopping value; hence we need a "fudge" factor which is called, naturally enough, FUDGE.

Now let's see how to make arcs using the faster BASICA CIRCLE command. An arc has a starting angle and an ending angle (in radians), as shown in Figure 3-22.

To make an arc, tack the starting angle and ending angle onto the end of the CIRCLE command. The syntax is

CIRCLE (xcenter,ycenter),radius,color,start,end

where *start* is the starting angle and *end* is the ending angle (in radians).

In the next example, we draw the same number of arcs as in the previous program. The positions are different in this program, but the programs are comparable because the arcs

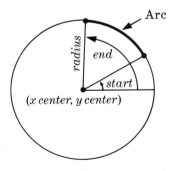

**Figure 3-22**

An Arc—Starting Angle and Ending Angle

are of the same lengths as in the previous program. We have also put a timer on this program so you can compare the speed of execution with the last program. You can see from the time output of the program in Figure 3-23 that it runs significantly faster (about 15 times faster). It is also much easier to understand. For example, there is only one FOR loop; the CIRCLE command takes care of what was the old inner FOR loop.

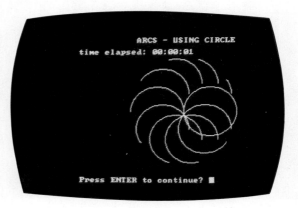

**Figure 3-23**

Making Arcs with the CIRCLE Command

EXAMPLE 3-21

## MAKING ARCS THE EASY WAY

Write a short program that draws ten arcs. This time use
the CIRCLE command. Use the computer's clock to time
the program. The new arcs are pictured in Figure 3-23.

## Solution

```
3560 ' ARCS - USING CIRCLE
3570 '
3580    T$ = "ARCS - USING CIRCLE"
3590    GOSUB 5000 ' pause & title
3600 '
3610 ' This uses the circle statement.
3620 '
3630    PI = 3.1415926535#
3640    R  = 40
3650 '
3660    TIME$="00:00:00"
3670    FOR EO = 0 TO 2*PI+.01 STEP PI/5
3680       Y = 100 - R*SIN(EO)
3690       X = 160 + R*COS(EO)
3700       CIRCLE (X,Y), R, 3, 0, EO
3710    NEXT EO
3720 '
3730    LOCATE 3,1
3740    PRINT "time elapsed: ";TIME$
3750 '
3760 '
```

Looking closely at the program, we see that the arcs are
produced by the CIRCLE statement on line 3700. The center
(X,Y) of this circle is recomputed each time through the
remaining FOR loop. The trigonometric functions in the FOR
loop cause this center to rotate about the center of the screen,
thus enhancing the picture. The radius R for each arc is
always the same, and the color is also always the same,
namely 3. Each arc always starts at an angle of 0 radians, but
each arc is longer than the previous one.

We could have eliminated the color parameter, but we

must still have the commas which mark its place in the command.

In the example the start and end angles were nonnegative. The CIRCLE command does something special if the angle is negative—it draws a radius. We will discuss this later when we present an example applications program that draws pie charts.

The last example in our "stand-alone" series shows how to "squash," or round out, circles. The last parameter in the CIRCLE command is called the *aspect ratio*. It is the ratio of the radius in the x-direction to the radius in the y-direction. When we change this quantity in the CIRCLE command, we get an ellipse. (See the full syntax of the CIRCLE command at the beginning of this section.)

If the aspect ratio is less than 1, the radius in the x-direction is equal to *radius* (as specified in the command) and the radius in the y-direction is equal to *radius*×*aspect*. If, on the other hand, the aspect ratio is greater than 1, the radius in the x-direction is equal to *radius/aspect*, and the radius in the y-direction is equal to *radius*. Figure 3-24 illustrates these rules. This scheme guarantees that *radius* (the specified radius) is always the *maximum* radius of the ellipse.

Our example program also illustrates the rules for aspect ratio. It has a FOR loop which steps through values for ASPECT from 0 to 9 by every tenth. If ASPECT is less than 1, the color is equal to 1 (cyan), and if ASPECT is greater

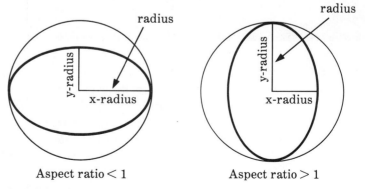

Aspect ratio < 1          Aspect ratio > 1

**Figure 3-24**

Explanation of Aspect Ratio
for CIRCLE Command

than or equal to 1, the color is equal to 2 (magenta). Thus, you can separate the cases as the figure is drawn. As the picture unfolds you will first see blue (cyan) ellipses that all have the same horizontal (x-direction) radius but are flattened vertically (y-direction). These ellipses have an aspect ratio of less than 1. Next you will see purple (magenta) ellipses that all have the same vertical radius (y-direction), but are flattened horizontally (x-direction). These ellipses have an aspect ratio greater than or equal to 1. All ellipses fit within the same circular region.

EXAMPLE 3-22

## DRAWING ELLIPSES

Write a short program that draws lots of ellipses. If the
aspect ratio is less than 1, color the ellipses cyan, but if the
aspect ratio is greater than 1, color the ellipses magenta.
The set of ellipses is shown in Figure 3-25.

## Solution

```
3770 ' ELLIPSES
3780 '
3790    T$ = "FAMILY OF ELLIPSES"
3800    COLOR 0,1
3810    GOSUB 5000 ' pause & title
3820 '
3830 ' This shows what you can do
3840 ' with the aspect ratio
3850 '
3860    PI = 3.1415926535#
3870    FOR ASPECT = 0 TO 9 STEP .1
3880       IF ASPECT<1 THEN C=1 ELSE C=2
3890       CIRCLE (160,100),60,C,,,ASPECT
3900    NEXT ASPECT
3910 '
3920    LOCATE 23,1
3930    END
3940 '
```

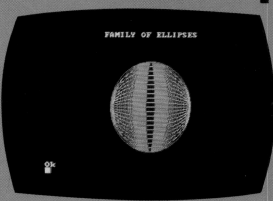

Figure 3-25
Ellipses

Notice that the arc-making parameters in the CIRCLE statement (line 3890) are absent but their places are held by commas.

At the end of the program we put a LOCATE statement (line 3920). This places the cursor out of the way when the program stops.

In the IBM PC there is a "default value" given to the aspect ratio when nothing is specified in the CIRCLE statement. This default value depends upon whether you are in medium- or high-resolution mode. The default for medium-resolution mode is 5/6 and for high-resolution mode is 5/12. This is consistent with the difference in resolution between these two modes being a doubling of resolution in the x-direction. These aspect ratios were designed to give a perfect circle in both cases, but in practice this does not always happen.

In theory, a TV screen has an aspect ratio such that the vertical side is three-quarters the size of the horizontal side. You can think of the screen as the lower three-quarters of a big square. With the $320 \times 200$ medium-resolution mode, this fictitious square is approximately $320 \times 267$, which gives an aspect ratio of 5/6. This is why IBM chose the 5/6 default value in the medium-resolution graphics mode.

Different TV sets and monitors will have slightly different aspect ratios. In fact, you can often make adjustments that will change the aspect ratio on a TV monitor. Thus, no matter what you do, a circle will never appear perfectly round for *all* displays. The aspect ratio can be adjusted for each site.

To finish this section on commands and their features, we present the first applications example program of this chapter. It produces a pie chart. A pie chart is a convenient way of presenting data in which each piece of data is part of a whole (total). The total is represented by the interior of a complete circle and each piece of data is represented by a different pie-shaped part (sector) of the interior of the circle.

In the following example, we use a special feature of the CIRCLE command called *radius drawing*. When it is used, the ends of arcs are automatically connected to the center of the circle by a straight line. To invoke this feature, you use negative angles for the beginning or ending angles of an arc.

EXAMPLE 3-23

## PIE CHART

Write a short interactive program that makes a pie chart.
The user should be allowed to enter as many items of data
as he or she wishes. Terminate such input with a negative
number. The pie chart is shown in Figure 3-26.

---

## Solution

```
100 ' PIE CHART
110 '
120 '
130    KEY OFF
140    SCREEN 1
150    CLS
160 '
170    PI=3.1415926535#
180    DIM SECTOR(25)
190 '
200    PRINT "To stop, enter a negative"
210    J = 0
220 ' INPUT LOOP
230       J = J+1
240       PRINT "size of sector";J;
250       INPUT SECTOR(J)
260       IF SECTOR(J)<0 THEN 300
270       TOTAL = TOTAL+SECTOR(J)
280    GOTO 220
290 '
300 ' CONTINUE
310    N=J-1
320 '
330    CLS
340    LOCATE 1,15
350    PRINT TOTAL; "Total";
360 '
370    BEGA=0
380    RADIUS=80
390 '
400    FOR J=1 TO N
410       ENDA=2*PI*SECTOR(J)/TOTAL+BEGA
420       MIDA=(BEGA+ENDA)/2
430 '
440       X = 160+COS(MIDA)*RADIUS*1.2
```

▶

# Example 3-23

## Solution, continued.

```
450        Y = 100-SIN(MIDA)*RADIUS*1
460        M$ = STR$(SECTOR(J))
470        LOCATE (Y+4)/8, X/8-LEN(M$)/2
480        PRINT M$;
490      '
500        A1 = -BEGA-.001
510        A2 = -ENDA
520        CIRCLE(160,100),RADIUS,,A1,A2
530      '
540        BEGA=ENDA
550    NEXT J
560    '
570    LOCATE 22
580    END
```

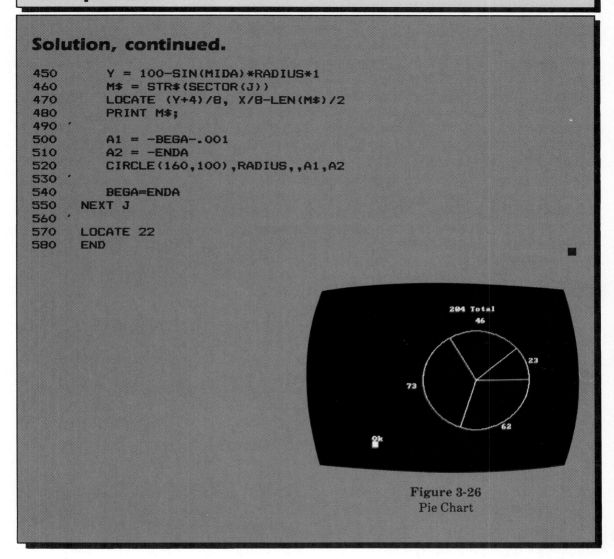

**Figure 3-26**
Pie Chart

Now let's look at the program in more detail. The first part of this program (lines 100-320) accepts data from the user, and the last part plots the pie chart. The user is allowed to enter as many values as he or she wants. To end data entry, the user types in a negative number.

In the part of the program that draws the pie chart, there is a main FOR loop that runs through the sectors (pieces) of the pie. Each sector is specified by a starting angle and an ending angle. The ending angle of one sector is the starting angle of the next sector. Within the FOR loop, the new ending angle is computed first, then a midpoint angle is obtained, and finally the sector is labeled. For positioning the labels, look at how we must transform from arc-circle (polar) coordinates to screen (x-y) coordinates, and finally to row-column coordinates for the text. The last part of the FOR loop actually draws the sector. Observe that the angles are negative to invoke the special "radius drawing" feature of the CIRCLE command.

We have just seen how to use the point-, line-, and circle-drawing commands one by one through a series of short examples and one real application. In the rest of this chapter, we will see how to put these commands together to perform further applications.

## ADVANCED GRAPHICS CONCEPTS

In this section we describe some simple but powerful techniques for drawing pictures with the point, line, and circle commands. You should consider this an introduction rather than a complete treatment. If you wish to know more, consult the books listed in Appendix D.

## Viewing Concepts— Coordinates and Transformations

The first concept is *coordinate systems* used in viewing an object. As we have seen in our example program segments, there is usually some *object* that we are trying to depict. Some of these objects are two-dimensional (2-D) and some are three-dimensional (3-D). Two-dimensional objects are flat, such as a piece of paper or the screen of your TV monitor. Such objects have only two dimensions: length and width. We can use two coordinates, like x and y, to represent the positions of the points they contain. Thus, the position of any point in a two-dimensional object is represented by a pair of numbers (x,y). Three-dimensional objects require an additional dimension, like depth, and an additional coordinate. The position of any point in a three-dimensional object is represented by a triple (x,y,z) of numbers. It is even possible to talk about objects that are four-dimensional and higher.

A given object will have some kind of natural coordinate system with a natural unit distance. For example, you can represent the position of one corner of a rectangular piece of property by the coordinates (0,0). Thus, the first coordinate will measure distance in feet from this point in the direction parallel to the front boundary and the second coordinate will measure distance in feet or meters back from this point in the direction parallel to the side boundary. This is illustrated in Figure 3-27.

On the other hand, the screen has its own natural coordinate system. For the IBM PC screen, the point (0,0) is in the upper-left corner. The first coordinate measures how many pixels you are to the right of this point and the second coordinate measures how many pixels you are down from this point.

The coordinate system for the object is usually referred to as the *user coordinate system* or *world coordinate system*. The coordinate system for the screen is usually referred to as the *screen coordinate system*. Other names for these coordinate systems are also commonly used. For example, instead of user or world coordinates we may say *object coordinates*, and instead of screen coordinates we may say *device coordinates* or *image coordinates*. Device coordinates is a handy term if we are trying to produce an image on a number of different devices, which may include video screens of different resolutions, digital plotters, or graphics printers.

When we want the computer to draw an object, the com-

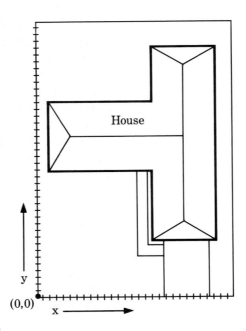

**Figure 3-27**

Natural Coordinate System
for a Piece of Property

puter needs to know the *screen* coordinates of the points in the *image* of the object on the screen. However, the data for the points is stored in the machine in user coordinates. Software (and sometimes hardware) is needed to convert the coordinate values associated with the object to the coordinates associated with the screen. This conversion process from user coordinates to screen coordinates is called a *viewing transformation*.

BASICA version 2 has built-in commands, VIEW and WINDOW, to simplify the process for the programmer, at least in 2-D. We will explain the basic ideas behind these commands and their syntax, and then show through example programs how they can be used to make programming easier.

**2-D Viewing Transformations**

To control and determine the 2-D viewing transformation we introduce two types of viewing regions: *viewports* and *windows*.

A *viewport* is a rectangular viewing region on the screen itself. Since the screen is rectangular, there is a natural rectangular region in the screen coordinate system that corresponds to the limits of the screen. In medium-resolution mode, these limits are 0 and 319 for $x$ and 0 and 199 for $y$. The viewport is initially the full screen. As we program, however, we can make the viewport smaller or larger than the actual screen. In fact, by making a number of small viewports (as illustrated in Figure 3-28) that correspond to different rectangles on the screen, we can present a whole series of pictures to the viewer at once, offering the possibility of making complicated programs very interactive.

You can control the placement of the viewport with the VIEW command. The full syntax for this command is

VIEW [[SCREEN][(u1,v1) − (u2,v2)[,[color][,[boundary]]]]]

where SCREEN is an optional specifier that controls the mapping, and $u1$, $v1$, $u2$, and $v2$ are numeric expressions that define the limits of the viewport or clipping window depending upon whether the SCREEN option is used (more on this later). The syntax works exactly the same way that the syntax in the LINE command specifies the limits of the box in its Box and Box Fill options. $u1$ and $u2$ determine the limits for the horizontal direction and $v1$ and $v2$ determine the limits for the vertical direction. We have used the variables $u$ and

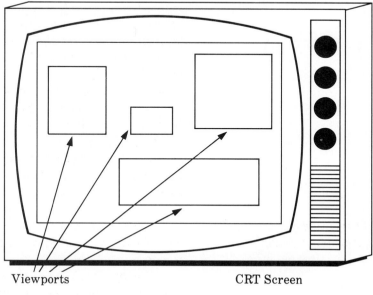

Viewports       CRT Screen

**Figure 3-28**

Viewports on the Screen

$v$ for the VIEW command to distinguish them from the x-and y-coordinates that are used in the WINDOW command. The variables $u$ and $v$ are screen coordinates. If you do not include the coordinates (u1,v1) − (u2,v2) in the command line, the viewport will be set to the entire screen.

The next parameter *color*, if used, is a numeric expression that specifies the color to fill the viewport; and *boundary*, if used, is a numeric expression that specifies the color of a boundary (frame) to be drawn around the viewport.

The CLS command only clears the area in the viewport, not the entire screen, if the viewport is defined to be smaller than the screen.

Just as the screen has viewing regions called viewports, the user coordinate space can have different viewing regions. These are called *windows*. When a picture is drawn, the current window in user space is mapped via the viewing transformation to the current viewport in screen space. This is shown in Figure 3-29.

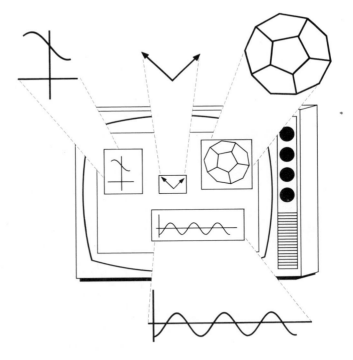

**Figure 3-29**

Windows Being Mapped to Viewports

The programmer controls the location of the window with the WINDOW command. The full syntax for this command is

WINDOW [[SCREEN] (x1,y1) − (x2,y2)]

where SCREEN is an optional specifier that controls the mapping, and $x1$, $y1$, $x2$, and $y2$ give the x and y limits of the window in the same way that $u1$, $v1$, $u2$, and $v2$ specify the limits of the viewport or clipping window in the VIEW command. If you do not include the coordinates (x1,y1) − (x2,y2), the window will be the same as the viewport.

The programmer can control the entire mapping process by controlling the location of the viewports and the windows. The general idea is that corners are mapped to corners. Initially, that is, after you type RUN or SCREEN commands but before setting any viewport or window, the viewport and the window are the same. For example, in the medium-resolution graphics mode, the viewport is given by

umin  =  0
vmin  =  0
umax  =  319
vmax  =  199

in screen coordinates, and the window is given by the same limits

xmin  =  0
ymin  =  0
xmax  =  319
ymax  =  199

in user coordinates. The point (umin,vmin) = (xmin,ymin) = (0,0) is in the upper-left corner of the screen, and the point (umax,vmax) = (xmax,ymax) = (319,199) is in the lower-right corner of the screen.

In this case, the corner point (xmin,ymin) of the window gets mapped to the corner point (umin,vmin) of the viewport and the corner point (xmax, ymax) of the window gets mapped to the corner point (umax,vmax) of the viewport. The effect is to ignore windows and viewports.

If you use the VIEW command with coordinates (u1,v1) − (u2,v2) but without the SCREEN option, the corners of the viewport are set by sorting these coordinates in the following way: The upper-left corner of the viewport is (umin,vmin), where umin is the minimum of u1 and u2, and vmin is the minimum of v1 and v2. The lower-right corner is (umax, vmax), where umax is the maximum of u1 and u2, and vmax is the maximum of v1 and v2. If you use the SCREEN option, the viewport is the entire screen and these coordinates specify the location of what is called the *clipping window*.

If you use the WINDOW command with coordinates (x1,y1) − (x2,y2), the corners of the window are set by these coordinates in the following way: One corner of the window is (xmin,ymin), where xmin is the minimum of x1 and x2, and ymin is the minimum of y1 and y2. The opposite corner is (xmax,ymax), where xmax is the maximum of x1 and x2, and ymax is the maximum of y1 and y2. If you do not use the SCREEN option, (xmin,ymin) is in the lower-left corner and (xmax,ymax) is in the upper-right corner. This is the normal case for Cartesian coordinates. However, if you do use the SCREEN option, the window is flipped upside down with (xmin,ymin) in the *upper*-left corner and (xmax,ymax) in the *lower*-right corner. This corresponds to the way screen coordinates are flipped upside down.

In version 1 of IBM PC Advanced BASIC, the VIEW and WINDOW commands were not available so the mapping process had to be explicitly controlled by the programmer. For those who have not yet obtained a copy of version 2, and for those who want to understand how the PC makes the viewing transformation, we will now describe the mathematics involved. All the formulas needed to implement the viewing transformation are included here.

## Deriving the Constants in the Viewing Transformation

In 2-D viewing transformations, the object is two-dimensional and so is its image on the screen. The viewing transformation can be accomplished by some stretching or shrinking (scaling), some shifting up, down, back, or forth (translation), and some flipping (y becomes −y). Another form of transformation, *rotation*, is discussed under "3-D Viewing Concepts."

There are two simple ideas that allow us to handle 2-D easily:

1. Each coordinate is handled separately.
2. The formula for the transformation is given by as simple a mathematical formula as possible.

As a result, we have two linear equations that have the user coordinates on the right-hand side and the screen coordinates on the left-hand side.

xscreen  =  a∗xuser + b

yscreen  =  c∗yuser + d

where *a*, *b*, *c*, and *d* are constants that determine the transformation.

Although these formulas can be understood in terms of scaling (shrinking and stretching) and translation (shifting back and forth or up and down), this is not how we choose to look at the situation. Instead, we prefer to keep the screen coordinates (*xscreen,yscreen*) and the user coordinates (xuser, yuser) in different "worlds." We can, however, think of these two different 2-D worlds as two slices of a 3-D object called a *viewing tube*. (See Figure 3-30 for an illustration.) This tube consists of the lines of sight from the object to the viewing screen and then to your eye. Such an approach will, indeed, lead to these formulas, but we will not attempt to derive this.

The constants *a*, *b*, *c*, and *d* completely determine the viewing transformation. We will now show how these constants can be determined if we are given the limits of the window and viewport.

Suppose that, as in our previous discussion, the screen coordinates are called *u* and *v* and the user coordinates are called *x* and *y*. The formula for the viewing transformation is

u  =  a∗x + b

v  =  c∗y + d

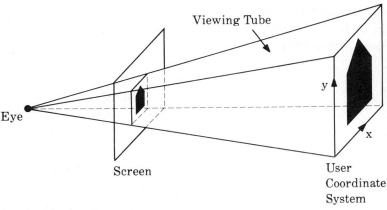

**Figure 3-30**

Viewing Tube

A given viewport is described by the conditions

umin $\leq$ u $\leq$ umax
vmin $\leq$ v $\leq$ vmax

If you use the VIEW command, the syntax

VIEW (umin,vmin) $-$ (umax,vmax)

would set up such a viewport in the machine. However, recall that if you specify the coordinates in the "wrong" order, that is, with *u1* greater than *u2*, the VIEW command will store them in the "right" order in the machine, with *umin* equal to the smaller of *u1* and *u2*, and so on.

The window is described by similar equations:

xmin $\leq$ x $\leq$ xmax
ymin $\leq$ y $\leq$ ymax

This time you can use the WINDOW command to specify these limits to the machine. For example:

WINDOW (xmin,ymin) $-$ (xmax,ymax)

Again, the machine will sort the values you give it to determine the correct minimum and maximum limits.

For this window to map to this viewport under the viewing transformation, we must have corner points of the window map to corner points of the viewport. How this is done depends upon whether you use the SCREEN option of the WINDOW command. Without the SCREEN option, the lower-left corner (xmin,ymin) of the window is mapped to the lower corner of the viewport, which happens to be (umin, vmax), and the upper-right corner (xmax,ymax) of the window is mapped to the upper-right corner of the viewport, which happens to be (umax,vmin). Notice how vmin and vmax are switched. With the SCREEN option, (xmin,ymin) is mapped to (umin,vmin) and (xmax,ymax) is mapped to (umax,vmax) so that window coordinates go in the same direction as viewport coordinates (upside down).

For purposes of this derivation, let's assume the SCREEN option is used in the WINDOW commands. When we plug into the transformation formulas, a set of four equations results:

umin = a*xmin + b
vmin = c*ymin + d
umax = a*xmax + b
vmax = c*ymax + d

Using algebra, it is possible to find formulas for $a$, $b$, $c$, and $d$ in terms of *umin, vmin, umax, vmax, xmin, ymin, xmax,* and *ymax.* These formulas are

a  =  (umax−umin)/(xmax−xmin)

b  =  umin−a*xmin (using $a$ from the previous equation)

c  =  (vmax−vmin)/(ymax−ymin)

d  =  vmin−c*ymin (using $c$ from the previous quation

Whenever you execute the VIEW or WINDOW commands, the machine automatically computes these constants and stores them, ready to be used as part of the viewing transformation. Our applications programs throughout the rest of this chapter will take advantage of the fact that these commands do all of this for you. If you do not have such commands, you will have to write a subroutine that computes these constants using the formulas. You will need to call this subroutine every time you change either the viewport or the window limits. In addition, you will need to include the viewing transformation functions

u  =  a*y + b

v  =  c*y + d

in your program. This is best done by defining BASIC functions as in the following commands:

DEF FNA(X)=VTA + VTB * X

DEF FNB(Y)=VTC + VTD * Y

But every time you plot a point, line, or circle you will need to invoke these functions explicitly. For example,

LINE −(FNA(X),FNB(Y)),C

draws a line from the old current position to the point whose user coordinates are (X,Y). You can see that the screen coordinates are computed as (FNA(X),FNB(Y)) within the command line.

**POINT and
PMAP Functions**

Now let's look at some functions that can be used for debugging programs that use viewing transformations. They are POINT and PMAP.

The POINT function can be used to return the color of any point. With version 2 of Advanced BASIC it can also return the current position both in user coordinates and screen coordinates.

It has two possible syntaxes:

v = POINT(x,y)

and

v = POINT(n)

where $x$ and $y$ are numeric expressions, and $n$ is an integer expression equal to 0, 1, 2, or 3.

More precisely, POINT(x,y) returns the color of the pixel at the point (x,y) in user coordinates, POINT(0) returns the x-coordinate of the current position in screen coordinates, POINT(1) returns the y-coordinate of the current position in screen coordinates, POINT(2) returns the x-coordinate of the current position in user coordinates, and POINT(3) returns the y-coordinate of the current position in user coordinates. For example,

X = POINT(0) : Y = POINT(1)

sets X equal to the x-coordinate of the current position and Y equal to the y-coordinate of the current position, both in screen coordinates. If your picture is just not doing what it is supposed to do and you cannot figure out what is going wrong, then add some PRINT statements such as

PRINT POINT(0);POINT(1);POINT(2);POINT(3)

near your POINT, LINE, and CIRCLE commands. They can often tell you what the problem is.

The PMAP function allows you to perform the viewing transformation in both directions. It is available only with version 2 of BASICA. Its syntax is

v = PMAP(x,n)

where $x$ is a numeric expression and $n$ is an integer expression equal to 0, 1, 2, or 3. If $n$ is 0, PMAP maps the x-coordinate from user coordinates to screen coordinates; if n is 1, PMAP maps y-coordinates from user coordinates to screen coordinates; if n is 2, PMAP maps x-coordinates from screen coordinates to user coordinates; and if n is 3, PMAP maps y-coordinates from screen coordinates to user coordinates.

For example,

PRINT PMAP(20,2); PMAP(30,3)

prints the x and y user coordinates of the screen point (20,30).

Let's see what this viewing transformation looks like in our first application example, the bar chart program. We begin with our centered title subroutine, given in Example 3-24.

EXAMPLE 3-24

## SIMPLE GRAPHICS PACKAGE (SGP)

Start a simple graphics package. Include a routine to print
a centered title.

### Solution

```
120 ' CENTERED TITLE
130 '
140 ' This part of the program
150 ' is a simple graphics package
160 ' which houses a useful subroutine.
170 '
180    GOTO 280 ' go to main program
190 '
200 ' SUBROUTINE - CENTERED TITLE
210 '
220 ' L$ is a string containing a title
230 '
240    LOCATE 1, (40-LEN(L$))/2
250    PRINT L$
260    RETURN
270 '
```

Now let's look at the program itself. The first few lines
consist of comments, and there is a GOTO command to
transfer control to the main program. Between this statement and the main program is our centered title subroutine.

Now let's add on a main program. Our first main program will make a bar chart.

EXAMPLE 3-25

## BAR CHART

Write a short program that makes a bar chart. Use the
simple graphics package provided in the last example. Put
the data for the bars in DATA statements. Use WINDOW
and VIEW so the chart can handle any values. The bar
chart is shown in Figure 3-31.

## Solution

```
100 ' BARCHART
110 '




280 ' MAIN PROGRAM - BARCHART
290 '
300 '
310   DATA 20
320   DATA    3.9,    5.3,    7.2,    9.6
330   DATA   12.9,   17.0,   23.2,   31.4
340   DATA   39.8,   50.2,   62.9,   76.0
350   DATA   92.0,  105.7,  122.8,  131.7
360   DATA  150.7,  179.3,  203.2,  211.0
370 '
380 ' Set up the screen
390   CLS : KEY OFF
400   SCREEN 1 ' medium resolution
410   COLOR 0, 1 ' bckgrnd & palette
420   VIEW (20,20)-(300,150),,3
430   WINDOW (0,0)-(1,250)
440 '
450   L$ = "SIMPLE BAR CHART"
460   GOSUB 200 ' print centered title
470 '
480   L$="US Population"
490   FOR I=1 TO LEN(L$)
500     LOCATE 3+I,1
```

▶

**Example 3-25**

## Solution, continued.

```
510      PRINT MID$(L$,I,1)
520    NEXT I
530  '
540    LOCATE 21,9
550    PRINT "Every ten years 1790-1980
560  '
570    READ N
580    DX = 1/N  : DDX = .75*DX : Y = 0
590  '
600    FOR I = 0 TO N-1
610      X=DX*I
620      READ DY
630      LINE (X,Y)-(X+DDX,Y+DY),1,BF
640    NEXT I
650  '
660    LOCATE 23
670    END
```

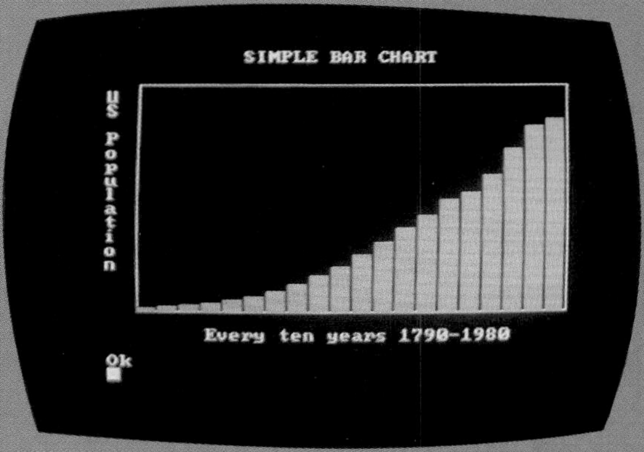

Figure 3-31
Bar Chart

The two lines at the beginning keep track of the name of your application program. The main program actually begins on line 280.

In the main program, the data for the bar chart comes first. This is given in DATA statements (lines 310-360). In practice, data should be located in a separate file. Since this is not a book about file management, we will not add this complication to our "simple" program.

Next we set up the screen. We clear it, turn the function key display off, and initialize it. We have chosen medium resolution so that we can use color: a black background color and palette 1, so that we have a white foreground.

Next we define our viewport and window with the VIEW and WINDOW commands. We have not used the SCREEN option with either; thus, we will have the user coordinates in the normal "right side up" manner for Cartesian coordinates, and we will have the viewport smaller than the screen. Notice that the boundary parameter in the VIEW command is used to draw a border around the viewport.

The window has x between 0 and 1 and y between 0 and 250. This is what we wanted for our particular chart. The viewport is defined by the coordinates (20,20)–(300,150), which is smaller than the screen. This allows room around the outside of our chart for labeling.

Next we print a title at the top of the screen. Notice that the GOSUB statements are all labeled so that you can tell at a glance what is going on. The next few lines (lines 480-520) put the message "US Population" down the side of the frame. Notice the use of LOCATE and MID$. At the bottom of the frame we place the message "Every ten years 1790-1980" (see lines 540-550).

We read the first piece of data. This is N, the number of data values for the graph. We define DX (the distance from the beginning of one bar to the beginning of the next bar) and DDX (the width of the bar). In this case we make DDX equal to three-quarters of DX. We also define Y = 0 to be the base of our bars.

Now we read and plot the data, one item at a time. The data is plotted in user coordinates. In this program the window (user frame) is given by xmin=0, xmax=1, ymin=0, and ymax=250. In these user coordinates, each bar goes from (X,Y) to (X+DDX, Y+DY). (X,Y) is the lower-left corner of the bar. Because X=DX*I and Y=0, this corner of the bar steps along the bottom side of the window as the FOR loop progresses. The LINE command (line 630), which actually draws the bar, uses the relative coordinates (DDX,DY). These coordinates define the width and height of the rectangular bar. DDX (the width) was explained earlier (three-quarters of DX), and DY (the height) is read as the data value.

Having the WINDOW, VIEWPORT, and viewing transformation built into the system saves many lines of code and speeds up the program. For example, the original version of this program, designed without these features, was 129 lines, but now it is only 66.

Next let's see how this same simple graphics package can be extended to help make a different type of graph—one that is generated by a formula rather than data and has curved lines instead of bars.

EXAMPLE 3-26

## 2-D FUNCTION PLOTTING

Write a short program that plots several functions of the form

$$y = f(x)$$

Plot each function with a different line style. Extend the simple graphics package given previously to include a function plotting subroutine that can be called to do this. The graphs are shown in Figure 3-32.

## Solution

```
100 ' FUNCTION 2D
110 '

180    GOTO 400 ' go to main program


280 ' SUBROUTINE - FUNCTION PLOTTER
290 '
300 ' FNF is the function to be plot
310 '
320    PSET (XMIN,FNF(XMIN))
330    FOR X = XMIN TO XMAX STEP XSTEP
340      LINE -(X,FNF(X)),C,,S
350    NEXT X
360 '
370    RETURN
380 '
390 '
400 ' main program - FUN2D
410 '
420    XMIN=-10:XMAX=10:YMIN=-10:YMAX=10
421    XSTEP = (XMAX-XMIN)/50
430 '
440 ' Set up the screen
450    CLS : KEY OFF
460    SCREEN 1     ' medium resolution
470    COLOR 0, 1 ' bckgrnd & palette
480    WINDOW (XMIN,YMIN)-(XMAX,YMAX)
490    VIEW (30,30) - (300,150),,3
500 '
```

▶

# Example 3-26

## Solution, continued.

```
510    L$="SIMPLE GRAPH OF A FUNCTION"
520    GOSUB 200 ' centered title
530  '
550  '
560  ' Plot the first function
570    DEF FNF(X) = -X
580    C = 2        ' color for graph
590    S = &HAAAA ' style = dotted
600    GOSUB 280  ' plot the function
610  '
620  ' Plot the second function
630    DEF FNF(X) = X
640    C = 2        ' color for graph
650    S = &H8000 ' style = sparse dots
660    GOSUB 280  ' plot the function
670  '
680  ' Plot the third function
690    DEF FNF(X) = COS(X)
700    C = 2        ' color for graph
710    S = &HF000 ' style = dashed
720    GOSUB 280  ' plot the function
730  '
740  ' Plot the fourth function
750    DEF FNF(X) = X*COS(X)
760    C = 2        ' color for graph
770    S = &HFFFF ' style = solid
780    GOSUB 280  ' plot the function
790  '
800    LOCATE 23,1
810    END
```

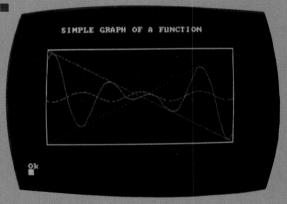

Figure 3-32
2-D Function Plots

To enter this program, load the centered title subroutine and start typing line 100 with the title FUN2D, and a line 110 which is "blank" (see lines 100-110 of the previous example). Then change line 180 as indicated and type in the rest of the program from line 280 onward.

The function plotting subroutine consists of a PSET command to place the current position at the beginning of the graph and a FOR loop (lines 330-350) to plot the function using the LINE command. The graph of the function is thus approximated by a series of short lines. The beginning and ending points, the step size, the color, the line style, and the formula for the function are all controlled by parameters defined outside the subroutine.

In the main program, the maximum and minimum values are defined and the step size is chosen (lines 420-421). For the step size we have decided to make 50 divisions across the window. With a window from −10 to 10 and a viewport from 30 to 300 in the horizontal direction, this gives a step size of about 5 pixels. Next the screen is set up as before and titled.

There are four functions to be plotted, and for each the formula is chosen by defining it as the function FNF, the color is chosen by setting C equal to it, the style is selected by setting S equal to it, and the function plotting routine is called.

Notice that only about the first five (leftmost) bits of the line style parameter are significant in this program. This is because the individual lines are only as long as the step size, which is about 5 pixels on the screen. Try a style of FF00 and notice that it produces a solid line for most of the functions in this program. The only exception is the last function, which has steep slopes, and thus will have larger numbers of pixels between steps on its graph.

In the next section we explain clipping and how it helps with zooming and panning.

## Clipping, Panning, and Zooming

As we have described, the window determines what part of the "world" or "user" space you want to see, and the viewport determines what part of the screen you want to see it on. For example, if we have a function that we want to graph, we can use the window limits to select a particular rectangular area of its graph to examine, perhaps selecting a wide range of values to show the general behavior of the function or perhaps zooming in on an area containing a small kink in the graph. Everything outside our window is *clipped* off.

Selecting different viewport limits will allow us to draw lots of small images on different parts of the screen or draw one big image that covers the entire screen.

In general, moving the window without changing its size is called *panning*, and changing the size of the window without moving it is called *zooming*. In the next example we illustrate panning and zooming.

EXAMPLE 3-27

# DRAWING A GLOBE

Display a picture of a white grid-like globe with a small
red "IBM" logo in its center. Let the user control zooming
and panning via the function keys. One view is shown in
Figure 3-33.

## Solution

```
100 ' GLOBE
110 '
120 ' SIMPLE 2D GRAPHICS PACKAGE
130 '
140 ' This part of the program
150 ' is a simple graphics package.
160 ' It houses useful subroutines.
170 '
180   GOTO 280 ' go to main program
190 '
200 ' SUBROUTINE - CENTERED TITLE
210 '
220 ' L$ is a string containing a title
230 '
240   LOCATE 1, (40-LEN(L$))/2
250   PRINT L$
260   RETURN
270 '
280 ' main program - GLOBE
290 '
300 ' Initial window parameters
310   X0 = 0  :  Y0 = 0  : RD = 20
320   DIM X(20,20), Y(20,20)
330 '
340 ' Set up the screen
350   SCREEN 1 ' medium resolution
360   COLOR 0, 1 ' bckgrnd & palette
370   CLS : KEY OFF
380 '
390 ' Print a wait message
400   LOCATE 12,18
410   PRINT "wait"
420 '
430 ' compute the grid
440 '
```

▶

## Example 3-27

## Solution, continued.

```
450 ' Grid constants
460   PI = 3.14159
470   R = 9    ' radius of globe
480   A = .7  ' tip angle of globe
490   COSA = COS(A) : SINA = SIN(A)
500 '
510 ' Grid values
520   FOR I = 0 TO 20
530    T = I*PI/10
540    COST=COS(T):SINT=SIN(T)
550    FOR J = 0 TO 10
560     S = J*PI/10
570     COSS=COS(S):SINS=SIN(S)
580     X(I,J) = R*COST*SINS
590     Y(I,J) = R*SINA*SINT*SINS+R*COSA*COSS
600    NEXT J
610   NEXT I
620 '
630 ' Set up the viewport
640   VIEW (60,20) - (260,180),,3
650 '
660   L$="WINDOWING A GLOBE"
670   GOSUB 200 ' centered title
680 '
690 ' Loop starts here
700 '
710   CLS
720 '
730 ' Set the window
740   WINDOW(X0-RD,Y0-RD)-(X0+RD,Y0+RD)
750 '
760 '
770 ' The logo
780 '
790    Y = .3
800    LINE (-.8 ,Y)-(-.5 ,Y),2
810    LINE (-.4 ,Y)-(-.12,Y),2
820    LINE ( .1 ,Y)-( .3 ,Y),2
830    LINE ( .6 ,Y)-( .8 ,Y),2
840 '
850    Y = .2
860    LINE (-.8 ,Y)-(-.5 ,Y),2
870    LINE (-.4 ,Y)-( 0 ,Y),2
880    LINE ( .1 ,Y)-( .35,Y),2
890    LINE ( .55,Y)-( .8 ,Y),2
900 '
```

▶

## Example 3-27

## Solution, continued.

```
910      Y = .1
920      LINE (-.7 ',Y)-(-.6 ,Y),2
930      LINE (-.3 ,Y)-(-.2 ,Y),2
940      LINE (-.05,Y)-( .05,Y),2
950      LINE ( .2 ,Y)-( .4 ,Y),2
960      LINE ( .5 ,Y)-( .7 ,Y),2
970    '
980      Y = 0
990      LINE (-.7 ,Y)-(-.6 ,Y),2
1000     LINE (-.3 ,Y)-(-.07,Y),2
1010     LINE ( .2 ,Y)-( .44,Y),2
1020     LINE ( .46,Y)-( .7 ,Y),2
1030   '
1040     Y = -.1
1050     LINE (-.7 ,Y)-(-.6 ,Y),2
1060     LINE (-.3 ,Y)-(-.07,Y),2
1070     LINE ( .2 ,Y)-( .3 ,Y),2
1080     LINE ( .31,Y)-( .59,Y),2
1090     LINE ( .6 ,Y)-( .7 ,Y),2
1100   '
1110     Y = -.2
1120     LINE (-.7 ,Y)-(-.6 ,Y),2
1130     LINE (-.3 ,Y)-(-.2 ,Y),2
1140     LINE (-.05,Y)-( .05,Y),2
1150     LINE ( .2 ,Y)-( .3 ,Y),2
1160     LINE ( .35,Y)-( .55,Y),2
1170     LINE ( .6 ,Y)-( .7 ,Y),2
1180   '
1190     Y = -.3
1200     LINE (-.8 ,Y)-(-.5 ,Y),2
1210     LINE (-.4 ,Y)-( 0 ,Y),2
1220     LINE ( .1 ,Y)-( .3 ,Y),2
1230     LINE ( .4 ,Y)-( .5 ,Y),2
1240     LINE ( .6 ,Y)-( .8 ,Y),2
1250   '
1260     Y = -.4
1270     LINE (-.8 ,Y)-(-.5 ,Y),2
1280     LINE (-.4 ,Y)-(-.12,Y),2
1290     LINE ( .1 ,Y)-( .3 ,Y),2
1300     LINE ( .45,Y)-( .45,Y),2
1310     LINE ( .6 ,Y)-( .8 ,Y),2
1320   '
1330   ' Latitudes
1340     ASPO = .67*COSA
1350     FOR S = 0 TO PI STEP PI/10
```

# Example 3-27

## Solution, continued.

```
1360     X = 0
1370     Y = R*COSA*COS(S)
1380     RO =R*SIN(S)
1390     CIRCLE (X,Y),RO,1,,,ASPO
1400    NEXT S
1410 '
1420 ' Longitudes
1430    FOR I = 0 TO 20
1440     PSET (X(I,0),Y(I,0))
1450     FOR J = 1 TO 10
1460      LINE -(X(I,J),Y(I,J))
1470     NEXT J
1480    NEXT I
1490 '
1500 ' Get the key
1510     A$ = INKEY$
1520     IF LEN(A$)<>2 THEN 1510
1530     ANS = ASC(MID$(A$,2,1))
1540     IF ANS = 72 THEN RD = RD*.9
1550     IF ANS = 80 THEN RD = RD/.9
1560     IF ANS = 75 THEN XO = XO-RD*.1
1570     IF ANS = 77 THEN XO = XO+RD*.1
1580 '
1590     GOTO 690
1600 '
1610 END
```

Figure 3-33
A View of the Globe

When this program runs you will first see a small red rectangle surrounded by a globe made of grid lines. The latitude lines of the globe are drawn in cyan and the longitude lines in magenta. The small red rectangle appears so small that you cannot see that it is the IBM logo. After the picture is drawn, you press a cursor key to zoom or pan for the next view of the picture. The CURSOR UP key will zoom in and the CURSOR DOWN key will zoom out. To move your view left or right, the CURSOR LEFT key will pan left, and the CURSOR RIGHT key will pan right.

As you zoom in by repeatedly pressing the CURSOR UP key, the red logo becomes clearer and clearer until it fills the whole window.

Now let's look at the listing. The first couple of lines give the title and the next few lines are the centered title subroutine. The main program begins on line 280.

In the main program the window parameters are centered at (x0,y0) = (0,0) with a radius of 20. Later these parameters will be used to define a window with coordinates (X0−RD, Y0−RD)−(X0+RD,Y0+RD). Then the screen is set as usual and a "wait" message is displayed.

Next, the coordinates of the grid points for the globe are computed and stored in an array X. It is important to compute as much as possible before the picture is actually drawn so that it can be drawn rapidly to make the program more interactive.

Once the main loop is entered, the window is defined. Notice that the window is the only thing that is changing each time through the loop. Next as part of the loop, the logo is drawn as a series of horizontal lines, and then the globe is drawn over it.

The latitudes are easy to draw using the CIRCLE command with aspect ratio; they are just ellipses that are flattened horizontally. However, the longitude lines cannot be drawn with the CIRCLE command because even though they appear elliptical, they are flattened in a slanted direction. Thus, the longitude lines must be approximated by a series of short line segments whose endpoints are stored in the array X.

At the bottom of the loop, the keyboard is polled for a cursor key. If a cursor is pressed, the window parameters are adjusted appropriately. The UP and DOWN CURSOR keys affect the radius RD, and the LEFT and RIGHT CURSOR keys affect the x-coordinate of the center of the window.

Even though the picture in this example appears to be 3-D, it uses only 2-D techniques. In the next section we describe how the 2-D ideas presented in this section can be extended to help us draw 3-D objects with 3-D techniques. This will allow us to depict things such as 3-D function plots and rotating houses.

## 3-D Viewing Concepts— Advanced Topics

Drawing pictures of three-dimensional objects is more complicated. Because of this, this section is more advanced than the others.

Although this section is a simplified treatment of 3-D graphics, it will allow you to show views of three-dimensional objects from any arbitrary angle. The objects in these programs will be represented in BASIC DATA statements, or a mathematical function may generate coordinate values. The views will be computed using transformations that take us from our three-dimensional *user* or *world coordinates* to the 2-D coordinates of the screen. Again, these transformations are called *viewing transformations*. In our treatment, the views will not have true perspective (with vanishing points); rather, they have what is called *parallel perspective*. This means they can be produced as a shadow or projection of a 3-D object onto a flat (2-D) screen using a light beam consisting of a set of parallel light rays (see Figure 3-34). This type of perspective is relatively easy to create. It is a good approximation of a projection in which the light comes from the sun. In this case we can think of the viewing transformation as a picture-taking process in which the viewing surface is like the film in a camera and the focal length of the camera is infinity.

Other types of perspective involve more mathematics than we can present here. See the books listed in Appendix D for detailed presentations of this rich subject.

To make things less complicated, we break up our 3-D viewing transformation into several stages. This is called a *pipeline* approach. You can think of the coordinates for the original 3-D object being put into one end of a "pipe" and the picture (in screen coordinates) coming out the other end. Along the pipe is a series of stations where stages of the computations are done. In this section we break up our transformations into three stages: first one or two 3-D-to-3-D rotations, then a 3-D-to-2-D parallel projection, and finally a standard 2-D viewing transformation, as shown in Figure 3-35.

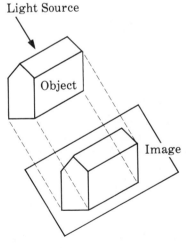

**Figure 3-34**

Parallel Perspective for Parallel Light Rays

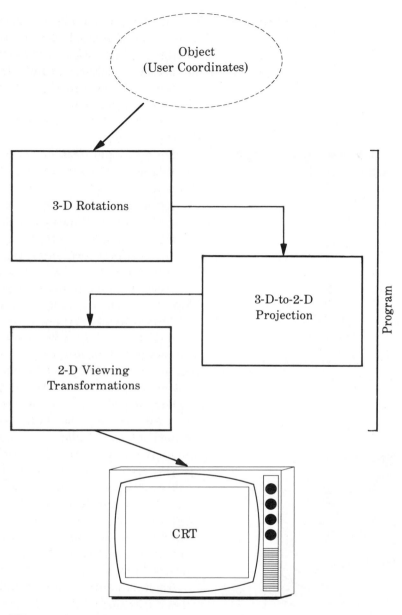

**Figure 3-35**

Pipeline for 3-D Viewing Transformations

We start with the first "station" along the "pipe." This is a 3-D-to-3-D transformation. Of the various possible types of 3-D-to-3-D transformations, we will just study 3-D rotations.

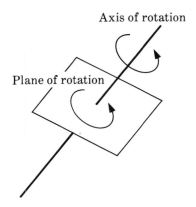

**Figure 3-36**

Typical 3-D Rotation

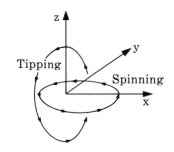

**Figure 3-37**

Spinning and Tipping

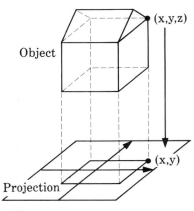

**Figure 3-38**

Simple 3-D-to-2-D Projection

This is enough to make the kinds of interesting pictures we show in our 3-D applications programs.

Every 3-D rotation is characterized by an *axis* of rotation and a *plane* of rotation, as illustrated in Figure 3-36. The axis of rotation is the set of points that do not move during the rotation. The plane of rotation is perpendicular to the axis of rotation and represents the points of maximum motion during the rotation.

The most general case of rotation can be expressed as a combination of a rotation centered at the origin and some translations. Any arbitrary rotation centered at the origin can be expressed as the composition or product of *principal rotations*. These are rotations whose plane of rotation is one of the principal planes formed by the coordinate axes. We will use two of these: spinning and tipping. For spinning, the plane of rotation is the xy-coordinate plane, and for tipping, the plane of rotation is the yz-plane (described graphically in Figure 3-37). Using these in combination allows you to view a 3-D object from any angle.

In Appendix A we describe the formulas for these principal rotations and derive the equations for the rotation that results when we combine them.

The next station in our graphics pipeline is a 3-D-to-2-D parallel projection. There are three principal parallel projections, one for each coordinate, giving a top, front, and side view of the object. There is an easy method to program this projection. It is called "forgetting."

You start with a 3-D coordinate system with coordinates (x,y,z) for a typical point. For each point, if you forget the z-coordinate of that point, you have the coordinates (x,y) which are its projection on the xy-plane. Plot these on an xy-coordinate system and you have a top view of the object with each point (x,y,z) *projected* to the corresponding point (x,y) on the xy-plane.

If you "forget" (or cancel) the y-coordinate, the point (x,y,z) is projected to the point (x,z) on the xz-plane. This is the side view. If you forget the x-coordinate, the point (x,y,z) is projected to the point (y,z) on the yz-plane. This is the front view. We will use this "forgetting" transformation in several different forms in our applications programs. The exact form depends upon how the 3-D axes are oriented with respect to the viewing screen. Figure 3-38 shows how forgetting the z-coordinate lets us project a house on the xy-plane.

The last step in the process is a standard 2-D viewing transformation.

In the following example program we show how to graph a function of two variables, which in turn results in a three-dimensional drawing. The example gives a simple graphics package. This contains just one subroutine that does an entire 3-D-to-2-D viewing transformation as described previously.

EXAMPLE 3-28

# 3-D SIMPLE GRAPHICS PACKAGE

Write a short extension to the 2-D SGP that does the 3-D viewing transformation as described in this section.

## Solution

```
280  ' 3D EXTENSION TO SGP
290  '
300    GOTO 520 - TO MAIN PROGRAM
310  '
320  ' SUBROUTINE - SET 3D TO 2D TRANS
330  '
340  ' COEFFICIENTS:
350  ' A11, A12, A13, A21, A22, A23
360  '
370    RD=3.14159/180 ' RAD TO DEG
380  '
390    A11=  COS(SPIN*RD)
400    A12=  SIN(SPIN*RD)
410    A13=  0
420    A21= -SIN(TIP*RD)*SIN(SPIN*RD)
430    A22=  SIN(TIP*RD)*COS(SPIN*RD)
440    A23=  COS(TIP*RD)
450  '
460    DEF FNX(X,Y,Z)=A11*X+A12*Y+A13*Z
470    DEF FNY(X,Y,Z)=A21*X+A22*Y+A23*Z
480  '
490    RETURN
500  '
510  '
```

In lines 460-470, we have the forgetting transformation. This is why only the first and second rows are needed. In more detail, we want the first 3-D coordinate (x-coordinate) to be mapped to the horizontal direction (x-coordinate) of the 2-D viewing screen and the second 3-D coordinate (y-coordinate) to be mapped to the vertical direction (y-coordinate) of the viewing screen. The third 3-D coordinate (z-coordinate) is forgotten because it is perpendicular to the 2-D coordinate system.

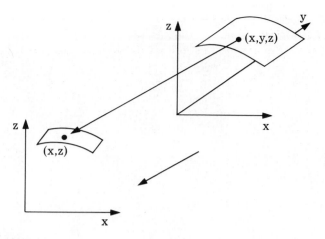

**Figure 3-39**

Forgetting Transformation
for FUN3D

Figure 3-39 shows the forgetting transformation for the y-coordinate.

Once we have figured all this out and encased it in this subroutine, we can forget about all its details and just use the resulting functions FNX and FNY.

The next program is the main portion of FUN3D. After you have loaded the centered title subroutine and typed in the extension, you can type in this program and save the whole thing as FUN3D. Do not forget to add lines 100-110 with the program name FUN3D. You will also have to modify the centered title routine to allow for an 80-column width. Just change the number 40 on line 240 to 80.

## Example 3-29

# 3-D FUNCTION PLOTTING

Write a short program that graphs a function of two variables on the three-dimensional coordinate system. Use the 3-D viewing transformation in the (extended) simple graphics package as described. Show the graph of the function f(x,y)=COS(x)*COS(y). The graphed function is shown in Figure 3-40.

# Solution

```
520 ' MAIN PROGRAM - FUN3D
530 '
540 ' Set up screen
550   SCREEN 2 ' high resolution
560   CLS:KEY OFF
570 '
580 ' 2D window and viewport
590   WINDOW (-5,-5) - (5, 5)
600   VIEW (120, 20) - (500, 198),,1
610 '
620 ' 3D limits
630   READ X3MIN,X3MAX,Y3MIN,Y3MAX
640   DATA -3, 3, -3, 3
650 '
660   SPIN=45
670   TIP=30
680 '
690 ' THE FUNCTION:
700   DEF FNF(X,Y) = COS(X)*COS(Y)
710 '
720   C = 1
730   XSP = (X3MAX-X3MIN)/20
740   YSP = (Y3MAX-Y3MIN)/20
750 '
760 '
770 ' MAIN LOOP
780 '
790   SCREEN 2
800   CLS:KEY OFF
810   L$ = "3D GRAPH OF A FUNCTION"
820   GOSUB 200 ' print centered title
830 '
```

▶

**Example 3-29**

## Solution, continued.

```
840    GOSUB 320 ' 3D to 2D transform
850  '
860   FOR X = X3MIN TO X3MAX STEP XSP
870    Y=Y3MIN : Z=FNF(X,Y)
880    PSET (FNX(X,Y,Z),FNY(X,Y,Z))
890    FOR Y = Y3MIN TO Y3MAX STEP YSP
900     Z = FNF(X,Y)
910     LINE -(FNX(X,Y,Z),FNY(X,Y,Z)),1
920    NEXT Y
930   NEXT X
940  '
950   FOR Y = Y3MIN TO Y3MAX STEP YSP
960    X=X3MIN : Z=FNF(X,Y)
970    PSET (FNX(X,Y,Z),FNY(X,Y,Z))
980    FOR X = X3MIN TO X3MAX STEP XSP
990     Z = FNF(X,Y)
1000     LINE -(FNX(X,Y,Z),FNY(X,Y,Z)),1
1010    NEXT X
1020   NEXT Y
1030  '
1040   INPUT"SPIN";SPIN
1050   INPUT"TIP";TIP
1060  '
1070   GOTO 770
```

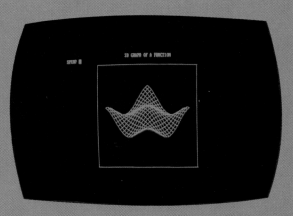

Figure 3-40
3-D Function Plotting

Our program graphs the function f(x,y) = COS(x)*COS(y) (see lines 690-760), but you can substitute a function of your own choice. The SPIN and TIP angles are specified in lines 660-670. Step sizes XSP and YSP for the grid are defined in lines 730-740. Twenty steps in both directions are used. Change this if you want.

The main loop of the program extends from 770 to 1070. There are two double FOR loops. Each draws a set of parallel cross sections of the surface which is the graph of the function. These two sets of cross sections cross to form a grid. Within the loops, values for X, Y, and Z are set with Z=f(X,Y) (using FNF). The viewing transformation functions FNU and FNV use these user coordinate values of X, Y, and Z. Then the PSET and LINE commands use the screen coordinate values returned from FNU and FNV.

## Using Data to Define Your Picture

Now let's discuss how to draw a different kind of 3-D picture. This kind of picture is *driven* by 3-D data and not a formula of some function. The data is more than the coordinates of all the points plotted in the picture. In addition to coordinate information we have included information on how to connect the points and even what surface they belong to. All this information is carefully structured to allow the program to efficiently construct a 3-D picture.

With this information structure there is an additional bonus. We will be able to compute which edges of the picture are hidden and which are visible. The particular algorithm we use requires that the object be convex—no arms sticking out or holes punched in. With this restriction, a house is a perfect candidate for drawing (if no chimney is allowed). The following examples give three listings that make up such a program.

The idea is simple: We go through a list of edges of the house with a FOR loop. For each edge, if either of its associated faces is visible, the edge is visible. You tell whether or not a face is visible by checking the third component of its *normal*. If this component is positive, the face is pointed toward you and therefore is visible. If the edge is visible, we draw it using the vertices associated with it in our data base.

We break the program into four parts: the 2-D SGP which you already have, a modification to the 3-D Simple Graphics Package extension, a data section, and a main program. As you type in the lines, you will notice certain gaps in the line numbers. We will fill in the gaps with some "paint" to make an example program in Chapter 5 when we show you the PAINT command. In that chapter we will show how to paint the house no matter what angle we view it from.

Let's look at the 3-D extension first. It is a scaled-down version of the 3-D extension for the previous program, FUN3D, and the axes are oriented differently because the application is different. Here the z-axis is "up" and the y-axis is "back" on your screen. Thus, the formulas are slightly different (see lines 360-440). In this case the subroutine just computes the composite of the spin and tip rotations and returns the results in the array C.

EXAMPLE 3-30

## THE HOUSE EXTENSION TO THE 3-D SGP

Modify the previous 3-D SGP extension to work with the
house program in the next examples. This time the z-axis is
"up" and the y-axis is "back" on your screen. Make this
routine compute the composite of the spin and tip rotation
and return the coefficients of the resulting matrix in an
array C.

## Solution

```
280 ' 3D EXTENSION TO SGP
290 '
300    GOTO 490 - TO MAIN PROGRAM
310 '
320 ' SUBROUTINE - 3D ROTATION MATRIX
330 '
340    RD=3.14159/180 ' RAD TO DEG
350 '
360    C11= COS(SPIN*RD)
370    C12= 0
380    C13=-SIN(SPIN*RD)
390    C21=-SIN(TIP*RD)*SIN(SPIN*RD)
400    C22= COS(TIP*RD)
410    C23=-SIN(TIP*RD)*COS(SPIN*RD)
420    C31= COS(TIP*RD)*SIN(SPIN*RD)
430    C32= SIN(TIP*RD)
440    C33= COS(TIP*RD)*COS(SPIN*RD)
450 '
460    RETURN
470 '
480 '
```

Now comes the data section. It is long because we want
some windows and a door on the house. Data for the window
and viewport transformations are first. Then come the (x,y,z)
coordinates of the vertices. There are 30 vertices (or points).
Next is the coordinate information for the faces. Here is
where some mathematics comes in. For each face (surface)
we give the (x,y,z) components of the outward normal. This is

a "vector" (arrow) that is perpendicular to the surface and points away from the center of the figure (described for our house in Figure 3-41). These are called the *face normals*. There are seven face normals for our house (front, back, two sides, floor, two sides to the roof).

Finally come the edges. The data for the edges consists of "pointers" (or indices) to vertices and faces. They are laid out as follows: There are four numbers for each edge. The first two numbers are indices into the vertex table. They point to the two vertices that determine the edge. The third and fourth numbers are indices into the face table and they point to the faces that bound the edge. Notice the repeats for those edges which have the same face on either side (for example, the eaves of the roof).

The scheme for the data can be better understood through the following example: On line 1780 of the program, there are the numbers 1, 2, 1, 7. The first and second numbers tell us that this edge goes from vertex 1 to vertex 2, and the third and fourth numbers tell us that this edge is bounded by faces 1 and 7. The coordinates of these vertices and the components of "normals" for these faces are found in the corresponding positions in the vertex and face data statements. For example, the coordinates for vertex number 1 are on line 1290, the very first line of coordinates in the vertex list. All of these numbers were determined by drawing a sketch of the house on graph paper (shown in Figure 3-42), numbering everything, and then entering the information into the computer.

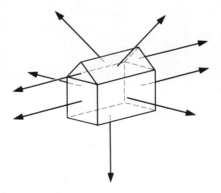

**Figure 3-41**

Face Normals

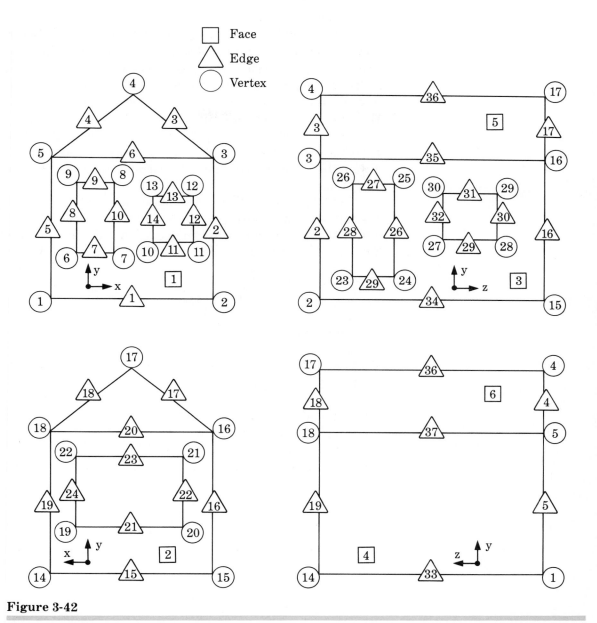

**Figure 3-42**

Sketch of House Showing the Parts

The coordinate system on the graph paper was chosen to make the job easy. You can see that the house lines up nicely with the coordinate axes. Even the normals are easy to compute. For example, face number 1 is parallel to the xy-coordinate plane, and therefore perpendicular to the z-axis.

By inspecting the graph in Figure 3-42, you can see that the outward normal for this face does, in fact, point in the direction of the z-axis. Therefore, we selected (0,0,1) for this normal. The hardest normals to determine are the ones associated with the roof. Here it helps to realize that there are no z-components to these normals. We simply drew a careful picture of the roof on the xy-plane and saw that for these normals the y-component was twice as long as the x-component. From this information the two normals we selected were (1,2,0) and (−1,2,0).

There are fancier ways to compute normals, but by "eyeballing" such a picture you can arrive at the correct answer faster than with most other methods, that is, provided that the faces are oriented so simply.

EXAMPLE 3-31

# DATA SECTION OF THE HOUSE PROGRAM

Write the data for the house program. Include the
coordinates for all the vertices and the "face normals."
For each edge, give the numbers (indices) of the vertices
on either end of it and the faces it bounds.

## Solution

```
490 ' DATA AREA - HOUSE            840 '
500 '                              850 ' data for faces
510 '                              860    DATA  7
520 ' data for vertices:           870    DATA  0,   0,   1
530    DATA  30                    880    DATA  0,   0,  -1
540    DATA -10, -10,  15          890    DATA  1,   0,   0
550    DATA  10, -10,  15          900    DATA -1,   0,   0
560    DATA  10,  10,  15          910    DATA  1,   2,   0
570    DATA   0,  15,  15          920    DATA -1,   2,   0
580    DATA -10,  10,  15          930    DATA  0,  -1,   0
590    DATA  -7,  -3,  15          940 '
600    DATA  -2,  -3,  15          950 ' data for edges
610    DATA  -2,   6,  15          960    DATA  37
620    DATA  -7,   6,  15          970    DATA  1, 2, 1, 7
630    DATA   2,   1,  15          980    DATA  2, 3, 1, 3
640    DATA   7,   1,  15          990    DATA  3, 4, 1, 5
650    DATA   7,   6,  15          1000   DATA  4, 5, 1, 6
660    DATA   2,   6,  15          1010   DATA  5, 1, 1, 4
670    DATA -10, -10, -15          1020   DATA  3, 5, 1, 1
680    DATA  10, -10, -15          1030   DATA  6, 7, 1, 1
690    DATA  10,  10, -15          1040   DATA  7, 8, 1, 1
700    DATA   0,  15, -15          1050   DATA  8, 9, 1, 1
710    DATA -10,  10, -15          1060   DATA  9, 6, 1, 1
720    DATA  -8,  -4, -15          1070   DATA 10,11, 1, 1
730    DATA   8,  -4, -15          1080   DATA 11,12, 1, 1
740    DATA   8,   7, -15          1090   DATA 12,13, 1, 1
750    DATA  -8,   7, -15          1100   DATA 13,10, 1, 1
760    DATA  10,  -8,  12          1110   DATA 14,15, 2, 7
770    DATA  10,  -8,   6          1120   DATA 15,16, 2, 3
780    DATA  10,   7,   6          1130   DATA 16,17, 2, 5
790    DATA  10,   7,  12          1140   DATA 17,18, 2, 6
800    DATA  10,  -2,   2          1150   DATA 18,14, 2, 4
810    DATA  10,  -2, -12          1160   DATA 16,18, 2, 2
820    DATA  10,   6, -12          1170   DATA 19,20, 2, 2
830    DATA  10,   6,   2          1180   DATA 20,21, 2, 2
```

▶

## Example 3-31

### Solution, continued.

```
1190    DATA 21,22, 2, 2          1270    DATA 29,30, 3, 3
1200    DATA 22,19, 2, 2          1280    DATA 30,27, 3, 3
1210    DATA 23,24, 3, 3          1290    DATA  1,14, 4, 7
1220    DATA 24,25, 3, 3          1300    DATA  2,15, 7, 3
1230    DATA 25,26, 3, 3          1310    DATA  3,16, 3, 5
1240    DATA 26,23, 3, 3          1320    DATA  4,17, 5, 6
1250    DATA 27,28, 3, 3          1330    DATA  5,18, 6, 4
1260    DATA 28,29, 3, 3          1340
```

EXAMPLE 3-32

# MAIN SECTION OF THE HOUSE PROGRAM

Write the main part of the program to draw a house.
Use the previous data for the house. The house should
be drawn with hidden edges not shown. The program
should repeatedly draw the house, each time from a view
slightly rotated from the last one. One view of the house
is pictured in Figure 3-43.

## Solution

```
1510 ' MAIN PROGRAM - HOUSE
1520 '
1530    CLS: KEY OFF
1540    SCREEN 1 ' high resolution
1550    LOCATE 12,18 : PRINT "wait"
1560 '
1570 ' set window & viewport
1580    WINDOW (-20,-20) - (20,20)
1590    VIEW (80,20) - (240,180)
1600 '
1610    DIM V(40,3), F(8,3), E(40,4)
1620    DIM P(20,5)
1630 '
1640 ' display angles
1650    SPIN=30
1660    TIP=20
1670 '
1680 ' MAIN LOOP
1690 '
1700    RESTORE 520
1710 '
1720 ' read vertex data
1730    READ NV
1740    FOR I=1 TO NV:FOR J=1 TO 3
1750      READ V(I,J)
1760    NEXT J:NEXT I
1770 '
1780 ' read face data
1790    READ NF
1800    FOR I=1 TO NF:FOR J=1 TO 3
1810      READ F(I,J)
1820    NEXT J:NEXT I
1830 '
```

▶

## Example 3-32

## Solution, Continued.

```
1840 ' read edge data
1850    READ NE
1860    FOR I=1 TO NE:FOR J=1 TO 4
1870      READ E(I,J)
1880    NEXT J:NEXT I
1890 '
1900    GOSUB 320 ' 3D ROTATION MATRIX
1910 '
1920 ' NOW ROTATE
1930 '
1940 ' the vertices:
1950    FOR I=1 TO NV
1960      X=V(I,1):Y=V(I,2):Z=V(I,3)
1970      V(I,1)=C11*X+C12*Y+C13*Z
1980      V(I,2)=C21*X+C22*Y+C23*Z
1990      V(I,3)=C31*X+C32*Y+C33*Z
2000    NEXT I
2010 '
2020 ' the faces:
2030    FOR I=1 TO NF
2040      X=F(I,1):Y=F(I,2):Z=F(I,3)
2050      F(I,1)=C11*X+C12*Y+C13*Z
2060      F(I,2)=C21*X+C22*Y+C23*Z
2070      F(I,3)=C31*X+C32*Y+C33*Z
2080    NEXT I
2090 '
2100 ' NOW DRAW IT
2110 '
2120    CLS:KEY OFF
2130 '
2140    L$="HOUSE"
2150    GOSUB 200 ' centered title
2160 '
2170    FOR I=1 TO NE
2180     IF F(E(I,3),3)>0 THEN 2220
2190     IF F(E(I,4),3)>0 THEN 2220
2200     GOTO 2240
2210 '
2220     PSET (V(E(I,1),1),V(E(I,1),2))
2230     LINE-(V(E(I,2),1),V(E(I,2),2))
2240    NEXT I
2250 '


2480    SPIN=SPIN+10
2490 '
2500    GOTO 1680 ' next picture
```

**Example 3-32**

**Solution, Continued.**

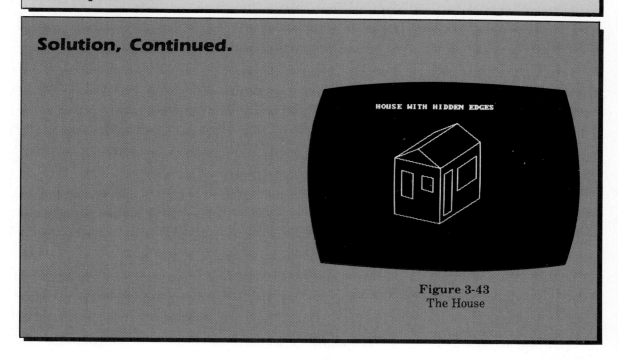

HOUSE WITH HIDDEN EDGES

Figure 3-43
The House

Now we get to the main program. Line 1680 is the beginning of the main loop. The loop extends to the bottom of the program. Once through the loop makes one view of the house. Each view is rotated (spin angle) by 10 degrees from the previous view. The vertex, face, and edge data are read each time, hence the RESTORE statement on line 1700 and the FOR loops around the READ statements on lines 1720-1880. After that, the rotation matrix is defined as a function of the current SPIN and TIP angles by calling the subroutine (see line 1900). Now we use this matrix to rotate the vertex and face data (see lines 1920-2080).

The *main* part of the main program is the heart of the method. The idea is simple: We go through the list of edges with a FOR loop. For each edge, if either of its associated faces is visible, then the edge is visible. You tell whether or not a face is visible by checking the third component of its "normal" (see lines 2180-2190). If this component is positive, the face is pointed toward you and therefore is visible. If the edge is visible, we draw it (lines 2220-2230) using the vertices associated with it.

## CONCLUSION

We have shown how to use the point, LINE, and CIRCLE commands to draw various kinds of computer graphics. We started with short simple programs that did very little and then presented techniques to draw some interesting pictures as part of some useful applications programs.

The techniques discussed include the idea of 2-D and 3-D viewing transformations. We have seen how a simple graphics package can be used to wrap this up in a way that allows an applications programmer to concentrate on just the coordinate system that is natural for the particular application.

Our applications range from pie charts, to bar charts, to 2-D and 3-D graphs of functions. We have even included a program that continually rotates and draws an object with hidden lines.

In Chapter 4, we will show how to use entirely different kinds of graphics commands—using BASIC strings to define shapes via the DRAW command. In Chapter 5, we will paint some of the objects drawn in this chapter.

# GRAPHICS DEFINITION LANGUAGE

# CONCEPTS

Concepts
  Graphics Definition Language
  Forward Differences
  Turtle Graphics
  Interactive Input
  Animation
  Recursion

Commands
  DRAW

Applications
  Space-Filling Curves
  Drawing Electronic Symbols

# INTRODUCTION

This chapter introduces the DRAW command and its associated Graphics Definition Language (GDL). The power of BASIC's string manipulation is brought to bear upon picture generation. You will see how to generate pictures by "driving" around the screen with this command language.

As in Chapter 3, we approach this material presenting a series of small, "stand-alone" program segments that demonstrate the GDL language. We will show how to draw a number of useful shapes such as stars, spirals, arrows, triangles, and polygons. Each example will introduce a new set of GDL commands.

Example applications programs include drawing space-filling curves and a program that generates some standard electronic symbols which you can move around the screen.

As in the last chapter, the "stand-alone" program segments are all part of one large program. This program has a "front end" consisting of initialization commands and a "back end" consisting of the same pause and title subroutines used in Chapter 3.

EXAMPLE 4-1

## INITIALIZING THE PROGRAM

Write a short program that initializes the screen in
medium-resolution mode with the screen clear and the
function key display off. This will prepare the display for
the examples in this chapter.

### Solution

```
100 ' CHAPTER 4 LESSONS
110 '
120    SCREEN 1     ' MEDIUM RESOLUTION
130    KEY OFF
140    CLS
150 '
```

## EXAMPLE 4-2

## PAUSE AND TITLE SUBROUTINES

Give the PAUSE and TITLE subroutines from the last chapter.

### Solution

```
2000 ' SUBROUTINE - PAUSE & TITLE PAGE
2010 '
2020    LOCATE 25,1
2030    INPUT"Press ENTER to continue";A
2040    CLS
2050    GOSUB 2080 ' CENTERED TITLE
2060    RETURN
2070 '
2080 ' SUBROUTINE - CENTERED TITLE
2090 '
2100    LOCATE 1,(40-LEN(T$))/2+1
2110    PRINT T$;
2120 '
2130    RETURN
2140 '
```

## DRAW COMMAND

Only one BASIC graphics command will be studied in this chapter—the DRAW command. This command has only one parameter (a BASIC string); however, you can use it to generate all sorts of shapes because this one string parameter can contain a whole series of special one-letter draw commands from a special command language called Graphics Definition Language (GDL).

More precisely, the syntax for the DRAW command is

DRAW string

where *string* is a string expression consisting of drawing commands in the GDL.

Let's begin our examination of this language. A summary list of its components is given in Table 4-1. We will discuss the rules for putting these components together to form command strings, but first let's begin with a detailed discussion of the syntax rules.

### M Command

The M command is the global move command. The M command has two different modes: relative and absolute. These modes correspond to and perform in much the same way as the relative and absolute modes work for the PSET, PRESET, LINE, and CIRCLE commands that we discussed in Chapter 3. In absolute mode the new coordinates *become* the new current position, and in relative mode the new coordinates are *added* to the current position.

The syntax, however, is quite different. Instead of using the key word STEP to indicate relative mode, we use a strategically placed plus or minus sign. To see how this works, look at the syntax for the M command in absolute mode. Absolute mode is used if the letter M is followed by an unsigned integer, followed by a comma, followed by another unsigned integer. The first unsigned integer is the new x-coordinate

Table 4-1

Components of the Graphics Definition Language (GDL)

| Class | Component | Use |
| --- | --- | --- |
| Special symbols | Comma (,) | x,y separator |
|  | Equals (=) | Variable marker |
|  | Semicolon (;) | End of command |
| Constants and variables | Numeric constant | Direction or location |
|  | Numeric variable | Direction |
|  | String variable | Part of command |
| Global move | M | Move to an absolute or relative x,y position |
| Local move | U | Move up |
|  | D | Move down |
|  | L | Move left |
|  | R | Move right |
|  | E | Move up and right |
|  | F | Move down and right |
|  | G | Move down and left |
|  | H | Move up and left |
| Move modifiers | B | Move without drawing |
|  | N | Move and return to beginning position |
| Attribute settings | A | Set angle (90°) |
|  | TA | Set angle (any angle) |
|  | C | Set color |
|  | S | Set scale |
| Command control | X | Execute substring |
| Area fill | P | Paint |

and the second unsigned integer is the new y-coordinate; that is, it will be of the form

Mx,y

where $x$ and $y$ are unsigned integers.

The effect of this command is to draw a line from the old current position to a new current position given by the x- and y-coordinates. For instance, "m5,21" would draw a line to the point 5,21.

Relative mode is used if there is a plus or a minus sign between the M and the first number (x-coordinate), making the x-coordinate an explicitly *signed* integer. The second number (y-coordinate) must also be a signed integer, but it does not have to display a plus sign if it is positive. The form will look like

Mx,y

where $x$ and $y$ are signed integers and $x$ has an explicit plus or minus sign. For instance, "m+5,21" would draw a line to a point 5 pixels to the right and 21 pixels down from the current position.

In our first example, we use the absolute form of the move to draw a large arrowhead on the screen.

EXAMPLE 4-3

## ABSOLUTE MOVES

Write a short program that draws a large arrow. Use GDL
absolute move commands. The result is shown in Figure
4-1.

## Solution

```
160  ' MOVES
170  '
180    T$="MOVES"
190    GOSUB 2080 ' title
200  '
210  ' Uses absolute global moves
220  '
230    DRAW "m160,20"
240    DRAW "m319,100m160,179"
250    DRAW "m160,100m319,100m0,100"
260  '
```

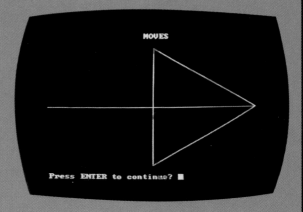

Figure 4-1
Large Arrow

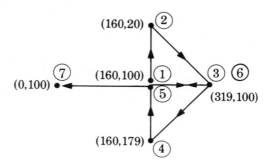

**Figure 4-2**

Drawing the Arrow

As shown in Figure 4-2, the graphics cursor begins at the center of the screen, drawing as it moves straight up to near the top. It then moves diagonally down and to the right until it reaches the center of the right side of the screen, then diagonally down and to the left until it is in the center near the bottom, then up to the center of the screen, then to the right until it reaches the center of the right side, and then finally to the left until it reaches the left side of the screen.

You can see from the listing that the command string can consist of a single move command, or several such commands can be joined together in the same string. It is also possible to put in semicolons to separate move commands (for example, line 240 could have been "m319,100;m160,179"). It is even possible to put spaces anywhere throughout the command string. You should also notice that the effect of several DRAW commands is cumulative. This means that you do *not* have to pack all your move commands into one command string. Thus, you can avoid writing programs with the DRAW command that are impossible to read because of their length or density.

Notice that the "m" is written in lowercase. Any of the GDL commands can be written in either upper- or lowercase. You will notice that if you type in your BASIC program in lowercase, most of it is automatically transformed to uppercase. This is not true for comments and strings like GDL command strings—they will stay in lowercase.

The next example illustrates relative moves. Here we draw a star pattern.

EXAMPLE 4-4

## RELATIVE MOVES

Write a short program that draws an eight-sided star. Use
only GDL relative moves. The star is shown in Figure 4-3.

## Solution

```
270 ' STAR
280 '
290     T$="STAR"
300     GOSUB 2000 ' title & pause
310 '
320 ' Uses relative global moves
330 '
340     DRAW "m+30,-75"
350     DRAW "m-75,+30"
360     DRAW "m+75,+30"
370     DRAW "m-30,-75"
380     DRAW "m-30,+75"
390     DRAW "m+75,-30"
400     DRAW "m-75,-30"
410     DRAW "m+30,+75"
420 '
```

Figure 4-3
Star

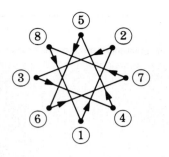

**Figure 4-4**

Drawing the Star

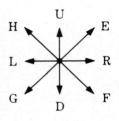

**Figure 4-5**

Local Moves

The graphics cursor starts in the center of the screen. It draws, zigzagging from one side to the other of the star as it draws its points, as shown in Figure 4-4.

In the program listing, notice the plus and minus signs before the first number (x-coordinate), forcing the move command into relative mode. We have also put signs in front of the second numbers (y-coordinates) because it looks prettier to have the symmetry between coordinates, and we could not remember whether or not it was necessary to put the sign on the second number. We believe it is better to be safe than sorry.

U, D, L, R, E, F, G, and H are commands for local moves. The four major directions are indicated by the appropriate initial: U for up, D for down, L for left, and R for right. Diagonal directions are also possible. The letters E, F, G, and H take you around the diagonal positions on a clock face moving clockwise, starting at 1:30 for E, 4:30 for F, 7:30 for G, and 10:30 for H, as pictured in Figure 4-5.

In the next example, we draw all these local moves in clockwise order, starting with U at 12:00. In this example, the graphics cursor begins at the center and turns around and around as it moves away from the center, thus forming a spiral. The spiral is squarish, but other effects are possible, as we shall see later.

EXAMPLE 4-5

## DRAWING A SPIRAL

Write a short program that draws a spiral. Use only GDL
local moves, calling them over and over again in their
natural "around the clock" order, u, e, r, f, d, g, l, h, as you
spiral outward. The spiral is shown in Figure 4-6.

## Solution

```
430 ' SPIRAL                          520     DRAW "e2"
440 '                                 530     DRAW "r=i;r2"
450   T$="SPIRAL"                      540     DRAW "f2"
460   GOSUB 2000 ' pause & title       550     DRAW "d=i;d4"
470 '                                  560     DRAW "g2"
480 ' Uses local moves                 570     DRAW "l=i;l6"
490 '                                  580     DRAW "h2"
500   FOR I=1 TO 150 STEP 8            590   NEXT I
510     DRAW "u=i;u0"                  600 '
```

Figure 4-6
Spiral

There are three possible forms for the syntax for these local move commands: (1) the command letter by itself, (2) the command letter followed by an unsigned integer, and (3) the letter followed by an equal sign, the name of a variable, and a semicolon. In the third case you can even have indexed variables, as long as the index is not an expression.

A letter by itself (first case) indicates a move by one unit (equal to one horizontal or vertical pixel length) in the indicated direction, while a letter followed by either an unsigned integer constant (second case) or by an "equals" variable (third case) allows you to move as many units as you specify in that direction. In the example, we have mixed the second and third cases (constants and variables). We have even included a case in which the constant is zero. In subsequent examples, you will see instances of the first case (the command letter by itself).

Running this program produces a spiral on the screen. Many different types of spirals are possible. This one has very little diagonal motion, giving it a squarish appearance. It would be quite possible to replace lines 520, 540, 560, and 580 by lines that move by the amount "i" and then by the amount 1, 3, 5, or 7, respectively.

Lots of variations are possible by changing the order of these local moves. It is even possible to produce a pattern which is star-like or has little spikes. For example, to make spikes, make the changes in lines 500-590, as indicated in Table 4-2.

**Table 4-2**

Changes in the SPIRAL Subprogram to Make Spikes

| Change From: | | To: | |
|---|---|---|---|
| 500 | FOR I=1 TO 150 STEP 8 | 500 | FOR I=1 TO 150 STEP 16 |
| 510 | DRAW "u=i;u0" | 510 | DRAW "u=i;u0" |
| 520 | DRAW "e2" | 520 | DRAW "h2" |
| 530 | DRAW "r=i;r2" | 530 | DRAW "r=i;r4" |
| 540 | DRAW "f2" | 540 | DRAW "e2" |
| 550 | DRAW "d=i;d4" | 550 | DRAW "d=i;d8" |
| 560 | DRAW "g2" | 560 | DRAW "f2" |
| 570 | DRAW "l=i;l6" | 570 | DRAW "l=i;l12" |
| 580 | DRAW "h2" | 580 | DRAW "g2" |
| 590 | NEXT I | 590 | NEXT I |

To make a star-like spiral, make the spikes grow by replacing lines 520, 540, 560, and 580 in Table 4-2 with the lines in Figure 4-7.

**B and N Modifiers**

In our next two examples we show how to use the B and N prefixes in the GDL string. They can be used with either the global or local move commands studied so far.

The B stands for begin. This command causes the next command to be executed as a move without drawing a line. It allows you to place the unseen graphics cursor anywhere on the screen without unsightly scratches or scrapes on your drawing. The B command will only modify one move command; thus, you need to put it in front of each "unseen" move. In the next example we have shown how to use the B command to "pick up the video pen" so that the figures we are drawing do not merge together into one big mess.

```
520     DRAW "h=i;h2"
540     DRAW "e=i;e6"
560     DRAW "f=i;f10"
580     DRAW "g=i;g14"
```

**Figure 4-7**

More Changes in SPIRAL Program

**EXAMPLE 4-6**

## ARROWS IN AN ARC

Write a short program that draws a set of small arrows
shooting out over an arc. Use the B command to help
position the arrows. The arc of arrows is shown in
Figure 4-8.

## Solution

```
610 ' ARROWS
620 '
630    T$="ARROWS"
640    GOSUB 2000 ' pause & title
650 '
660 ' Uses B prefix
670 '
680    DRAW "bm10,100;"
690 '
700    FOR I=1 TO 24
710      DRAW "bu10bd=i;br10"
720      DRAW "r20d4e4h4d4l20"
730    NEXT I
740 '
```

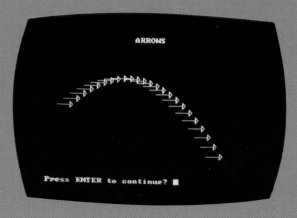

Figure 4-8
Arrows in an Arc

Notice the initial global move in line 680. This puts the graphics cursor in the desired position to start the drawing. The FOR loop, lines 700-730, draws the entire picture. The command string "r20d4e4h4d4l20" is used to draw an arrow (as in Figure 4-9). Notice that we finish the arrow with the current position in the same place as it was when we started. It is a good idea to draw each subfigure so that the current position returns to its starting point. This is a boon when you want to use these subfigures in a complex drawing because you can work at a higher level, placing subfigures at various positions on the screen without worrying how the current position is affected by the current subfigure.

If you look at Figure 4-8, you will see that the arrows follow an arc. This is controlled by line 710, in which we move up by a constant amount, down by a variable amount, and then over by a constant amount. This represents the *difference* in position between the tails of the arrows. In this case the differences are given by the formula

$i - 10$

which is a *linear* formula. If the *differences* are linear, the absolute positions are *quadratic* and we will see a parabola, which is the correct shape for a trajectory. This method is used in computer graphics to good effect, allowing curves to be generated by fast processes that are linear. Generating curves in this way is called the method of *forward difference*.

The next example shows how to use the N prefix. This command causes the current position to remain as it was before executing the command. This prefix affects only the very next move command, so it is not helpful for returning the current position to the starting point for a whole subfigure.

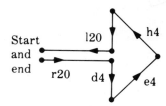

**Figure 4-9**

Diagram of a Small Arrow

EXAMPLE 4-7

## DRAWING AN ASTERISK

Write a short program that draws an asterisk. Use the N
prefix to keep the current position at the center of the
asterisk as each of the eight arms is drawn. The asterisk is
shown in Figure 4-10.

## Solution

```
750 ' ASTERISK                    800 ' Uses N prefix
760 '                             810 '
770   T$="ASTERISK"               820   DRAW "nu30nr30nd30nl30"
780   GOSUB 2000 ' pause & title  830   DRAW "ne20nf20ng20nh20"
790 '                             840 '
```

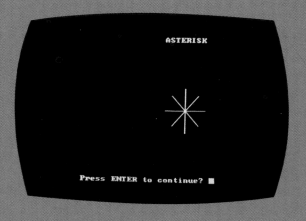

Figure 4-10
Asterisk

In this example, we have chosen to display a simple star or
asterisk. The current position starts out at the center of the
asterisk and remains there after drawing in each of the eight
possible directions. We have chosen to draw the four major
directions first (line 820), and then the diagonals (line 830),
but you can give them in any order since the "pen" (current
position) always returns to the center each time.

## Setting Color

The C command in the GDL language stands for color, and it sets the color for subsequent move commands until the next C command. Its syntax is similar to that of the local move commands, except that you are not allowed to have the letter C alone without following it with a semicolon. If you use just "c;" a value of zero will be assumed. Normally, you can have C followed by an unsigned integer (such as "c2") or an equal sign, followed by a variable name, followed by a semicolon (such as "c=clr1;").

The rules for associating numbers with colors are the same here as in Chapter 3. In the medium-resolution mode you can use the numbers 0, 1, 2, or 3 to specify four different colors, and in the high-resolution mode, you can use the numbers 0 and 1 to specify the two colors. The default is the current foreground color. However, the default is not reset when you clear the screen. The initial color is, however, reset to this default value whenever you run a program.

EXAMPLE 4-8

## DRAWING RECTANGLES

Write a program that draws an array of rectangles of
different colors on the screen. Use the C command to set
the color for each rectangle. Draw two copies of the
rectangles immediately next to each other horizontally to
get better color on NTSC monitors. The screen is shown in
Figure 4-11.

### Solution

```
850 ' RECTANGLES                    1010 '
860 '                               1020    WD=10 : HT=15
870    T$="RECTANGLES"              1030 '
880    GOSUB 2000 ' pause & title   1040 ' Now display it all over the
890 '                               1050 ' screen and in different
900 ' Uses color                    1060 ' colors.
910 '                               1070 '
920 ' It shows how to define and    1080    FOR I=0 TO 15
930 ' position a rectangle.         1090      FOR J=0 TO 7
940 '                               1100        PRESET (20*I,20*J+20)
950 ' First define a rectangle of   1110        XCOLOR=(I+J) MOD 4
960 ' width wd and height ht.       1120        DRAW "c=XCOLOR;"
970 '                               1130        DRAW REC$+"br"+REC$
980    REC$="r=WD;d=HT;1=WD;u=HT;"  1140      NEXT J
990 '                               1150    NEXT I
1000 ' Set the size.                1160 '
```

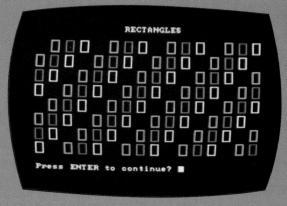

Figure 4-11
Rectangles in Color

In this example, we define a shape, in this case a rectangle with the string REC$="r=WD;d=HT;l=WD;u=HT". Here WD stands for width and HT stands for height. Notice that each of these variables is used in several places in the string. You can easily generalize this idea by defining your own shapes with their own variables, some of which may appear several times in the command string.

The actual drawing is done within the double FOR loop indexed by I and J, starting on lines 1080 and 1090. For each value of I and J, the position of the rectangle is computed in a PRESET command. Thus, we see that the current position that is set by the point, line, and circle drawing commands of the last chapter is the same current position (our invisible cursor) set by the move commands in this chapter.

Notice that the color "cycles" through the values 0, 1, 2, and 3. You will not see the boxes that are colored with the number 0 because 0 indicates the background color. In the DRAW command itself, the string is computed by concatenating three strings together; that is, we are allowed to bring the power of string manipulation to bear upon this powerful graphics language. The effect of this concatenation is to draw the rectangle twice with the two copies one horizontal position apart. This ensures true colors for an NTSC monitor.

**Setting the Angle**

The next example illustrates how to use the A command, which sets the *angle* for all subsequent move commands until the next A command. Only four angles are allowed: 0, 90, 180, and 270 degrees. With version 2.0 of BASICA, there is an easy way to turn by any angle. We will discuss this method (the TA command) in the next section.

When you first run a program and until you invoke the first A command, a default angle value of 0 is used. The syntax for this command is the same as for the COLOR command. The number you give it should be 0, 1, 2, or 3, which corresponds directly to the possible angles. In other words, the angle of rotation is 90 degrees times the number you specify in the A command. When objects are rotated by 90 or 270 degrees, they are drawn with the aspect ratio of 4/3. (See the discussion of the CIRCLE command in Chapter 3 for an explanation of aspect ratio.) What this means is that rotated objects are drawn so that they appear undistorted if you happen to be using an ideal TV monitor.

**EXAMPLE 4-9**

## ARROWS TURNING

Write a short program that draws arrows spiraling out
from the center of the screen. Use the A command to
change the angle for each arm of the spiral. The picture of
the arrows turning is shown in Figure 4-12.

### Solution

```
1170 ' ARROWS TURNING              1260     FOR I=0 TO 11
1180 '                             1270       A = I MOD 4
1190     T$="ARROWS TURNING"       1280       FOR J=1 TO I
1200     GOSUB 2000 ' pause & title 1290          DRAW "a=A;"
1210 '                             1300          DRAW "r10d4e4h4d4l10"
1220 ' Uses angle                  1310          DRAW "br19"
1230 '                             1320       NEXT J
1240     DRAW "c3"                 1330     NEXT I
1250 '                             1340 '
```

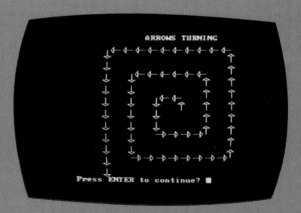

Figure 4-12
Arrows Turning

Notice that the angle for our example program is computed using the MOD function. This keeps the angle number cycling through the values 0, 1, 2, and 3 (see line 1270). Line 1290 is actually where the angle is set. Line 1300 draws a single arrow, and line 1310 generates a move to the next tail position without drawing (it uses the B prefix). We use practically the same arrow in this example as we did in Example 4-6.

Notice the double FOR loop. The outer FOR loop (lines 1260-1330) controls the angle, making the various arms of the spiral. The inner FOR loop (lines 1280-1320) repeats the arrow in the same direction for the correct length of one particular arm of the spiral. You can see that we used the same idea for producing spirals as in Example 4-5. However, this time the arms are made out of multiple copies of a subfigure rather than multiple move commands.

**Turning by Degrees**

Version 2 of Advanced BASIC has a method to turn, point, or travel in practically any direction. It is done by the TA command. The syntax is the same as the A command except that the parameter can have any value between −360 and 360. It sets the number of degrees by which all subsequent GDL commands are rotated. For example, if we first have

DRAW "TA30"

the up, down, left, and right directions are all turned counterclockwise by 30 degrees. Positive angles will turn these directions in a counterclockwise direction, and negative angles will turn these directions in a clockwise direction.

In the next example we show how TA and turning can be used to produce spirals that appear to be smoothly rounded.

**EXAMPLE 4-10**

## ROUNDED SPIRAL

Write a short program that draws a rounded spiral. Use
the TA command. The spiral is shown in Figure 4-13.

___

### Solution

```
1350 ' ROUNDED SPIRAL
1360 '
1370   T$="ROUNDED SPIRAL"
1380   GOSUB 2000 ' pause & title
1390 '
1400 ' Uses TA command
1410 '
1420   DRAW "c2"
1430   FOR I=1 TO 200
1440    A=10*I MOD 360:X=I/11
1450     DRAW "ta=a;r=x;"
1460   NEXT I
1470 '
```

Figure 4-13
Rounded Spiral

In this program, the angle gradually turns as the length of the move gradually increases. That is the basic idea behind smooth spiraling.

Looking at the program in detail, we see that first the color is changed to magenta and then a FOR loop draws the spiral. There are 200 steps to the spiral. At every step the angle is 10 times I (the step number), and the distance traveled in the right direction is I divided by 11. Both of these are increasing functions of the step size I. Line 1450 contains the TA command to make the turn and the R command to make the move.

The next example shows how to draw circles of various sizes using the TA command. To make a circle, you gradually turn, but move the same amount at each step.

**EXAMPLE 4-11**

## SPIRALING CIRCLES

Write a short program that draws circles of various sizes.
Make the circles form a spiral with the TA command. The
circles are shown in Figure 4-14.

## Solution

```
1480 ' SPIRALING CIRCLES
1490 '
1500    T$="SPIRALING CIRCLES"
1510    GOSUB 2000 ' pause & title
1520 '
1530 ' Uses TA command
1540 '
1550    FOR I = 1 TO 100 STEP 2
1560     T=10*I MOD 360:C=(I MOD 3)+1
1570     DRAW "bm160,100;ta=t;br=i;c=c;"
1580     FOR A = -180 TO 180 STEP 120-I
1590      DRAW "ta=a;u2" :NEXT A
1600    NEXT I
1610 '
```

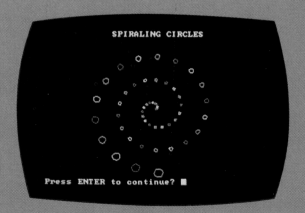

Figure 4-14
Spiraling Circles

Looking at the listing we see that there are 50 circles drawn in the main FOR loop (lines 1550-1600) indexed by I. For each circle, the starting point is determined by moving from the center of the screen along a line I units long at an angle of 10×I degrees. Thus, the starting points are moving out as they turn around the center of the screen. This gives the spiraling effect. Notice that we had to use the MOD function on the angle. This is because error messages will stop the program whenever the angle is larger than 360. Using MOD on the angle with an argument of 360 gives the equivalent angle between −360 and 360. Notice that we also use the MOD operator to help change the color of the circles as we step along.

Each circle is drawn with the smaller FOR loop (lines 1580-1590). Here we make a complete turn gradually from −180 to 180 degrees while moving a constant amount each step. The step size is a decreasing function of I, the index of the main loop. At first, the step size is large, causing small circles to be drawn, and as the step size decreases the circles become larger. Thus, as the circles spiral out, they become larger. You can also control the size of the circles by changing the size of the move in line 1590. In our case, it is "u2," that is, two units in the up direction. If we changed it to four units, the circles would be twice as large.

**Adjusting the Scale**

In the next example we introduce the scale command. It uses the letter S, and it sets a scale factor for all subsequent move commands until the next S command. Its syntax is the same as the C command except for the allowable values for the number you give it. You must be careful when using the S command because only multiples of 4 between 0 and 252 should be used (that is, 0, 4, 8, ..., 252). The default value is 4. The number actually scales subsequent moves by one-fourth the number you specify. This means that a value of 4 does not enlarge the drawing, a value of 8 doubles its size, a value of 12 triples its size, and so on. We observed some strange effects when we used other numbers in one of the programs in the next section.

The example below draws lots of triangles, each larger than the previous one.

EXAMPLE 4-12

## GROWING TRIANGLES

Write a short program that draws triangles. Use the S
command to scale the triangles so that they gradually
become larger. Use as few letters as possible to define your
typical triangle in the GDL language. The triangles are
shown in Figure 4-15.

---

## Solution

```
1620 ' TRIANGLES                      1710 '
1630 '                                1720    DRAW "bm210,10;c3a0"
1640    T$="TRIANGLES"                1730 '
1650    GOSUB 2000 ' pause & title    1740    FOR K=1 TO 18
1660 '                                1750     SZ=4*K
1670 ' Uses scale                     1760     DRAW "s=SZ;"
1680 '                                1770     DRAW "bg"+TR$
1690 ' First define the triangle.     1780    NEXT K
1700    TR$= "UFL"                     1790 '
```

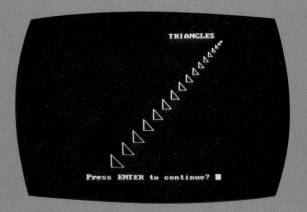

Figure 4-15
Growing Triangles

The original triangle is very small—it's just defined by the primitive string "UFL" (see line 1700). In the FOR loop (lines 1740-1780), we blow it up to as much as 18 times its original size. Each time we draw it, we move out of the way of the previous triangle. This is the purpose of the "bg" string on line 1770.

## X Command

The last example in our series uses the X command. The X command acts like a subroutine call in that it causes any command string you name to be executed right on the spot. The syntax is the letter X followed by the name of an external string variable containing GDL commands followed by a semicolon. The semicolon *must* be present so that BASIC knows when the name of the string has ended. It is possible to have indexed string variables as long as the index is not an expression.

EXAMPLE 4-13

## POLYGONS WITH THE X COMMAND

Write a short program that draws octagons. Use the X
command to execute a string that contains GDL commands
specifying the shape of the octagon. The polygons are
shown in Figure 4-16.

## Solution

```
1800 ' POLYGON                          1900.  FIG$="reuhlgdf"
1810 '                                   1910   DRAW "bm120,180"
1820    T$="POLYGONS"                    1920 '
1830    GOSUB 2000 ' pause & title       1930   FOR A = 8 TO 224 STEP 12
1840 '                                   1940      DRAW "s=A;xFIG$;"
1850 ' Uses the X command                1950   NEXT A
1860 '                                   1960 '
1870 ' It shows a family of octagons. 1970   LOCATE 22
1880 '                                   1980   END
1890 '                                   1990 '
```

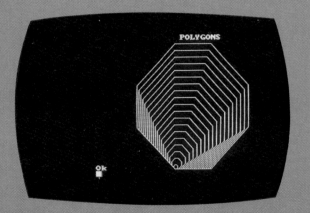

Figure 4-16
Polygons

Using GDL language, an octagon is defined and stored in the string variable called FIG$. The FOR loop from lines 1930-1950 draws the various copies of the figure. This loop has just one DRAW command. Within this DRAW command, the scale factor is set and then the string FIG$ is executed. We see that the X command was not really necessary. Instead, we could have concatenated the strings "s=A" and FIG$. In the next section we will give an example of a situation in which the X command is useful.

There is one more GDL command, namely the P command (for paint), that allows you to fill in areas with color. However, we will discuss it in Chapter 5, which presents a full discussion of area filling.

# GRAPHICS CONCEPTS

## Turtle Graphics

The DRAW command and its associated command language provide capabilities that are similar to but definitely not the same as *turtle graphics*. Turtle graphics is part of a computer language called *LOGO*. This is an exciting new language that has been designed to help children understand computers and geometry. It was inspired by Jean Piaget, who is famous for his theories of human development.

In LOGO you can move a graphics cursor called a *turtle* around the screen. As with the IBM GDL, you can move this graphics cursor backward and forward and make it turn. Just as we found spirals to be such a natural thing to do in IBM GDL, turtles also love to make spirals. (See the August 1982 issue of *BYTE* magazine for some examples of turtle spirals.)

There are, however, fundamental differences between the IBM GDL and turtle graphics. For example, the commands to move the turtle are expressed in full words that are an integral part of the LOGO language. In IBM GDL, the move commands are given by single letters hidden in strings. There are also other important differences. A turtle in LOGO always has a heading that is the direction in which it faces. You can instruct the turtle to go forward or backward by a specified number of steps, but you *cannot* directly tell it to go left or right so many steps. Instead, you must first instruct it to change its heading left or right by so many degrees, and then tell it to move forward in that direction. On the other hand, with the IBM GDL you can go in eight different directions relative to its heading, and you can change its heading to any integer angle between $-360$ and $+360$ degrees.

**A Space-Filling Curve**

The next example contains some advanced ideas, both in the application and in the methods. The application is topology, the branch of mathematics that studies the shapes of objects. For a good introduction to this branch of mathematics, see *Introduction to Topology and Modern Analysis* by George F. Simmons (McGraw-Hill, 1963). A graphics computer is a handy tool in topology because it can quickly and dynamically generate mathematical shapes that might take a person hours or even days to draw. The resulting pictures are very useful, for they often provide instant understanding of some very difficult ideas. In this example we look at the idea of a space-filling curve (see pages 341-342 of Simmons's book). When you run this program you might be able to see how such a curve can be constructed as a limiting case of a series of pictures of increasing intricacy that fill more and more of the screen.

This example also serves as a very good illustration of the X command. You can think of the X command as kind of a subroutine call in GDL. One of the most abstract concepts associated with subroutine calls is the idea of *recursion*. Very simply, recursion happens whenever a routine eventually calls itself. The ability to do recursion is built into such modern languages as Pascal. It is a good tool for performing all kinds of operations, including some sorting procedures. In this example we use recursion to put more and more corners in the curve so that it eventually turns in every possible direction, filling a whole area on the screen. In other words, we have a series of subroutines that make corners, but each time the "stuff" that makes the corner is made by calling other subroutines that make a series of smaller corners, and so on.

Since recursion is not a part of IBM GDL, or even BASIC, we will have to manufacture it as part of our program. We use string arrays to do this. The index of the array is used to keep track of the *level*, which is a measure of the number of returns from subroutines that are currently pending as the program progresses.

**EXAMPLE 4-14**

# SPACE-FILLING CURVES

Write a reasonably short program that draws space-filling
curves. Use the X command with the idea of recursion. The
space-filling curve is shown in Figure 4-17.

## Solution

```
100 ' SPACE-FILLING CURVE
110 '
120 ' This example uses the draw
130 ' command with the string
140 ' operator "X".
150 '
160   SCREEN 1 ' medium resolution
170   KEY OFF
180   CLS
190   LOCATE 12,18
200   PRINT "wait"
210 '
220   DIM UU$(10), UR$(10), UL$(10)
230   DIM DD$(10), DR$(10), DL$(10)
240   DIM RU$(10), RD$(10), RR$(10)
250   DIM LU$(10), LD$(10), LL$(10)
260 '
270 ' The following strings define
280 ' our primitive motions.
290 '
300   UU$(0)="u"
310   UR$(0)="u"
320   UL$(0)="u"
330   DD$(0)="d"
340   DR$(0)="d"
350   DL$(0)="d"
360   RU$(0)="r"
370   RD$(0)="r"
380   RR$(0)="r"
390   LU$(0)="l"
400   LD$(0)="l"
410   LL$(0)="l"
420 '
430 ' Now make the strings to
440 ' unfold the pattern.
450 '
460   FOR K= 1 TO 10
```

▶

## Example 4-14

## Solution, Continued.

```
470 ' Package the srings in the
480 ' form:
490 '        x**$(k-1);
500 '
510    MUU$="xuu$("+STR$(K-1)+");"
520    MUR$="xur$("+STR$(K-1)+");"
530    MUL$="xul$("+STR$(K-1)+");"
540    MDD$="xdd$("+STR$(K-1)+");"
550    MDR$="xdr$("+STR$(K-1)+");"
560    MDL$="xdl$("+STR$(K-1)+");"
570    MRU$="xru$("+STR$(K-1)+");"
580    MRD$="xrd$("+STR$(K-1)+");"
590    MRR$="xrr$("+STR$(K-1)+");"
600    MLU$="xlu$("+STR$(K-1)+");"
610    MLD$="xld$("+STR$(K-1)+");"
620    MLL$="xll$("+STR$(K-1)+");"
630 '
640 ' Define the level changers
650 '
660    UU$(K)=MUR$+MRU$+MUL$+MLU$
670    UR$(K)=MUU$+MUR$+MRD$+MDR$
680    UL$(K)=MUR$+MRU$+MUL$+MLL$
690    DD$(K)=MDL$+MLD$+MDR$+MRD$
700    DR$(K)=MDL$+MLD$+MDR$+MRR$
710    DL$(K)=MDD$+MDL$+MLU$+MUL$
720    RU$(K)=MRR$+MRU$+MUL$+MLU$
730    RD$(K)=MRU$+MUR$+MRD$+MDD$
740    RR$(K)=MRU$+MUR$+MRD$+MDR$
750    LU$(K)=MLD$+MDL$+MLU$+MUU$
760    LD$(K)=MLL$+MLD$+MDR$+MRD$
770    LL$(K)=MLD$+MDL$+MLU$+MUL$
780 '
790    NEXT K
800 '
810 ' Now start the process
820 '
830    FOR K = 0 TO 6
840 '
850    SIDE = 2^(K+1)
860    FSCALE=508/SIDE
870    HSCALE=FSCALE/2
880 '
890    CLS
900    LOCATE 1,1
910    PRINT "Level";K;
```

▶

## Example 4-14

## Solution, Continued.

```
920     PRINT ":  Fills a";
930     PRINT SIDE;"by";SIDE;"grid"
940 '
950 ' The following DRAW commands
960 ' just help to locate the start
970 ' of the curve.
980 '
990     DRAW "bm90,90;s=HSCALE;bf"
1000     DRAW "s=FSCALE;"
1010 '
1020 ' Here is the only real DRAW
1030 ' command in the program.
1040 '
1050   DRAW UR$(K)+RD$(K)+DL$(K)+LU$(K)
1060 '
1070     LOCATE 22,1
1080     INPUT"press ENTER to cont";ANS$
1090 '
1100     NEXT K
```

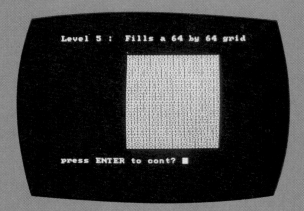

Figure 4-17
Space-Filling Curve

In our program, the subroutines are represented by command strings and the level is tracked in a reverse way by the index K. The index K starts out high, and as the level *increases*, the number K *decreases*. When the index K has decreased to 0, there are no more *calls* and the *returns* start to get resolved.

In lines 220 through 790, the following command strings are defined for K = 0 through 10:

UU\$(K), UR\$(K), UL\$(K),

DD\$(K), DR\$(K), DL\$(K),

RU\$(K), RD\$(K), RR\$(K),

LU\$(K), LD\$(K), LL\$(K)

These are our subroutines. The letters indicate the kind of moves that these subroutines will perform. For example, UR\$ performs a "U" for up, and then an "R" for right.

When K=0, these strings are specially defined to be the move indicated by the first letter of their name. For example, UL\$(0) is just "U". This is the most primitive level — no more calls, so the program can go no deeper than the level it is on.

As the program runs, watch all of this unravel. At first, you see only a simple shape, namely a square. But as the pictures continue to be drawn, you see more and more kinks in the path — each stage of kink smaller than the previous stage. The limiting case of this sequence of paths is the actual space-filling curve. We can never get the actual curve for several reasons. One is the limited resolution of the screen, and another is the infinite amount of time needed to take the limit. Our program does continue until it reaches the resolution of the screen.

While this example illustrated some fairly sophisticated applications, the next example shows the other end of the spectrum of applications, namely how the IBM PC can be used to write games.

## Animation and the Cursor Keys

The next application example illustrates an extremely important area of computer graphics: interactive input.

The cursor keys control the motion on the screen. Press the CURSOR RIGHT key and the object moves to the right. Press the CURSOR LEFT key to move the object to the left, CURSOR UP to move it up, and CURSOR DOWN to move it down.

## Interactive Input

The cursor keys provide the IBM PC with built-in interactive input facilities. With these keys we will be able to move various parts of a picture around, perhaps for an animated game or for developing a design (a room design or design of an electronic circuit). When you press one of the cursor keys while a program is running, the program is actually interrupted to process that key stroke.

IBM BASIC is designed to handle interrupts from as many as 14 different keys. These include the function keys (the ten keys on the left side of your keyboard) and the cursor keys (the four keys marked with arrows on the right side of your keyboard). These keys are assigned numbers from 1 to 10 for the function keys and 11 to 14 for the cursor keys.

Normally these keys will not interrupt your program. You must do three things before an interrupt will happen successfully. You must enable each key that you want to use in this way; you must declare the location (line number) of an interrupt service subroutine for each key that you want to use; and you must write an interrupt service routine for each such key that you have enabled. Now let's discuss each step in more detail.

Normally interrupts are disabled, which means that these special keys behave like any other keys. This means that while your program is running, you can use the INPUT or INKEY\$ statements to wait for combinations of (or single) keystrokes which involve these or any other keys.

Interrupts are *enabled* by the KEY(n) ON command, where $n$ is a number from 1 to 14. An interrupt from key number $n$ can only happen after the KEY(n) ON has been executed. The syntax for this command is

KEY(n) ON        (enable interrupts from key number $n$)

You can use the KEY(n) OFF command to disable any further interrupts from that key, and you can use the KEY(n) STOP command to temporarily stop processing any interrupts from that key. Any interrupt will be processed upon execution of a subsequent KEY(n) ON command for that key. The syntax for these commands is

KEY(n) OFF        (disable interrupts from key number $n$)
KEY(n) STOP       (stop interrupts from key number $n$)

Interrupt service subroutines are declared with the ON KEY command (not to be confused with the KEY(n) ON or even the KEY ON command). This command allows you to place your interrupt service routine wherever you want in your BASIC program. The syntax is

ON KEY(n) GOSUB line

where *n* is the number of the key and *line* is the line number of the interrupt service routine you have written for that key.

Now let's look at the interrupt service routines themselves. The purpose of these routines is to take care of the keystroke quickly with the least amount of disruption to the main program. When a program is running, BASIC checks for interrupts before executing each BASIC statement. If interrupts are declared (ON KEY statement), enabled (KEY(n) ON statement), but not stopped, then whenever that key is pressed, the declared interrupt service subroutine is automatically called. It is interesting to note that while an interrupt subroutine is executing, the corresponding interrupt key is automatically stopped (equivalent to putting the KEY(n) STOP command at the beginning of the subroutine).

An interrupt service routine in IBM PC BASIC looks very much like any other type of BASIC subroutine. In particular, it must end with a RETURN statement; and like any other kind of subroutine, after a RETURN statement, control returns to the main program to exactly the next statement after the one where it left off.

A typical program might contain four such interrupt subroutines, one for each cursor key. These subroutines are usually very short.

It is interesting to note that IBM BASIC mimics the interrupt facilities of its 8088 central processing unit. For the 8088 CPU, there is a section of memory that holds the locations of all the interrupt service routines. The programmer must load these locations to "declare" these routines. There are also processor instructions that can enable and disable interrupts. In contrast to interrupts in BASIC, these processor instructions disable or enable almost all interrupts at once (there are some that cannot be disabled). The interrupt service routines for the 8088 are in machine language, although they might have been written in a higher-level language such as assembly language or PL/I. Each such routine must end in a return instruction, but in this case, the return instruction is a slightly different kind of return than the one used for ordinary subroutines for this processor. The difference is that more information is "saved" (and thus must eventually be restored upon return) when interrupt subroutines are executed.

## Drawing Symbols

One of the tasks to which the DRAW command is particularly well suited is drawing medium-sized symbols. We have included an example application program that draws electronic symbols and extensively uses the cursor key's interrupts for moving objects.

The program has three parts: symbol construction, general display, and symbol move. In the symbol construction section, four kinds of electronic gate symbols are constructed. For various reasons, the symbols are constructed in sections. It is simply easier to work with smaller pieces, and we would like to avoid "wrap-around," an effect that happens when the program lines are longer than the number of characters across the screen. The symbols were designed by laying them out on fine graph paper, as in Figure 4-18. The curved lines were approximated by sequences of dots on the grid points of the graph paper. Then the result was translated into a series of local moves right on the graph paper.

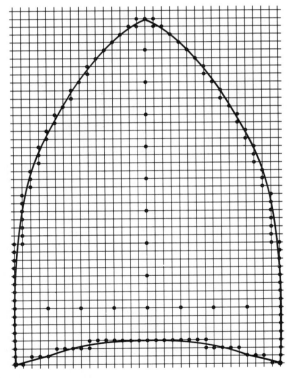

Figure 4-18

Constructing a Command String for a
Section of a Symbol

EXAMPLE 4-15

## ELECTRONIC SYMBOLS

Write a short GDL program that displays the symbols for
the AND, OR, NOT, and XOR gates. After these gates are
drawn, allow the user to move a gate around the screen.
Use the cursor keys with interrupts to move the figure and
function keys to select which type of gate is being moved.
A picture of the symbols is shown in Figure 4-19.

## Solution

```
100 ' ELECTRONIC SYMBOLS
110 '
120 ' This program displays the
130 ' following electronic symbols:
140 '    1)   AND gate
150 '    2)   OR  gate
160 '    3)   NOT gate
170 '    4)   XOR gate
180 '
190    SCREEN 1
200    KEY OFF
210    CLS
220    LOCATE 1,8
230    PRINT "Some Electronic Symbols"
240 '
250 ' First define them
260 '
270 ' 1) the AND gate
280 ' upper left
290    ULAND$="u16r24"
300 ' upper right
310    URAND$="rrrfrrfrfrfffdfdfddfddd"
320 ' lower right
330    LRAND$="dddgddgdgdgggglglgllglll"
340 ' lower left
350    LLAND$="124u16"
360 ' now put them together
370    GAND$=ULAND$+URAND$+LRAND$+LLAND$
380 '
390 ' 2) the OR gate
400 ' upper left
410    ULOR$="u7huuuhuuhu"
420 ' upper right
```

▶

**Example 4-15**

## Solution, Continued.

```
430     UROR$="r17frrrfrrfrrfrfrffrfrf7d"
440   ' lower right
450     LROR$="dg7lglgglglgllgllgllgl17"
460   ' lower left
470     LLOR$="ueuueuuueu7"
480   ' now put them together
490     GOR$  = ULOR$+UROR$+LROR$+LLOR$
500   '
510   ' 3) the NOT gate
520   ' upper right
530     URNOT$="frffrffrffrffrffrffrffrf"
540   ' top
550     TNOT$="u16"+URNOT$
560   ' circle
570     CIRNOT$="uerrfddgllhu"
580   ' lower right
590     LRNOT$="glgglgglgglgglgglgglgglg"
600   ' bottom
610     BNOT$=LRNOT$+"u16"
620   ' now put it all together
630     GNOT$=TNOT$+CIRNOT$+BNOT$
640   '
650   ' 4) the XOR gate
660   ' left side
670     LSXOR$="bd16"+LLOR$+ULOR$
680   ' right side
690     RSXOR$="bd16br8"+GOR$+"bl8"
700     GXOR$=LSXOR$+RSXOR$
710   '
720   ' Now draw them
730   '
740     LOCATE 9,6 : PRINT "AND gate"
750     DRAW "bm40,40"+GAND$
760   '
770     LOCATE 9,26 : PRINT "OR gate"
780     DRAW "bm200,40"+GOR$
790   '
800     LOCATE 21,6 : PRINT "NOT gate"
810     DRAW "bm40,136"+GNOT$
820   '
830     LOCATE 21,26 : PRINT "XOR gate"
840     DRAW "bm200,136"+GXOR$
850   '
860     LOCATE 25
870     INPUT "Press ENTER to cont";ANS$
880     CLS
```

▶

## Example 4-15

### Solution, Continued.

```
890  '
900  ' now let the user move one
910  '
920     ON KEY(1)   GOSUB 1660
930     ON KEY(2)   GOSUB 1710
940     ON KEY(3)   GOSUB 1760
950     ON KEY(4)   GOSUB 1810
960     ON KEY(5)   GOSUB 1860
970     ON KEY(11)  GOSUB 1420
980     ON KEY(12)  GOSUB 1480
990     ON KEY(13)  GOSUB 1540
1000    ON KEY(14)  GOSUB 1600
1010 '
1020    X$=GAND$
1030    Y$=X$
1040    X=160:Y=100
1050    SSTEP=4
1060    PNEW=1
1070    DONE=0
1080 '
1090    LOCATE 1,13
1100    PRINT "MOVE THE SYMBOL"
1110 '
1120    LOCATE 25
1130    PRINT "F1:AND   ";
1140    PRINT "F2:OR    ";
1150    PRINT "F3:NOT   ";
1160    PRINT "F4:XOR   ";
1170    PRINT "F5:exit";
1180 '
1190    KEY(1)   ON
1200    KEY(2)   ON
1210    KEY(3)   ON
1220    KEY(4)   ON
1230    KEY(5)   ON
1240    KEY(11)  ON
1250    KEY(12)  ON
1260    KEY(13)  ON
1270    KEY(14)  ON
1280 '
1290 ' main loop
1300 '
1310    IF DONE=1 THEN 1890
1320    IF PNEW=0 THEN 1290
1330 '
1340    PNEW=0
```

▶

## Example 4-15

### Solution, Continued.

```
1350    Z$=Y$
1360    MOV$="bm0,0br=x;bd=y;c3"
1370    DRAW "c0"+X$+MOV$+Z$
1380    X$=Z$
1390  '
1400    GOTO 1290
1410  '
1420  ' cursor up
1430    IF Y<= 30 THEN Y=30:GOTO 1460
1440    Y=Y-SSTEP
1450    PNEW=1
1460    RETURN
1470  '
1480  ' cursor left
1490    IF X<= 20 THEN X=20:GOTO 1520
1500    X=X-SSTEP
1510    PNEW=1
1520    RETURN
1530  '
1540  ' cursor right
1550    IF X>=270 THEN X=270:GOTO 1580
1560    X=X+SSTEP
1570    PNEW=1
1580    RETURN
1590  '
1600  ' cursor down
1610    IF Y>=160 THEN Y=160:GOTO 1640
1620    Y=Y+SSTEP
1630    PNEW=1
1640    RETURN
1650  '
1660  ' select AND
1670    Y$=GAND$
1680    PNEW=1
1690    RETURN
1700  '
1710  ' select OR
1720    Y$=GOR$
1730    PNEW=1
1740    RETURN
1750  '
1760  ' select NOT
1770    Y$=GNOT$
1780    PNEW=1
1790    RETURN
```

▶

**Example 4-15**

## Solution, Continued.

```
1800 '
1810 ' select XOR
1820    Y$=GXOR$
1830    PNEW=1
1840    RETURN
1850 '
1860 ' exit
1870    DONE=1
1875 RETURN
1880 '
1890    END
```

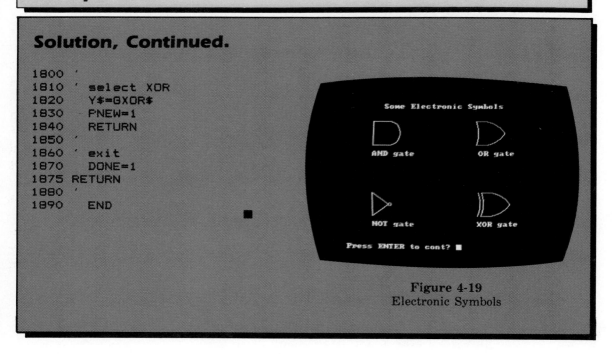

Figure 4-19
Electronic Symbols

    In the general display section of this program (lines 720-840), we show all four symbols with labels. Notice the use of the LOCATE command to position the labels. Combining text and graphics in this way is sometimes time-consuming because of the difficulty of lining up the two different kinds of coordinate systems. We have found a fairly good method —it's called trial and error.

    The symbol move section uses some of the same principles discussed in conjunction with the last example. Again, we are using the interrupt structure in IBM BASIC. This time, however, we do not keep on displaying the figure over and over. Instead, there is a variable called PNEW that tells us whenever a new picture should be drawn. If PNEW is zero, no new picture should be drawn and the program loops back. Otherwise, it drops through this loop and redraws the symbol.

    You can see that we have now activated the function keys as well as the cursor keys in this program. We use F1 to select the AND gate, F2 to select the OR gate, F3 to select the NOT gate, and F4 to select the XOR gate.

Notice how F5 is used to exit the program. We have followed the policy that interrupt service routines should only update variables, and not really *do* anything. In light of this, we have programmed the service routine for an exit so that it updates the variable DONE. The main loop has a check to see if DONE has become 1, thus signaling that the user wants to stop the program. If so, it then jumps to the last statement in the program, which is an END statement. This scheme is a good approach because it never causes any unresolved RETURN statements. The pending RETURN statement from any interrupt service routine is always executed. It is possible to use this idea to successfully step up and down a whole hierarchy of loops while using interactive input.

This program could be the basis of a sophisticated Computer Aided Design (CAD) program in which you could control the positions of several gates on the screen and hook them up in different ways to form a circuit.

# CONCLUSION

In this chapter we have presented a number of topics while discussing the DRAW command and what you can do with it. The major topic is its associated Graphics Definition Language, but other topics included recursion, animation, interactive input, and symbol design. These last topics go beyond a discussion of the syntax of the graphics commands, and provide some very interesting and useful graphics techniques.

# AREA FILLING

# CONCEPTS

**Concepts**
    Region Filling
    Comparison with Box Fill

**Commands**
    PAINT

**Applications**
    Coloring Pie Charts
    Coloring 3-D Objects
    Drawing a Background Scene

# INTRODUCTION

This chapter introduces the powerful PAINT command. Region filling (as exemplified by the PAINT command) is compared to and contrasted with scan conversion of polygons (an approach exemplified by the LINE command with the BF option). The advantages and disadvantages of each approach and the theory behind each are discussed. BASIC programs show various ways the PAINT command can be used to color in a picture.

In this chapter we will again use a series of "stand-alone" example programs that are housed in a larger program. The "front end" (lines 100-150) and the "back end" (lines 5000-5140) of this example program are the same as in Chapter 3, except that line 100 now should read

100 ' CHAPTER 5 LESSONS

# PAINT COMMAND

The PAINT command allows the user to fill any enclosed region on the screen with color. To use this command, you must make sure that the region is completely surrounded with a color called the *boundary* color. You do this by using any combination of the point, LINE, CIRCLE, and DRAW commands that we studied in previous chapters. With the PAINT command you "plant" a "seed" of color in the region, and this seed "grows" by filling the region with the desired color.

The full syntax for the PAINT command is

PAINT (x,y) [[,paintcolor [,boundary][,background]]

where $(x,y)$ are the coordinates (relative or absolute) of the point where you plant the "seed," *paintcolor* is an expression that specifies the desired new color or texture for the interior of the region, *boundary* is an expression that specifies the color of the boundary, and *background* is an expression that controls the conditions for continuing to paint over areas already painted.

The *paintcolor* parameter can be either an integer or a string expression. If it is an integer, it specifies the color number for painting solid areas; if it is a string, it specifies a texture. We will discuss texture later in this chapter, as well as explain how the *background* parameter is used.

The PAINT command has many options, but we will start with the simplest case and build toward the more complex ones. We start with

PAINT (x,y)

You can see that only the coordinates of the "seed" are given. Both the color of the boundary and the paint color default to the foreground color.

Although this command looks simple, it can be used to paint a complex region. But we need to draw a complicated boundary first. Our first example shows how this form of the PAINT command can be used to fill in a moderately complex region. We will draw the outline of a picket fence, and then use the PAINT command to "whitewash" it.

EXAMPLE 5-1

## PAINTING A COMPLEX REGION

Draw a picket fence with an arch and paint it white using
the simplest form of the PAINT command. The painted
fence is pictured in Figure 5-1.

## Solution

```
160 ' PAINTED PICKET FENCE
170 '
180    T$="PICKET FENCE"
190    GOSUB 5090 ' title
200    COLOR 2,1
210 '
220 ' first draw the outline
230 '
240 ' main middle section
250    DRAW "bm20,60"
260    FOR I=1 TO 7
270       DRAW "f10d10r20u10e10"
280       DRAW "bm-30,+30r20d20l20u20"
290       DRAW "bm -0,+30r20d20l20u20"
300       DRAW "bm-10,+40r10u10r20d10r10"
310       DRAW "bu100"
320    NEXT I
330 '
340 ' end posts
350    DRAW "bm20,60g10d90r10"
360    DRAW "bm300,60f10d90l10"
370 '
380 ' arch
390    PI=3.1416
400    CIRCLE (180,70), 30,, 0, PI
410    CIRCLE (180,70), 50,, 0, PI
420    PRESET (140,60)
430 '
440 ' Now paint it
450 '
460    PAINT (160,115)
470 '
480 '
```

## Example 5-1

### Solution, continued.

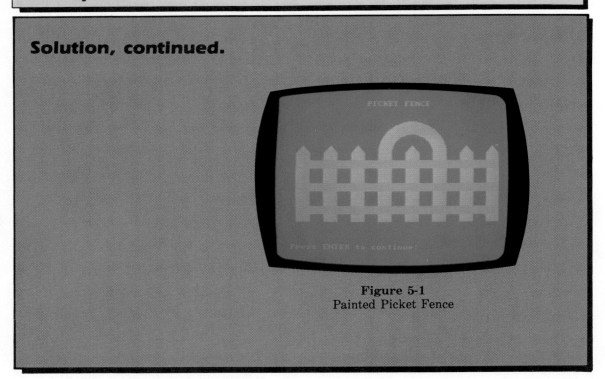

**Figure 5-1**
Painted Picket Fence

In this example, the fence is constructed in lines 220-420 and painted in line 460. Notice how easy it is to paint the fence once you have drawn its boundary.

The fence is outlined in the foreground color, the default color for commands such as DRAW and CIRCLE. This is also the default color for the boundary color, so no color need be specified anywhere in the program.

The symmetry of the fence is exploited during its construction by using a FOR loop (lines 260-320) to replicate a section of fence seven times across the screen. Within this FOR loop, the DRAW command and its associated GDL provide an efficient way to encode a top U-shaped piece (line 270), two middle rectangles (lines 280 and 290), and a bottom upside-down U-shaped piece (line 300). We see a correspondence between the lines of code and the parts of the picture—four parts of boundary in four lines of code. A fifth line (line 310) moves the current position to the correct position to draw the next section of fence during the next pass through the

FOR loop. After the FOR loop, the ends of the fence are completed with more DRAW commands (lines 350-360).

We have decided to put an arch in the fence. This arch could be the top of a gate or a trellis for some climbing vines. The arch is constructed using CIRCLE commands (lines 400-410), one for the outside of the arch, and one for the inside. Notice that the two CIRCLE commands actually draw 180 degree arcs, as specified by the start and stop parameters for angles.

The PRESET command on line 420 looks useless but is really quite necessary. It punches a pin hole in the boundary between the inside of the fence and the inside of the arch, thus making the entire fence and arch one region. As in the story about the Dutch boy at the dike, only one small hole is necessary to cause a large flood, as you will see when this program is run. This will also serve to point out the importance of *completely* surrounding the region you want to paint by the boundary color. If we punched that tiny hole in the boundary between the fence and an area we did not want colored, we would have quite a mess.

On line 460, painting begins. There is no specification of color in the PAINT statement on line 420, so we must use the foreground color for both the paint and the boundary.

The coordinates of the seed are (160,115). This is where you begin to paint. This seed points to a spot near the center of the fence, but definitely inside the fence. You might try starting at other points inside the fence, near the top, near the bottom, on either side, or even in the arch. What do you think will happen if you start painting outside the fence? The next example will explain this.

When the program runs, you see the background turn green (see the COLOR statement in line 200). Next, the outline of the fence is drawn in sections and the arch appears. Then we see paint begin to flow into the fence. Both the paint and the outline of the fence are white, which is the foreground color for the particular graphics state we are in (palette 1 in the medium-resolution mode). This is how we get the fence whitewashed with white paint.

As you watch the fence being painted, you will see that the paint first flows from the seed position throughout the rest of the fence. You can temporarily stop the action of the PAINT command by pressing the CONTROL and NUMLOCK keys at the same time, and you can restart it by pressing any other key.

You will see different effects depending upon the version of Advanced BASIC you are using.

In version 1 of BASICA, the paint flows entirely across one horizontal line of the fence, and then flows upward a line at a time until it reaches a row of rectangular holes. (These holes were drawn in the FOR loop.) It then fills the parts of the posts alongside these holes one at a time in a right-to-left order. Once the holes are cleared, it again paints all the way across. Eventually, it paints all the way to the top of the fence, and then fills in the arch. After the upper half of the fence has been painted, the bottom half is painted in a similar manner.

The method used in version 1 uses BASIC's *stack* to keep track of the areas yet to be painted. The *IBM BASIC* manual warns you that you may run out of stack space if you have a very complex region. It also tells you how to gain more room for the stack. In version 2, the paint flows evenly outward from the seed position, moving upward and downward at the same time. We have found that this method does not use the stack, so the IBM warning no longer applies.

Painting methods fall into a class of algorithms called *scan line* algorithms (not to be confused with a scan conversion algorithm, which we will discuss later in this chapter). For our screen, a scan line is a horizontal row of dots on the screen. By looking closely at the screen you can see that either painting method works by coloring entire portions of the scan lines that cross the region. This is how we get the name scan line for this type of algorithm. You should understand that whatever method BASIC uses to paint, it uses quite a bit of intelligence to compute how to paint the entire region as fast as it does without missing any spots.

The next example demonstrates what happens when we place the seed in different regions of the same picture. The seed can be placed anywhere within the interior of the region you want to color. Since a picture is normally divided into a number of regions, you must specify the location of the seed to indicate which region you want to color.

EXAMPLE 5-2

## PAINTING DIFFERENT REGIONS OF THE SAME PICTURE

Draw a sun pattern and paint different regions by placing the seed point in different places. Mark the seed position with an asterisk after painting. The five pictures are shown in Figure 5-2.

---

## Solution

```
490 ' SUN
500 '
510 ' asterisk for pointing to seed
520    ASTERISK$="c2s40nunrndnlnenfngnh"
530 '
540    GOTO 860 ' skip the subroutine
550 '
560 ' SUBROUTINE - OUTLINE THE SUN
570 '
580    GOSUB 5000 ' pause & title
590 '
600 ' separate title from picture
610    LINE (0,12)-(319,12)
620 '
630 ' Draw star pattern
640 '
650    PSET   (150,20)
660    LINE - (165,70)
670    LINE - (230,40)
680    LINE - (180,95)
690    LINE - (220,140)
700    LINE - (170,130)
710    LINE - (170,180)
720    LINE - (135,140)
730    LINE - ( 90,170)
740    LINE - (100,120)
750    LINE - ( 50,110)
760    LINE - (100, 90)
770    LINE - ( 85, 40)
780    LINE - (135, 65)
790    LINE - (150, 20)
800 '
810 ' circle in center
820    CIRCLE (140,95), 25
```

▶

## Example 5-2

Example 5-2

## Solution, continued.

```
830 '
840    RETURN
850 '
860 ' Now demonstrate paint command
870 '
880    T$="SUN - UNFILLED"
890    GOSUB 560 ' outline the sun
900    COLOR 9,1
910 '
920    T$="SUN - CENTER FILLED"
930    GOSUB 560 ' outline the sun
940    PAINT (140,95)
950    PSET (140,95):DRAW ASTERISK$
960 '
970    T$="SUN - MIDDLE FILLED"
980    GOSUB 560 ' outline the sun
990    PAINT (180,100)
1000   PSET (180,100):DRAW ASTERISK$
1010 '
1020   T$="SUN - OUTSIDE FILLED"
1030   GOSUB 560 ' outline the sun
1040   PAINT (240,100)
1050   PSET (240,100):DRAW ASTERISK$
1060 '
1070   T$="SUN - CENTER & OUTSIDE"
1080   GOSUB 560 ' outline the sun
1090   PAINT (160,95)
1100   PSET (160,95):DRAW ASTERISK$
1110   PAINT (180,50)
1120   PSET (180,50):DRAW ASTERISK$
1130 '
1140 '
```

Figure 5-2
Sun Pictures

Example 5-2

## Solution, continued.

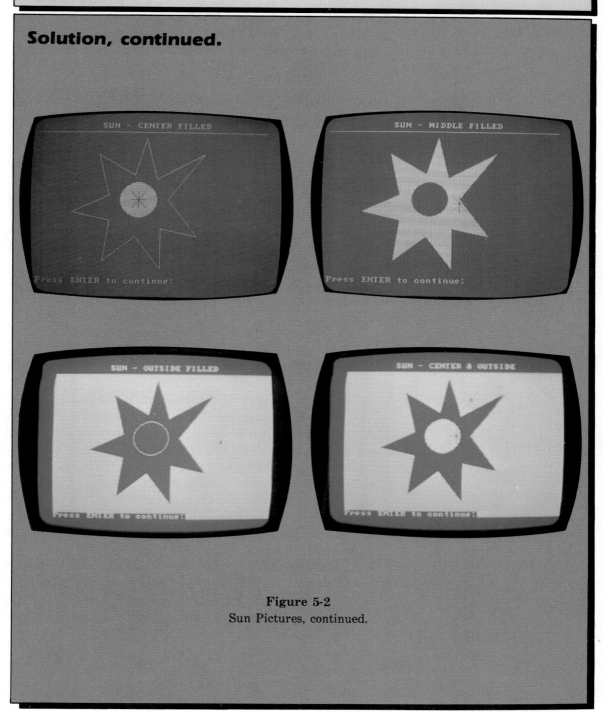

Figure 5-2
Sun Pictures, continued.

In this example we draw a picture of a sun that has a round center and a star-like corona. The picture consists of three regions. The paint seed is placed in each of these regions in turn, and finally in two regions at once. After painting, we point out the position of the seed by marking it with a red asterisk. It might seem more natural to mark the seed location before painting begins, but unfortunately that would cause two serious problems: The marker would be painted over, and the painting would be messy because the marker would punch a hole in the boundary of the region. This happens when the seed is close to the boundary.

In this example program, the job of drawing the sun's boundaries is encapsulated in a subroutine. This "outliner" subroutine also calls the pause and title subroutine and draws a line across the top of the screen to separate the title from the picture. Such a line is needed to prevent the title from being washed away when we paint the outermost region of the figure.

The actual picture consists of a star shape and a circle in its center. The star is done with a PSET statement (line 650), followed by a series of LINE statements (lines 660-790).

The star and circle divide the picture into the following three regions: the center (inside the circle), the middle (outside the circle and inside the star pattern), and the area outside both.

The main program for this example starts on line 860. First we set the background to blue (the second parameter of the COLOR statement in line 900), and then we call the outline subroutine to draw the boundaries of the star shape and circle without painting anything. Next we fill in only the center, then just the middle, and then just the outside. Finally we fill in both the center and the outside. Notice that the boundaries of the screen serve as a boundary for the outside region; that is, painting the outside region does not continue to infinity, taking an infinite time to complete its work.

Again with this example you will be able to see the paint flow across the region. Painting does not appear to be an instantaneous process. You might want to watch carefully and try to predict which areas will be painted first and which areas will be saved for last.

## Painting with Other Colors

Now let's add some color to the PAINT command. First let's see what we can do with just the *paintcolor* expression. We use the syntax

PAINT (x,y), paintcolor

where *paintcolor* is an expression that specifies the color you want to paint the interior of the region. In this form, the boundary must be the same color that we use to paint the region. If it is not, there might be areas inside the region that do not get painted.

In the next example we draw a 3-D cube and color each of its visible faces with a different color. The first face is colored with the Box Fill option of the LINE command, but the other two are first outlined with LINE commands and then filled with the PAINT command.

**EXAMPLE 5-3**

## PAINTING A CUBE

Paint the faces of a cube with different colors. Use only one
color parameter for the PAINT command. Use the BF (Box
Fill) option for one face. The cube is shown in Figure 5-3.

---

## Solution

```
1150 ' BLOCK
1160 '
1170    T$="BLOCK"
1180    GOSUB 5000 ' title & pause
1190    COLOR 0,0
1200 '
1210 ' Use same color for interior
1220 ' and boundary
1230 '
1240 ' front face (just Box Fill)
1250    PSET (100,150),  1
1260    LINE -(180,80),  1, BF
1270 '
1280 ' top face (needs PAINT)
1290    PSET (100,80),   2
1300    LINE -(180,80),  2
1310    LINE -(210,50),  2
1320    LINE -(130,50),  2
1330    LINE -(100,80),  2
1340    PAINT (120,70),  2
1350 '
1360 ' side face (needs PAINT)
1370    PSET (180,150),  3
1380    LINE -(210,120), 3
1390    LINE -(210,50),  3
1400    LINE -(180,80),  3
1410    LINE -(180,150), 3
1420    PAINT (200,100), 3
1430 '
```

## Example 5-3

### Solution, continued.

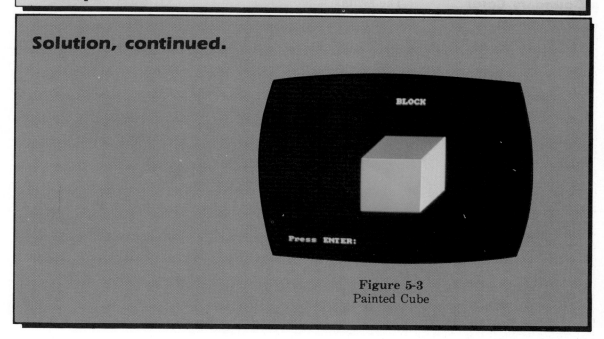

Figure 5-3
Painted Cube

In this subprogram, after the title appears, the background color is changed to color 0 with palette 0 (with the COLOR command on line 1190). This selection causes color 0 (the background color) to appear black, color 1 to appear green, color 2 to appear red, and color 3 to appear yellow. (The *IBM BASIC* manual lists brown instead of yellow for this last color, but it looks yellow to us.)

The front face of our cube is a rectangle; thus, it can be colored using the BF (Box Fill) option of the LINE command. It is easier to program Box Fill than the PAINT command because only one BASIC statement is required with this form. It also runs much faster. Later in this chapter we will discuss the differences between these two methods in more detail. Color 1 (green) is specified as part of the LINE command.

The top face is drawn next. It is not a rectangle, and thus cannot be filled with the LINE command. The face is first outlined in color 2 (red) using one PSET command and four LINE commands. Then the inside is painted with this same color (see the PAINT command on line 1340).

The side face is outlined and painted in color 3 (yellow) in a similar manner to the top face.

## PAINT with a Boundary Color

Let's explore the PAINT command's *boundary* parameter. The syntax is

PAINT (x,y), paintcolor, boundary

Here the boundary can be a different color from the interior. The next example shows this in action.

EXAMPLE 5-4

## CUBE WITH DESIGNS

Paint some designs on the face of the cube we drew in
Example 5-3. Use the most advanced form of the PAINT
command. This will allow the boundary to be a different
color from the interior. The designed cube is pictured in
Figure 5-4.

## Solution

```
1440 ' DESIGNS ON BLOCK
1450 '
1460 ' hold that picture
1470   LOCATE 25,1
1480   PRINT"Press ENTER:";
1490   ANS$=INPUT$(1)
1500 '
1510 ' Uses different color for
1520 ' than interior
1530 '
1540 ' letter A on front
1550 ' boundary = color 0
1560   PSET  (110,140), 0
1570   LINE -(135,90),  0
1580   LINE -(145,90),  0
1590   LINE -(170,140), 0
1600   LINE -(160,140), 0
1610   LINE -(155,130), 0
1620   LINE -(125,130), 0
1630   LINE -(120,140), 0
1640   LINE -(110,140), 0
1650   PSET  (130,120), 0
1660   LINE -(150,120), 0
1670   LINE -(140,100), 0
1680   LINE -(130,120), 0
1690   PAINT STEP(-1,-1), 2, 0
1700 '
1710 ' number one on side

1720 ' boundary = color 2
1730   PSET  (185,135), 2
1740   LINE -(205,115), 2
1750   LINE -(205,105), 2
1760   LINE -(200,110), 2
1770   LINE -(200,75),  2
1780   LINE -(185,90),  2
1790   LINE -(185,100), 2
1800   LINE -(190,95),  2
1810   LINE -(190,120), 2
1820   LINE -(185,125), 2
1830   LINE -(185,135), 2
1840 '
1850 ' interior = color 0
1860   PAINT STEP(1,-2), 0, 2
1870 '
1880 ' square on top
1890 ' boundary = color 3
1900   PSET  (140,75)
1910   DRAW "s8r3er3er2erere2"
1920   DRAW "u2h212g1g"
1930   DRAW "h21g1"
1940   DRAW "g4dgdfd"
1950 '
1960 ' interior = color 1
1970   PAINT (155,65), 1, 3
1980 '
1990 '
```

■

**Example 5-4**

**Solution, continued.**

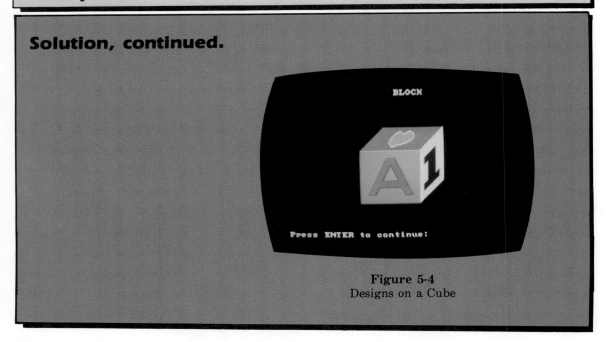

Figure 5-4
Designs on a Cube

This program uses the same cube as was drawn in the previous example. This is why you do not use the "pause and title" routine that clears the screen between these two examples. Instead, we use a "hold that picture" routine.

The three faces of the cube are each given a different design. The front face is designed first. We outline a block letter "A" in black (color 0) against the green (color 1) already there, and then we paint the interior of this block letter red (color 2) (see line 1690). Here we have an illustration of the full power of the PAINT command with all its options.

Notice how we have used relative coordinates for the seed, "stepping" a little into the region from the last point drawn on the boundary (line 1690). This is only effective if you paint the interior right after outlining the boundary.

For the side face (already colored 3 for yellow), we outline a block number "1" in red (color 2), and then fill it with black (color 0).

The top side (already red—color 2) is decorated with a heart whose border is yellow (color 3), and whose interior is green (color 1).

It is interesting to note what happens if you already have a color in a region. Actually, this will always be the case, since every point has to be *some* color. There are several important rules which must be followed:

1. Surround the region completely with the boundary color.
2. Do not use the boundary color for points that are not on the boundary.
3. Do not use the paint color inside the region before it is painted.

If you follow these rules the result is simple: If a point in the interior of the region is colored with any color other than the background color, it will subsequently be colored with the paint color.

We should note that often you can get away with breaking rule number 3, but sometimes the PAINT command will prematurely stop painting if you do.

**Tiling**

Version 2 of Advanced BASIC has the ability to fill areas on the screen with texture; that is, a pattern, which is not just one solid color. IBM calls this process *tiling*. It is accomplished by using a string expression instead of a numeric expression for the *paintcolor* in the PAINT command. Basically, this string contains a *mask* for a sample rectangular patch of the texture or tiling. This patch is replicated like a wallpaper pattern to cover the entire area to be tiled, but of course, like wallpaper, the pattern is cut so only those portions of the pattern that fall within the area to be covered are shown.

Each row of the tiling patch is stored in individual characters of the tiling string. There can be as many as 64 characters in a tiling string and thus as many as 64 rows in a tiling patch.

Each row of the tiling patch corresponds to one byte of video RAM. With the medium-resolution graphics mode this gives four pixels in each row of the tiling patch; in the high-resolution mode this is eight pixels per tiling row.

The individual copies of the tiling patch are aligned with the screen in a simple way. Horizontally, each row of each patch fits precisely within a byte of the video RAM. Since there are 80 bytes across the screen, there are exactly 80 possible horizontal positions for the patches. Vertically, the possible patch positions repeat themselves, starting from the top of the screen and going toward the bottom. This means that if a tiling string has length $n$, the patch pattern repeats itself vertically every $n$ scan lines with the first row of the patch always falling on a scan line position that is an even multiple of $n$.

If you need to know the particular row of the pattern that will fall on a given scan line, you can use the following formula, which uses the MOD operator:

row = scanline MOD n

where *row* is the row of the tiling patch, counting 0 as the top of the tiling patch, and *scanline* is the scan line, counting 0 as the top scan line of the screen.

As we discussed in Chapter 2, in medium-resolution mode, each pixel requires a 2-bit binary number that determines its color. Four of these 2-bit numbers are packed into a byte of the video RAM. When you are tiling, you have to indicate each row of the tiling pattern in this packed form. For example, if you want a row of the pattern to consist of four pixels with the color numbers 3, 0, 1, and 2, you would compute the byte value in the following way:

3 0 1 2 (decimal) = 11 00 01 10 (binary) =
11000110 (binary) = C6 (hexadecimal)

These byte values in turn are used in place of ASCII codes for characters in the tiling string. The easiest way to do this is to use the CHR$ function. For example, suppose you want to have a tiling pattern that consists of one row of pixels with colors 0, 0, 2, 2 and a second row with colors 3, 3, 1, 1. The first row has the byte value

00 00 10 10 (binary) = 00001010 (binary) =
0A (hexadecimal)

and the second row has the byte value

11 11 01 01 (binary) = 11110101 (binary) =
F5 (hexadecimal)

Thus, as the first character has ASCII code 0A (hexadecimal) and the second character has ASCII code F5 (hexadecimal), we pack these together to form the tiling string

CHR$(&H0A) + CHR$(&HF5)

In our next example, we will demonstrate how to fill areas on the screen with two-row patterns like this one.

EXAMPLE 5-5

## COLORFUL PATTERNS

Write a short program that draws boxes filled with colorful
patterns in a quilt-like array. Use two-character tiling
strings. The pattern is shown in Figure 5-5.

---

## Solution

```
2000  ' COLOR PATTERNS
2010  '
2020    T$="COLOR PATTERNS"
2030    GOSUB 5000 ' pause and title
2040    COLOR 0,1
2050  '
2060  ' draw the boxes
2070    FOR X = 50 TO 290 STEP 15
2080      LINE (X,20)-(X,180)
2090    NEXT X
2100  '
2110    FOR Y = 20 TO 180 STEP 10
2120      LINE (50,Y)-(290,Y)
2130    NEXT Y
2140  '
2150  ' fill with color pattern
2160    FOR I1 = 0 TO 3
2170      FOR I2 = 0 TO 3
2180        ROW1$ = CHR$(80*I1+5*I2)
2190        X = 51 + 15*(4*I1+I2)
2200        FOR I3 = 0 TO 3
2210          FOR I4 = 0 TO 3
2220            IF I1+I2+I3+I4 = 0 THEN 2260
2230            ROW2$ = CHR$(80*I3+5*I4)
2240            Y = 21 + 10*(4*I3+I4)
2250            PAINT (X,Y), ROW1$+ROW2$
2260          NEXT I4
2270        NEXT I3
2280      NEXT I2
2290    NEXT I1
2300  '
```

Example 5-5

**Solution, continued.**

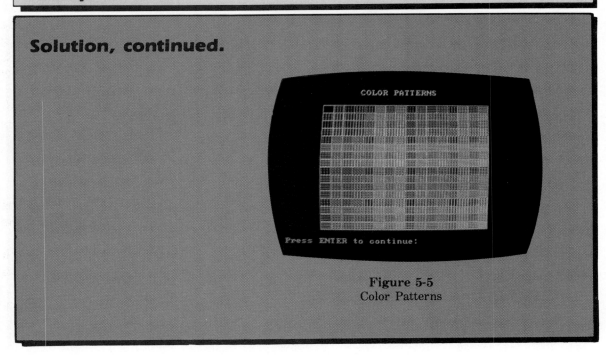

Figure 5-5
Color Patterns

When this program runs, you will see a 16 × 16 quilt-like array of samples of various two-row tiling patterns, each one a little different from the other. Because of problems with NTSC color encoding, we have doubled each pixel horizontally, giving two double pixels per row of the tiling patch. Since there are two rows in each patch, each patch has a total of four double pixels. Each of the four double pixels can be any one of four colors. Our picture shows all 256 possibilities.

Looking at the listing, you see a quadruple nested FOR loop. The indices I1, I2, I3, and I4 each range from 0 to 3. Each index corresponds to a different double pixel, and in this way, we include all four colors for all four double pixel positions in the pattern.

The indices I1 and I2 determine the first row of the pattern. This is done in line 2180 with the formula

ROW1 = CHR$(80*I1 + 5*I2)

To understand better what this does, let's rewrite it as

$$ROW1 = CHR\$(64*I1 + 16*I1 + 4*I2 + I2)$$

The coefficients 64, 16, 4, and 1 shift the colors into their correct bit positions of the tiling byte. For example, multiplying I1 by 64 shifts the value I1 into the top two bits (bits 7 and 6) of the byte, while multiplying this same quantity by 16 shifts it into the next two bits (bits 5 and 4). Thus, for the first row we have colors I1, I1, I2, I2.

The indices I1 and I2 also determine the horizontal position for the pattern within our array. The formula on line 2190

$$X = 51 + 15*(4*I1 + I2)$$

takes care of this.

Similarly, the indices I3 and I4 determine the second row of the pattern and also determine the vertical position for the pattern in our array.

Note the IF statement on line 2220. It prevents tiling with a string of zero-valued rows. Such a choice would cause an error in BASICA.

Our next example illustrates how tiling can create new colors for NTSC color generation.

EXAMPLE 5-6

## NTSC COLORS

Show a Venn diagram of the primary colors red, green,
and blue and the secondary color combinations these colors
generate. Use a tiling pattern to fool an NTSC monitor into
producing more colors than the four normally possible, as
shown in Figure 5-6.

## Solution

```
2310 ' NTSC COLORS
2320 '
2330   T$="NTSC COLORS"
2340   GOSUB 5000 ' pause and title
2350   COLOR 9,2
2360 '
2370   WINDOW (-3,-3)-(  3,  3)
2380   VIEW (50,0)-(270,180),,3
2390 '
2400 ' carve out Venn diagram regions
2410   CIRCLE (  0 ,-1),1.5
2420   CIRCLE (-.87,.5),1.5
2430   CIRCLE ( .87,.5),1.5
2440 '
2450 ' fill in the regions
2460   PAINT (   0,  2),CHR$(&H33),3
2470   PAINT (   0, -1),CHR$(&HAA),3
2480   PAINT (-.87, .5),CHR$(&H55),3
2490   PAINT (   0,  1),CHR$(&H11),3
2500   PAINT (-.87,-.5),CHR$(&HFF),3
2510   PAINT ( .87,-.5),CHR$(&H22),3
2520   PAINT (   0,  0),CHR$(&HCC),3
2530 '
2540 ' RESTORE WINDOW AND VIEWPORT
2550   WINDOW:VIEW
2560 '
```

## Example 5-6

### Solution, continued.

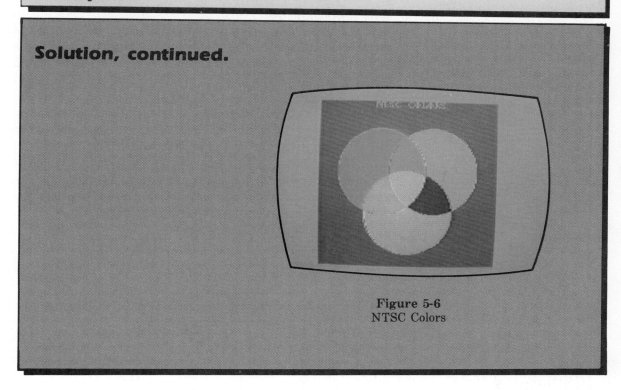

**Figure 5-6**
NTSC Colors

When this program runs on an NTSC monitor, you will first see the background turn blue. Blue is used for the background color because we are using palette number 0, which has the colors green, red, and yellow. This then provides all three primary colors plus a complementary color to one of the primary colors. More explicitly, red, green, and blue are primary, and yellow is complementary to blue. With such an arrangement, we have the basic tools we need to explore coloring.

After setting the background, the program draws the three intersecting circles of a Venn diagram and begins to color in the surrounding area and the regions cut off by these circles. The surrounding area is colored with the pattern 33 (all patterns are specified in hexadecimal), which corresponds to the color pattern "blue, yellow, blue, yellow." In this order (blue on even pixels and yellow on odd pixels), we see black. The major areas within the circles are next colored with the primary colors (except blue, which is already colored). We see the patterns AA in the bottom circle, which is "red, red, red, red," and 55 in the left circle, which is "green, green, green, green."

The intersections then are painted. For the intersection of the green and blue circles, we have the pattern 11, which is "blue, green, blue, green." The result appears to be cyan, a bluish green color. For the intersection of the red and green circles, we have the pattern FF, which is "yellow, yellow, yellow, yellow." For the intersection of the red and blue circles, we have the pattern 22, which is "red, red, red, red." The result is actually magenta (a purplish color). The intersection of all three circles is colored with the pattern CC, which is "yellow, blue, yellow, blue." This appears as a light gray. The colors we obtain for the intersections are what is predicted by color theory when colors are added together.

Our next example demonstrates how to make wallpaper.

EXAMPLE 5-7

## WALLPAPER

Draw a wall with a window and a door in it and use tiling
to paper it with wallpaper. The wallpaper should have a
red background with rows of hearts, and the rows should
alternate in color between yellow and green. The wallpaper
is pictured in Figure 5-7.

## Solution

```
2570 ' WALLPAPER
2580 '
2590    T$="WALLPAPER"
2600    GOSUB 5000 ' pause and title
2610    COLOR 0,0
2620 '
2630 ' draw room
2640    LINE (40,40)-(260,180),,B
2650    LINE (70,80)-(160,160),,B
2660    LINE (180,80)-(230,180),3,BF
2670    LINE (190,90)-(220,140),0,BF
2680    CIRCLE (225,135),2,2
2690    PAINT  (225,135),2,2
2700 '
2710 ' define wallpaper
2720    WP1$=CHR$(&HAA)+CHR$(&HAA)
2730    WP2$=CHR$(&H66)+CHR$(&H56)
2740    WP3$=CHR$(&H9A)+CHR$(&HAA)
2750    WP4$=CHR$(&HAA)+CHR$(&HEE)
2760    WP5$=CHR$(&HEF)+CHR$(&HAB)
2770    WP$=WP1$+WP2$+WP3$+WP4$+WP5$
2780 '
2790 ' paste it up
2800    PAINT (50,50),WP$,3
2810 '
```

## Example 5-7

**Solution, continued.**

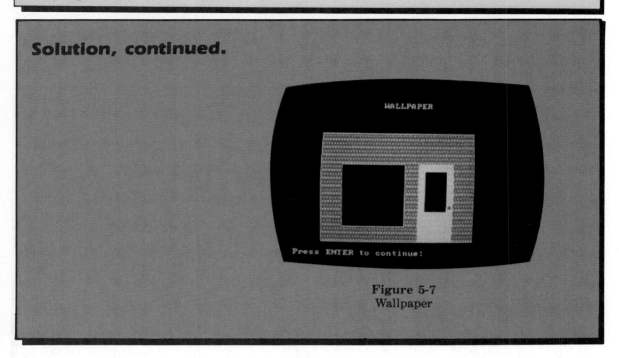

**Figure 5-7**
Wallpaper

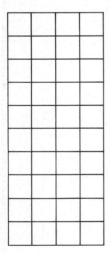

**Figure 5-8**

Tiling Patch for Wallpaper

We see the outline of the wall, door, and window drawn in lines 2630-2690. There is even a door knob to be painted red. In lines 2710-2770, the wallpaper pattern is defined. Figure 5-8 shows the tiling patch. A single line (line 2800) starts the wallpaper off its rolls and onto the wall.

Our next example illustrates what can go wrong and how it can be fixed using the *background* parameter of the PAINT command. This parameter is used to relax the conditions under which the PAINT command senses that it is tiling over where it has already been and thus stops. This parameter is a one-character string and can only be used if the paint color is a string. To be effective, it must agree with at least one character of the tiling string, but an error occurs if it agrees with more than two consecutive characters of the tiling string. It causes the PAINT command to continue tiling over an area that already contains the byte pattern specified in this parameter.

EXAMPLE 5-8

## BACKGROUND

Draw a rectangle filled with a color and then try to tile it
with a tiling pattern that has a row with the same pattern
as the original for the rectangle.

Next show a rectangle filled with the same color and
tiled with the same pattern. This time, however, include a
background parameter with the original color to allow the
tiling process to run to completion.

Finally, show what happens if you try to tile a region
that is already tiled with vertical lines of the border color.
The three examples are shown in Figure 5-9.

## Solution

```
2820 ' BACKGROUND
2830 '
2840   T$="BACKGROUND"
2850   GOSUB 5000 ' pause and title
2860   COLOR 0,1
2870 '
2880 ' set up tiling
2890   TILE$=CHR$(&HF0)+CHR$(&HAA)
2900 '
2910 ' first box - no background param
2920   LINE  (20,20)-( 70,150),2,BF
2930   LINE  (20,20)-( 70,150),,B
2940   PAINT(45,75),TILE$,3
2950 '
2960 ' second box - with background
2970   LINE  (135,20)-(185,150),2,BF
2980   LINE  (135,20)-(185,150),,B
2990   PAINT(160,75),TILE$,3,CHR$(&HAA)
3000 '
3010 ' third box - blocking pattern
3020   LINE  (250,20)-(300,150),,B
3030   PAINT (275,75),CHR$(&HC0),3
3040   PAINT(275,75),TILE$,3,CHR$(&HAA)
3050 '
```

**Example 5-8**

## Solution, continued.

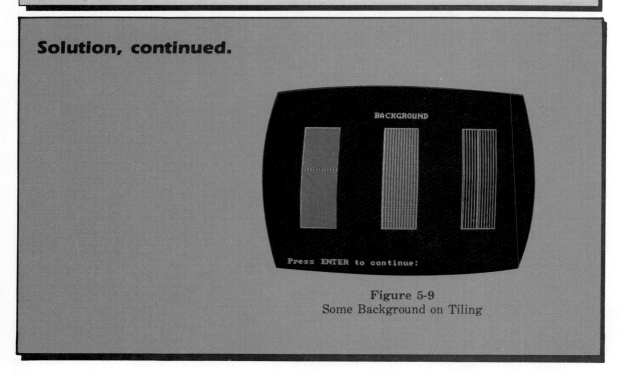

**Figure 5-9**
Some Background on Tiling

When this program runs, you will first see a magenta rectangle bordered by white on the left of the screen. Then you will see a double row of dashed lines run across the middle of this rectangle. This is an aborted attempt at tiling. The tiling pattern is shown in Figure 5-10.

The second row of this pattern matches what was already there in the background. The PAINT command stops because it decides that it already has been there even though it really has not.

| White | White | Black | Black |
|---------|---------|---------|---------|
| Magenta | Magenta | Magenta | Magenta |

**Figure 5-10**

Tiling Pattern for Example 5-8

Next you see a second box in the center of the screen with the same interior and border colors as before. This box is tiled with the same tiling that was unsuccessfully attempted before. However, this time it is successful because we have now added the background parameter with the pattern "magenta, magenta, magenta, magenta," so that the tiling does not stop when this byte is encountered in the area.

The last rectangle drawn in this program first gets tiled with the pattern "white, black, black, black." This causes vertical lines that are the same color as the border to appear in the rectangle. When the PAINT command in line 3040 attempts to tile this, only a thin vertical strip is filled in because the intrusion of boundary color blocks off further tiling.

In general, tiling or painting requires that the surface to be covered be properly prepared for the paint to "stick." For example, if it already contains either the border color or the paint color or tiling pattern, there may be a problem, because painting may stop prematurely. The purpose of the background parameter is to add a bit of primer into the paint to help it stick better. If your paint still doesn't stick, you should try to clean the area first, removing any paint or tiling pattern from it, and certainly removing any border color.

Let's try to "baffle" the computer. We will present the computer with a region that is so complex that (in version 1 of BASICA) it cannot remember enough details to finish painting. Appropriately enough, this region is made of lots of tiny baffles that prevent the color from flowing directly across the scan lines. We do this to show you a limitation of the PAINT command in version 1 and how to get around it. Version 2 of Advanced BASIC will paint this region successfully.

EXAMPLE 5-9

## BAFFLES

Give version 1 of BASICA a region to color that is more
complex than it can handle. The region will be rectangular,
filled with lots of boundary segments that act as little
baffle barriers during the painting process. The partially
painted drawing is shown in Figure 5-11.

## Solution

```
3060 ' BAFFLES
3070 '
3080   T$="BAFFLES"
3090   GOSUB 5000 ' pause and title
3100   COLOR 0,1
3110 '
3120 ' draw the baffle (double width)
3130   LINE (20,20)-(284,166),,B
3140   LINE (21,20)-(285,166),,B
3150   DRAW "C3S4"
3160   FOR J= 20 TO 160 STEP 8
3170   PSET (20,J)
3180    FOR I = 20 TO 280 STEP 12
3190      DRAW "d6ru6bf4br2d6lu6be4br2"
3200    NEXT I
3210   NEXT J
3220 '
3230 ' now paint it
3240   PAINT (163,100),2,3
3250 '
```

**Example 5-9**

**Solution, continued.**

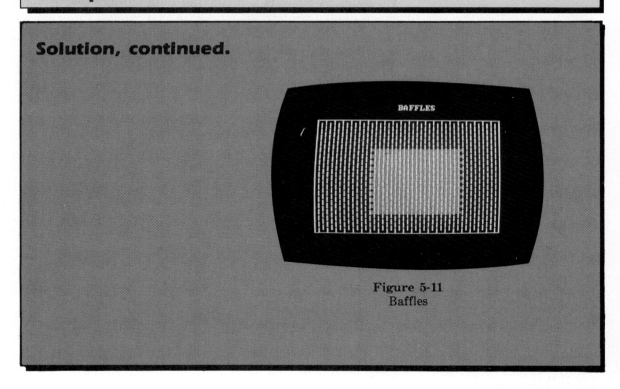

Figure 5-11
Baffles

In this example, you see that a large rectangle is drawn in the foreground color (in double pixels horizontally to get a better white color), and then lots of staggered small vertical double lines are drawn inside this rectangle with a double FOR loop. They are also drawn in the foreground color. This makes a region with a rather simple outside boundary, but a very complex inner boundary. We might use such a design for the inside of a muffler or some kind of filter.

After the figure is drawn, a PAINT command attempts to fill in the interior around all those baffles. When you run this program with version 1 of BASICA, you will find that only a small portion of the interior is painted before the computer runs out of memory (at least that is what the computer says when the program suddenly stops running in the middle of painting this region).

With version 2, there is no problem. The reason for this halt in version 1 is that the painting algorithm uses a *stack* in its main memory to store the locations of places that it cannot yet paint. A *stack* is a method of data storage that is very much like an "in box" on a desk, in that the last thing stored is the first thing removed from storage. On a 64K machine, the stack normally has only 512 bytes assigned to it. If the computer is asked to store more information here than there is room for, it refuses and returns the error message "Out of memory."

Fortunately, there is something you can do about this dilemma. The CLEAR statement allows you to allot more memory to the stack. Try giving the command

CLEAR ,, 1000

This assigns 1000 bytes of storage to the stack. If you run the program (by typing GOTO 3050), the painting will proceed much further. We found that about 2402 bytes of storage were needed to make the program run to completion. Thus, giving the command

CLEAR ,, 2402

should "clear" up any difficulties.

In version 2 of Advanced BASIC, the PAINT command does not use the stack for this purpose and, in fact, just continues to paint in all directions at once until it is finished.

## PAINT AND BOX FILL COMPARED

Now let's compare the Box Fill option of the LINE command with the PAINT command. The two are similar in that they both can be used to fill in regions on the screen with any available color. However, only the PAINT command can color with tiling.

When two things that can do the same task are compared, the obvious question is: "Which is better?" The usual answer is: "It depends upon what you are using it for." This response definitely applies to this case.

Superficially, the Box Fill option is best for filling rectangular regions. As we saw in an earlier example, it is easier to program and faster in performance than the PAINT command on such regions. The PAINT command, on the other hand, is better for filling any shape whose boundaries are not composed of a few horizontal and vertical lines.

There is, however, a deeper difference between these commands. The Box Fill method belongs to a class of graphics procedures called *scan conversion* algorithms, while the PAINT command is classified as a *filling* operation.

Scan conversion algorithms like the Box Fill option of the LINE command draw a figure on the screen without any input from what is already on the screen. Thus, it does not matter if there is some "paint" already on the screen; this kind of operation writes over what was there.

On the other hand, filling operations, such as the PAINT command, depend upon what is already on the screen. Thus, special attention is required by the programmer to make sure that the various images on the screen do not interfere with each other. However, there are circumstances where this is a hindrance. For example, there are certain algorithms for drawing 3-D scenes in which the scene is painted starting from the most distant objects, then the objects just in front of these, and so on, until you color the nearest objects. At each stage, the new objects will obscure parts of old objects and thus are painted right over anything previously painted, no matter what colors are there. This is sometimes what we want, but the PAINT command is not designed to work this way.

Filling operations like the PAINT command do have certain advantages. For example, there are some regions that must be constructed on the screen because their boundaries are pieced together as combinations of DRAW, CIRCLE, LINE, and PSET commands.

Because of these differences, it is best to have both commands available, and in fact, it would be nice to have a generalization of the Box Fill option of the LINE command to draw filled images of other types of figures such as polygons and circles. A general polygon scan conversion operation is included in many high-powered graphics systems. If you think about it, you'll agree that almost any shape can be approximated by polygons. For example, you saw how polygons can approximate circles.

## P OPTION OF THE DRAW COMMAND

Version 2 of Advanced BASIC has the ability to paint areas on the screen as part of the GDL of the DRAW command. That is, you may now include a command within the command string of DRAW that causes areas to be filled in with color. The syntax is

P paintcolor,boundary

where *paintcolor* is the paint color and *boundary* is the boundary color, as in the PAINT command. Both parameters must be present or else an error occurs. The effect of this command is to paint the area surrounded by the boundary color with the paint color starting at the current position as the seed.

For an example of how to use this new GDL command, we will now show how to draw and color a bug. This bug will be used in Chapter 6.

**EXAMPLE 5-10**

## A PAINTED BUG IN GDL

Draw and color a bug. Use only GDL commands.
The bug is shown in Figure 5-12.

---

## Solution

```
3260 ' BUG                          3380 ' draw the body and legs
3270 '                              3390   DRAW "rf2e2f2b14f2"
3280   T$="BUG"                     3400   DRAW "d2f2nd2h2d6"
3290   GOSUB 5000 ' title           3410   DRAW "g2f2nd2h2g2l"
3300   COLOR 0,1    palette         3420   DRAW "lh2g2nd2e2h2"
3310 '   background                 3430   DRAW "u6g2nd2e2u2"
3320 ' initial position and size    3440   DRAW "e2h2g2br4e2r"
3330   DRAW "c3bm160,101s16"        3450 '
3340 '          Color white         3460 ' now paint the body and head
3350 ' draw the head                3470   DRAW "bm160,101"
3360   DRAW "bu6re2u2h2l2g2d2f2r"   3480   DRAW "p2,3 bu8 p1,3"
3370 '                              3490 '
```

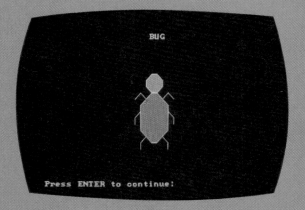

Figure 5-12
A Bug on the Screen

When this program runs you should see a large bug appear on the screen. The body is magenta; the head is cyan. In Chapter 6 we will use a smaller version of the bug. The size of the bug can easily be modified through the use of the scale command on line 3330.

You should take a close look at the combination of DRAW commands that is used to make the bug. Figure 5-13 shows how the bug is constructed. Observe how the head is outlined first (line 3360) and then the body and legs (lines 3380-3440). The legs are done at the same time as the body because to do them separately would require a lot of "move without draw" steps. In fact, we found that drawing the legs alone took up as much room as drawing both at once.

Painting the bug is done in line 3480. Note that the P command uses the current position as the seed. This is why the current position is moved to the center of the body in line 3470. You can see that in line 3480 the P command is first

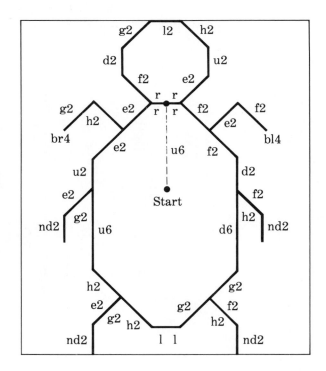

**Figure 5-13**

Diagram of the Bug

used to paint with magenta (color 2) within a boundary of white (color 3), then the current position is moved up to the center of the head, and then the P command is used again to paint with cyan (color 1) within a boundary of white.

# PAINT APPLICATIONS

Now we come to our example applications programs for the PAINT command. These programs are longer but more useful than the lesson examples. They include enhanced versions of two programs already presented in Chapter 3, the pie chart program and the house program.

**Colored Pie Charts**

Our first example applications program draws a colored pie chart. This program is a revision of the program in Example 3-23. In Chapter 3 we had point, line, and circle drawing commands, but no easy way to fill in pie-shaped regions. Now we have the PAINT command.

## EXAMPLE 5-11

## FILLED PIE CHART

Modify the program in Example 3-23 so that it now fills in
each sector with color. The output is pictured in Figure
5-14.

## Solution

```
540        X = 160+COS(MIDA)*RADIUS/2
543        Y = 100-SIN(MIDA)*RADIUS/2
546        PAINT (X,Y),(J MOD 4),3
```

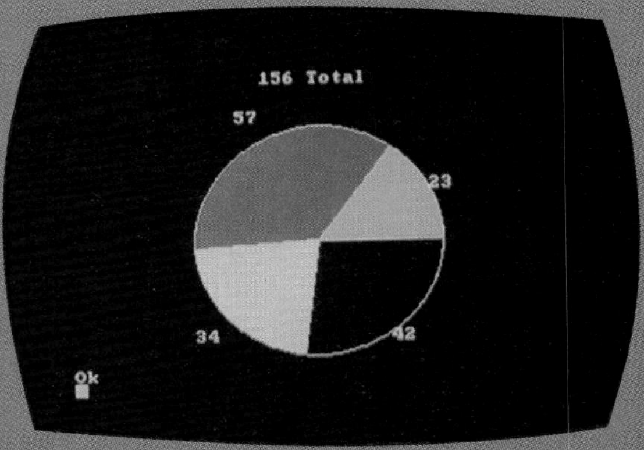

**Figure 5-14**
Colored Pie Chart

The new lines contain the new instructions to fill the pie
sections. The first two lines (lines 540 and 543) are used to
compute the coordinates of the paint seed for each sector. A
point in the absolute center of the sector is chosen (angle =
midpoint angle and radius = one half the radius of the pie).
Notice how the MOD function (line 546) is used to "cycle" the
paint number as we go around the pie. Here we are actually
using an expression, not just a constant or variable, as the
*paintcolor* parameter. Also notice that since the pie is out-

lined in the foreground color, we must specify 3 as the value for the boundary color parameter.

**Painted 3-D Objects**

Our next applications example shows how to add some color to a 3-D object. In this case, we use the 3-D drawing of a house from Chapter 3 and paint the roof, walls, and windows different colors.

**EXAMPLE 5-12**

## PAINTED HOUSE

Modify the house drawing program presented in Example
3-32 so that it now paints the house with a selection of
colors. A painted house is shown in Figure 5-15.

## Solution

```
1350 ' data for paint
1360    DATA 13
1370    DATA    0,   0,   15,  1,  1
1380    DATA    0,  12,   15,  1,  1
1390    DATA   -5,   0,   15,  1,  3
1400    DATA    5,   3,   15,  1,  3
1410    DATA    0,  -8,  -15,  2,  1
1420    DATA    0,  12,  -15,  2,  1
1430    DATA    0,   0,  -15,  2,  3
1440    DATA   10,   0,    4,  3,  1
1450    DATA   10,   0,   10,  3,  3
1460    DATA   10,   0,  -10,  3,  3
1470    DATA  -10,   0,    0,  4,  1
1480    DATA    4,  13,    0,  5,  2
1490    DATA   -4,  13,    0,  6,  2
1500 '
```

```
2140    L$="PAINTED HOUSE"
```

```
2260 ' NOW PAINT IT
2270 '
2280 ' read paint data
2290    READ NP
2300    FOR I=1 TO NP:FOR J=1 TO 5
2310      READ P(I,J)
2320    NEXT J:NEXT I
2330 '
2340 ' rotate the paint areas:
2350    FOR I=1 TO NP
2360      X=P(I,1):Y=P(I,2):Z=P(I,3)
2370      P(I,1)=C11*X+C12*Y+C13*Z
```

▶

## Example 5-12

### Solution, continued.

```
2380        P(I,2)=C21*X+C22*Y+C23*Z
2390        P(I,3)=C31*X+C32*Y+C33*Z
2400     NEXT I
2410   '
2420   ' now paint it
2430     FOR I=1 TO NP
2440        IF F(P(I,4),3)<=0 THEN 2460
2450        PAINT (P(I,1),P(I,2)),P(I,5),3
2460     NEXT I
2470   '
```

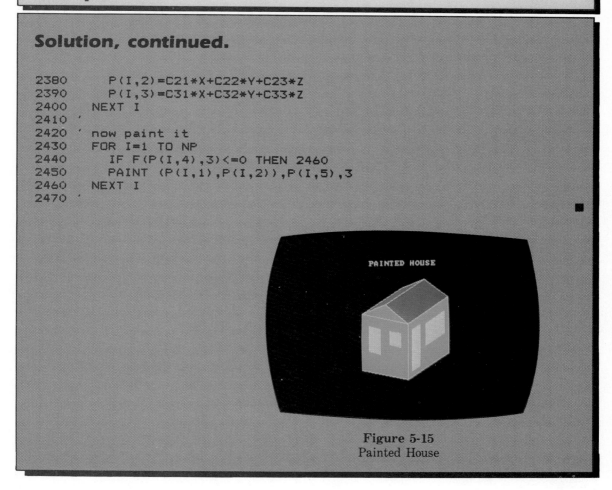

Figure 5-15
Painted House

Lines 1350-1500, 2140 and 2260-2470 are added to the program. In the first section, new data is stored to locate the 3-D paint seed points on the surface of the house.

The second new section (lines 3120-3330) contains instructions to read in these seed points, transform them via the current viewing transformation, and paint with them if they are visible. Notice that their visibility is determined only by the visibility of the plane they are on. Line 2980 is also changed to point out that we now have paint for our house.

Our last example applications program of this chapter shows a background scene.

EXAMPLE 5-13

## BACKGROUND SCENE

Draw a background scene showing a road and a landing
strip with an airplane on it. There should be telephone
poles along the road, mountains in the distance, and the
sun shining in the sky. The scene is given in Figure 5-16.

## Solution

```
100 ' BACKGROUND
110 '
120     SCREEN 1
130     COLOR 3,0
140     CLS
150     KEY OFF
160 '
170 ' border
180     LINE (  0,  0)-(319,199),3,BF
190 '
200 ' grass
210     LINE ( 40,185)-(280, 95),1,BF
220 '
230 ' sky
240     LINE ( 40, 95)-(280, 20),0,BF
250 '
260 ' frame
270     LINE ( 40,185)-(280, 20),3,B
280 '
290 ' horizon
300     LINE ( 40, 95)-(280, 95),3
310 '
320 ' mountains
330 '
340     PSET  (40,95)
350     LINE -(80,57)
360     LINE -(82,60)
370     LINE -(85,57)
380     LINE -(108,78)
390 '
400     PSET  (100,70)
410     LINE -(110,60)
420     LINE -(132,82)
430 '
440     PSET  (120,90)
450     LINE -(160,58)
```

▶

# Example 5-13

## Solution, continued.

```
460    LINE -(194,84)
470 '
480    PSET  (187,87)
490    LINE -(202,77)
500    LINE -(224,89)
510 '
520    PSET  (222,90)
530    LINE -(230,86)
540    LINE -(250,95)
550 '
560    PSET  (245,95)
570    LINE -(253,92)
580    LINE -(265,95)
590 '
600 ' paint mountains
610    PAINT (50,90), 3, 3
620 '
630 ' sun
640 '
650    CIRCLE (245,50), 10, 2
660    PAINT  (245,50),  2, 2
670    LINE   (242,42)-(240,20), 2
680    LINE   (243,42)-(241,20), 2
690    LINE   (248,40)-(260,20), 2
700    LINE   (249,40)-(261,20), 2
710    LINE   (253,42)-(280,30), 2
720    LINE   (254,42)-(281,30), 2
730    LINE   (254,47)-(280,44), 2
740    LINE   (255,47)-(281,44), 2
750    LINE   (255,50)-(280,60), 2
760    LINE   (256,50)-(281,60), 2
770    LINE   (254,54)-(280,70), 2
780    LINE   (255,54)-(281,70), 2
790    LINE   (252,57)-(280,87), 2
800    LINE   (253,57)-(281,87), 2
810    LINE   (247,58)-(250,92), 2
820    LINE   (248,58)-(251,92), 2
830    LINE   (242,57)-(227,87), 2
840    LINE   (243,57)-(228,87), 2
850    LINE   (238,55)-(207,80), 2
860    LINE   (239,55)-(208,80), 2
870    LINE   (237,53)-(168,63), 2
880    LINE   (238,53)-(167,63), 2
890    LINE   (150,65)-(120,70), 2
900    LINE   (150,65)-(121,70), 2
910    LINE   ( 55,80)-( 40,83), 2
920    LINE   (235,50)-(200,40), 2
```

▶

**Example 5-13**

## Solution, continued.

```
930    LINE    (191,37)-(130,20), 2
940    LINE    (237,45)-(195,20), 2
950    LINE    (238,42)-(220,20), 2
960  '
970  ' clouds
980  '
990    CIRCLE  (194,39), 7,2,,,.2
1000   PAINT   (194,39), 3,2
1010   CIRCLE  (186,42), 8,2,,,.2
1020   PAINT   (186,42), 3,2
1030   CIRCLE  (177,47),10,2,,,.2
1040   PAINT   (177,47), 3,2
1050   CIRCLE  (135,50), 5,2,,,.2
1060   PAINT   (135,50), 3,2
1070   CIRCLE  (126,52), 8,2,,,.2
1080   PAINT   (126,52), 3,2
1090   CIRCLE  (112,57),15,2,,,.2
1100   PAINT   (112,57), 3,2
1110 '
1120 ' runway
1130   PSET    (230,185)
1140   LINE   -(248,103)
1150   LINE   -(242,103)
1160   LINE   -(140,185)
1170 '
1180 ' paint runway
1190   PAINT   (220,130), 3, 3
1200 '
1210 ' center line of runway
1220   LINE    (215,150)-(245,105),2
1230 '
1240 ' airplane
1250 '
1260 ' wing
1270   DRAW  "c2bm175,160"
1280   DRAW  "m240,165m+4,-5u3"
1290   DRAW  "m182,152m-4,+3m-4,+6"
1300 '
1310 ' nose
1320   DRAW  "c2bm206,154"
1330   DRAW  "e5r2e2r2f3d3fg2"
1340 '
1350 ' fusillage
1360   DRAW  "bm202,162m-8,+13"
1370   DRAW  "bm197,177m+11,-9m+4,-6"
1380 '
```

▶

## Example 5-13

## Solution, continued.

```
1390 ' tail
1400    DRAW "bm197,177m+4,+1dg"
1410    DRAW "m-20,-1u2m+8,-1"
1420    DRAW "u10r2m+4,+9"
1430 '
1440 ' paint airplane
1450    PAINT (210,157), 2, 2
1460    PAINT (215,153), 2, 2
1470    PAINT (205,165), 2, 2
1480 '
1490 ' define road functions
1500    DEF FNX(T)= 205*T - 145
1510    DEF FNY(T)=  95*T + 65
1520    DEF FNS(T)=  10*SIN(2*T)
1530 '
1540    R0=30 ' half the road width
1550    U0=R0*COS(-2.7):V0=R0*SIN(-2.7)
1560 '
1570 ' left side of road
1580    PSET (40, 157)
1590    FOR T= 1 TO 15 STEP .1
1600       X=(FNX(T)+U0+FNS(T))/T
1610       Y=(FNY(T)+V0+FNS(T))/T
1620       LINE -(X,Y)
1630    NEXT T
1640    LINE -(205,95)
1650 '
1660 ' right side of road
1670    PSET (90,185)
1680    FOR T= 1 TO 15 STEP .1
1690       X=(FNX(T)-U0+FNS(T))/T
1700       Y=(FNY(T)-V0+FNS(T))/T
1710       LINE -(X,Y)
1720    NEXT T
1730    LINE -(205,95)
1740 '
1750 ' paint the road
1760    PAINT (60,170)
1770 '
1780 ' center of road
1790    FOR T= 1 TO 10 STEP .3
1800       X=(FNX(T)+FNS(T))/T
1810       Y=(FNY(T)+FNS(T))/T
1820       PSET (X,Y),2
1830    NEXT T
1840 '
```

▶

**Example 5-13**

## Solution, continued.

```
1850 ' telephone posts
1860 '
1870    HTL=100
1880    WTL=5
1890    WBR=30
1900    HBR=85
1910 '
1920    FOR T= 1.2 TO 30 STEP 1
1930 '
1940       X=(FNX(T)+U0+FNS(T))/T
1950       Y=(FNY(T)+V0+FNS(T))/T
1960       X=2*INT(X/2)+1 ' make it odd
1970       PSET  (X,Y)
1980       LINE -STEP(0,-HTL/T),2
1990       LINE -STEP (1,0)
2000       LINE -STEP(0,+HTL/T),1
2010 '
2020       X=X-WBR/2/T : Y=Y-HBR/T
2030       X=2*INT(X/2)+1 ' make it odd
2040       PSET  (X,Y)
2050       FOR J=1 TO WBR/2/T+1
2060          LINE -STEP(0,+WTL/T),2
2070          PSET  STEP(1,0)
2080          LINE -STEP(0,-WTL/T),1
2090          PSET  STEP(1,0)
2100       NEXT J
2110 '
2120    NEXT T
2130 '
```

Figure 5-16
Background Scene

In this example, we set the background color to 3 (blue for sky) and the palette to 0 (green for the grass and yellow for the sun).

Notice that we use the Box Fill option of the LINE command to fill in large rectangular regions such as the border, sky, and grass. The program would (and does) run much slower with the PAINT commands.

After the border, sky, grass, frame, and horizon are drawn, the mountains are sketched in and colored yellow.

The sun is outlined in red and filled with yellow. Then yellow rays are drawn out in all directions. Double lines are used to get a better yellow on NTSC monitors.

Next elliptical clouds are drawn using the CIRCLE command and painted with the PAINT command. The clouds are colored yellow with red boundaries. Unfortunately, we do not have white available in this palette for the clouds.

A runway is drawn next using the LINE command and filled with the PAINT command. Since the center stripe is neither the boundary color nor the paint color, it must be drawn after the runway region is filled. We used yellow for the runway and red for the center stripes.

The airplane is a small complex figure with lots of turns and twists; thus, we used the IBM Graphics Definition Language (GDL) with the DRAW command. We painted it bright red.

The road is constructed so that it vanishes off into the horizon. The mathematics used to define it is essentially correct, but beyond the scope of this book. (More complete descriptions can be found in chapters on 3-D viewing transformations in advanced books on computer graphics.) It seems to work better than a few methods we tried first.

Finally the telephone poles are drawn. With NTSC color monitors, they appear black. Actually, this is a trick. We found that alternate vertical lines of red and green, with red on odd-numbered lines and green on even-numbered lines, produced black. This is because we managed to fool the NTSC color encoding scheme. On an RGB monitor you will see the stripes. Thus, for NTSC color we have a five-color picture with only four colors available. Notice that the telephone poles consist of two parts, the post and the cross bar. The cross bar requires a FOR loop to produce the alternating color pattern.

# CONCLUSION

In this chapter we have explored the hows and whys of the powerful PAINT command. We have shown how to use it in its simplest form in which a planted "seed" grows within the area bounded by the foreground color, and we have shown how to use it in its fanciest form in which we can specify a tiling pattern for the interior, any color for the boundary, and a background "primer." We have also shown how to make the computer run out of memory (in version 1 of BASICA) by presenting it with a region too complex for it to color, and then how to solve this problem by allotting more memory to a special area called a stack.

We have shown by way of a step-by-step example how the PAINT command works and have contrasted it with another coloring method available as an option under the LINE command. Upon reflection, we decided that we wanted both of these commands and in fact, we would like to have extensions of what the LINE command could do.

We presented three applications examples, two of which came from an earlier chapter. For these, we can now add color. The last example shows how to use all sorts of graphics commands, including the PAINT command, to draw a background scene. We even showed how to produce a fifth color in the four-color mode that we were working in.

The next chapter will give us even more capability in that we will be able to capture anything that we can create with the methods explained so far and place it as many times as we want in many different places on the screen.

# IMAGE ARRAY PLOTTING

# CONCEPTS

Concepts
   Image Array Plotting
   Storage Considerations
   PUT Actions

Commands
   GET
   PUT

Applications
   Icon-based Computerized Lesson

IT GOT OUT TWO DAYS AGO, AND I HAVEN'T BEEN ABLE TO DO ANY GRAPHICS SINCE!

## INTRODUCTION

This chapter shows you how to use BASICA's GET and PUT commands to produce special effects including color processing and animation. The use of logical operators is discussed in relation to the PUT command. We will show how array plotting commands produce pictures faster and more easily than many other methods. We will also show how these commands can be used to make a simple teaching program that uses special symbols called *icons*.

This chapter again starts with a series of "stand-alone" example programs that are housed in a larger program. The "front end" (lines 100-150) and the "back end" (lines 5000-5140) of this example program are the same as in Chapter 5 except that line 100 now should read

100 ' CHAPTER 6 LESSONS

## THE COMMANDS

Since the PUT and GET commands work so closely together, we will explain them together. In particular, our first example will use both these commands.

The GET command allows the user to store the contents of any rectangular region of the screen into an array, and the PUT command allows the user to place the contents of such an array back onto the screen.

First, let's look at syntax. The syntax of the GET command is

GET (x1,y1)—(x2,y2), array

where $(x1,y1)—(x2,y2)$ specifies the rectangular region on the screen that is being saved, and *array* is the name of the array in which the contents of this region are to be stored.

The coordinates $(x1,y1)—(x2,y2)$ specify a rectangle almost in the same way as they do in the block option of the LINE command. That is, $(x1,y1)$ and $(x2,y2)$ specify the coordinates of opposite corners of the rectangle. The coordinates can be either relative or absolute (STEP or no STEP). You should be aware however that both "corners" must be mentioned explicitly in the GET command, whereas the first "corner" is optional in the LINE command. Unlike other commands, the GET command has no options. This is because it really does only one job.

The last parameter of the GET command can be any type of array: integer, real, double-precision, or string. You must make sure, however, that enough storage has been allotted to the array before the GET statement is invoked. Allotting storage is done with the DIM statement. We will look at this shortly in connection with our first example.

Now let's look at the PUT command and its syntax. Its full syntax is

PUT (x,y), array [, action]

Here $(x1,y1)$ represents the coordinates (relative or absolute) of a spot on the screen where the upper-left corner of the image will be placed, and *array* is the array where the image was stored. The last parameter, *action*, is optional. It will allow us to perform all sorts of "magic," but for now we ignore it and start our examples with the simplified syntax

PUT (x,y), array

In our first example, we get a bug shape and put it all over the screen.

EXAMPLE 6-1

## BUGS

Get and put bugs on your screen. Use the simplest form of
these commands. The bugs are shown in Figure 6-1.

## Solution

```
160 ' BUGS '
170 '
180   T$="BUGS"
190   GOSUB 3080 ' title
200   COLOR 0,1
210 '
220 ' set up the storage arrays
230 '
240   DIM BUG0(54), BUG1(54)
250   DIM BUG2(54), BUG3(54)
260 '
270 ' define limits of the region
280 '
290   X1=160-15:Y1=101-13
300   X2=160+15:Y2=101+13
310 '
320   GOTO 590 ' go to main program
330 '
340 ' SUBROUTINE - DRAW BUG
350 '
360 '  initialize
370   LINE (X1,Y1)-(X2,Y2),0,BF
380   DRAW "c3bm160,101"
390 '
400 '  draw the head
410   DRAW "bu6re2u2h2l2g2d2f2r"
420 '
430 '  draw the body and legs
440   DRAW "rf2e2f2b14f2"
450   DRAW "d2f2nd2h2d6"
460   DRAW "g2f2nd2h2g2l"
470   DRAW "lh2g2nd2e2h2"
480   DRAW "u6g2nd2e2u2"
490   DRAW "e2h2g2br4e2r"
500 '
510 '  now paint the body and head
520 '
```

▶

# Example 6-1

## Solution, continued.

```
530     DRAW "bm160,101"
540     DRAW "p2,3 bu8 p1,3"
550  '
560  '
570     RETURN
580  '
590  ' draw the bug
600     GOSUB 340 ' draw bug
610  '
620  ' now get it
630     GET (X1,Y1)-(X2,Y2), BUG0
640  '
650  ' clear the bug
660     LINE (X1,Y1)-(X2,Y2),0,BF
670  '
680  ' now put it all over the screen
690  '
700     FOR X= 26 TO 260 STEP 26
710      FOR Y= 133 TO 25 STEP -26
720       PUT(X,Y), BUG0
730      NEXT Y
740     NEXT X
750  '
760  '
```

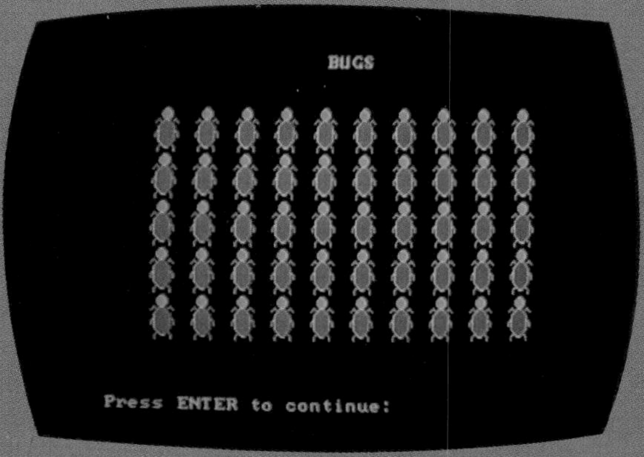

Figure 6-1
Bugs on the Screen

This example is longer than the lesson examples of previous chapters, but its length illustrates one of our main points—how the GET and PUT commands are used to access images that have been produced by other methods. Twenty-five of 60 lines in the listing are devoted to the subroutine (lines 340-570) that draws only one copy of the bug. Drawing the bug has been put in a subroutine because we will need other bugs drawn later. We will call upon this subroutine when that happens.

Now let's look at the rest of this listing. Before the subroutine, some important preliminary steps are taken care of, such as lines 220-250 where space in memory is allotted to the arrays in which we will be storing our bugs. We use the familiar DIM statement to dimension the bug arrays.

After the DIM statements but before the subroutine that draws the bug, we define variables X1, X2, Y1, and Y2. They define the limits of the rectangle around the bug. Notice that we use expressions like $160-13$ instead of equivalent constants such as 147 to define these quantities. This makes the program easier to read because it clearly shows that the rectangle is centered at (160,101) and it clearly shows that the rectangle extends 13 units out from the center in each horizontal and vertical direction. The values X1, X2, Y1, and Y2 are used in the GET statement and also in the LINE with Block Fill to erase the bug from the center of the screen. Notice the direct correspondence between these variable names and the names used to describe the syntax of these commands.

The main program continues after the subroutine. First the subroutine is called to draw a single copy of the bug on the screen, then the bug is "captured" with the GET command (line 630), and finally a whole field of bugs is output to the screen with the PUT command (lines 700-740). Notice how few statements are needed to put so many bugs on the screen. It is also interesting to compare the time needed to draw the original bug with the time needed to transfer it to the screen with the PUT statement. Putting the bug with the PUT command works more than eight times faster than drawing and painting the bug with the DRAW command.

**Determining Array Size**

You might wonder how large an array is needed to store an image. You can find out with a binary search; that is, you dimension the array to be very large and get the program working. This is your upper estimate of the amount of storage you will need. Your lower estimate is zero. Then you average your upper and lower estimates. If the program runs with this average estimate in the DIM statement, then this is your new upper estimate. If not, then it is your new lower estimate. Now get the average and repeat the process a few more times. The method "converges" quite quickly; that is, soon the upper and lower estimates will be equal. If you want a more scientific method, the formula is

$$\# \ bytes = 4 + INT((x*bitsperpixel + 7)/8)*y$$

where $x$ is the length (in pixels) of the horizontal side of the rectangle, $y$ is the length (in pixels) of its vertical side, and *bitsperpixel* is 2 for medium-resolution mode and 1 for high-resolution mode. In this example, we can put our bug into a $31 \times 27$ rectangle and we are in the medium-resolution mode. Thus, the number of bytes is

$$\# \ bytes = 4 + INT((31*2 + 7)/8)*27 = 220$$

Each real number takes up 4 bytes of storage; hence we need 220/4, or 55 units of storage for an array of real numbers. To compute the actual number used in the DIM statement, we subtract 1 (BASIC starts the array address at 0) from 55, getting 54 for the number in the DIM statements (lines 230-240) of our example program.

Table 6-1 lists the amounts of storage taken up by the various data types when used with the GET command. You use these numbers to compute the dimension needed for the GET with other types of data.

If you are like us and don't believe the computation given above, then why don't you try this out on the first example in the following way: Try reducing the argument to DIM for BUG0 to 53 and then running the program. You should get

Table 6-1

Storage Used by Each Data Type

| Data Type | Number of Bytes |
|---|---|
| Integer | 2 |
| Real | 4 |
| Double-precision Real | 8 |
| Character | 3 |

the error message "Illegal function call in 630", telling you there is something wrong with the GET statement in line 630. The error message means that there is really something wrong with line 240, the DIM statement, namely that there is not enough room in the array to store the picture. If you now reset the dimension number to 54, the program will run fine. Later we will take a closer look at how pictures are stored in arrays and see why this formula is true.

## PUT — The Action Parameter

The full syntax of the PUT command is

PUT (x,y), array [, action]

In our next example, the optional *action* parameter in the PUT command plays an important role even though it is hidden as a default. The *action* parameter controls the combining of the image stored in the array with what is already on the screen; that is, how paint "sticks" to the screen. From what we have done so far, you might think that the contents of the array are transferred directly from the array to the screen, but the IBM PC is more complicated and more clever than that. The possible values for *action* are XOR, PSET, PRESET, AND, and OR; and if you don't specify one, XOR is used as the default.

To understand what is happening, recall that the picture you see on the screen is stored in a special area of memory called *screen memory* or *video RAM*. This screen memory is part of your Color/Graphics Adapter. The electronic circuitry on this board constantly scans through this memory to make the video signal that drives your color monitor. To change the picture, you change the contents of the bits in the screen memory. Of course, the computer software does this for you as it obeys your BASIC commands.

When the GET statement is executed, the contents of the screen bits are transferred into corresponding bit positions in the named array. When the PUT statement is executed, bits are taken from the array *and* from what is already in the screen memory, and *combined* according to the indicated *action*. The result is then placed back in screen memory (as shown in Figure 6-2). Many useful and interesting effects can be achieved, depending upon which *action* is chosen. We will now investigate such possibilities in a step-by-step manner.

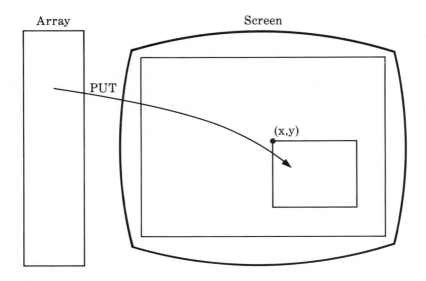

Array    Screen

PUT

(x,y)

**Figure 6-2**

Putting the Bits into Place

**XOR Action**

We start with the default mode for the PUT action and see how it works. In doing so, we will be introducing a little logic.

The logical *exclusive OR* bit operator is the default action of PUT. This operator is called XOR for short. The XOR truth table is given in Table 6-2; note that 0 means false and 1 means true. This table shows that x XOR y is true when x or y, but not both are true.

To see how the default form of PUT works and why the XOR action is such an appropriate default, we present our second example. It PUTs the bug figures on a multicolored background. We will see how the action of XOR on the bits in screen memory creates some interesting effects with color.

**Table 6-2**

Truth Table for XOR

| x | y | x XOR y |
|---|---|---------|
| 0 | 0 | 0 |
| 0 | 1 | 1 |
| 1 | 0 | 1 |
| 1 | 1 | 0 |

## EXAMPLE 6-2

## MULTICOLORED BUGS ON A MULTICOLORED SCREEN

Put some multicolored bugs on a multicolored screen.
The bugs are shown in Figure 6-3.

---

## Solution

```
770 ' BUGS ON BACKGROUNDS
780 '
790 ' use XOR default
800 '
810    T$="BUGS ON BACKGROUND"
820    GOSUB 2990 ' title & pause
830    COLOR 0,0
840 '
850 ' GET a new bug
860 '
870    DRAW "a3":GOSUB 340 'draw bug
880    GET (X1,Y1)-(X2,Y2), BUG3
890 '
900 ' draw the four-color background
910 '
920    LINE (  0, 25)-(141, 94),0,BF
930    LINE (141, 25)-(286, 94),1,BF
940    LINE (  0, 95)-(141,164),2,BF
950    LINE (141, 95)-(286,164),3,BF
960 '
970 ' now put the bug all over
980 ' the background
990 '
1000   FOR X= 26 TO 260 STEP 52
1010    FOR Y= 133 TO 25 STEP -26
1020     PUT(X,Y), BUG3
1030    NEXT Y
1040   NEXT X
1050 '
1060 '
```

**Example 6-2**

**Solution, continued.**

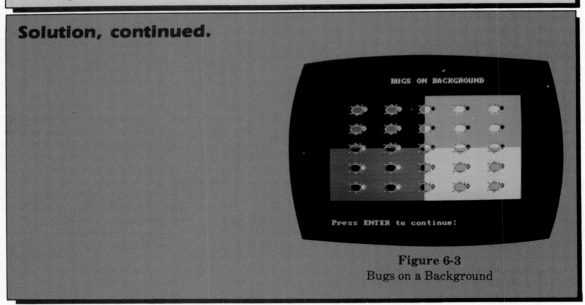

**Figure 6-3**
Bugs on a Background

The bug has four different colors (including the area immediately surrounding it), and the background has four different colors. Thus, this single example demonstrates all the possible color combinations from the array and from the screen.

This time we draw the bug facing to the right. The DRAW "a3" command that appears just before the bug-drawing routine sets the drawing angle to 270 degrees.

Next the background is drawn using a sequence of four Box Fill LINE commands, each with a different color. The palette is 0 and the background color is black, so the colors are black, green, red, and yellow, as we have seen before.

In this case, we have divided the screen into four sections with black in the upper-left portion, green in the upper-right portion, red in the lower-left portion, and yellow in the lower right portion (as pictured in Figure 6-4). Finally, at the end of the listing, the bugs are drawn in a double FOR loop. Note that the bugs in the upper left (against the black background) appear to have green heads (color 1), red bodies (color 2), and yellow legs (color 3). The area immediately surrounding the bug is black (color 0) (as pictured in Figure 6-4).

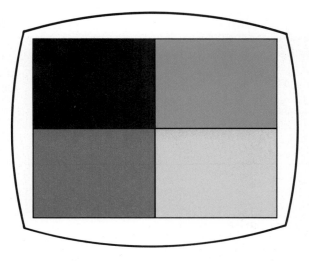 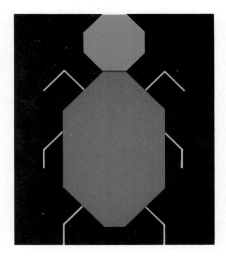

**Figure 6-4**

Screen Colors

These are the true colors for the bug in this color state (background 0 and palette 0). You can see that various parts of the bug take on different colors when put against other background colors. For example, in the lower-right portion (against a yellow background), the bugs have red heads (color 2), green bodies (color 1), and black legs (color 0). It appears that the colors have been switched in some way. This is exactly what the XOR action does, as we shall soon see.

To understand this better, we need to look at a few more ideas. Examine the truth table for the XOR bit operator (see Table 6-2). This really is a "truth" table if you think of 0 representing false and 1 representing true. Then the XOR operation can be interpreted as true just when either of the two, but not both, operands are true.

Another way to look at this is to hold y fixed and see how the result depends upon x (see Table 6-3). We see that if y is 0, the result is the some as x, but if y is 1, the result is just the opposite of x. This is the switching effect that we mentioned earlier.

Like the other logical operators, the XOR operator works in a bit-by-bit manner. This means that to specify what the operation does, we only have to say what it does to an individual bit. The effect on the whole picture is then obtained by applying the rule to every bit in an entire region of the screen.

**Table 6-3**

Another View of the XOR Function

| y=0 | | | y=1 | |
|---|---|---|---|---|
| x | x XOR y | | x | x XOR y |
| 0 | 0 | | 0 | 1 |
| 1 | 1 | | 1 | 0 |

**Table 6-4**

Representation of Colors in Binary

| Binary | Decimal | Color in Palette 0 | Color in Palette 1 |
|---|---|---|---|
| 00 | 0 | Background | Background |
| 01 | 1 | Green | Cyan |
| 10 | 2 | Red | Magenta |
| 11 | 3 | Brown | White |

Recall that in the high-resolution mode, each bit of screen memory corresponds to a single dot on the screen. If the bit is 0, the dot will appear black; and if the bit is 1, the dot will appear light (white on a standard TV and green on a green phosphor screen). However, in the colorful medium-resolution mode, the bits in screen memory are grouped in pairs to encode the color of the dots on the screen. The binary number system is used. This system is shown in Table 6-4.

To compute the action on the colors, we need to break down all the coloring information to the bit level, apply the XOR to each bit position, and take the result and interpret it again as coloring information. Table 6-5 shows in tabular form the results of XOR on the color numbers for the medium-resolution mode.

For example, suppose that x is 2 and y is 3. In the binary system, x is 10 and y is 11. Using the original truth table for the XOR operation, we combine the first bit from x with the first bit from y and the second bit from x with the second bit from y. We get the binary number 01. Thus, the result is the decimal number 1, as in Table 6-5.

**Table 6-5**

Effect of XOR on the Color Numbers

| | | y | | | |
|---|---|---|---|---|---|
| | | 0 | 1 | 2 | 3 |
| | 0 | 0 | 1 | 2 | 3 |
| x | 1 | 1 | 0 | 3 | 2 |
| | 2 | 2 | 3 | 0 | 1 |
| | 3 | 3 | 2 | 1 | 0 |

**Table 6-6**

Bug Colors on Each Screen Color
in Palette 0

| As stored in array | | | As placed on screen | |
|---|---|---|---|---|
| | | Screen Color = 0 (Black) | | |
| Black | 0 | 0 | Black | (Surrounding) |
| Green | 1 | 1 | Green | (Head) |
| Red | 2 | 2 | Red | (Body) |
| Yellow | 3 | 3 | Yellow | (Legs) |
| | | Screen Color = 0 (Green) | | |
| Black | 0 | 1 | Green | (Surrounding) |
| Green | 1 | 0 | Black | (Head) |
| Red | 2 | 3 | Yellow | (Body) |
| Yellow | 3 | 2 | Red | (Legs) |
| | | Screen Color = 2 (Red) | | |
| Black | 0 | 2 | Red | (Surrounding) |
| Green | 1 | 3 | Yellow | (Head) |
| Red | 2 | 0 | Black | (Body) |
| Yellow | 3 | 1 | Green | (Legs) |
| | | Screen Color = 3 (Yellow) | | |
| Black | 0 | 3 | Yellow | (Surrounding) |
| Green | 1 | 2 | Red | (Head) |
| Red | 2 | 1 | Green | (Body) |
| Yellow | 3 | 0 | Black | (Legs) |

Now let's look at the bugs again, organizing this table in a different way. Let x be the screen color that is stored in screen memory before the operation and y the bug color as stored in the array. Then we form four tables, one for each screen color in palette 0 (see Table 6-6).

We see from Table 6-6 that if the screen has color 0, the resulting image will have the same colors as originally stored in the bug array. This confirms our observations about the bugs in the upper-left (black) corner of our example.

We also see that if the screen color is 3 (yellow), the colors of the resulting image will be in reversed order. This agrees with our observations about the bugs in the lower-right (yellow) corner of our example.

The colors for the bugs in the other corners can also be seen in this table.

Now take a look at the bugs that cross over two different background colors—in particular, a bug in the center of the screen that has four different colors over the main part of its body because its body overlaps all four different background colors. We can again use the color table. The original body color is 2 (red), so we use the third column (under number 2) of the color table. You can see that the following colors hold:

0 XOR 2 = 2 (red) in upper-left corner

1 XOR 2 = 3 (yellow) in upper-right corner

2 XOR 2 = 0 (black) in lower-left corner

3 XOR 2 = 1 (green) in lower-right corner

Notice that none of the bugs blends into the background regardless of what color there is originally. This is a very handy property that we will use in our application program. The reason the background colors do not blend is given in the following general rules about the XOR action:

1. Putting the background color onto the screen with the PUT XOR action will not change the current screen color.
2. Two different color numbers in the original image will remain different color numbers when put onto the screen with the XOR action.

These rules can be verified by looking at the color number table for the XOR operation.

A word of warning is in order for rule 2: If the background color is the same as one of the nonbackground colors, distinct color numbers may not appear as distinct colors on the screen. For example, if the background color is 7 (white) and the palette is 1 (set by the statement COLOR 7, 1), both the background color and the foreground color will appear the same color (white) even though they have different color numbers. If you execute a different COLOR statement such as COLOR 0, 1, these colors will again appear distinct.

These rules make sense if the background color is constant over the region where the image is to appear, as we will see by looking at the opposite extreme; that is, when a copy of the image is already on the screen exactly where you are going to put that very image. A remarkable thing occurs: *the image disappears.* That is, putting the image twice with the XOR action returns the screen to what it was originally. This has immediate applications to animation.

In the next example, we run a bug around and around the screen using the nondestructive background erasing feature of the (default action) XOR operator. Later we will see how to change the action operator.

EXAMPLE 6-3

## ANIMATED BUG

Use the PUT command with its default XOR action to
animate a bug so that it races around a black screen. If
a key is pressed, stop the bug at the end of a complete
circuit. A picture of the bug running is given in
Figure 6-5.

## Solution

```
1070 ' ANIMATED BUG
1080 '
1090 ' use XOR default
1100 '
1110    T$="ANIMATED BUG"
1120    GOSUB 2990 ' title & pause
1130    COLOR 0,0
1140 '
1150    GOTO 1530 ' main program
1160 '
1170 ' SUBROUTINE  - MOVE BUG
1180 '
1190    LOCATE 25,1
1200    PRINT "Press any key to stop."
1210 '
1220    WHILE LEN(INKEY$)=0
1230 '
1240    X=260
1250    FOR Y = 110 TO 50 STEP -10
1260      PUT (X,Y), BUG0
1270      PUT (X,Y), BUG0
1280    NEXT Y
1290 '
1300    Y=30
1310    FOR X = 240 TO 60 STEP -10
1320      PUT (X,Y), BUG1
1330      PUT (X,Y), BUG1
1340    NEXT X
1350 '
1360    X=40
1370    FOR Y = 50 TO 110 STEP 10
1380      PUT (X,Y), BUG2
1390      PUT (X,Y), BUG2
1400    NEXT Y
```

▶

# Example 6-3

## Solution, continued.

```
1410 '                                    1630 ' clear the bug
1420   FOR X = 60 TO 240 STEP 10          1640   LINE (X1,Y1)-(X2,Y2),0,BF
1430    Y=130                             1650 '
1440    PUT (X,Y), BUG3                   1660 ' now run them around
1450    PUT (X,Y), BUG3                   1670 '
1460   NEXT X                             1680   GOSUB 1170 ' move bug
1470 '                                    1690 '
1480   WEND                               1700 '
1490   LOCATE 10,15
1500   PRINT "Goodbye, bug"
1510   RETURN
1520 '
1530 ' main program
1540 '
1550 ' get some more bugs
1560 '
1570   DRAW "a1":GOSUB 340 ' draw bug
1580   GET (X1,Y1)-(X2,Y2), BUG1
1590 '
1600   DRAW "a2":GOSUB 340 ' draw bug
1610   GET (X1,Y1)-(X2,Y2), BUG2
1620 '
```

Figure 6-5
Bug Racing Around the Screen

The first part of this example consists of a subroutine to move the bug. It consists of four FOR loops encased in a WHILE loop. Each FOR loop moves the bug along one side of the screen, and the WHILE loop keeps it moving while no keys are pressed. In more detail, the first FOR loop (lines 1250-1280) runs the bug up the right side of the screen. Notice that the x-position is held fixed at 260, and the y-position is controlled by the limits of the FOR loop, which range from 110 to 50 in steps of 10. Recall that these x- and y-positions are the coordinates of the upper-left corner of the rectangular region that holds the bug. Notice that the inside of the FOR loop consists of two identical PUT statements, one to place the bug and one to erase the bug.

Normally, you would put some kind of delay procedure between the placing of the image and the erasing of the image, and in fact, have a very short distance between the old erase and the next place. Trial and error have convinced us that the method presented gives the best results for this computer running this example. The loop structure seems to keep the place, then erase, then place, then erase rapidly and evenly enough to fool the viewer into thinking the bug is moving. The speed of the PUT command is not actually fast enough to give flicker-free motion, but the effect is reasonably good. You can use this information to figure out a way to slow down the bug.

Each FOR loop uses a different copy of the bug. This is so that the bug always faces the direction in which it is moving. Thus, four different bug images are needed. They are stored in the arrays BUG0, BUG1, BUG2, and BUG3. Since the WHILE loop, which encloses all the FOR loops, continues as long as no key on the keyboard has been pressed, the bug must finish a full circuit around the screen before coming to a stop when you do press a key.

After the subroutine we have the main program. Here we get two more bug images (unused until now); we clear the bug away from the center of the screen; and then we call the subroutine to move the bug around the screen.

You might think from the last example that animation only works on a black background, but this is not so. Our next example shows that we can run the bug around just as easily on a multicolored background.

EXAMPLE 6-4

## ANIMATED BUG ON MULTICOLORED BACKGROUND

Use the PUT command with its default XOR action to animate a bug on a multicolored background. The bug is shown in Figure 6-6.

---

## Solution

```
1710 ' ANIMATION ON BACKGROUND
1720 '
1730   T$="ANIMATION ON BACKGROUND"
1740   GOSUB 2990 ' title & pause
1750   COLOR 0,0
1760 '
1770 ' Now run them on a background
1780 '
1790   LINE (  0, 25)-(141, 94),0,BF
1800   LINE (141, 25)-(286, 94),1,BF
1810   LINE (  0, 95)-(141,164),2,BF
1820   LINE (141, 95)-(286,164),3,BF
1830 '
1840   GOSUB 1170 ' move the bug
1850 '
1860 '
```

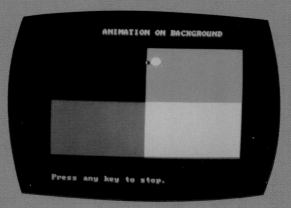

Figure 6-6
Bug Racing Around the Multicolored Screen

It is really amazing that this example works in that we don't lose the bug. This depends upon the formula

$$( x \text{ XOR } ( x \text{ XOR } y )) = y$$

no matter what $x$ or $y$ is. This formula means that if you start with a screen color y, put an object of color x onto it with the PUT XOR action (getting color x XOR y), and then put the same object of color x onto it again (getting the full left-hand side of the formula), you will actually have the color y back on the screen again.

Proving this formula is beyond the scope of this book, but it can easily be done with the truth tables.

As the listing in Example 6-4 shows, it is easy to make the XOR action work with all the routines that we have already developed. We just need to draw the background (again using four Box Fill LINE commands) and call the routine to move the bug.

You will notice that as the bug goes around and around the screen, it changes color so that you can always see it, but it never permanently changes what was already on the screen.

Our next example shows exactly what is stored in an array when a GET statement is executed. We will print a character in the upper-left corner of the screen, use the GET command to put it into an array, and print the contents of this array on the screen.

EXAMPLE 6-5

## PEEK AT LETTERS

With BASICA print an "A" in the upper-left corner of the
screen, capture it in an array using the GET statement,
and display the contents of this array on the screen.
Display the first two entries (the size of the rectangular
region) in decimal and the rest in binary. The output is
shown in Figure 6-7.

## Solution

```
1870 ' PEEK AT LETTERS
1880 '
1890    T$="PEEK AT LETTERS"
1900    GOSUB 2990 ' pause and title
1910    SCREEN 1
1920    COLOR 0,1
1930 '
1940    DIM A%(9)
1950 '
1960    LOCATE 1,1
1970    PRINT "A"
1980    GET (0,0)-(7,7), A%
1990 '
2000    LOCATE 5,1
2010    PRINT "The contents of A%:"
2020    PRINT
2030    PRINT A%(0), A%(1)
2040    PRINT
2050 '
2060    FOR K = 2 TO 9
2070     X = A%(K)
2080     FOR D = 0 TO 15
2090      LOCATE ,16-D
2100      PRINT USING "#"; X AND 1;
2110      X=INT(X/2)
2120     NEXT D
2130     PRINT
2140    NEXT K
2150 '
2160 '
```

**Example 6-5**

**Solution, continued.**

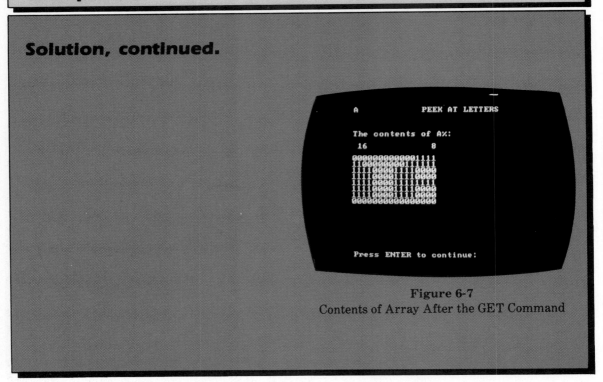

Figure 6-7
Contents of Array After the GET Command

Notice that the letter has its left and right halves reversed. This happens because the bytes that make up the integers in which we store the pattern are switched when they are used to store the image. This is peculiar to the way the 8088 microprocessor handles memory.

The first number in the array gives the number of bits needed horizontally (for each row). Since we are in medium-resolution mode, two bits are needed for each dot horizontally. In the GET statement, the x-coordinates run from 0 to 7. This means that the rectangle has 8 columns of dots. Multiplying this by the number of bits per dot (2) gives us 16, which is the correct value for the first entry of A%.

The second number in the array gives the number of rows of dots in the rectangle. The GET statement has y-coordinates running from 16 to 23 or 8 dots vertically. This agrees with the second number displayed on the screen.

The next numbers are displayed in binary because they correspond to the actual bits taken from the screen by the GET command. If you look closely at the pattern of 0s and 1s for these eight numbers, you will see the left side of the "A" on the right and the right side of the "A" on the left. The reason for this switch has to do with the way the numbers are stored in the machine and how the central processor accesses data. That is, the lower 8 bits of the number were stored first, and the upper 8 bits of the number second.

For this example, you should understand that the third entry of A% (a 16-bit number) holds the first row of the rectangle, the fourth entry of A% (also a 16-bit number) holds the second row, and so on.

Notice that the array A% has integer entries. As we mentioned previously, any data type will work for the PUT and GET commands. We have chosen integer entries because they are the easiest to manipulate with ordinary arithmetic and logical operations. In particular, the first two entries (the sizing information) are actually stored as integers. If you use real arrays, the bits will still be stored in binary, but the resulting arrays will be harder to decipher. String arrays can also be used. Again, the bits are stored in binary. However, it is fairly easy to decipher the results.

In the program, we use a well-known method of creating the expansion into binary representation; that is, repeated divisions by 2. In this method each time we divide by 2, the remainder yields a new binary digit of the binary representation. Notice that the digits of the binary expansion are computed from right to left. The LOCATE command allows us to put them directly on the screen in this reverse order. As the program runs, you can see the digits shuffle into place.

Perhaps you would like to use the PEEK command to see what bugs look like when they are stored in a matrix. We wrote a program that uses the GET command to put a bug into an integer matrix A% and then print out the bits of A% as 0s and 1s. Figure 6-8 shows the contents of A%.

Our program had to unscramble the bits of A% to produce the picture in Figure 6-8. The first two entries of A% helped us by showing us the width and height in bits of the rectangular area of the screen stored in A%.

Notice that there are 62 bits horizontally. We found that this is rounded up to an even multiple of 8 to make 64 bits or 8 bytes per row. The bytes are then packed two at a time, low byte then high byte, into the 16-bit integer entries of A%.

```
0000000000000000000000000000000000000000000000000000000000000000
0000000000000000000000000000000000000000000000000000000000000000
0000000000000000000000000011111000000000000000000000000000000000
0000000000000000000000001101010111000000000000000000000000000000
0000000000000000000000011010101010111000000000000000000000000000
0000000000000000000000011010101010111000000000000000000000000000
0000000000000000000000011010101010111000000000000000000000000000
0000000000000000000000011010101110000000000000000000000000000000
0000000000000000000110000011111000000110000000000000000000000000
0000000000000000011001100111010101100110011000000000000000000000
0000000000000011000000111010101010110000001100000000000000000000
0000000000000000000001110101010101010110000000000000000000000000
0000000000000000000011101010101010101011000000000000000000000000
0000000000000000000011101010101010101011000000000000000000000000
0000000000000000000011101010101010101011000000000000000000000000
0000000000000000001111101010101010101011100000000000000000000000
0000000000000000110011101010101010101011001100000000000000000000
0000000000000000110011101010101010101011001100000000000000000000
0000000000000000110011101010101010101011001100000000000000000000
0000000000000000000111010101010101010110000000000000000000000000
0000000000000000000111010101010101010110000000000000000000000000
0000000000000000000011101010101010110000000000000000000000000000
0000000000000000000001110101010110000000000000000000000000000000
0000000000000000000011001110101011001100000000000000000000000000
0000000000000000000110000011111000000110000000000000000000000000
0000000000000000000110000000000000000011000000000000000000000000
0000000000000000000110000000000000000011000000000000000000000000
```

**Figure 6-8**

The Bits of a Bug

Thus, each row of the picture is stored in four successive entries of A%. For example, the first row is stored in

A%(2), A%(3), A%(4), A%(5)

and the second row in

A%(6), A%(7), A%(8), A%(9)

and so on. Because of the low-high order, we told our program to print out the bits of each A%(I) in the order

bit 7, bit 6, bit 5, bit 4, bit 3, bit 2, bit 1, bit 0,
bit 15, bit 14, bit 13, bit 12, bit 11, bit 10, bit 9, bit 8

This flipped the bytes back into place in the program's output.

In the resulting picture, every two bits represents a pixel. Grouping the digits in pairs, you can see that pixels outside the bug correspond to 00s, all the pixels around the boundary of the bug correspond to 11s, pixels inside the head correspond to 01s, and pixels inside the body correspond to 10s. Thus, you can see precisely how the colors for the bug are stored as bits in the video RAM.

## PSET and PRESET Actions

With the PSET and PRESET action parameters, the new image overwrites whatever was previously on the screen instead of combining with it. The PSET action produces a direct image of what you are putting and the PRESET action produces a reverse image, much like a photographic negative.

The truth table for PSET is given in Table 6-7, and the truth table for PRESET is given in Table 6-8. Notice that neither of these actions pays any attention to what was on the screen.

In the next example, we apply what we learned in the previous example to magnify text. We show how to expand letters on the screen vertically by a factor of three. This technique can easily be generalized to expand lettering or pictures by any scale factor.

The idea is to print each letter in a normal size at a corner of the screen using the normal PRINT statement, and then get the letter into an array. The information in this array is then copied into another array, but during the copying process we repeat the bytes. The resulting array is then put back on the screen, producing a magnified version of the original letter.

**Table 6-7**

Truth Table for PSET

| x | y | x PSET y |
|---|---|----------|
| 0 | 0 | 0 |
| 0 | 1 | 0 |
| 1 | 0 | 1 |
| 1 | 1 | 1 |

**Table 6-8**

Truth Table for PRESET

| x | y | x PRESET y |
|---|---|------------|
| 0 | 0 | 1 |
| 0 | 1 | 1 |
| 1 | 0 | 0 |
| 1 | 1 | 0 |

EXAMPLE 6-6

## TALL LETTERS

Display some letters on the screen with the vertical scale
magnified by a factor of three. Show the result on the
screen against a background of text of ordinary height. Use
the PSET and PRESET actions for the PUT command to
help display the enlarged lettering in direct and reversed
mode. The resulting screen is shown in Figure 6-9.

## Solution

```
2170 ' TALL LETTERS
2180 '
2190   T$="TALL LETTERS"
2200   GOSUB 2990 ' pause and title
2210   SCREEN 1
2220   COLOR 0,1
2230 '
2240   LOCATE 6,1
2250    FOR I = 6 TO 20
2260      PRINT SPACE$(6);
2270      FOR J = 1 TO 2
2280        PRINT "small letters ";
2290      NEXT J
2300      PRINT
2310    NEXT I
2320 '
2330   DIM LO%(10), L1%(26)
2340 '
2350   M$=" Tall Letters "
2360 '
2370   X1=160-4*LEN(M$)-12
2380   L1%(0)=16 : L1%(1)=24
2390 '
2400   FOR I = 1 TO LEN(M$)
2410 '
2420     LOCATE 1,1 :PRINT MID$(M$,I,1)
2430     GET (0,0)-(7,7), LO%
2440 '
2450 '   stretch the letter
2460     FOR K = 0 TO 7
2470       L1%(3*K+2)=LO%(K+2)
2480       L1%(3*K+3)=LO%(K+2)
```

▶

## Example 6-6

### Solution, continued.

```
2490      L1%(3*K+4)=L0%(K+2)
2500    NEXT K
2510 '
2520 '   put it into place
2530    PUT (X1+8*I,76),  L1%, PSET
2540    PUT (X1+8*I,100), L1%, PRESET
2550 '
2560    NEXT I
2570 '
2580 '
```

Figure 6-9
Tall Lettering

In this example, the ordinary background lettering is printed first. The message "small letters" was chosen for obvious reasons. A double FOR loop is used to create this background display with its horizontal and vertical repetitions of the message.

Next we set up two arrays L0% and L1%. The first one is dimensioned with nine elements to hold one image of a normal-sized letter, and the second is dimensioned with 25 elements to hold the expanded image of a single letter. Next the message "Tall Letters" is placed in the string variable M$. Then X1 is defined to give the base for the horizontal positions of the letters. It will be used in the PUT commands. Next we set the horizontal and vertical sizing information. The horizontal size is 16 bits, just as before, but the vertical size is three times larger than it was (24 bits). Next we have a FOR loop that goes through the letters of the message. For each letter of the message, we print the letter by itself in the upper-left corner, we GET it, and then go into a smaller FOR loop that causes each row of the original array to be copied three times into the second array. This multiple copying is really all there is to magnifying lettering or any kind of picture. Finally, we PUT the expanded letter in two different places on the screen, once using the PSET action option, and a second time right below using the PRESET action option. The PSET produces a direct image and the PRESET produces a reverse image like a photographic negative. In both cases, the new image overwrites the old small lettering.

**AND and OR Actions**

There are two more possible actions for the PUT statement: AND and OR. Like the XOR, these operators work direcly on the bits. The truth tables are given in Tables 6-9 and 6-10.

**Table 6-9**

Truth Table for AND

| x | y | x AND y |
|---|---|---------|
| 0 | 0 | 0 |
| 0 | 1 | 0 |
| 1 | 0 | 0 |
| 1 | 1 | 1 |

**Table 6-10**

Truth Table for OR

| x | y | x OR y |
|---|---|--------|
| 0 | 0 | 0 |
| 0 | 1 | 1 |
| 1 | 0 | 1 |
| 1 | 1 | 1 |

From these tables, the color number "truth" tables for the medium-resolution mode can be computed. They are shown in Tables 6-11 and 6-12.

You can see that there is a lot of "color collapse." That is, for a given background, several colors in the image will become the same color when put on the screen. For example, if the background is 2 and the image is being put onto the screen with the AND option, both color 0 and color 1 will collapse to color 0.

In our next example, we will use the AND and OR options to "filter" the image we created in the last example, producing some different colors out of the white lettering.

**Table 6-11**

Effect of AND on the Color Numbers

|   |   | y | | | |
|---|---|---|---|---|---|
|   |   | 0 | 1 | 2 | 3 |
|   | 0 | 0 | 0 | 0 | 0 |
| x | 1 | 0 | 1 | 0 | 1 |
|   | 2 | 0 | 0 | 2 | 2 |
|   | 3 | 0 | 1 | 2 | 3 |

**Table 6-12**

Effect of OR on the Color Numbers

|   |   | y | | | |
|---|---|---|---|---|---|
|   |   | 0 | 1 | 2 | 3 |
|   | 0 | 0 | 1 | 2 | 3 |
|   | 1 | 1 | 1 | 3 | 3 |
| x | 2 | 2 | 3 | 2 | 3 |
|   | 3 | 3 | 3 | 3 | 3 |

EXAMPLE 6-7

## COLOR FILTER

Run the Tall Lettering example through a "color filter"
using the AND and OR actions of the PUT command.
Using a thin horizontal line, filter the image first with a
red NTSC filter, then restore the image, and filter with
a blue RGB filter. The output is shown in Figure 6-10.

## Solution

```
2590 ' COLOR FILTER
2600 '
2610    T$="COLOR FILTER"
2620    GOSUB 3080 ' title
2630 '
2640    DIM FILTER%(81)
2650 '
2660    FILTER%(0)=640
2670    FILTER%(1)=1
2680 '
2690 ' load the filter pattern
2700    FOR I= 0 TO 39
2710      FILTER%(I+2)=&HCCCC
2720    NEXT I
2730 '
2740 ' now filter the screen
2750    FOR J = 0 TO 199
2760      PUT (0,J), FILTER%, AND
2770    NEXT J
2780 '
2790 ' restore the missing elements
2800    FOR J = 199 TO 0 STEP -1
2810      GET (0,J)-(318,J), FILTER%
2820      PUT (1,J), FILTER%, OR
2830    NEXT J
2840 '
2850 ' set up another filter pattern
2860    FILTER%(0) = 640
2870    FILTER%(1) = 1
2880    FOR I= 0 TO 39
2890      FILTER%(I+2)=&H5555
2900    NEXT I
2910 '
2920 ' now filter the screen
```

▶

## Example 6-7

## Solution, continued.

```
2930    FOR J = 0 TO 199
2940       PUT (0,J), FILTER%, AND
2950    NEXT J
2960 '
```

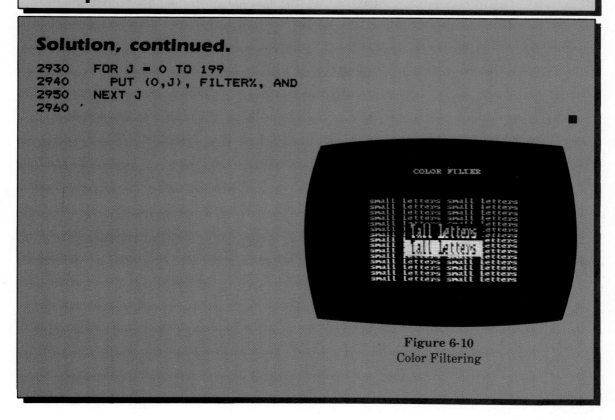

**Figure 6-10**
Color Filtering

The first step is to define the filter. It consists of an array that when put on the screen will correspond to a 320 horizontal by 1 vertical rectangle. This is a single line of dots on the screen. By placing a certain pattern along a single row, we create what is called a *mask* for our filtering. In general, a mask is something that allows you to "see" certain parts of an object, but not other parts of it. In computer programming, masks are often constructed out of bits with a 0 indicating what should be hidden and a 1 indicating what should be seen. In our example, the first filter we define has the following binary pattern for each of its integer entries:

1100110011001100

We will use it to mask the bits on the screen, 16 bits at a time. Starting from the left, this number indicates that we will show two bits, hide two bits, then show two bits, and so on.

IBM PC BASIC does not allow the direct input of numbers in binary. The best we can do is hexadecimal. In this representation, we group the binary digits in groups of fours and convert each group into a single hexadecimal digit.

Thus, sixteen bits of our filter is the quantity

$$1100110011001100 = 1100 \quad 1100 \quad 1100 \quad 1100$$
$$= C \qquad C \qquad C \qquad C$$
$$= CCCC \text{ (hexadecimal)}$$

In line 2710, we use the PUT command to compare this filter to each line on the screen 16 bits at a time with a FOR loop indexed by the screen lines 0 through 199. The AND action is specified in the PUT statement. This means that each line of the screen will be combined with the AND action against the filter pattern (bit-by-bit) and placed back on the screen. The 0s in the filter will cause zero results for those bit positions and the 1s in the filter will cause the original bits to stay intact on the screen. The effect of this particular filter is to clear (make equal to zero) every other dot on the screen. The visual effect is quite colorful on an NTSC monitor. When the program runs we see a horizontal line lowering down the screen. On an NTSC monitor, the letters are orange above the line, and they are still white below the line.

The next step is to put the white color back by copying bits back to the places they were cleared from. To do this we copy bits from the dot just to the left. We use a FOR loop that scans through all the rows starting from the bottom toward the top (just for the sake of variety). In this loop, we first get the row into our one line filter FILTER%, and then we put it back, shifted over by one dot position. We use the OR action in the PUT statement. The fact that this works depends upon the following property of the OR operator. If a color number is being combined according to the OR action with a zero, the result will be the same as the original color number. This allows us to "add" the colors into place. We will see a line going from the bottom of the screen upward that restores the white color. Notice that the text is restored to almost the same condition that it was originally, but not quite. When text is printed by the IBM PC in graphics mode, dots are usually, but not always, doubled horizontally on the screen to give the best white color. Our method depends upon the doubling. Those dots that are not doubled will either be removed or will be doubled after our filtration exercise.

The last thing we do is to set up the filter again and filter out every other bit of the program. The integer that now makes our filter is

$$0101010101010101 = 0101 \quad 0101 \quad 0101 \quad 0101$$
$$= 5 \quad\quad 5 \quad\quad 5 \quad\quad 5$$
$$= 5555 \text{ (hexadecimal)}$$

This time we see a line going down the screen painting the text blue as it goes. The result is blue on both NTSC and RGB monitors.

Now let's see how the mechanics of the GET and PUT commands can be used in a computerized lesson.

# APPLICATIONS PROGRAMMING

In this section we show how to use the GET and PUT commands to create a computerized lesson. With the GET and PUT commands we can place carefully designed, symbolic, graphic images called *icons* anywhere on the screen on top of a background drawn earlier in the program. By using the default XOR action for the PUT command, we write these images over a complicated background without fear of destroying any part of that background. To remove any icon, we simply use the PUT command a second time in the same spot and all traces of it disappear. The background is then correctly reinstated.

In our example, we draw a picture of a small computer system, including a tray to store several floppy disks, a pair of floppy disk drives, a CRT screen, and a keyboard. These objects form the background of the scene. In the foreground, we use drawings of various forms of a human hand. We will call these drawings *icons* because, like statues, they are meant to suggest a real object without appearing or moving in a completely realistic manner. In such a computerized lesson we can use these symbols to indicate that certain actions are being performed. For example, selecting a floppy disk from the disk tray is represented by a drawing of a hand pointing toward the disks in the tray.

The user can use the cursor keys to move the icons around

the screen. As an icon is moved from one place to another, it may change form. If we move the icon from the disk tray area to the disk drive area, it will change from a pointing hand into a hand grasping a floppy disk, ready to insert the disk into one of the drives.

What we have provided in this example merely represents a skeleton for a larger (and longer) program that would take a user step-by-step through a complicated procedure like creating a new disk and backing up a set of files.

EXAMPLE 6-8

## ICONS

Write a program that illustrates how to use a floppy disk
operating system. Show the floppy disks stored in trays, the
floppy disk drives, and the keyboard. Allow the user to
move hands on the screen to select disks from the disk
trays and move selected disks to the drives where they may
be inserted into the drives. Show the hands moving onto
the keyboard to type commands. An example of the screen
is shown in Figure 6-11.

## Solution

```
100 ' DOS DEMO
110 '
120    SCREEN 1
130    CLS:KEY OFF
140 '
150    DIM HP%(800), HG%(800), HK%(800)
160 '
170 ' define hand icons
180 '
190 ' open hand
200    HO1$ ="e8u8f4d12r28d4l20"
210    HO2$ ="r24d4l24r20d4l20r16d4l36"
220    HO$ = HO1$ + HO2$
230 '
240 ' hand pointing
250    HP1$ = HO1$
260    HP2$ = "r8d4l8r8d4l8r8d4l28"
270    HP$  = HP1$+HP2$
280    CLS
290    DRAW HP$
300 ' LINE (160,80)-STEP(40,40),,B
310    GET (160,80)-STEP(40,40),HP%
320 '
330 ' hand grasping floppy disk
340    HG1$ = "u4h2u8e2u16f4d12r16"
350    HG2$ = "d10g2d4u4e2u10"
360    HG3$ = "r5u30l30d30r5"
370    HG4$ = "bu13br8r2eu2h12gd2f"
380    HG5$ = "bu6u8r2d8l2"
390    HG$  = HG1$+HG2$+HG3$+HG4$+HG5$
```

▶

## Example 6-8

### Solution, continued.

```
400     CLS
410     DRAW HG$
420   ' LINE (150,50)-STEP(40,50),,B
430     GET (150,50)-STEP(40,50),HG%
440   '
450   ' hands for keyboards
460   ' left hand:
470     HKL1$ = "u36r4d16u20r4d20u24r4"
480     HKL2$ = "d24u20r4d26"
490     HKL3$ = "r4e6r4d2g12d4g2"
500     HKL$ = HKL1$+HKL2$+HKL3$
510   ' right hand:
520     HKR1$ = "u36l4d16u20l4d20u24l4"
530     HKR2$ = "d24u20l4d26"
540     HKR3$ = "l4h6l4d2f12d4f2"
550     HKR$ = HKR1$+HKR2$+HKR3$
560     CLS
570     DRAW "bm125,100"+HKL$
580     DRAW "bm195,100"+HKR$
590   ' LINE (125,55)-STEP(70,45),,B
600     GET (125,55)-STEP(70,45),HK%
610     CLS
620   '
630   ' LINE (0,0)-(319,199),,B
640   ' define disk trays
650   '
660     LINE (50,150)-(90,54),,B
670   '
680     FOR I = 1 TO 6
690        Y = 150 - 16*I
700        LINE(50,Y)-(90,Y)
710        LOCATE Y/8+1, 8
720        PRINT "#";
730        PRINT USING "#"; I
740     NEXT I
750   '
760   '
770   ' define disk drives
780   '
790     LINE (120,130)-(170,90),,B
800     LINE (120,110)-(170,110)
810   '
820     LINE (130,118)-(160,122),,B
830     LINE (130, 98)-(160,102),,B
840   '
850   ' define terminal
```

▶

# Example 6-8

## Solution, continued.

```
860 '
870 ' crt screen
880    LINE (200, 20)-(300,110),,B
890    LINE (210, 30)-(290,100),,B
900 '
910 ' keyboard
920    LINE (200,120)-(300,160),,B
930    LINE (225,130)-(290,155),,B
940    FOR Y = 130 TO 155 STEP 5
950      LINE (225,Y)-(290,Y)
960      LINE (210,Y)-(220,Y)
970    NEXT Y
980    FOR X = 225 TO 290 STEP 5
990      LINE (X,130)-(X,155)
1000   NEXT X
1010   LINE (210,130)-(220,155),,B
1020   LINE (215,130)-(215,155)
1030 '
1040   LOCATE 25,2
1050   PRINT "Use the cursor keys to ";
1060   PRINT "move the hand.";
1070 ' set up cursor keys
1080   ON KEY(11) GOSUB 1430 ' up
1090   ON KEY(12) GOSUB 1480 ' left
1100   ON KEY(13) GOSUB 1540 ' right
1110   ON KEY(14) GOSUB 1600 ' down
1120 '
1130   XPOS = 1
1140   YPOS = 1
1150 '
1160   KEY(11) ON
1170   KEY(12) ON
1180   KEY(13) ON
1190   KEY(14) ON
1200 '
1210 ' main loop
1220 '
1230   ON XPOS GOTO 1260,1320,1380
1240   GOTO 1210
1250 '
1260 ' pointing to disk tray
1270   Y = YPOS
1280   PUT (5,136 - 16*Y), HP%
1290   PUT (5,136 - 16*Y), HP%
1300   GOTO 1210
```

▶

Example 6-8

## Solution, continued.

```
1310 '                              1480 ' cursor left
1320 ' inserting a disk             1490   IF XPOS=1 THEN 1520
1330   Y = YPOS                     1500   XPOS = XPOS-1
1340   PUT (125, 156 - 10*Y), HG%   1510   YPOS = 1
1350   PUT (125, 156 - 10*Y), HG%   1520   RETURN
1360   GOTO 1210                    1530 '
1370 '                              1540 ' cursor right
1380 ' typing a command             1550   IF XPOS=3 THEN 1580
1390   PUT (220,150), HK%           1560   XPOS = XPOS+1
1400   PUT (220,150), HK%           1570   YPOS = 1
1410   GOTO 1210                    1580   RETURN
1420 '                              1590 '
1430 ' cursor up                    1600 ' cursor down
1440   IF YPOS = 6 THEN 1460        1610   IF YPOS = 1 THEN 1630
1450   YPOS = YPOS+1                1620   YPOS = YPOS-1
1460   RETURN                       1630   RETURN
1470 '                              1640 '
```

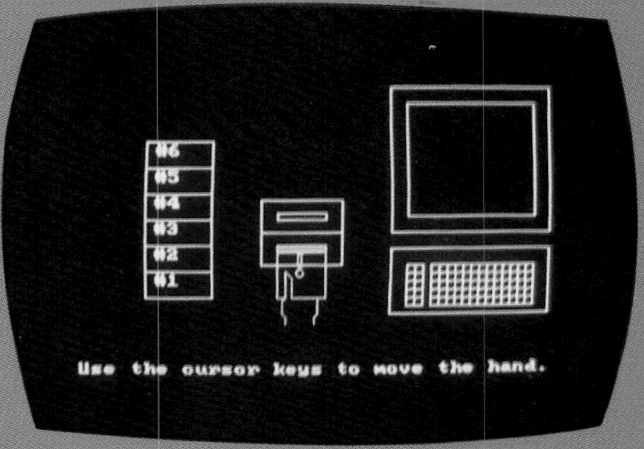

Figure 6-11
Icons

Let's go through this program step by step. In line 150, we dimension the various arrays that store the hand icons. We have used identifying letters for these arrays that suggest the particular position or function of each icon. In particular, HP% is where the *H*and *P*ointing is stored, HG% is where the *H*and *G*rasping the disk is stored, and HK% is where the

*H*ands on the *K*eyboard are stored. The percent signs indicate that these are integer arrays.

The next several lines of this listing contain commands to draw and then save each icon. In each case, a string is built up that contains DRAW commands in the IBM PC GDL. The string is drawn and a rectangular region surrounding the resulting image is saved into the array with the GET command. You may notice that in between the DRAW and the GET commands are LINE commands in the Box mode. They are really comment lines since they start with apostrophes. If you were to remove the apostrophes, these commands would be activated and would draw boxes around each icon figure. There is even a command (line 630) that draws a box around the whole screen. These boxes are useful when you debug your program. With the boxes present, you can better see how to position and GET your icons during program development.

After the icons are defined and stored, we start drawing the background picture. We must wait until the icons have been drawn unless we can find a big enough area of blank screen in our background picture. Remember that the GET statement gets *everything* inside the indicated rectangle. The background scene is drawn in lines 630-1020. First the disk trays are constructed, then the disk drives, and finally the CRT and keyboard. A lot of LINE commands accomplish this task.

Next comes the main loop. The cursor keys are set up for interactive interrupts (the ON KEY statements in lines 1080-1110 and the KEY ON statements in lines 1160-1190). Recall that ON KEY statements define the interrupt service routines and the KEY ON statements actually activate the keys for interrupt mode. The main loop dispatches to particular sections of code that handle various situations. The horizontal position of the icon (XPOS) determines which situation is appropriate. You can refine this so that other conditions can also be used in the dispatching process.

Each state or situation is handled in its own section of the program. In each case we need to position the icon. Other actions can be handled as well. For example, when you are in the keyboard position (extreme right position of the screen), you might want to have the user type some text onto the screen. The situation could get complicated if you want to interpret what the user types in.

Notice that the XPOS and YPOS variables are used at

most once per loop through the dispatching and situation handling process. This is because they might be updated at any time. There are certain crucial places where variables cannot be changed in midstream. For example, if the position of the icon is changed between the two PUT statements that place it and remove it, it will not be properly erased. This is why we copy the variable YPOS, which can be updated by the interrupt service routines, to the variable Y, which is used to help position the two PUT commands. Then YPOS can be updated as much as we want while Y is used to draw the picture.

The interrupt routines come last. They merely update the x-and y-position variables and return. In this case, the variables XPOS and YPOS are used for communicating the updated information to the main loop.

You are welcome to take this very basic example and expand it into something of use to you in your particular situation. You might want to turn it into a teaching tool for your employees who are learning about floppy disks and floppy disk operating systems.

# CONCLUSION

In this chapter, we have studied the image array commands GET and PUT. These commands can be used in a variety of ways from animation, to filtering out parts of the picture, to achieving interesting color effects. In this respect you can use the GET and PUT commands to control the very bits that make the picture on the screen.

The applications program in this chapter illustrates computerized learning, an area where tremendous growth is expected in the next few years. The graphics on the IBM PC now provide the necessary tools to make such lessons relatively easy to produce.

# CUSTOM AND GRAPHICS CHARACTERS

# CONCEPTS

**Concepts**
    Character Graphics
    Custom Characters
    Character Animation
    Page Flipping

**Commands**
    LOCATE
    PRINT
    COLOR
    SCREEN

**Applications**
    Font Editor
    Walking Man
    Ping-Pong Game
    Animation with Page Flipping

# INTRODUCTION

This chapter explains character graphics on the IBM PC. We will describe what character graphics is about and what is involved in producing custom character cells on the IBM PC graphics screen. We will also show how to assemble these characters on the screen to generate graphics effects, such as animation.

Character generation in both the text modes and graphics modes will be explored. We will see the important difference between these two modes and will discuss the advantages and disadvantages of each, including some interesting side effects each generates.

In the text modes, we will see how the characters are hard-wired into place with *codes* that are stored in a compact format in the screen memory. Taking up a fraction of the 16,384 bytes of screen memory, these codes allow plenty of room in video memory for such effects as separate coloring for the foreground and background of each character on the screen. There is even room to store copies of several different full screens of characters, and thus allow "page flipping."

In the graphics modes, we will see how the characters are painted on the screen by software and how, in these modes, the patterns for the characters are stored in tables in memory. Next, we will set up our own table to define 128 of the 256 available characters and demonstrate a simple but powerful font editor to customize these characters.

Several applications programs will be presented, including a simple Ping-Pong game using character graphics and a simple animation program that uses custom-defined characters.

In this chapter we depart from our usual practice of having one large lesson program. Instead, we give individual short examples as needed to explain various concepts. Later in the chapter we return to our normal format with the applications programs.

The important commands for character graphics (in either text or graphics modes) are LOCATE, PRINT, COLOR, and SCREEN. You can also use the commands CLS and WIDTH and the functions and system variables CSRLIN, POS, SCREEN, SPC, and TAB. In addition, all the string commands, functions, and operations are used. In this chapter, we will discuss only the first four commands and first three functions in detail.

# CHARACTERS AND CHARACTER GRAPHICS

We define character graphics as the use of *characters* (placed in character cells) to draw pictures. This is different from the graphics we have been studying so far, which is referred to as *all points addressable* (APA) graphics. With APA graphics each pixel (dot) on the screen can be individually located and changed independently from all the rest. APA graphics requires an APA display, such as the IBM PC Color/Graphics Adapter in graphics mode.

In contrast, character graphics breaks the screen into a moderately large number of small blocks. In the 80-column text mode there are 2000 such blocks arranged as an array with 80 blocks horizontally and 25 blocks vertically. Character graphics can be done either via hardware on a video *text* display, such as the Color/Graphics Adapter in *text* mode, or through software on an APA display, such as the Color/

Graphics Adapter in *graphics* mode. We will discuss both approaches.

In character graphics each block is called a character *cell*. On the Color/Graphics Adapter in any of its modes, each cell contains an array or matrix, which is 8 dots horizontally by 8 dots vertically. In this way, each dot on the screen may be located by specifying a *cell* position and then a *dot* position within that cell. This gives a very different and more difficult algorithm for specifying and plotting points and the other geometric shapes mentioned.

Instead of trying to make character graphics display points, lines, and circles as is so easy with APA graphics, it is better to take approaches that take advantage of its cellular nature.

In character graphics, the cells are designed to hold the dot matrix patterns for characters, that is, symbols for the letters of the alphabet, digits for a numbering system, punctuation marks, and special graphics characters.

In the most rudimentary character graphics, only text is placed on the screen by putting these dot patterns in the various cells. The screen becomes what is often called a "glass teletype" machine. The IBM PC will do more than this.

To help steer the course between APA graphics and the "glass teletype," the IBM PC has provided an extended character set including more than one hundred special built-in shapes (available only in text modes) and even a way for you to design your own custom characters (available only in graphics modes). The custom characters can be defined only in the graphics modes because they require APA capabilities that are available only in those modes. As a result, you cannot do many things with *custom* characters that are possible in the text modes, including color attributes for each character position and page flipping.

Effective character graphics depends upon the ability to control each character cell (block) of the screen. In an $8 \times 8$ cell there are 64 dots. The possible patterns you can display in such cells are calculated by taking 2 to the 64th—about 1.84E19, a rather large number! Out of all these only 256 are selectable at one time on the IBM PC. This is limiting, but not quite as limiting as these numbers seem to indicate. Perhaps four or five thousand combinations would suffice for many purposes. The problem with having a lot of combinations is finding a way to represent them in the computer's memory. The IBM PC uses 8 bits to encode the 256 numbers that select among the 256 different patterns. Each possible 8-bit pattern points to an $8 \times 8$ representation of the pattern in memory. Thus, each character only takes up a byte of main memory to specify its shape. If we used another entire byte to encode the shape, then with a total of 16 bits we could specify as many as 65,536 different patterns. We have seen already how a second byte is used to encode color; thus, such a 16-bit selection scheme would make a total of *three* bytes for each character position.

# LOCATING AND MAKING CHARACTERS

The easiest way to get characters on the screen is with the BASICA commands such as PRINT and LOCATE. These commands, and a few related functions, are described in the following sections.

## CSRLIN, POS, and SCREEN Functions

BASICA has several functions that tell you the condition of the cursor and the screen. The CSRLIN function returns the row, and the POS function returns the column that the cursor is currently on. CSRLIN requires no argument, but POS requires a dummy argument. Technically speaking, CSRLIN is a system variable, while POS is a built-in function. The following example will set X equal to the current cursor column and Y equal to the current cursor row:

X = POS(0)

Y = CSRLIN

The SCREEN function can be used to return both the ASCII code and the attributes of a character on the screen. Its syntax is

x = SCREEN(row,column[,z])

where *row* is a numeric expression that specifies a row number between 1 and 25, and *column* is a numeric expression that specifies a column number between 1 and 40 (for 40-column displays) or 1 and 80 (for 80-column displays). The optional parameter *z* specifies whether you want the ASCII code or the attribute byte. If *z* is 0 (the default value), you use the ASCII code for the character position at that column and row number; if $z$ is nonzero, you use the value of the attribute byte in that position. The attribute byte is encoded with blink, foreground, and color information, as described in Chapter 2. In the graphics modes there is a similar function, POINT, which returns the color of any pixel on the screen.

## LOCATE Command

The LOCATE command has been used a number of times in our examples and applications programs. Its purpose is to position the text cursor on the screen. It is also used to specify the position for the next text to be printed. Its syntax is

LOCATE [row] [,[column] [,cursor] [,[start] [,stop]]]

All parameters here are optional. An omitted parameter retains its original value.

The first two parameters give the current row and column for positioning the cursor. We have already used the LOCATE statement with just these first two parameters in a number of our examples to position text for labeling.

The last three parameters (*cursor*, *start*, and *stop*) only take effect in the text modes. The third parameter, *cursor*, tells whether or not the cursor is to be visible. A 0 means off (invisible) and a 1 means on (visible).

The last two parameters, *start* and *stop*, control the size of the cursor (see Figure 7-1). With the Color/Graphics Adapter, the lines in a character position in text mode are numbered from 0 to 7 with 0 at the top. The *start* parameter specifies the starting line for the cursor and the *stop* parameter specifies its ending line.

As an example,

LOCATE 1,1,1,0,7

will make a cursor visible in the upper-left corner of the screen. It will occupy the entire rectangle for that character position (see Figure 7-2).

If the start position is greater than the stop position, the cursor is broken into two pieces, starting with the start line, running to the bottom, and then wrapping around the top to end at the end line. For example,

LOCATE 1,1,1,7,0

will produce a cursor with a line at the bottom and a line at the top. If we just wanted the cursor to have such a shape

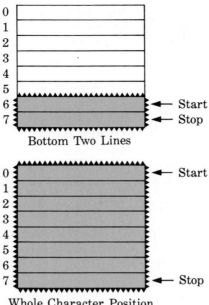

Bottom Two Lines

Whole Character Position

**Figure 7-1**

Cursor Start and Stop Lines

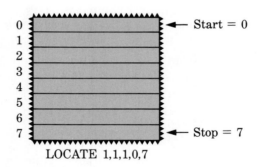

LOCATE 1,1,1,0,7

**Figure 7-2**

Default Block Cursor

without changing the cursor position or turning it on during program execution, we would use

    LOCATE ,,,7,0

Then when the program stopped, the cursor would appear as shown in Figure 7-3.

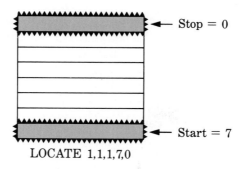

LOCATE 1,1,1,7,0

**Figure 7-3**

Cursor Altered with LOCATE

## PRINT Command

Everyone who has written a BASIC program knows what the PRINT statement is and how to use it. However, since it is the principal method of putting characters on the screen, we include a brief discussion of this command.

The full syntax of the PRINT command is

PRINT [list of expressions] [; or ,]

The list of expressions can include numeric or string expressions. The value of each expression is placed across the screen in order from left to right. The expressions in the list can be separated by commas, semicolons, or one or more spaces. In general, commas cause wide spacing on the screen, semicolons no spacing, and spaces between items act the same as semicolons.

On the IBM PC, each line is divided into "print zones" of 14 character positions each. For the 40-column character modes there are two zones, and for the 80-column character modes there are five zones. A comma in the list causes the value of the next item to be printed starting at the beginning of the next print zone; whereas a semicolon in the list causes the value of the next item to appear right after the previous item. Since numerical values are displayed with a trailing space, semicolons will not jam them together in an unreadable form. Strings, however, do not have any extra spaces in front or in back; thus, they can be placed right next to each other. Most people quickly learn to take this into account in their programming.

A comma or semicolon *after* the list of expressions will cause the next PRINT statement to continue its output on the same line, spacing it accordingly. For example,

PRINT "HI";
PRINT "THERE"

will cause

HITHERE

to be printed.

Now let's explore some other ways of putting characters on the screen besides printing them. They include using various graphics commands to plot or place characters on the screen, and using the PEEK and POKE statements to directly modify the screen memory.

## Alternate Ways to Put Text on the Screen

In the chapters on the graphics commands, we learned how to create all sorts of shapes. They can easily include characters. However, any such method of producing characters can never be done as easily as printing the characters. For example, an "A" can be made with the following DRAW command:

DRAW "bd7u6e3rf3d6bu4l6"

As you can see, this is a lot less efficient than using the PRINT statement. We have used a string of 17 command characters just to indicate one printed character. There are, however, certain advantages to using graphics commands. For example, drawn characters can be scaled up in size, whereas printed characters cannot.

In the last chapter, we saw how the PUT statement can be used to produce enlarged images of characters that have already been printed. Again, this process is far from direct, but offers some interesting possibilities.

Another method is to use POKE. In Chapter 2 we explored how the Color/Graphics Adapter's "hardware" mapped the extended ASCII codes and attributes in text modes to the screen. We saw how to use POKE to generate characters on the screen. In the medium-resolution graphics mode, we will now use PEEK to look at the built-in tables that are used to generate characters. We will then use the POKE statement in a font editing program statement to help define new characters.

# GRAPHICS MODE CHARACTERS

Now let's see what is involved in generating characters in a graphics mode. In these modes, the shapes of the characters are stored in memory in special tables. This is in contrast to the text modes, in which the character dot patterns are stored in a special ROM (Read-Only Memory), which is not accessible by the user.

In the graphics modes, ASCII codes 128 through 255 (the upper half) are treated differently than ASCII codes 0 through 127 (the lower half). For the lower half, a pattern table is permanently stored in main memory in ROM as part of the BIOS. On the other hand, there are no built-in tables for the characters in the upper half (ASCII codes 128 through 255) in graphics modes. Instead the user is free to set up a custom table for the upper half, and in fact, must do so to get anything but incomprehensible symbols for ASCII codes in this range.

We will show you a font editor to help you design your own custom characters for ASCII codes 128 to 255. But first, we present a program that uses PEEK to help us examine the ROM table that holds the dot patterns for any of the permanent characters (ASCII codes 0 through 127). You can find the table for these permanent characters near the end of the assembly language listing of the BIOS in the *IBM PC Technical Reference* manual. Our program will give a magnified visual display of what is stored in this table. Consider this example a preliminary step to the font editor.

EXAMPLE 7-1

# ENLARGED CHARACTERS

Design a program to display a magnified dot pattern for
the permanently stored characters in medium-resolution
graphics mode. An example of the output is shown in
Figure 7-4.

## Solution

```
100 ' CHARACTER ENLARGEMENT
110 '
120 ' This program displays
130 ' charcters in enlarged form.
140 '
150 '
160     SCREEN 1
170     CLS
180 '
190     CBASE = &HFA6E
200     DEF SEG = &HF000
210     LOCATE 1,11
220     PRINT "ENLARGED CHARACTERS"
230 '
240 ' MAIN LOOP
250     LOCATE 20,1
260     PRINT "ASCII CODE:        ";
270     LOCATE 20, 13
280     INPUT ACODE
290     IF ACODE>127 THEN 380
300     LOCATE 5,5
310     PRINT CHR$(ACODE)
320     LOCATE 7,5
330     PRINT USING "###";ACODE;
340     PRINT SPACE$(20);
350     GOSUB 430 ' load character
360     GOTO 240
370 '
380 ' error: acode>127
390     LOCATE 23,18
400     PRINT"too large";
410     GOTO 240
420 '
430 ' SUBROUTINE - LOAD CHARACTER
440     LOCATE 23,18
450     PRINT"wait      ";
```

▶

**Example 7-1**

## Solution, Continued.

```
460    FOR I= 0 TO 7
470      AO=PEEK(CBASE+8*(ACODE)+I)
480      FOR J= 0 TO 7
490        X% = AO AND 1
500        IF X% THEN X$="#" ELSE X$=" "
510        LOCATE 5+I,18+(7-J):PRINT X$
520        AO = INT(AO/2)
530      NEXT J
540    NEXT I
550    LOCATE 23,18
560    PRINT"          ";
570    RETURN
580    '
590    END
```

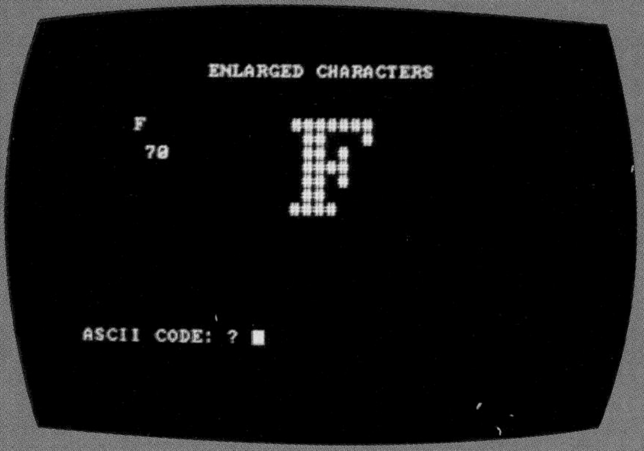

Figure 7-4
Enlarged Characters

Let's look at this program in detail. First the screen is put into medium-resolution graphics mode and is cleared. Next, in lines 190 and 200, we define the offset and the segment number of the ROM character table. These numbers were determined by looking at the assembly language listing in the *IBM PC Technical Reference* manual.*

---

*For details on segments, see *8086/8088 16-Bit Microprocessor Primer* by Christopher Morgan and Mitch Waite (Peterborough, N.H.: Byte Books, 1982).

```
#######.
.##...#.
.##.#...
.####...
.##.#...
.##.....
####....
........
```

**Figure 7-5**

An Enlarged F

Next the screen is titled, followed by the main loop. In the main loop, the ASCII code is requested from the user, and the corresponding symbol is displayed on the screen. We call the subroutine that loads the character onto the screen in the enlarged format and then loop back for more.

Looking at the subroutine (lines 430-570) in detail, we see that a PEEK statement transfers a byte from the table and pulls it apart bit-by-bit, displaying each bit as a space or "#" on the screen, depending upon whether its value is 0 or 1. Each byte represents one row of the dot matrix for the character. The algorithm used is a simple conversion to the binary representation of the number, as discussed in Chapter 6.

Now let's look at one particular pattern. If we run the program for the ASCII code 70, we would see the enlarged pattern of the letter "F," as shown in Figure 7-5.

In Chapter 2 we saw how the medium-resolution mode has twice the resolution with the NTSC color-encoding format. As a result, to get a true white dot, all dots must be doubled horizontally. But notice that this is not true for every dot in the pattern. Specifically, the serifs on the two arms of the letter are only one pixel wide. However, when you look at the character as it appears in a normal size on the screen, it looks as white as other characters in which every dot is doubled. We see that it is possible to use a small number of single dots with a blue tint to increase the resolution without changing the overall color of the character too much.

Now let's look at the font editor. In contrast to the last program, the font editor can only modify those characters whose ASCII code is greater than 127. These characters are stored in RAM rather than ROM and thus can be changed, that is, edited.

You can use this program to load dot matrix patterns onto the screen from anywhere in the extended ASCII code (values 0-255), modify that pattern with cursor controls, and then save it as part of the second half of the extended ASCII code (values 127-255).

EXAMPLE 7-2

# FONT EDITOR

Design a font editing tool for creating the dot patterns
for characters with ASCII codes from 128 to 255 in the
medium-resolution graphics mode. An example of the
screen is shown in Figure 7-6.

## Solution

```
100 ' FONT EDITOR
110 '
120 ' This program allows you to
130 ' create and modify characters
140 ' with ASCII codes from 128 to
150 ' 255 in the medium resolution
160 ' mode.
170 '
180     DIM A(7,7)
190     SCREEN 1
200     CLS
210 '
220 ' define keys
230     KEY OFF
240     KEY 1,"":KEY 2,""
250     KEY 3,"":KEY 4,""
260     KEY 10,CHR$(27)
270 '
280 ' set up pointer to characters
290     CBASE = &H4000
300     DEF SEG=0
310     POKE &H7C, 0
320     POKE &H7D, &H40
330     POKE &H7E, PEEK(&H510)
340     POKE &H7F, PEEK(&H511)
350     DEF SEG
360 '
370     ACODE = 128
380 '
390 ' Set up screen
400 '
410     LOCATE 1,14
420     PRINT "FONT EDITOR"
430     FOR J=1 TO 8
440       LOCATE 4+J,18
450       PRINT "........";
```

▶

## Example 7-2

## Solution, Continued.

```
460     NEXT J
470   '
480     LOCATE 4, 1
490     PRINT "ASCII CODE: ";
500   '
510     LOCATE 1,30
520     PRINT "CURSOR"
530     LOCATE 2,30
540     PRINT "D DRAW"
550     LOCATE 3,30
560     PRINT "E ERASE"
570     LOCATE 4,30
580     PRINT "M MOVE"
590     LOCATE 6,1
600     PRINT "F1 -1   F2 +1";
610     LOCATE 7,1
620     PRINT "F3 -5   F4 +5";
630     LOCATE 6,30
640     PRINT "CHARACTER";
650     LOCATE 7,30
660     PRINT "C CLEAR";
670     LOCATE 8,30
680     PRINT "L LOAD";
690     LOCATE 9,30
700     PRINT "S SAVE";
710     LOCATE 11,30
720     PRINT "F10 ESCAPE";
730   '
740     GOSUB 1710 ' display all chars
750   '
760   ' GO TO MAIN LOOP
770     GOTO 1850
780   '
790   ' SUBROUTINE - PLACE CURSOR
800     BLINK%=(BLINK%+1) MOD 20
810     IF BLINK%<10 THEN 880 ELSE 830
820   '
830   ' cursor off
840     IF A(ROW,COLUMN)=0 THEN CH$="."
850     IF A(ROW,COLUMN)=1 THEN CH$="#"
860     GOTO 930
870   '
880   ' cursor on
890     IF CURS=-1 THEN CH$="-"
900     IF CURS= 0 THEN CH$="*"
910     IF CURS= 1 THEN CH$="+"
```

▶

Example 7-2

## Solution, Continued.

```
920  '
930      LOCATE 5+ROW,18+COLUMN
940      PRINT CH$;
950      RETURN
960  '
970  ' SUBROUTINE - REMOVE CURSOR
980      IF A(ROW,COLUMN)=0 THEN CH$="."
990      IF A(ROW,COLUMN)=1 THEN CH$="#"
1000     LOCATE 5+ROW,18+COLUMN
1010     PRINT CH$;
1020     RETURN
1030 '
1040 ' SUBROUTINE - SHOW CODE & SYMBOL
1050     LOCATE 4, 13
1060     PRINT USING "###"; ACODE;
1070     CH=ACODE
1080     IF CH>6 AND CH<14 THEN CH=32
1090     LOCATE 10, 10
1100     PRINT CHR$(CH);
1110     RETURN
1120 '
1130 ' SUBROUTINE - CLEAR CHAR
1140     LOCATE 23,18
1150     PRINT "wait"
1160     FOR I= 0 TO 7
1170        LOCATE 5+I,18
1180        PRINT "........";
1190        FOR J= 0 TO 7
1200        A(I,7-J)=0
1210        NEXT J
1220     NEXT I
1230     LOCATE 23,18
1240     PRINT "      "
1250     RETURN
1260 '
1270 ' SUBROUTINE - SAVE CHARACTER
1280     IF ACODE<128 THEN 1430
1290     LOCATE 23,18:PRINT "wait";
1300     FOR I= 0 TO 7
1310        A0=0
1320        FOR J= 0 TO 7
1330           A0 = A0 + A0 + A(I,J)
1340        NEXT J
1350        POKE CBASE+8*(ACODE-128)+I,A0
1360     NEXT I
1370     I=INT(ACODE/32):J=ACODE MOD 32
```

▶

## Example 7-2

## Solution, Continued.

```
1380    LOCATE 15+I,1+J
1390    PRINT CHR$(ACODE)
1400    LOCATE 23,18:PRINT "     ";
1410    RETURN
1420  '
1430    LOCATE 23,10
1440    PRINT "cannot save ASCII<128";
1445 FOR I=1 TO 1000: NEXT I
1450    LOCATE 23,10
1460    PRINT "                      ";
1470    RETURN
1480  '
1490  ' SUBROUTINE - LOAD CHARACTER
1500    LOCATE 23,18
1510    PRINT "wait"
1520    DEF SEG
1530    COFF = CBASE+8*(ACODE-128)
1540    IF ACODE>127 THEN 1570
1550     DEF SEG=&HF000
1560     COFF=&HFA6E+8*ACODE
1570    FOR I= 0 TO 7
1580      A%=PEEK(COFF+I)
1590      FOR J= 0 TO 7
1600       X% = A% AND 1
1610       A(I,7-J)=X%
1620       IF X% THEN X$="#" ELSE X$="."
1630        LOCATE 5+I,18+(7-J):PRINT X$
1640       A% = INT(A%/2)
1650      NEXT J
1660    NEXT I
1670    DEF SEG
1680    LOCATE 23,18:PRINT "     ";
1690    RETURN
1700  '
1710  ' SUBROUTINE - DISPLAY ALL SYM
1720    LOCATE 23,18:PRINT "wait";
1730    FOR I= 0 TO 7
1740     LOCATE 15+I,1
1750     FOR J= 0 TO 31
1760      CH=32*I+J
1770       IF CH>6 AND CH<14 THEN CH=32
1780      PRINT CHR$(CH);
1790     NEXT J
1800     PRINT
1810    NEXT I
1820    LOCATE 23,18:PRINT "     ";
```

▶

# Example 7-2

## Solution, Continued.

```
1830    RETURN
1840  '
1850  ' main program
1860  '
1870  ' Set cursor
1880    ROW=0 : COLUMN=0 : CURS=0
1890  '
1900  ' new ascii
1910    GOSUB 1040 ' show code & symbol
1920  '
1930  ' main loop
1940    BLINK%=0
1950    IF CURS=-1 THEN A(ROW,COLUMN)=0
1960    IF CURS=+1 THEN A(ROW,COLUMN)=1
1970  '
1980  ' blink entry
1990    GOSUB 790  ' place cursor
2000  '
2010    A$=INKEY$
2020    DEF SEG: POKE 106,0 ' CLEAR BUF
2030    IF LEN(A$) = 0 THEN 1980
2040    IF LEN(A$) = 1 THEN 2080
2050    IF LEN(A$) = 2 THEN 2190
2060    GOTO 1980
2070  '
2080  ' length is 1
2090    CODE1=ASC(A$) AND &H5F
2100    IF CODE1 = 27 THEN 3190 ' esc
2110    IF CODE1 = ASC("E") THEN 2880
2120    IF CODE1 = ASC("M") THEN 2920
2130    IF CODE1 = ASC("D") THEN 2960
2140    IF CODE1 = ASC("C") THEN 3230
2150    IF CODE1 = ASC("L") THEN 3270
2160    IF CODE1 = ASC("S") THEN 3310
2170    GOTO 1980
2180  '
2190    IF ASC(A$)<>0 THEN 1930
2200    CODE2=ASC(RIGHT$(A$,1))
2210    GOSUB 970  ' remove cursor
2220  '
2230  ' cursor
2240    IF CODE2=71 THEN 2400 ' home
2250    IF CODE2=73 THEN 2470 ' upper r
2260    IF CODE2=79 THEN 2540 ' lower l
2270    IF CODE2=81 THEN 2610 ' lwer rgh
2280    IF CODE2=72 THEN 2680 ' curs up
```

▶

## Example 7-2

## Solution, Continued.

```
2290     IF CODE2=75 THEN 2730 ' curs lft
2300     IF CODE2=77 THEN 2780 ' curs rgh
2310     IF CODE2=80 THEN 2830 ' curs dwn
2320 '
2330 ' ascii code
2340     IF CODE2=59 THEN 3000 ' -1
2350     IF CODE2=60 THEN 3050 ' +1
2360     IF CODE2=61 THEN 3100 ' -5
2370     IF CODE2=62 THEN 3140 ' +5
2380     GOTO 1980
2390 '
2400 ' upper left
2410 '   IF ROW=0 THEN ROW=8
2420     IF COLUMN=0 THEN COLUMN=8
2430     ROW=ROW-1
2440     COLUMN=COLUMN-1
2450     GOTO 1930
2460 '
2470 ' upper right
2480     IF ROW=0 THEN ROW=8
2490     IF COLUMN=7 THEN COLUMN=-1
2500     ROW=ROW-1
2510     COLUMN=COLUMN+1
2520     GOTO 1930
2530 '
2540 ' lower left
2550     IF ROW=7 THEN ROW=-1
2560     IF COLUMN=0 THEN COLUMN=8
2570     ROW=ROW+1
2580     COLUMN=COLUMN-1
2590     GOTO 1930
2600 '
2610 ' lower right
2620     IF ROW=7 THEN ROW=-1
2630     IF COLUMN=7 THEN COLUMN=-1
2640     ROW=ROW+1
2650     COLUMN=COLUMN+1
2660     GOTO 1930
2670 '
2680 ' curs up
2690     IF ROW = 0 THEN ROW = 8
2700     ROW=ROW-1
2710     GOTO 1930
2720 '
2730 ' curs left
2740     IF COLUMN=0 THEN COLUMN = 8
```

▶

## Example 7-2

## Solution, Continued.

```
2750    COLUMN=COLUMN-1
2760    GOTO 1930
2770    '
2780    ' curs right
2790    IF COLUMN=7 THEN COLUMN = -1
2800    COLUMN=COLUMN+1
2810    GOTO 1930
2820    '
2830    ' curs down
2840    IF ROW=7 THEN ROW = -1
2850    ROW=ROW+1
2860    GOTO 1930
2870    '
2880    ' erase
2890    CURS=-1
2900    GOTO 1930
2910    '
2920    ' move
2930    CURS=0
2940    GOTO 1930
2950    '
2960    ' draw
2970    CURS=+1
2980    GOTO 1930
2990    '
3000    ' ascii -1
3010    IF ACODE=0 THEN 3030
3020    ACODE =ACODE-1
3030    GOTO 1900
3040    '
3050    ' ascii +1
3060    IF ACODE=255 THEN 3080
3070    ACODE =ACODE+1
3080    GOTO 1900
3090    '
3100    ' ascii -5
3110    IF ACODE<5 THEN 3130
3120    ACODE =ACODE-5
3130    GOTO 1900
3140    ' ascii +5
3150    IF ACODE>250 THEN 3170
3160    ACODE =ACODE+5
3170    GOTO 1900
3180    '
3190    ' escape from program
```

```
3200    LOCATE 23,1
3210    GOTO 3350
3220    '
3230    ' clear
3240    GOSUB 1130 ' clear
3250    GOTO 1840
3260    '
3270    ' load
3280    GOSUB 1490 ' load
3290    GOTO 1840
3300    '
3310    ' save
3320    GOSUB 1270 ' save
3330    GOTO 1900
3340    '
3350    END
```

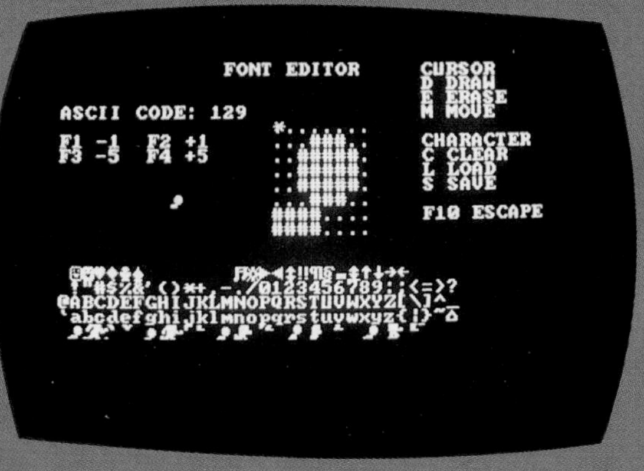

Figure 7-6
Font Editor

Before we describe how this program works, let's describe how you operate it. When the program signs on, it displays an enlarged dot matrix work area in the center of the screen. A cursor blinks in one of the dot positions of this matrix. You can move the cursor up, down, left, and right within the work area by means of the cursor keys. In addition, you can move the cursor diagonally by means of the "corner" keys next to the cursor keys (see Figure 7-7). Moving diagonally facilitates the drawing of diagonal parts of the character symbols.

On the right of the screen is a display of the cursor and character commands. With cursor commands, D (DRAW) causes the cursor to turn dots on wherever it goes, E (ERASE) causes the cursor to turn dots off wherever it goes, and M (MOVE) allows the cursor to move nondestructively around the dot matrix work area. With character commands, C (CLEAR) clears the dot matrix, L (LOAD) loads the dot matrix work area on the screen from the dot matrix of the current ASCII code (as indicated on the left side of the screen), and S (SAVE) saves the dot matrix on the screen into memory for the current ASCII code. Finally, function key F10 allows you to exit the program.

On the left side of the screen, the current ASCII code and the current symbol for that code are displayed. The symbol

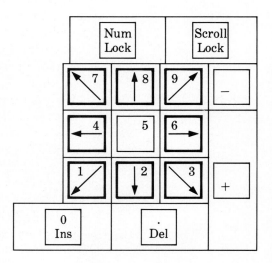

**Figure 7-7**

Corner and Cursor Keys for
the Font Editor

will not necessarily agree with the dot matrix work area on the screen until after a LOAD or SAVE command is typed. You can increase or decrease the current ASCII code in steps of 1 or 5 by means of the function keys F1, F2, F3, and F4, as indicated on the screen. You can think of F1 and F2 as the "local" keys, because they increase or decrease the current ASCII character by 1, and F3 and F4 as the "express" keys, because they increase or decrease the current ASCII value by 5. At the bottom of the screen the complete extended ASCII code in 4 rows of 64 characters is displayed.

Now let's look at how this program works. The matrix A is dimensioned as $7 \times 7$ to hold the $8 \times 8$ pattern for the character symbol currently being edited. The screen is set to medium-resolution mode and is cleared; the function keys at the bottom of the screen are turned off, and the function keys F1, F2, F3, F4, and F10 are redefined. In lines 280-350, an area in memory is reserved for the characters, and pointers are set up so BASIC knows how to find these characters. The characters will be stored in memory starting at address 4000 (hexadecimal), or 16,384 bytes into the BASIC data segment. This allows plenty of room for the BASIC font editor program, which uses about 8K.

As documented in the *IBM PC Technical Reference* manual, the operating system and BASIC maintain certain "pointers" (locations containing addresses of other locations) in the bottom segment of memory (segment number 0). Some of these pointers indicate where the patterns for our text characters can be found. Since we are defining our own set of characters, we need to initialize these pointers.

In particular, locations 7C through 7F (hexadecimal) contain a 4-byte pointer to the tables for defining the characters with ASCII codes 128-255. The bytes 7C and 7D contain the offset (which we set in lines 310-320 to 4000 hexadecimal), and bytes 7E and 7F contain the segment number (which we set in lines 330-340 to the segment number for the BASIC data segment as stored in bytes 510 and 511).

After loading these values we set the BASIC data segment back to its default value. We also set an initial value of 128 for the current character ASCII code (128 is the first one we can edit).

The next section of the program (lines 390-750) sets up the screen with such things as a title, work area, various labels, and a display of all characters.

Now we jump to the main program, skipping over several useful subroutines that are used to place and remove the cursor from the work area, show the ASCII code and symbol on the screen, load the character from memory onto the screen, save the current character, and display all characters.

The main program has several entry points for its basic loop structure. Line 1870 (set cursor) is used every time a new character is loaded from memory, line 1900 (new ascii) is used every time the current ASCII code is changed, line 1930 (main loop) is used every time the cursor is moved, and line 1980 (blink entry) is used if no key or a wrong key was pressed. This entry keeps the cursor in the work area blinking. The blink happens every 20 cycles of this loop. The subroutine that places the cursor (lines 790-950) does the blinking.

The next section (lines 2010-2380) gets your keystroke (through the INKEY$ function) and tries to match it with the appropriate action. Some keystrokes cause a string of length 1 and some cause a string of length 2. A length 0 indicates that no key was pressed. The double character strings correspond to keys on the left and right sides of the keyboard, namely the function and cursor keys. We wish to use the regular cursor keys plus the keys at the corner positions. We will use these corner keys to indicate diagonal motions. Because of this, we cannot use interrupt I/O, as in several of the examples in previous chapters.

After the main loop there are procedures to service the various keystrokes (lines 2400-3330). They include moving the cursor, selecting a new character, and exiting the program. We will not describe them, but you are welcome to explore the code yourself.

You should note there is no direct provision in our program for permanently saving a character set. However, this can easily be done using the BSAVE command. The following line can be used to save the current character table in the file CTABLE.BAS:

BSAVE "CTABLE", &H4000, 1024

Now when you want to use this character set in another program (graphics mode only), you reload this table by setting the desired segment where you want the character set with the DEF SEG command and the BLOAD command.

For example, you can retrieve the file you saved with the command

BLOAD "CTABLE"

You must also set the pointers in low memory to point to this offset and segment, as we did in lines 300-350. Once this is done, the characters should be available for your use. In the next example we will demonstrate how to use custom characters that have been defined using this font editor.

# CHARACTER ANIMATION

In this section we present a short example of how custom characters can be used to create animation. In particular, we shall show how to make a program that displays a little man walking on your screen.* The man is constructed by drawing him on graph paper in a series of five positions. Each position is called an animation *frame*. Each frame is broken up into six 8 × 8 blocks. We have a separate custom character for each block of each frame. This requires a total of 30 custom characters. The characters, shown in Figure 7-8, are placed in the dot matrices for extended ASCII codes 128 through 157 with the font editor.

The main idea of the animation program is to display these frames in sequence over and over again. This is called the *animation sequence*. Thus, as the program "walks" through the animation sequence, the man walks on the screen. To do this, the program merely prints these custom characters on the screen in the right positions, using the LOCATE command in the right sequence.

Before you run the program, run the font editor from the last example, and form all of the ASCII codes shown in Figure 7-8. After you exit the font editor, save the new characters with the command

BSAVE "WALKCHAR", &H4000, 1024

---

*Our patterns for the walking man are courtesy of Mitch Waite and are from *Computer Animation Primer* by David Fox and Mitch Waite (Peterborough, N.H.: Byte Books, 1982).

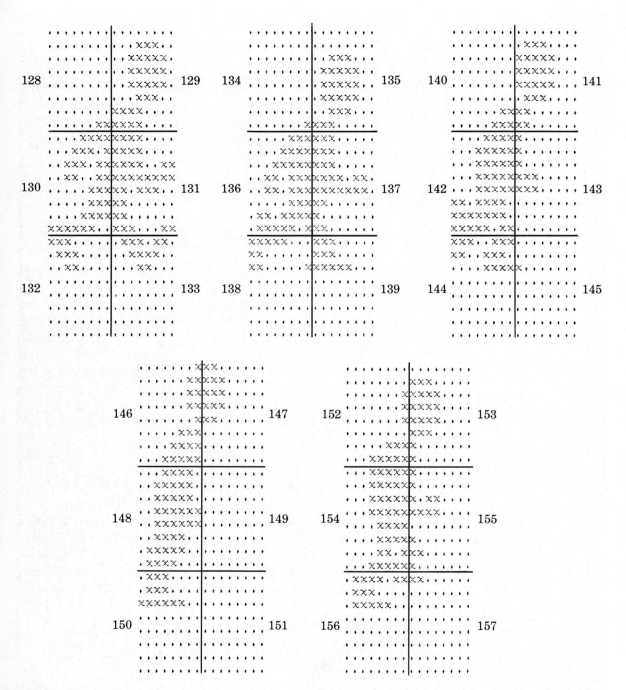

**Figure 7-8**

Dot Matrices for the Frames
of the Walking Man

EXAMPLE 7-3

## WALKING MAN

Make an animation program in which a man walks on
your screen. Break the man into blocks with each block
controlled by custom characters. One frame of the
animation is shown in Figure 7-9.

## Solution

```
100 ' WALKING MAN                   255     CLEAR , &H8000
110 '                               260     DEF SEG=0
120    GOTO 250                     270     POKE &H7C,0
130 '                               280     POKE &H7D,&H40
140 ' subroutine - frame            290     POKE &H7E,PEEK(&H510)
150    G=128+6*F                    300     POKE &H7F,PEEK(&H511)
160    LOCATE 10,10                 310     DEF SEG
170    PRINT CHR$(G+0);CHR$(G+1)    320     BLOAD "WALKCHAR",&H8000
180    LOCATE 11,10                 330 '
190    PRINT CHR$(G+2);CHR$(G+3)    340     SCREEN 1 : CLS
200    LOCATE 12,10                 350 '
210    PRINT CHR$(G+4);CHR$(G+5)    360 ' main loop
220    FOR I=1 TO 20:NEXT           370     FOR F = 0 TO 4
230    RETURN                       380     GOSUB 130 ' frame
240 '                               390     NEXT F
250 ' load walk characters          400     GOTO 370
```

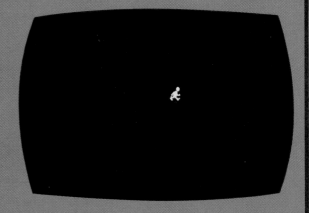

Figure 7-9
Walking Man

The program is short and simple. Each frame is drawn with the subroutine (lines 140-230). In this subroutine, we compute an offset G from F, the frame number. G selects the particular section of the extended ASCII code containing the custom characters for that frame. For each of the three rows of the man, we use the LOCATE command to set the position of the cursor and then print with the CHR$ function to place two custom characters on that row. At the end of the subroutine is a delay loop (line 220).

The main part of the program extends from line 360 to line 400. It first loads our character set and then runs through the five frames (with F from 0 to 4) over and over again in an endless loop, producing the animation sequence.

Next, we turn our attention to some fun and games. We will show how the colorful text mode can be used to make a Ping-Pong game.

# COLORING TEXT CHARACTERS

In Chapter 3 we saw that each character on the screen can be colored separately by placing attributes directly into memory. However, the "official" way to set the coloring of characters in the text mode is by the COLOR command. In previous chapters, we used this command to set the foreground palette and the background color in the medium-resolution graphics mode. Here we will explore how to use it to color characters in the 40-column text mode.

In text mode, the syntax for the COLOR statement is

COLOR [foreground] [,background] [,border]

Here, *foreground* is the foreground color for the next characters to be printed, *background* is the background color for the next characters to be printed, and *border* is the color of the border. Any omitted parameters retain their old values. The same numerical color codes are used, as discussed in the previous chapters.

Now we present a simple Ping-Pong game to illustrate the use of the COLOR statement. This program will illustrate a number of other ideas, including animation.

In this game, there are two players. Player #1 (on the left side of the screen) uses the function keys F1 and F3 to move the left paddle up or down, and player #2 uses the CURSOR UP and CURSOR DOWN keys to move the right paddle up and down. The ball can bounce off the paddles or the side walls. If the ball hits a paddle off-center, it is deflected at an angle. Each time a player lets the ball get past (go out of bounds), the game stops and the other player gets a point. Play is resumed by hitting any key.

This program uses the SOUND command to make the play more interesting.

EXAMPLE 7-4

## PING-PONG GAME

Design a Ping-Pong game. Use the COLOR statement to color the walls, paddles, and ball different colors. The playing field is shown in Figure 7-10.

---

## Solution

```
100 '  PING-PONG GAME
110 '
120    SCREEN 0,1   ' text mode
130    KEY OFF
140    S$=SPACE$(37)
150 '
160    ON KEY(1)   GOSUB 1490
170    ON KEY(3)   GOSUB 1550
180    ON KEY(11)  GOSUB 1610
190    ON KEY(14)  GOSUB 1670
200 '
210 ' start
220 '
230    KEY(1)   ON
240    KEY(3)   ON
250    KEY(11) ON
260    KEY(14) ON
270 '
280 ' starting position
290    Y1   = 12 : Y1SCR = Y1
300    Y2   = 12 : Y2SCR = Y1
310    XOLD = 20 : YOLD  = 12
320    DELX =  1 : DELY  =  0
330    PAD1 = -1 : PAD2  = -1
340    BCOUNT=0
350 '
360    COLOR 15,0
370    CLS
380 ' print the scores
390    LOCATE 1,1 : PRINT PLAYER1;
400    LOCATE 1,35: PRINT PLAYER2;
410 '
420 ' side walls
430    COLOR   1,1
440    LOCATE  2,2 : PRINT S$;
450    LOCATE 24,2 : PRINT S$;
460    COLOR  15,0
```

▶

## Example 7-4

## Solution, continued.

```
470 '
480 ' main loop
490    SND = 0 ' sound off
500 '
510 ' update paddle #1 if needed
520    IF NOT(PAD1 OR PAD2) THEN 820
530    IF NOT PAD1 THEN 670
540    PAD1=0
550 ' erase old paddle
560    COLOR 15,0
570    LOCATE Y1SCR-1, 1,0: PRINT " ";
580    LOCATE Y1SCR  , 1,0: PRINT " ";
590    LOCATE Y1SCR+1, 1,0: PRINT " ";
600 ' make new paddle
610    Y1SCR = Y1
620    COLOR 15,4
630    LOCATE Y1SCR-1, 1,0: PRINT " ";
640    LOCATE Y1SCR  , 1,0: PRINT " ";
650    LOCATE Y1SCR+1, 1,0: PRINT " ";
660 '
670 ' update paddle #2 if needed
680    IF NOT PAD2 THEN 820
690    PAD2=0
700 ' erase old paddle
710    COLOR 15,0
720    LOCATE Y2SCR-1, 39,0:PRINT " ";
730    LOCATE Y2SCR  , 39,0:PRINT " ";
740    LOCATE Y2SCR+1, 39,0:PRINT " ";
750 ' make new paddle
760    Y2SCR = Y2
770    COLOR 15,2
780    LOCATE Y2SCR-1, 39,0:PRINT " ";
790    LOCATE Y2SCR  , 39,0:PRINT " ";
800    LOCATE Y2SCR+1, 39,0:PRINT " ";
810 '
820 ' update position of ball
830    IF BCOUNT<>0 THEN 860
840    X = XOLD + DELX
850    Y = YOLD + DELY
860    BCOUNT=(BCOUNT+1) MOD 2
870 '
880    IF X<>2 THEN 1040 ' out on left?
890      SND = 500
900      DELX = 1
910      IF Y < Y1SCR-1 THEN 980
920      IF Y > Y1SCR+1 THEN 980
```

▶

## Example 7-4

## Solution, continued.

```
930        IF Y = Y1SCR-1 THEN 960
940        IF Y = Y1SCR+1 THEN 970
950        DELY =  0 : SND=500  :GOTO 1200
960        DELY = -1 : SND=1000 :GOTO 1200
970        DELY =  1 : SND=1000 :GOTO 1200
980        COLOR 15,0
990        LOCATE YOLD,3,0:PRINT " ";
1000        LOCATE Y, 2,0  :PRINT "*out";
1010        PLAYER2=PLAYER2+1
1020        GOTO 1320
1030 '
1040     IF X<>38 THEN 1210 'out on rght?
1050      SND = 500
1060      DELX = -1
1070      IF Y < Y2SCR-1 THEN 1140
1080      IF Y > Y2SCR+1 THEN 1140
1090      IF Y = Y2SCR-1 THEN 1120
1100      IF Y = Y2SCR+1 THEN 1130
1110      DELY =  0 : SND=500  :GOTO 1200
1120      DELY = -1 : SND=1000:GOTO 1200
1130      DELY =  1 : SND=1000:GOTO 1200
1140      COLOR 15,0
1150      LOCATE YOLD, 37,0:PRINT " "
1160      LOCATE Y,35,0    :PRINT "out*"
1170      PLAYER1=PLAYER1+1
1180      GOTO 1320
1190 '
1200 ' hit side walls?
1210    IF Y =  3 THEN DELY =  1:SND=600
1220    IF Y = 23 THEN DELY = -1:SND=600
1230 '
1240 ' redraw the ball
1250    COLOR 14,0
1260    LOCATE YOLD,XOLD,0 : PRINT " ";
1270    LOCATE Y, X,0      : PRINT "*";
1280    XOLD = X : YOLD = Y
1290    IF SND THEN SOUND SND,2
1300    GOTO 480 ' back for more
1310 '
1320 ' out of bounds
1330    KEY(1) OFF
1340    KEY(3) OFF
1350    KEY(11) OFF
1360    KEY(14) OFF
1370 '
1380 ' glissando
```

▶

## Example 7-4

## Solution, continued.

```
1390    FOR I=2000 TO 400 STEP -100
1400      SOUND I,1
1410    NEXT I
1420  ' clear buffer for pause
1430    DEF SEG : POKE 106,0
1440    LOCATE 25,1
1450    PRINT"press any key to restart";
1460    A$=INPUT$(1)
1470    GOTO 210 ' restart game
1480  '
1490  ' player #1 up
1500    Y1 = Y1 - 1
1510    IF Y1 < 2 THEN Y1 = 24
1520    PAD1 = -1
1530    RETURN
1540  '
1550  ' player #1 down
1560    Y1 = Y1 + 1
1570    IF Y1 > 24 THEN Y1 = 2
1580    PAD1 = -1
1590    RETURN
1600  '
1610  ' player #2 up
1620    Y2 = Y2 - 1
1630    IF Y2 < 2  THEN Y2 = 24
1640    PAD2 = -1
1650    RETURN
1660  '
1670  ' player #2 down
1680    Y2 = Y2 + 1
1690    IF Y2 > 24 THEN Y2 = 2
1700    PAD2 = -1
1710    RETURN
```

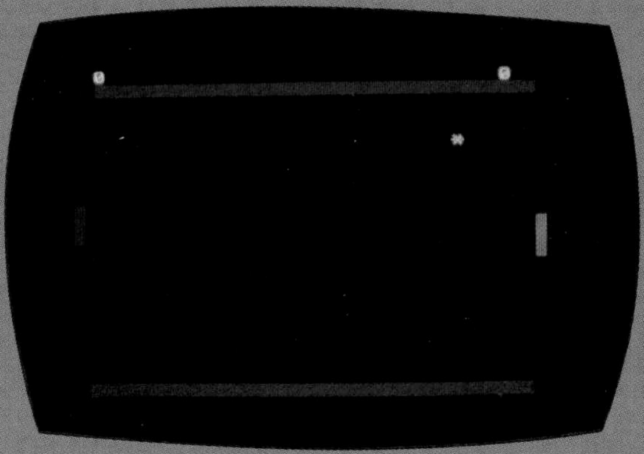

Figure 7-10
Ping-Pong Game

Looking at this example closely, we see that the program uses interrupt I/O (see Chapter 4 for details). There is a main loop (lines 480-1300) in which the positions of the ball and the paddles are updated as needed. Service routines (lines 1490-1710) respond to the four active keys used in this game by updating the variables Y1 and Y2, which control the position of the paddles. There is a special routine (lines 880-1180) to handle the cases when the ball goes out of bounds. Notice that the function keys are disabled during this routine and that the DEF SEG and POKE 160,0 commands are used to clear the buffer before the INPUT$ function is used to stop the game temporarily. This makes a clean break in the play. Without this POKE, the switch from interrupt-driven I/O to the INPUT$ function I/O will not work correctly.

Now let's see how the COLOR statement is used in this program. First look at the side walls. You can see that they are ASCII spaces whose background color is blue. The paddles are also colored spaces. One paddle is colored green and the other red. To move a paddle (lines 510-800), we erase the old paddle by setting the background color to black and placing spaces over the old paddle position. Then we write the new paddle by setting the background color appropriately and again placing spaces. This time the spaces are in the new paddle position.

The ball is a yellow asterisk. The foreground color is used with the intensity bit on. Notice in lines 1240-1290 that the ball is replaced right after it is erased. XOLD and YOLD help keep track of where the ball was last time so that the erasure works properly.

# PAGE FLIPPING

In the *text* mode only, the SCREEN command can be used to create animated effects using what is called *page flipping*. We have already seen how the SCREEN command can be used to put the graphics adapter into text mode or into the two graphics modes; we now explore its additional purpose associated with page flipping, namely, the assignment of the active and the visible page.

The syntax for the SCREEN command is

SCREEN [mode] [,[burst] [,[apage] [,[vpage]]]

Here, *mode* and *burst* are defined as before, and the last two quantities (*apage* and *vpage*) determine the active and visible pages, respectively.

In the text modes, the screen memory is divided into several *pages*. The 40-character text mode has four pages. At any particular time only one page is active and only one is visible. The active page is the page on which you can print or place your cursor. The visible page is the one that is currently being displayed. Normally, both of these pages are the same. The ability to draw on a page that is not visible is the secret of certain types of animation. Unfortunately, the IBM PC falls short in this area. You cannot define custom characters or invoke graphics commands while you use page flipping. This would require twice the amount of screen memory that is available.

Because of these limitations, our page flipping example will be rather limited. We will simply show an expanding double-walled box. Other effects are possible, but it is difficult to draw things with the limited choices a fixed character set offers. Perhaps once you see how this method works, you will be able to mix in your creative character capabilities to achieve some interesting effects.

EXAMPLE 7-5

## SIMPLE ANIMATION SEQUENCE

Use page flipping to make an animation sequence. Use all
four pages of the 40-character text mode. Show a box
getting larger and smaller. The box is shown in Figure
7-11.

## Solution

```
100 ' ANIMATION SEQUENCE
110 '
120   FOR I = 0 TO 3
130 '
140   SCREEN 0, 0, I, I
150   CLS
160 '
170 ' draw a box
180 '
190 ' top
200   L$=STRING$(2*I+1,205)
210   L$=CHR$(201)+L$+CHR$(187)
220   LOCATE 10-I,18-I:PRINT L$;
230 '
240 ' middle
250   L$=STRING$(2*I+1,32)
260   L$=CHR$(186)+L$+CHR$(186)
270   FOR J = 1 TO 2*I+1
280     LOCATE 10-I+J,18-I: PRINT L$;
290   NEXT J
300 '
310 ' bottom
320   L$=STRING$(2*I+1,205)
330   L$=CHR$(200)+L$+CHR$(188)
340   LOCATE 10+I+2,18-I:PRINT L$;
350 '
360   NEXT I
370 '
380 ' animation sequence
390 '
400   SCREEN 0,0,0,0
410   GOSUB 580
420   SCREEN 0,0,1,1
430   GOSUB 580
440   SCREEN 0,0,2,2
```

▶

Example 7-5

## Solution, continued.

```
450     GOSUB 580
460     SCREEN 0,0,3,3
470     GOSUB 580
480     SCREEN 0,0,3,3
490     GOSUB 580
500     SCREEN 0,0,2,2
510     GOSUB 580
520     SCREEN 0,0,1,1
530     GOSUB 580
540     SCREEN 0,0,0,0
550     GOSUB 580
560     GOTO 380
570     '
580     ' SUBROUTINE - DELAY
590     FOR K=1 TO 40:NEXT K
600     RETURN
```

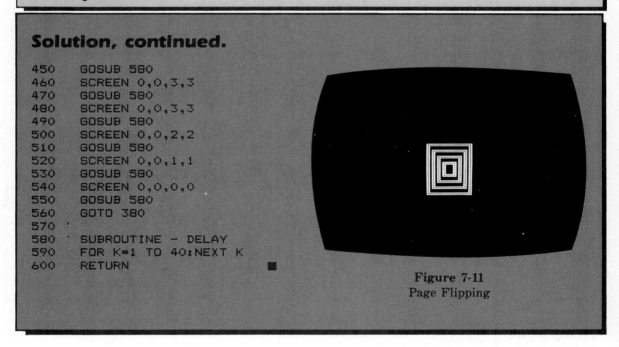

Figure 7-11
Page Flipping

Lines 120-360 contain a FOR loop that draws a different-sized box in each of the four pages of the screen. The index of the FOR loop is used to specify the page as well as the size of the box. You can see the boxes being drawn. This is not yet animation.

The rest of the program does the page flipping. See how fast the pages flip. In fact, we must introduce a delay to slow down the flipping so that we do not see double or triple images of the boxes.

## CONCLUSION

In this chapter, we have discussed character graphics and have investigated how characters are stored and generated in the various modes of the IBM PC. We have also seen how character graphics can be used in games and animation.

# SPECIAL PROGRAMMING ON THE COLOR/ GRAPHICS ADAPTER

# CONCEPTS

**Concepts**
6845 Video Controller Chip
Memory and I/O Ports
Video Timing

**Commands**
OUT
IN

**Applications**
Special Text and Graphics Modes

# INTRODUCTION

This chapter explores some deeper levels of your IBM PC. You will learn how to program the Motorola 6845 video controller chip, which lies at the heart of your Color/Graphics Adapter. You will see how to send the chip commands to create new text and graphics modes. You will also see how to program some bits that correspond to switch settings on the adapter board.

In previous chapters we have seen that it is possible to accomplish quite a bit with only the BASIC graphics commands for changing modes: SCREEN, WIDTH, and COLOR. In this chapter we show how even more is possible with special programming.

This special programming uses the OUT command in BASIC to send bytes to a special set of addresses housed in what is called the *I/O space* of the machine. Using this BASIC command will enable us to access the I/O space directly and thus program the Color/Graphics Adapter and the video chip that makes it run.

With this added control, we will show you how to do such things as squeeze the display, scroll it horizontally and vertically, and completely reformat it. We will also introduce you to some new, more colorful graphics modes.

# THE 6845 I/O PORTS

As we indicated in the introduction to this chapter, we will be communicating directly with the adapter board and its video chip through I/O ports. These ports are individual addressable 8-bit cells in the I/O space of the computer. The I/O space is like main memory only with a smaller range and with special, more limited ways to access it. Both memory cells and ports have bits that can be modified. However, not all bits in an I/O port need to be changeable. I/O ports are usually connected electronically to the I/O devices in your system rather than to any memory; thus, instead of storing a bit pattern in a cell, you are really sending bits to a device in your system. I/O ports help the programmer interface with such devices as printers, keyboards, communication lines, and video boards. To see which ports to use and what to put in them, you can browse through the *IBM PC Technical Reference* manual. The I/O devices in your system and the I/O locations (ports) that are hooked to them are described here.

On older 8-bit machines other than the IBM, there are only 256 I/O ports with addresses 0 through 255. With the newer 8088 16-bit microprocessor that the IBM PC uses, the I/O space has 65,536 ports. However, only a small number of these are actually used.

We will be interested in the seven I/O ports that are used to access the Color/Graphics Adapter. They are shown in Table 8-1. In Chapter 9, we will look at the ports that are

Table 8-1

Color/Graphics Adapter Ports

| Addresses (in hex) | Description |
| --- | --- |
| 3D0 | 6845 index register |
| 3D1 | 6845 data register |
| 3D8 | Mode control |
| 3D9 | Color select |
| 3DA | Status[*] |
| 3DB | Clear light pen[*] |
| 3DC | Preset light pen[*] |

[*]Not covered in this book

connected to the Monochrome Adapter. We will be interested in only four of the Color/Graphics Adapter ports—the ones that directly control modes and colors. Two of the other ports are used in conjunction with a light pen, which we will not use, and one other is used for status, which we will not need. Of the four ports we *will* use, two provide direct access to the Motorola 6845 video chip, and two are used to set certain bits on other parts of the adapter board.

# PROGRAMMING
# THE 6845 VIDEO CONTROLLER

The Motorola 6845 video chip acts as the "traffic manager" for the Color/Graphics Adapter. Its job is to provide the horizontal and vertical synchronization video signals and the digital addresses that scan through the video RAM as the picture is being displayed. The video chip also provides information for scanning through the rows of the dot matrix for each row of characters. The chip is designed by Motorola for display of text, but the clever IBM engineers have made it do double duty: displaying both text and graphics.

This video chip has 18 internal 8-bit memory cells called *registers*. These registers can be individually programmed (loaded with values that you specify). These registers hold such information as the number of bytes per line and the number of lines that are displayed on the screen. Fortunately, the computer automatically loads these registers for you upon start-up and whenever you change modes. However, we will see how to override these selections.

In Table 8-2, we show the two output port addresses that are used to do special programming of the 6845 video chip on the Color/Graphics Adapter. Through these ports we will send bits to all 18 internal registers of the 6845 video chip to change some timing parameters of that chip.

Now let's take a closer look at these two ports. Port 3D0 (hex) is called the index register. When you send a number between 0 and 17 to this port, you tell the chip which of the 18 internal registers of the 6845 you wish to access next. To make this selection, use the BASIC command

OUT &H3D0, number

**Table 8-2**

**Output Port Addresses for the 6845 Video Controller**

| Port address (in hex) | Name of register | Description |
| --- | --- | --- |
| 3D0 | Index | Selects internal register on the 6845 |
| 3D1 | Data | Holds data for the register selected with port 3D0 |

where *number* is a number from 0 to 17 (decimal) corresponding to one of the 18 registers. This command only "sets up" a communications channel or pathway. It does not in itself send any useful information to the chip or the board. You can think of it as opening the proper "door" to the desired internal register.

To send information, the previous command would then be followed by another command

OUT &H3D1, value

where *value* is the value that you want to send to the previously selected 6845 *internal* register. Note that the address in this case is the address of the data port. This command sends the value to the adapter where it goes into the 6845 internal register that you just selected with the previous OUT command.

Most of the internal registers are *write-only*, which means you can only send data to them. However, registers 12 through 17 are *read-write*, which means you can also read their internal values. To read the value of a register, put the number of the register on port 3D0 (hex) as we did before, and then give the command

IN &HD31, variable

The *variable* will then contain the value. Table 8-3 lists what these internal registers do.

The first four registers (0-3) control the horizontal timing and the next five registers (4-8) control the vertical timing. Before we start detailed discussions of each register, it is important for you to recall what was said in Chapter 1 about

**Table 8-3**

**6845 Internal Registers**

| Register number | Function | Initial Values 40-column text | 80-column text | Graphics |
|---|---|---|---|---|
| 0 | Horizontal time total | 56 | 113 | 56 |
| 1 | Horizontal bytes displayed | 40 | 80 | 40 |
| 2 | Horizontal synchronization position | 45 | 90 | 45 |
| 3 | Horizontal synchronization width | 10 | 10 | 10 |
| 4 | Vertical lines total | 31 | 31 | 127 |
| 5 | Vertical adjust | 6 | 6 | 6 |
| 6 | Vertical lines displayed | 25 | 25 | 100 |
| 7 | Vertical synchronization position | 28 | 28 | 112 |
| 8 | Interlace mode | 2 | 2 | 2 |
| 9 | Maximum scan line | 7 | 7 | 1 |
| 10 | Cursor start | 6 | 6 | 6 |
| 11 | Cursor end | 7 | 7 | 7 |
| 12* | Memory start address (high) | 0 | 0 | 0 |
| 13* | Memory start address (low) | 0 | 0 | 0 |
| 14* | Cursor address (high) | 0 | 0 | 0 |
| 15* | Cursor address (low) | 0 | 0 | 0 |
| 16* | Light pen (high) | | | |
| 17* | Light pen (low) | | | |

*Can be read from or written to

how a TV picture is generated. In particular, you should remember that the picture is generated by an electron beam traveling through a zigzag *raster scan* pattern on the face of the picture tube. This pattern consists of two hundred left-to-right *scan lines* that are swept out one by one as the beam moves from the top to the bottom of the screen. Each trip through the raster is called a *field*. With an interlaced display, two fields form a *frame* to make a complete picture.

At the beginning of each horizontal line and at the beginning of each field, the IBM PC sends special synchronization signals so that a TV or video monitor can correctly follow and then reproduce this raster pattern.

The first nine internal registers of the 6845 control the timing of the horizontal and vertical motions described here, including the timing of the synchronization signals. The parameters in these registers specify both the total time (including retrace time) and the time that the picture is actually being displayed. Fortunately, the parameters in these internal registers allow you to make the actual display time as small a part of the total as you need to ensure that the active part of the display will fall well within the visible part of the screen. Other registers can also be used to move the display to the left or to the right on the screen so that it is properly centered.

The ultimate timing of the signals put out by the video chip is based upon a special character clock signal that is supplied by the Color/Graphics Adapter on which the video chip is mounted. This timing signal oscillates at a frequency that depends upon the graphics or text mode that the board is set for. The frequency at which this signal oscillates is called the *character clock* frequency. We will see later how to set a certain bit that tells the board which of two possible frequencies to generate.

In the 80-column text mode, the character clock frequency is half the 3.579545 megahertz color subcarrier frequency described in Chapter 1. Thus, the character clock frequency is 1.7897725 megahertz in this mode. As a result, each color clock cycle takes about 279.4 nanoseconds (billionths of a second), and each character clock cycle takes about 559 nanoseconds. Thus, in this mode each character clock takes *two* color clock cycles. This means that there can be at most two color changes horizontally across each character in the 80-column mode if you use an ordinary NTSC color TV.

For all the other modes, the clock frequency is one-quarter the color subcarrier frequency, which means that for these modes each character clock takes *four* color clock cycles. This provides much better color resolution with four possible color changes horizontally across each character. We will use these numbers later to figure out how to program the 6845 video chip.

# INDIVIDUAL REGISTERS OF THE 6845

The 6845 internal registers are grouped into horizontal control, vertical control, internal control, cursor control, and memory scanning control. We start with the horizontal control registers. These control the timing of the individual scan lines of the display.

Our examples in this section require the TEXT program that is given in Example 2-1. It displays an uppercase "A" in 40-column text mode with all its possible attributes.

## Horizontal Registers

Register 0, *horizontal time total*, determines the total number of character clock cycles per horizontal line of the display. It actually contains one less than the total. This is because if we count from 0 to this number we will arrive at the desired total. Some of the 6845 registers work in this manner (counting from 0), and some contain the actual count. There is some inconsistency in the way these registers are designed. This is because they are set up in a way that is natural for the chip and not for those who have to program it.

This horizontal time total (register 0) determines the total time from when the beam starts one scan to when it starts the next scan line. This includes time that the beam is on for display as well as when it is off during overscan and retrace. For the 80-column text mode, the IBM PC automatically sets register 0 equal to 113, and thus the true total is 114. Since each character clock cycle in this mode is equal to two color clock cycles, each line will take 228 color clocks. This is almost, but not exactly, equal to the IEEE standard of 227.5 color clocks per line. But most monitors will forgive a discrepancy quite a bit larger; that is, they will adjust to produce a good picture even if the timing is not exactly the standard.

In the other modes, the IBM PC sets register 0 to the value of 56, which gives a true total of 57 character clocks per line. Since in these modes each character clock is worth four color clocks, each horizontal line contains 228 color clocks, the same as we just found for the 80-character text mode.

As an example of how you can program this register, type the following line at the end of the program from Example 2-1:

```
310    OUT &H3D0, 0 : OUT &H3D1, 55
```

You should see the display stretch a bit because a horizontal total smaller than the usual 56 is being used to cover the same size line on the screen. Thus, register 0 allows us to shrink and stretch the display. Looking closely at this line of code, you can see that register 0 is selected with the first OUT command (to the 6845 index port), and then the value 55 is loaded into that register (through the 6845 data port) with the second OUT command. Other values may make your screen unreadable.

Register 1, *horizontal bytes displayed*, determines the actual number of character positions or bytes of the video RAM that are displayed per line. This number must be less than the horizontal total discussed previously. For a striking example of how this register works, type in the following line at the end of the example right after the last line you just typed in:

```
320    OUT &H3D0, 1 : OUT &H3D1, 32
```

You will see the display suddenly squeeze itself, showing only 32 characters per line instead of the usual 40. You will see the blue border fill up the space left by the missing eight characters per line. Notice that this particular line of BASIC changes the mapping so that the first 32 characters map to the first line on the screen, the second 32 characters map to the second line, and so on. This is a key to producing new modes.

Register 2, *horizontal synchronization position*, is used to position the display horizontally. You can load almost any value between 1 and the horizontal time total into this register. However, some values may cause the display to disappear or become illegible. This depends somewhat upon your TV or monitor. For the 80-column text mode, the IBM PC automatically loads this register with the value 90, and for all other modes, it loads 45 into this register. You can think of the synchronization signal as following the time period in which the characters are displayed. This is just the opposite view of the usual one in which the horizontal synchronization signal is said to start the line. As a result, you should choose large values—between the value in register 1 and the value in register 2—for this parameter. To see how this register works, try adding the following lines to our modified example:

```
330    FOR I = 32 TO 46
340        OUT &H3D0, 3 : OUT &H3D1, I
350        FOR J = 1 TO 1000 : NEXT J
360    NEXT I
```

When you run this, you should see the display move horizontally across the screen. Here we use a range from 32 to 46 for the horizontal synchronization position. These should be "safe" positions that do not cause problems with the display. Notice that the FOR loop on line 350 (indexed by J) is used to slow down the program so that you can more easily study what happens.

Register 3, *horizontal synchronization width*, will not produce any interesting effects. It must be wide enough for the TV or monitor to detect and lock onto. In all modes, it is set to 10.

## Vertical Registers

Now we come to the vertical registers. These registers control the number of scan lines on the display and the number of scan lines per character.

Register 4, *vertical lines total*, controls the total number of lines per field (one full screen), including lines that are not seen because of vertical retrace time. Unlike register 0, which controls the horizontal time total, changing this register will probably not shrink or stretch your picture. Register 4 actually contains 1 less than the total number of rows of characters in a field. To get the number of scan lines in one field of the picture, we have to consider two other registers: register 9, which is called *maximum scan line*, and register 5, which is called *vertical adjust*. For the monitor to work properly, this total must be fairly close to what the monitor is adjusted to expect.

Register 9 determines the number of scan lines per character row and thus the maximum height of the characters in the text modes. Again, you have to add 1 to get the total number of scan lines per row of characters. Register 5 determines an extra number of scan lines to add to the screen to get the actual number of scan lines in one field. This is necessary because the number calculated by using just registers 4 and 9 is not precise enough.

The total number of scan lines per field is the total number of character rows times the total number of scan lines per row plus the vertical adjust. In terms of the contents of these registers, it is

$$((REG4+1)*(REG9+1))+(REG5)$$

where *REG4* is the contents of register 4, *REG9* the contents of register 9, and *REG5* is the contents of register 5.

Just using registers 4 and 9 will not allow you to select a value that is exact to the nearest integer. Thus, we need the vertical adjust register to give this precision. It is interesting to note that the IEEE standard specifies this number to be 262.5, which is a whole number plus *half* a scan line.

**Vertical Values in Text Modes.** In the text modes, register 4, vertical lines total, is set to 31 (one less than the actual value); register 9, maximum scan line, is set to 7 (again, one less than the total number); and register 5, vertical adjust, is set equal to 6. This gives a total of

$$(31+1)*(7+1) + 6 = 262$$

scan lines. Comparing this with the IEEE standard of 262.5 lines per field, we see that it is close, but not perfect.

**Vertical Values in Graphics Modes.** For the graphics modes, the situation is more complicated. Here we have rows of pixels instead of rows of characters. In these modes, the vertical lines total is set to 127, the maximum scan line is 1, and the vertical adjust is 6. The answer, however, comes out the same:

$$(127+1)*(1+1) + 6 = 262$$

The added complication lies in the fact that the maximum scan line is 1 so that there are exactly *two* scan lines per "character row" in graphics mode, that is, two rows of pixels per "character row."

You should keep in mind that the 6845 chip is designed for text display by Motorola but is being cleverly used by IBM to display graphics while in the graphics modes. Thus, the graphics mappings are achieved by using character mapping schemes to put the pixels on the screen. It turns out that in the graphics modes, for each "character row," the first scan line of dots is taken from the first half of the video RAM and the second line of dots is taken from the second half of the video RAM. Putting it another way, the video RAM is divided into two "banks" that are "interlaced" to make the whole picture.

You might wonder why such a complicated scheme was used in the graphics modes. The answer lies in the fact that the registers cannot hold numbers large enough to do this mapping in a more straightforward manner. For example, register 4, vertical total, is only 7 bits wide, and thus the highest number it can store is 127; and register 5, vertical adjust, is only 5 bits wide, and thus the maximum number it can store is 31. If we reduced the number of scan lines per character row to 1 (by setting register 9 to 0), we would not be able to reach a total of scan lines to any more than

$$127 + 31 = 158$$

scan lines per field. The monitor or TV would not be able to handle this; the picture would exhibit a severe case of "flips" (as if the vertical hold knob needed adjusting). You are welcome to experiment with these registers. You will find that your picture moves up or down or starts to flip depending upon how you set them.

**More Vertical Registers**

Register 6, *vertical lines displayed*, offers some interesting programming possibilities. With it we can make a picture gradually unroll before our eyes. It specifies the number of character rows that are actually displayed. In the text modes it is set to 25 for the 25 rows of characters in these modes, and in the graphics modes it is set to 100. Since each character row consists of two rows of pixels, we have the 200 rows of pixels for the graphics modes. Try adding the following lines to the modified example:

```
295     GOTO 400
400     FOR I = 0 TO 100
410        OUT &H3D0, 6 : OUT &H3D1, I
420        FOR J = 1 TO 10 : NEXT J
430     NEXT I
```

When you run this you will see the color pattern being drawn. Then the picture disappears with a possible flipping of the picture. It then starts to appear line by line from top to bottom.

Register 7, *vertical synchronization position*, can be used to align the picture vertically just as register 2, horizontal synchronization position, is used to align the position horizontally. Try various values for this register. We will use this register later to make a small adjustment in our new low-resolution mode.

Register 8, *interlace mode*, can be used to put the picture into three different configurations with regard to interlace.

Register 8 can accept four different values: 0, 1, 2, and 3 (shown in Table 8-4). Of these, the values 0 and 2 give the same result, which is a noninterlaced picture. This means that each field is identical, one field makes an entire frame, and thus the frame rate is doubled, drastically reducing

**Table 8-4**

**Interlace Modes**

| Code | Function |
|------|----------|
| 0 | Noninterlaced; fields repeat exactly |
| 1 | Interlaced; fields repeat but are displaced |
| 2 | Noninterlaced; fields repeat exactly |
| 3 | Interlaced; fields are different |

flicker. However, the picture has only half the number of scan lines as a fully interlaced display. This is the interlace mode used by all the IBM PC text and graphics modes. It is the only interlace mode that produces a clear picture on the IBM PC.

For the second interlace mode, the value 1 is loaded into register 8. This gives an interlaced display in which the two fields repeat the same information, first on the even lines for the first field and then on the odd lines for the second field. When this mode is selected on the IBM PC, the picture suffers a severe case of the jitters. We do not recommend this mode.

The third mode is when 3 is loaded into register 8. In this case, the display is interlaced and the alternate fields display different pictures. Here lines 0, 2, 4, 6, and so on, of a character are on even-numbered fields, and lines 1, 3, 5, 7, and so on, of a character are on odd-numbered fields. On a normal TV there will be quite a bit of flicker. However, the vertical resolution is twice as good. As we mentioned earlier, one way to reduce flicker is to use a long-persistence phosphor monitor. Many monochrome monitors are available with this feature. There are now long-persistence phosphors available for color monitors.

## 50-Line 80-Column Text Display

Let's see how we can use this fourth interlace mode to create a display with twice the usual vertical resolution. It will have to be in the text mode because there is not enough memory to support such a display in the graphics modes.

**EXAMPLE 8-1**

## 50-LINE TEXT MODE

Create a text display mode that has a 50-line format. Use
the full interlace mode. To demonstrate this format, fill
the screen with the letter "A." The output is shown in
Figure 8-1.

## Solution

```
100 ' INTERLACED TEXT
110 '
120 ' Displays text in interlaced
130 ' mode.
140 '
150    SCREEN 0,0
160    WIDTH 80
170    CLS
180    OUT &H3D0,8: OUT &H3D1,3
190 '
200    PRINT TAB(12);"INTERLACED TEXT"
210 '
220    DEF SEG = &HB800
230    FOR I = 3 TO 49
240     FOR J = 0 TO 79
250      POKE 160*I+2*J,65
260     NEXT J
270    NEXT I
280 '
290 '
```

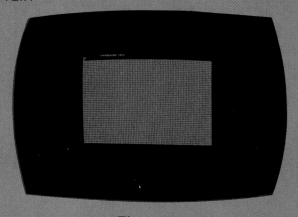

Figure 8-1
50-Line Text Mode

In this example, we first set the screen to text mode and
turn off the color with the SCREEN statement. The color is
turned off to make the display more readable. Next the

WIDTH statement is used to select the 80-character text mode. The screen is cleared with the CLS command.

Now comes the special programming. In line 180 we select register 8, interlace mode, and then place a 3 in it, thus specifying the fully interlaced mode that doubles the resolution vertically.

Next the PRINT statement puts the title on the top row of the screen. Then we fill 80 characters per row for rows 3 through 49 with the letter "A" by placing the ASCII code for that letter in every other memory location (the even-addressed ones) for the appropriate number of bytes of the video RAM. Recall that it takes two bytes to specify each character position. Notice that the DEF SEG command sets up the video RAM as the data segment for subsequent POKE commands into memory.

When the example runs you might notice flecks across the screen. These occur because of contentions between the central processor (the 8088) and the video display circuitry. They both want to access the video RAM at the same time. For the usual modes, the circuitry is designed to avoid this kind of contention by locking out the central processor at those key times when the bytes are needed by the display circuitry. However, when we use special programming we may not be in step with the timing that is designed to do this.

If you use an ordinary TV, you will also see quite a bit of flicker. It is also possible that there will be a certain amount of waviness in the picture. The letters may appear too small for you to read. IBM does not support this mode and so it has not tried to "tune" the adapter to work cleanly under these conditions. Further experimenting may lead to better production of this mode.

## Scrolling Register

The final set of internal registers we wish to examine are registers 12 and 13. These registers hold the memory address that corresponds to the beginning of the picture. This is called the *start address*. It is a 14-bit quantity that is a memory offset added to the beginning of the video RAM to get the starting scan address. The upper 6 bits are contained in register 12 and the lower 8 bits are contained in register 13. By placing different values into this register, you can make the display scroll up and down. Even more interesting effects can be produced.

EXAMPLE 8-2

## SCROLLING

Use the starting address parameter to cause scrolling in
the 40-character text mode. Add the following statements to
the TEXT program (Example 2-1). The output is shown in
Figure 8-2.

## Solution

```
310
320    FOR ROW =   0 TO 8
330       START = 80*ROW
340       STARTH = INT(START/256)
350       STARTL = START MOD 256
360       OUT &H3D0,12:OUT &H3D1,STARTH
370       OUT &H3D0,13:OUT &H3D1,STARTL
380       FOR J=1 TO 40:NEXT J
390    NEXT ROW
400    GOTO 320
```

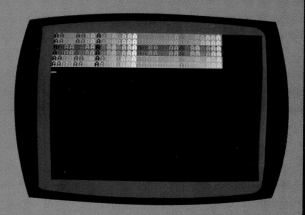

Figure 8-2
Scrolling

This section of code can be added to any program that
produces a display in the 40-character mode. Let's see what it

does and how it does it. When this section runs you will see the display repeatedly scroll up, each time starting from its original position.

Looking at the code you will see that the FOR loop is indexed by the variable ROW, which is the number of rows that the display is to be scrolled. Each row takes up 80 bytes, so we multiply ROW by 80 to get the starting scan address offset. Before we can send this to the registers, we must separate this number into its upper 6 bits and its lower 8 bits. This is done in lines 340 and 350. STARTH is the upper part and STARTL is the lower part. In lines 360 and 370 these are sent out to registers 12 and 13 respectively. Line 380 provides a short delay to slow down the scrolling so that you can more easily see it. Line 400 is a GOTO that loops this scrolling in an endless loop.

It is possible to increment the starting scan address by various amounts to get different kinds of effects. If we increment it by a couple of bytes each time, the display will appear to scroll to the left (and creep slowly upward). If we increment the starting scan address by a large amount, such as a whole screen worth of bytes, we will get page flipping, which is useful for animation. We explored the IBM PC's built-in page flipping in Chapter 7.

The other 6845 internal registers that are used for cursor and light pen control will not be discussed in this book.

# PROGRAMMING THE COLOR/GRAPHICS ADAPTER

Now let's discuss the bits that control various electronic switches on the board itself. Some of these bits are set by the SCREEN and COLOR commands as they do their mode setting, but we will see here how to set them directly. Table 8-5 shows the two ports that contain these bits. There are two types of these bits: *mode* bits, which determine the particular *mode* of the adapter (graphics versus text, or 40-column versus 80-column), and *color* bits, which determine background, border, and palette colors.

**Table 8-5**

**Output Port Addresses for the Color/Graphics Adapter**

| Port address (in hex) | Function |
|---|---|
| 3D8 | Graphics and text modes |
| 3D9 | Color of background, border, and palette |

Port 3D8 (hex) is connected to six important bits on the board. You can think of each of these bits as an ON/OFF switch that controls some particular circuit on the board. Table 8-6 shows these bits and their functions.

Each of these bits can be set whichever way you want. However, only certain combinations will occur in the four modes supplied by IBM. For example, in the $640 \times 200$ high-resolution black-and-white mode, bit 0 is always off for the slower timing, bit 1 is always on to select the graphics mapping, bit 2 is always on to select black-and-white mode, bit 3 is on so that you can see the picture, bit 4 is on to select the higher-resolution graphics mode, and bit 5 is set either way because it does not have any effect in the graphics modes.

Now let's examine these bits in more detail and try to see how they work.

Bit 0 controls the selection of two possible speeds for the character clock signal. We discussed earlier that this is fed

**Table 8-6**

**Mode Bits for the Color/Graphics Adapter**

| Bit | Function | Bit = 0 | Bit = 1 |
|---|---|---|---|
| 0 | Speed of character clock signal | Slow (40-column text or graphics) | Fast (80-column text) |
| 1 | Text or graphics mode | Text | Graphics |
| 2 | Color or black-and-white | Color | Black-and-white |
| 3 | Display picture | No picture | Normal picture |
| 4 | High- or low-resolution graphics | $320 \times 200$ medium-resolution | $640 \times 200$ high-resolution |
| 5 | Function of bit 7 in character attribute bytes | Blinking | Intensity |

into the 6845 video controller chip to provide a fixed *clock* for the operation of the chip as it sends out the bytes. It sends a regular sequence of electrical pulses into the chip through a pin called *CLOCK* and the timing of all signals coming out of this chip is in multiples of the pulses provided by this basic clock signal. For example, the horizontal synchronization signal produced by the 6845 on the Color/Graphics Adapter occurs as a multiple of the pulses of this clock, the exact number of which is determined by the contents of the internal register 0. A value of 1 in bit 0 of port 3D8 (hex) causes this character clock to oscillate at a fast speed for operation with the 80-column character text mode, while a value of 0 in this bit produces a slower speed, which is used with all other text and graphics modes. The particular frequencies for this clock were discussed earlier in this chapter.

Bit 1 controls the mapping of individual bytes from the video RAM onto the screen. You should understand that the 6845 video chip was designed only for display of text. Thus, the graphics modes are produced by a special design of the board that "fools" the chip into thinking it is displaying characters when it is really displaying graphics. In the text and graphics modes, the actual data bytes that make up the characters or graphics do not go through the video chip itself. The chip only produces the digital addressing information and the video synchronization signals, but no data signals. The board itself contains other logic that processes the data, grabbing it from the video RAM, converting it from digital on/off information to a standard video signal, and delivering it to the video output, as shown in Figure 8-3. This logic on the board can be set up so the *graphics serializer* grabs the data directly for the graphic modes (bit 1 = 1), or it can run the data through the *character ROM* (read-only memory), where the dot patterns for the characters are stored for the text modes (bit 1 = 0).

Let's look more carefully at how text is mapped to the screen. Assume that each character is housed in an 8 × 8 matrix; that is, each character occupies 8 pixels on 8 different scan lines (as shown in Figure 8-4). The 8-dot pattern for each scan line of each character is stored as a byte in character ROM. Thus, each of the 256 different characters requires 8 bytes of storage in this ROM, so the ROM must have a storage capacity of 2048 bytes.

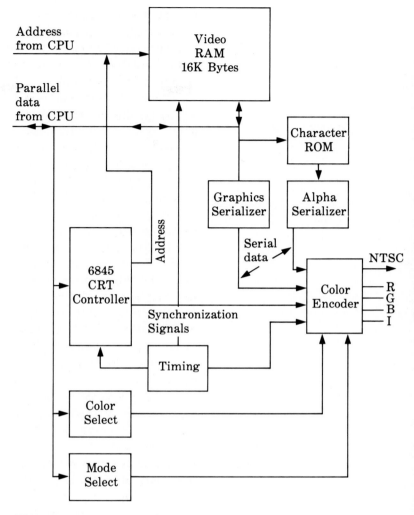

**Figure 8-3**

Block Diagram of Mapping Hardware

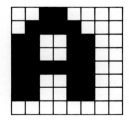

**Figure 8-4**

Character Dot Matrix

Now look at what happens when a scan line of the picture is displayed. This scan line consists of a certain line from the dot matrix of all the characters in a given row of text on the screen. The line is specified by a 3-bit number which ranges from 000 (0 decimal) for the top line to 111 (7 decimal) for the bottom line of the dot matrix for the characters. These 3 bits are output by the 6845 video chip.

As the beam traverses this scan line on the screen, the 6845 video chip scans through the video RAM where the

ASCII codes for these characters are stored. The 8-bit ASCII codes are combined with the 3-bit line number to give 11-bit numbers that are fed to the character ROM. This 11-bit number is just the right size to specify one of 2048 bytes, which is exactly how many bytes are stored in this ROM. Immediately after the 11-bit number is delivered to the ROM, it outputs the corresponding byte, which specifies the appropriate dot pattern. This byte is then sent to the alpha serializer that outputs the video signal dot-by-dot.

From this, you can see that graphics mapping schemes are potentially simpler than text mapping schemes because they are more direct. However, they may put a bigger strain on the system because there are normally more bytes fetched from memory during the same time period for a graphics display than for a text display.

Bit 2 controls the color. If no color is desired (a value of 1 in this register), no color subcarrier is produced, and there is no color burst signal at the beginning of each horizontal line.

Bit 3 is called the video enable bit. Putting a 0 in this bit will blank the whole picture. This might be a good idea in a program that changes graphics modes, especially if the picture tends to flash into strange patterns during such a change.

Bit 4 selects between a two-bits-per-pixel mapping and a one-bit-per-pixel mapping mode, and thus selects between the medium-resolution graphics mode and the high-resolution graphics mode.

In the two-bits-per-pixel mode, each byte is divided into four pairs of bits. Each pair maps to a single pixel on the screen, which can be any one of four colors depending upon how the two bits are set. If they are both 0, the dot appears with color 0, and so on.

In the one-bit-per-pixel mode, each of the eight bits in each byte maps to a different pixel on the screen, which can be either off or on depending upon whether the bit is 0 or 1.

Bit 5 selects how the attribute bytes work (blinking versus intensity). It is effective only in the text modes. For a dramatic demonstration of how it works, try typing the following lines at the end of the TEXT program (Example 2-1):

```
305    FOR I = 1 TO 1000 : NEXT I
310    OUT &H3D8, &H8
```

When you run this program, at first the right half of the displayed characters will blink on and off because the blink bit is on for these characters. Then the OUT statement will change the value of bit 5 from 1 to 0, and you will see the display suddenly change from its blinking mode to a constant, but more colorful display. The blink bit now functions as an intensity bit for the background. You will see that the background now shows all 16 possible color combinations.

Now that we have discussed all these mode bits, let's compare the roles of just two of these bits in combination, bits 1 and 4. The choice of modes is determined by these two bits. Bit 1 controls text versus graphics, and bit 4 controls the mapping of the bits to the pixels (one bit per pixel versus two bits per pixel). In other words, bit 1 controls the mapping of the *bytes* and bit 4 controls the mapping of the *bits* within the bytes. There are four possibilities:

1. Bit 1 equals 0 and bit 4 equals 0. This is the normal case for both text modes.
2. Bit 1 equals 0 and bit 4 equals 1. This combination is not used for any legitimate mode. We have examined the display and have found that it definitely uses byte mapping for text. However, on the bit level there are problems in that half the dots are missing.
3. Bit 1 equals 1 and bit 4 equals 0. This is the normal colorful medium-resolution graphics mode.
4. Bit 1 equals 1 and bit 4 equals 1. This is the black-and-white high-resolution graphics mode.

Table 8-7 summarizes in tabular form the bit settings within this port for the standard modes.

Table 8-7

**Bit Settings for Standard Modes**

| Columns | Text or Graphics | Color or Black-and-white | Bit 5 | Bit 4 | Bit 3 | Bit 2 | Bit 1 | Bit 0 |
|---|---|---|---|---|---|---|---|---|
| 40 | Text | Black-and-white | 1 | 0 | 1 | 1 | 0 | 0 |
| 40 | Text | Color | 1 | 0 | 1 | 0 | 0 | 0 |
| 80 | Text | Black-and-white | 1 | 0 | 1 | 1 | 0 | 1 |
| 80 | Text | Color | 1 | 0 | 1 | 0 | 0 | 1 |
| Medium-resolution | Graphics | Black-and-white | 0 | 0 | 1 | 1 | 1 | 0 |
| Medium-resolution | Graphics | Color | 0 | 0 | 1 | 0 | 1 | 0 |
| High-resolution | Graphics | Black-and-white | 0 | 1 | 1 | 1 | 1 | 0 |

**Table 8-8**

Color Bits in the Color Port

| Bit | Description |
|-----|-------------|
| 0-3 | Four-bit color of border (text) or background (graphics) |
| 4 | Intensity of background (text) |
| 5 | Selects palette 0 or 1 |
| 6-7 | Not used |

Before we can really control the machine, there is one more port that is of interest to us, port 3D9 (hex). It contains bits that set the border and background colors. There is also a bit that selects one of the two palettes used in the medium-resolution mode. Table 8-8 shows what these various color bits do.

Now let's experiment with all these registers, mode bits, and color bits to produce some colorful *new* modes. We should warn you, however, that modes other than the ones supported by IBM will have certain defects, like flecks or color problems. This is because the hardware has not been "tuned" to work under these conditions.

# NEW MODES

We will now show you how to design two new graphics modes for the Color/Graphics Adapter. Remember, these modes are not "real" graphics modes, but they show you some of the capabilities of your IBM PC.

## Special 16-Color, 80 × 100 Graphics Mode

The first mode we wish to produce is an 80 × 100 graphics type of mode with 16 colors for each pixel on the screen. We will set up the mode bits (port 3D8 (hex)) as follows:

Bit 0 = 1 (fast character clock)

Bit 1 = 0 (text)

Bit 2 = 0 (color)

Bit 3 = 1 (video signal enabled)

Bit 4 = 0 (usual text bit mapping)

Bit 5 = 0 (blink off)

Thus we will load the value 9 into port 3D8 (hex). We will also set the color bits (port 3D9 (hex)) as follows:

Bit 0 = 0

Bit 1 = 1 (border color = green)

Bit 2 = 0

Bit 3 = 0

Bit 4 = 0

Bit 5 = 0

Thus we will load the value 2 into port 3D9 (hex). This will make the border color green. We found that the natural choice, a black border (a value of 0), did not produce any color on our NTSC monitor.

The 6845 internal registers also need to be set up. We would like to have 80 character clocks per line. This implies that the horizontal values should be set the same as for the 80-column text mode, as shown in the following:

Register 0 = 113 (horizontal time total)

Register 1 = 80 (horizontal bytes displayed)

Register 2 = 90 (horizontal synchronization position)

Register 3 = 10 (horizontal synchronization width)

The vertical timing should have 100 lines of character rows, each of which consists of two scan lines. This is the same as the following graphics modes:

Register 4 = 127 (vertical lines total)

Register 5 =   6 (vertical adjust)

Register 6 = 100 (vertical lines displayed)

Register 7 = 106 (vertical synchronization position)

Register 8 =   0 (interlace mode)

Register 9 =   1 (maximum scan line)

We will leave the other registers alone.

Since we have a new mode, we need a new way of plotting points. Let's develop a subroutine to do this. The subroutine should use the x- and y-coordinates of any point to compute the memory position (in video RAM) for that point for our special mapping. First we develop a formula. Let $X$ be the variable that holds the x-coordinate and let $Y$ be the variable in charge of the y-coordinate. Now each point uses two bytes horizontally and each horizontal line uses 160 bytes. A quick calculation reveals the following formulas for the byte offset address for the two corresponding bytes:

Data byte:      $160*Y + 2*X$

Attribute byte: $160*Y + 2*X + 1$

We will actually use the second address, since it contains the coloring information (the attribute byte). If we use a space for all our character positions (ASCII code equal to 32), we can control the color of each position via its background color. If C is the desired color, then multiplying C by 16 will give the correct background color because the background color is stored in the upper four bits of the attribute byte.

Here is an example program that will display things in this new mode.

## EXAMPLE 8-3

### 80 X 100 16-COLOR MODE

Write a program that displays graphics in a new mode that is 80 pixels horizontal by 100 pixels vertical with 16 colors for each pixel. Write subroutines to initialize and clear the screen and to plot points given their x- and y-coordinates and color. Use these subroutines in a demonstration program that shows all 16 colors in a color bar and some diagonal lines to show the resolution. The new mode is shown in Figure 8-5.

---

## Solution

```
100  ' 80 by 100 graphics mode
110  '
120     GOTO 380 ' go to main program
130  '
140  ' subroutine - initialize & clear
150     SCREEN 1,1
160     WIDTH 80
170     SCREEN 0,1
180     KEY OFF
190  '
200     OUT &H3D0,4 : OUT &H3D1,127
210     OUT &H3D0,5 : OUT &H3D1,6
220     OUT &H3D0,6 : OUT &H3D1,100
230     OUT &H3D0,7 : OUT &H3D1,112
240     OUT &H3D0,8 : OUT &H3D1,0
250     OUT &H3D0,9 : OUT &H3D1,1
260     FOR J=1 TO 100:NEXT J
270     OUT &H3D9,2
280     FOR J=1 TO 10:NEXT J
290  '
300     DEF SEG = &HB800
310     RETURN
320  '
330  ' subroutine - plot a point
340     M = 160*Y + 2*X + 1
350     POKE M, 16*C
360     RETURN
370  '
380  ' main program
390  '
400     GOSUB 140 ' initialize & clear
```

▶

## Example 8-3

### Solution, continued.

```
410 '                                 620      GOSUB 330 ' plot (x,y)
420 ' set up some color bars          630    NEXT X
430   FOR C = 0 TO 15                  640 '
440     FOR X = 4*C+8 TO 4*C+11        650   C = 2
450       FOR Y = 10 TO 15
460         GOSUB 330 ' plot (x,y)
470       NEXT Y
480     NEXT X
490   NEXT C
500 '
510 ' draw some lines
520 '
530   C = 1
540   Y = 20
550   FOR X = 0 TO 79
560     GOSUB 330 ' plot (x,y)
570   NEXT X
580 '
590   C = 4
600   Y = 99
610   FOR X = 0 TO 79
```

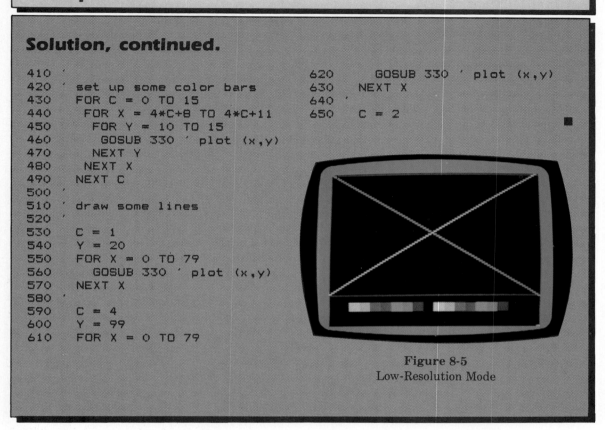

Figure 8-5
Low-Resolution Mode

Looking through this example in detail, we see that there are two subroutines and a main program.

The first subroutine (lines 150-310) initializes and clears the screen in our new mode. In detail, it sets up the mode to graphics, selects the 80-column width, and then sets the mode to text. Since there is a forced change of mode, the video RAM is cleared. Next the function keys are turned off with the KEY OFF statement.

Since we are in the 80-column text mode, all the horizontal timing parameters are set for our new mode. Thus, we only have to set the vertical timing parameters. These are set up as specified by the graphics modes, with the exception that the vertical synchronization is set to 112 to raise the picture because it was low.

Finally, the mode bits in port 3D8 (hex) are set to the value 9, and the color bits in port 3D9 (hex) are set to 2, as we indicated earlier.

The second subroutine (lines 340-360) plots points, given their x- and y-coordinates and their color. The algorithm was discussed previously.

The main program first draws a small square of each of the 16 possible colors. We call this the *color bar*. Next the program draws a series of horizontal and diagonal lines in different colors. Since there is no line plotting routine, it is all done with FOR loops that contain calls to the point plotting subroutine.

You will have to reboot your system after running this program since you cannot give any more commands. This example is only meant to show the possibilities of new modes.

## Other Special Graphics Modes

We have just shown how to create a new mode that has an 80 ×100 resolution with 16 colors. It is possible to modify this mode to create a mode with the same number of colors, but twice the horizontal resolution (that is, 160 × 100). This can be done by using an ASCII character for each character position whose symbol is half foreground and half background color. A search through the ASCII code table reveals that an ASCII value of 221 or 222 will do. Suppose we pick 222. For this case, the background color controls the left pixel and the foreground color controls the right pixel. With this choice, the attribute byte is used to color the two pixels contained in the corresponding character position. The upper nibble (upper four bits) controls the background, and hence the left pixel, and the lower nibble (lower four bits) controls the foreground and hence the right pixel. This makes the point plotter subroutine more complicated. When you plot any point you must make sure that you do not disturb its neighbors. This can be done with a little logic.

An algorithm for plotting in this mode should proceed as follows: First, you must use the PEEK command to move the appropriate byte of video RAM into a BASIC variable. Then you must strip off the old color value of the pixel by combining a certain pattern with the variable containing this byte with the AND operator. Next you must bring in the new color by combining the new value with the stripped byte using either AND or OR operator. Finally, the result of all of this must be placed back into memory with a POKE command. We leave the implementation of this to you.

Other modes can be created in other ways. For example, we could use the $320 \times 200$ medium-resolution graphics mode with a different point plotting function to get more colors with half the horizontal resolution (that is, $160 \times 200$ in 16 colors). This would depend upon using the peculiarities of NTSC video output and cannot be done with an RGB video output. The following lines show what the point plotter routine for this mode would look like:

```
200 ' subroutine - plot point
210   C1 = C/4
220   C2 = C MOD 4
230   PSET (2*X,Y),    C1
240   PSET (2*X+1,Y),  C2
250   RETURN
```

The input to this routine is given in the variables $X$, $Y$, and $C$. The first two variables hold the x- and y-coordinates of the point. Note that $X$ is supposed to range from 0 to 159, while Y ranges from 0 to 199. The third variable $C$ contains the color. It ranges from 0 to 15.

The algorithm behind this subroutine relies upon the fact that two medium-resolution pixels reside in one color clock position. The color that appears within that color clock position depends upon what colors are set for both of these medium-resolution pixels. There are 16 possibilities for each color clock position (one pixel in our new mode) since there are four possible colors for each of the two pixels that comprise it. The algorithm just takes a number in $C$, splits it into its lower two bits and upper two bits, and then plots these values in two adjacent medium-resolution pixels. The horizontal positions of these two pixels are just $2 \times X$ and $2 \times X+1$. You are welcome to type in this subroutine and make up your own program to test it out.

# CONCLUSION

In this chapter we explored ways to program the Color/Graphics Adapter and its video chip directly. We saw how to use OUT command to do this. Once we mapped out all the bits involved, we showed how to develop new modes. We saw that we could set certain parameters according to the way they are set for one mode and set certain other parameters according to other modes to get entirely new modes. In particular, we actually demonstrated the existence of a 16-color 80 × 100 graphics mode, and we explained two ways you could create 16-color 160 × 100 graphics modes.

# GRAPHICS ON
# THE MONOCHROME
# DISPLAY

# CONCEPTS

Concepts
   Design of the Monochrome Adapter
   Character Graphics

Commands
   PRINT
   LOCATE
   WIDTH
   COLOR

Applications
   Bar Charts
   Character Graphics Editor

# INTRODUCTION

This chapter explores making graphics on the IBM PC Monochrome Display Unit. We will see that although the Monochrome Adapter is more limited in its graphics capabilities than the Color/Graphics Adapter, it is well designed for putting images on the terminal—the job for which it was intended. In spite of the Monochrome Adapter's limitations, it can still produce very useful graphics.

We will look closely at this adapter and its display unit, comparing them with the Color/Graphics Adapter. You will see that the Monochrome Adapter has only one display mode, which is a high-density text mode with 80 characters horizontally by 25 characters vertically. This mode has special high definition in that each character sits in a $9 \times 14$ dot matrix.

We will show the similarity between this text mode and the text modes available on the Color/Graphics Adapter. You will see how to extend what we learned in Chapter 7 about text modes on the Color/Graphics Adapter to program the Monochrome Adapter effectively. You will learn how to take advantage of the Monochrome Adapter's special built-in graphics characters and how to use the character attributes to cause such effects as blinking, high intensity, and underlining.

Since the Monochrome Adapter can display only text, we will be limited to character graphics (see Chapter 7 for a discussion and explanation of this area of computer graphics). We will, however, show how to work within this limitation to produce graphics that will have particular use in the business world, such as bar charts and business forms. We will also discuss other applications, such as animated games.

## MONOCHROME EQUIPMENT

The IBM PC Monochrome Adapter and Display Unit are two separate pieces of equipment. The *adapter* is a printed circuit board that fits inside the IBM PC, and the *display unit* is a video monitor that connects to the Monochrome Adapter through a special cable. The Monochrome Adapter and Display Unit are designed to deliver a clear, crisp display of text suitable for word processing and computer terminal uses. The IBM engineers achieved this high-density, high-quality image in part by selecting an 80-column by 25-row display, in part by selecting a density dot matrix for the characters, in part by using a digital method of transmitting the video signal to the display, and in part by using a long-persistence phosphor on the display screen. The Monochrome Adapter and Display Unit do, however, have the disadvantage of not being compatible with standard video signals used in the United States. In this section we will explore these various ideas in detail.

**Screen Display Format**

The Monochrome Adapter's display format of 80 columns and 25 rows of characters is important for the uses for which it was designed. This size is the current standard for display devices for today's computer systems. On larger systems (minicomputers and mainframes) these displays are handled by CRT terminals. Since the IBM PC is a modern, self-contained computer system, it needs the built-in equivalent of a CRT terminal. Both the Color/Graphics Adapter (with a monitor) and the Monochrome Adapter and Display Unit can supply this essential function. However, the Monochrome Adapter looks and performs more like a traditional computer terminal, while the Color/Graphics Adapter looks and performs more like the display device of many other personal computers. In this regard, the 80-column, green phosphor display of the Monochrome Display provides a more traditional environment for systems development (editors, debuggers, and so on), business applications (data base management), and word processing.

Users of the first generation of personal computers were not so fortunate. Most of these early users were stuck with displays that had 64 columns and 16 rows of characters, producing cramped results with excessive wraparound. In these cases, there were often logical lines generated by the computer that were too long for the screen and hence had to be awkwardly broken into two or more physical lines on the screen.

A particular area in which output to a terminal is extremely critical is text editing. Perhaps more computer time is spent in editing textual information than in any other task. This comes about because of the inefficient manner in which people produce information in comparison to what machines can do, and because a large portion of computer input is textual. Of course, once speech recognition is working effectively, the situation may turn around.

An 8 1/2 × 11-inch sheet of paper usually corresponds to 80 columns by 60 rows of text. Most applications use less than this to give adequate room for margins. Very often 72 columns by 55 rows of text will actually be printed. Thus, in the horizontal direction, the IBM Monochrome Display and the Color/Graphics Adapter (in high-resolution text mode) are both well-suited to handle 8 1/2-inch wide text formats. In the vertical direction, however, there are severe limitations. The standard 25 display lines cannot show even half a page of text. The IBM display is not alone in this regard, for very few computer displays can do better. Perhaps future standards will have 60 or more lines of text. When this happens, we will be able to work with documents page by page rather than several lines at a time as on the IBM PC. This will allow us to produce documents that look better and read better.

We have shown you in Chapter 8 how to produce a 50-line display on the Color/Graphics Adapter. However, the results were not very readable because the characters were too short vertically in comparison to their width horizontally. This means they had the wrong aspect ratio. A 60-line display would produce an even worse aspect ratio. Some manufacturers and indeed some owners of personal computers have managed to turn the screen on its side and make the text go across the *narrow direction* to achieve a much better aspect ratio. Meanwhile, IBM's decision to have 25 rows of characters keeps the cost of the system down and the readability of the text on the screen up.

**Character Display Format**

The IBM PC Monochrome Adapter Unit uses a $9 \times 14$ dot matrix for each character. Such a dense dot matrix provides the possibility of adding detail to each symbol on the screen, and it also allows a great deal of flexibility in adjusting the relative placement of characters. Both of these factors make the screen easier to read and character graphics easier to design.

You should understand that most characters do not use the entire $9 \times 14$ dot matrix. For example, each capital letter occupies a $7 \times 9$ dot matrix that sits inside the total $9 \times 14$ matrix (shown in Figure 9-1). The smaller $7 \times 9$ matrix does not include the leftmost and rightmost columns of the larger matrix, and it also does not include the upper two rows and bottom three rows of the larger matrix. This means that there will always be at least two dot positions horizontally and five dot positions vertically between capital letters. Most of the lowercase letters fit within this smaller matrix, but some, like "g," "p," and "q," descend two rows below, reaching the next-to-bottom row of the full matrix. Thus, in a mixture of upper- and lowercase letters, there will always be at least three dot positions vertically between letters.

There are some symbols, like the caret ($\wedge$), that reach the very top row, and there are block characters that fill the entire dot matrix. There are also some special graphics symbols for drawing single and double lines and corners; some of them reach the bottom row, some reach the very top row, some reach the leftmost column, and some reach the rightmost column. These symbols are of special interest to us

**Figure 9-1**

Upper- and Lowercase Letters on the
Monochrome Unit

because they form building blocks for graphics. We will discuss them in more detail later.

It is interesting to compare the characters available on the Color/Graphics display with those displayed on the Monochrome Display. *The same set of characters is displayed on both devices;* however, they look quite different because the dot matrix representations for any given character differ significantly between the two adapters. The character tables in the *IBM BASIC Reference* manual and the *Technical Reference* manual work for both adapters in spite of this difference. The tables give only the extended ASCII code for each screen character together with an equivalent *typeset* character, which does not correspond exactly to the dot matrix for the character on either adapter.

On the Color/Graphics Adapter each character position has an $8 \times 8$ dot matrix. However, each capital letter is contained in a smaller $7 \times 7$ dot matrix that consists of the upper 7 rows and the 7 leftmost columns of the total matrix (shown in Figure 9-2). As a result, capital letters on this display are separated at most by only *one* dot position horizontally and one dot position vertically. Lowercase letters, such as "g" and "p," descend to the bottom row of the total dot matrix and in this way can merge into an upper- or lowercase letter on the line below. Because of the smaller dot matrix for all charac-

**Figure 9-2**

Capital A on the Color/Graphics
8 × 8 Dot Matrix

ters and the merging of some characters, text on the color
display is definitely harder to read. This only points out how
the Monochrome Display is better suited for the display of
pure text.

**Video Timing**

When you use the Monochrome Adapter, you cannot substitute an ordinary TV or TV monitor for the Monochrome
Display Unit. Likewise, you cannot use the Monochrome Display Unit as a monitor for the standard video signals produced by ordinary television broadcasts, for the Color/Graph-
ics Adapter, or for many other personal computers. The main
reason for this incompatibility is a difference in timing
between the video signals.

The whole issue of video timing on the IBM PC can be
understood in terms of the frequency at which dots, character
lines, screen lines, and the whole screen are generated. Let's
start with dots. For the Monochrome Adapter, the dots that
make up the characters are generated at a rate of 16,257,000
per second. In the language of electrical engineers, that is
16.257 megahertz. This frequency is called the *dot clock frequency*. On the high-resolution text mode of the Color/Graph-
ics Adapter, the dot clock frequency runs at a slightly slower

rate of 14,318,180 dots per second. It is interesting to consider that these rates are several times the speed at which the CPU operates. Finely tuned crystals on the adapter boards generate and precisely maintain these high dot frequencies. To get the sharpest possible image, your TV or video monitor must be able to handle video signals consisting of square waves at such frequencies.

Monitors are rated according to the highest dot frequency they can handle. This is called their *bandwidth*. The Monochrome Display is rated for a 16-megahertz bandwidth, which works fine with the 16.257-megahertz dot clock frequency produced by the Monochrome Adapter. If a monitor is not able to handle dot clock frequencies that are fed to it, the resulting image will be somewhat blurred. The same would happen if you could use an ordinary TV with the Monochrome Adapter. TVs are not designed to handle such high frequencies because they have bandwidths of 4 megahertz at most and thus are not as suitable for high-resolution displays as the Monochrome Display Unit. There are, however, other video monitors that do as well as or better than the Monochrome Adapter. We should warn you that there are some subtle nuances to understanding these ratings, so manufacturers of video monitors are now advertising the horizontal resolution of their equipment.

All the other timing signals on the adapter can be derived from the dot clock. For example, on the Monochrome Adapter each line of the dot matrix of a character position contains 9 dots; thus, the adapter generates these individual character lines of the dot matrix at a rate of 16,257,000 divided by 9, or 1,806,333 lines per second. This is called the *character clock frequency*. This frequency is fed into the Motorola 6845 video chip on the adapter through its clock input, providing a basis for all its timing signals. This character clock frequency is the frequency at which the video chip has to fetch new 9-bit words from the character ROM. Both the character ROM and the video chip must be able to work at this speed—a reasonable requirement for such circuitry in today's microcomputers. If we had to operate this type of equipment at the original dot clock frequency, we would have to pay considerably more money.

Let's examine some of the other frequencies in the Adapter. Consider the *horizontal frequency*, the number of screen lines per second. On the Monochrome Adapter, the 6845 video chip is programmed to display 80 characters per line, but it has to be told to allow for a total time of 98 characters per line. The extra time is needed for overscanning and horizontal retrace (shown graphically in Figure 9-3). Both the characters displayed per line (80) and the total characters per line (98) have to be conveyed to the 6845 chip by loading its internal registers. With 98 character lines in each screen line, we divide the character clock frequency by 98 to get a horizontal frequency of about 18,432 screen lines per second. The Monochrome Display Unit is set up to expect this number as its horizontal frequency for display. On the other hand, ordinary televisions and video monitors in the United States are designed to accept a horizontal frequency of about 15,734 lines per second.

Now we look at the *frame rate*. The Monochrome Adapter displays 25 rows of characters, and each character row contains 14 screen lines. Thus 350 lines need to be displayed on the screen. However, another 20 lines are needed for vertical retrace, yielding a total of 370 lines per screen with only 350 visible. These values have to be conveyed to the video chip by loading them into certain of its internal registers. Dividing

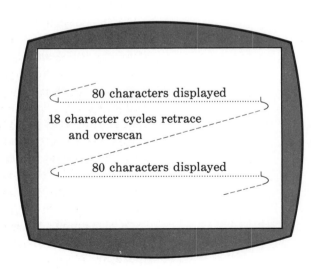

**Figure 9-3**

Displaying 80 Characters per Line
with Retrace

the horizontal frequency (18,432 lines per second) by 370 gives 49.82 screens (frames) per second. This is sometimes called the *refresh rate*. Our calculations give a refresh rate of almost 50 frames per second, nearly that specified in the IBM manuals. Most monitors and TVs in the United States will not accept a video signal with this slower refresh rate. However, 50 cycles per second is the standard frequency for European TVs. Since many companies that make video equipment for sale in the United States also make versions of such equipment for Europe, monitors tuned for this lower frequency should be available by special request from many sources other than IBM.

## Digital Versus Analog

There is also a difference in the way that the video signals are sent from the Monochrome Adapter through the connectors and cable to the Monochrome Display Unit. An ordinary television signal can be carried over one wire (with a ground wire for return). This signal has a range of voltages and thus may be considered an analog signal. In contrast, the video signals for the Monochrome Unit are carried over a collection of wires in digital form. These wires carry the basic video signal that turns the electron beam on and off as it scans the screen, and in addition, signals that control vertical synchronization, horizontal synchronization, and highlighting. There are also a couple of ground lines.

A digital format for these lines means that each signal line alternates between two voltage levels. These levels correspond to the yes/no logic inside the computer as it scans through a picture that has been stored as digital information in the computer's memory. Incidentally, these two voltage levels are the same as are used inside the IBM PC (and a lot of other computers as well) and are sent "as is" from the Adapter to the Display Unit.

The digital method of transmission has a number of advantages that help produce the best possible picture. First, each part of the total signal is carried separately. This is because the parts have to be separated eventually to operate the various components inside the monitor. The processes of combining the separate parts of the signal in the Adapter and then separating them in the Display Unit would cause a loss of information in transmission and thus a loss of definition (an increase in fuzziness) in the resulting picture. In general, it is best to have as few steps as possible in processing information because each *internal* step can introduce errors or noise that degrade the final results.

Another advantage to the digital method is the reduction of noise from *external* sources as the signal travels from the Monochrome Adapter to the Display Unit. With the digital method, only "pure" information is transmitted over the cable to the Display Unit. Because it is encoded in electrical signals alternating between two voltages, any extraneous signals that creep in should affect the voltages only slightly — not enough to change any of the digital information carried by these voltages.

It is interesting to note the tremendous similarity between the wiring of the video output produced by the Monochrome Adapter and the output produced by the RGB of the Color/ Graphics Adapter. In fact, if you look closely at the back of the IBM PC, you will see that the same type of 9-pin D shell connector is used for both of these adapters. This similarity is not just superficial; it extends to the way the parts of the video signal are assigned to the various pins on the connectors. For both adapters, the video signals are transmitted in digital form over a collection of signal lines, and most of these signals are carried over the same wires on both adapters. For example, on both adapters, pins 1 and 2 are ground, pin 6 carries highlighting information, pin 8 carries the horizontal synchronization, and pin 9 carries the vertical synchronization. However, the basic monochrome video signal from the Monochrome Adapter is carried over pin 7, which is not used by the Color/Graphics Adapter, while the three separate red, green, and blue (RGB) signals from the Color/Graphics Adapter are carried over pins 3, 4, and 5, which are not used by the Monochrome Display (but are produced by the Monochrome Adapter). Thus, even though you can physically plug the Monochrome Display Unit into the output of the Color/ Graphics Adapter without causing any sparks to fly, such an arrangement will not produce any picture. This pseudo-compatibility has many advantages: easier and less costly testing, as well as the prevention of catastrophes when absent-minded technicians plug in the wrong device.

**The Phosphor**

The choice of long-persistence phosphor on the CRT screen of the Monochrome Display Unit is important. With such a phosphor, light remains for a longer time after the phosphor is energized by the electron beam that draws the picture on the face of the tube. This is important since the picture is "refreshed" only so often (50 times a second on the Monochrome Display Unit). Since the phosphor dots that make up the picture are energized only so often, the amount of energy that is fed to each bright dot on the screen is actually rapidly oscillating in intensity. If an ordinary phosphor is used on the screen, the amount of light put out by a bright dot will also rapidly oscillate. If this oscillation is fast enough, it is not perceived and the picture appears to be steady. If the oscillation is too slow, the picture will appear to flicker. Even if the oscillation is fast enough to give the illusion of steadiness, this oscillation in light levels is still present and can fatigue your eyes. Using a long-persistence phosphor smoothes this oscillation because, with such a phosphor, light is produced for a longer time after the phosphor is energized. Thus each dot continues to produce light even when it is not being directly energized by the beam. The result is a very even, steady picture that will cause less strain on the user's eyes.

In the next section we will look further into the details of operation of the Monochrome Adapter, investigating how to program its single text mode.

# PROGRAMMING THE MONOCHROME UNIT

Before discussing how to program the Monochrome Adapter we should say a few words about switching back and forth between the two displays.

## Switching Between the Two Adapters

To switch between adapters you must have both adapters installed. The secret to doing this lies in a certain byte of memory used by BASICA and the operating system to store the switch settings that you have set for your monitors and other pieces of equipment, such as disk drives and memory. This byte is located in segment 0 at offset 410 (hex). Bits 4 and 5 of this byte specify the type of monitor, as shown in Table 9-1.

IBM supplies programs to switch between these two monitors, but you can do this yourself with your own program or just with a few BASIC commands. Starting with the Mono-

**Table 9-1**

Switch Settings for Monitors

| Type of monitor | Bit 5 | Bit 4 |
|---|---|---|
| None | 0 | 0 |
| Color/Graphics Adapter with low-resolution monitor | 1 | 0 |
| Color/Graphics Adapter with high-resolution monitor | 0 | 1 |
| Monochrome Adapter *or* both adapters | 1 | 1 |

chrome Adapter as the current display device, enter the following:

```
DEF SEG=0
X=PEEK(&H410)
POKE &H410,(X AND &HCF) OR &H10
```

The first line sets BASICA's data segment so that it starts at 0. This is where the system parameters are located, including the system's copy of the equipment byte. The second line picks up this byte, and the third line computes and puts back a new value into the same location. The new value is computed using some logic. First the old byte is combined with a bit pattern 11001111 (written as &HCF) with the AND function. This clears the two bits (4 and 5) that control the monitor settings. Next the result is combined with the bit pattern 00010000 (written as &H10) with the OR function. This inserts a new value for these bits into the byte.

At this point your cursor should be showing on the Monochrome Display, but anything you type should be on the Color/Graphics Adapter's display. Bits 5 and 4 of the equipment byte say you have the Color/Graphics Adapter with a low-resolution monitor, but the change is not complete. Now type

SCREEN 1

At this point the computer system sets the medium-resolution graphics mode on the Color/Graphics Adapter and you see your cursor in this mode on the Color/Graphics Adapter. If you now type

    SCREEN 0

you will go into text mode, but you will see no cursor. To get the proper cursor, type

    LOCATE ,,1,6,7

This turns on the cursor and places it at the bottom two rows of the dot matrix in which it resides.

If you now want to go back to the Monochrome Display, type

    DEF SEG=0 (if SEG has been changed)
    X=PEEK(&H410)
    POKE &H410, (X OR &H30)
    SCREEN 1
    SCREEN 0
    WIDTH 80
    LOCATE ,,1,12,13

Here we set both bits 4 and 5 to 1, change the mode (with the two SCREEN commands), set the width to 80, which is the proper size for the Monochrome Adapter, and set the cursor for the Monochrome Display Unit.

## The Programmer's Model

As with the Color/Graphics Adapter, you may program the Monochrome Adapter in a number of ways. It is convenient to view these ways in terms of *levels* of programming. At the highest level is what you can do with the BASICA statements PRINT, LOCATE, COLOR, and WIDTH. At this level the programmer does not have to understand the internal details of how the adapter works—just what it is capable of doing under the action of these commands. This understanding is called the *programmer's model* of the machine. Lower levels of programming require more knowledge of the equipment by the programmer, and hence they have a more complicated programmer's model. These lower levels use the POKE command to change the contents of the screen memory directly and use the OUT command to modify registers on the adapter and the internal registers of the Motorola 6845 video chip.

For the Monochrome Adapter, a programmer's model includes the fact that each character position on the 80-column by 25-row screen corresponds to a unique pair of memory cells that controls what appears in that particular character position. Physically, all these memory cells are located on the Monochrome Adapter and are "mapped" as part of main memory. A high-level programmer does not have to know this, but lower-level programmers do have to understand more about how this works.

The programmer's model at any level should also include some memory cells that store information about the cursor such as its location and its shape. Physically, these cells are inside the Motorola 6845 video chip, but again, a high-level programmer does not have to know exactly where these cells are located.

It is helpful to realize there is a strong similarity between the way the Monochrome Adapter works in this regard and the way the high-resolution text mode is set up on the Color/Graphics Adapter. The programmer's model for both machines is quite similar. In particular, the screen is the same dimension in both cases, and there is an ASCII code memory cell and an attribute memory cell for each character position on the screen. As we observed, the same ASCII codes work on both adapters but with slightly different dot patterns resulting on the screen. In both cases, we also have attributes called foreground, background, and blink. However, attributes work differently from one adapter to another. Instead of controlling background and foreground colors, as on the Color/Graphics Adapter, the attribute cells on the Monochrome Adapter control underlining, highlighting, blinking, and reverse video for the character positions. We will look at this more closely when we examine the COLOR statement.

Next we will look at the PRINT, COLOR, LOCATE, and WIDTH statements and how these commands are used to control our programmer's model of the Monochrome Adapter.

**High-Level Programming**

If we restrict ourselves to using just the PRINT, COLOR, LOCATE, and WIDTH commands while using the Monochrome Adapter, we will do high-level programming. We start with a few brief comments about the PRINT command.

**PRINT Command.** We will not need to discuss the PRINT command in much detail because it has been explained in Chapter 6 and is a standard part of BASIC. It suffices to say that the PRINT command allows us to print messages and numerical values on the screen according to a set of rules that is standard to most BASICs and that it has the usual syntax. The only unusual aspect might be the size of the print fields—the same as for the Color/Graphics Adapter.

**COLOR Command.** The COLOR command controls the attributes for all characters that are printed by subsequent PRINT statements. The current attributes stay in one setting until the next COLOR statement. Characters that have already been printed do not suddenly change attributes when a new COLOR statement is executed.

When used with the Monochrome Adapter, the full syntax for the COLOR statement is

COLOR [totalforeground][,background]

where *totalforeground* is given by

totalforeground = foreground + 16 * blink

The quantities *foreground*, *blink*, and *background* are described in detail below.

Notice that we have omitted the third parameter, *bordercolor*, from this command. This is because bordercolor has no effect on the Monochrome Adapter.

For each character position on the Monochrome Adapter, there are three attributes that are stored in different parts of its attribute memory cell. These attributes are called *foreground*, *blink*, and *background*, the same as they are on the Color/Graphics Adapter. However, they do quite different things and follow somewhat complex rules as they interact with each other. The various combinations of *foreground* and *background* are described in Table 9-2.

The first attribute for the Monochrome Adapter is called *foreground*; it controls both the foreground intensity and whether or not the character is underlined. It ranges from 0 to 15, but only a few of these values produce different results.

The second attribute is called *background*. It ranges from 0 to 7, and it controls whether or not the symbol is reversed, but only if the foreground color is 0 or 8.

The third attribute is called *blink*. It controls whether or

# Table 9-2

Foreground and Background Attributes

| | | Foreground | | | | | |
|---|---|---|---|---|---|---|---|
| | | 0 | 1 | 2 → 7 | 8 | 9 | 10 → 15 |
| | 0 | Off | Underlined and normal intensity | | Off | Underlined and high intensity | |
| Background | 1<br>↓<br>6 | Normal intensity | | Normal intensity | High intensity | | High intensity |
| | 7 | Reversed and normal intensity | | | Reversed and normal intensity | | |

not the character blinks. In the COLOR statement, this attribute is combined with the first according to the formula given in conjunction with the syntax for the COLOR command.

To see exactly what happens in each case for the COLOR command, run the TEXT program from Example 2-2 on the Monochrome Adapter. You should see 8 rows of characters, one for each possible value for the background, ranging from 0 for the top row to 7 for the bottom row (as in Figure 9-4). There are 32 columns, one for each possible value for the total foreground, ranging from 0 for the leftmost column to 31 for the rightmost column. You should look closely at rows 0 and 7, which contain the key values for the background. You should also look at columns 0 and 8, which correspond to the foreground "colors" that allow the background to do its best job.

**LOCATE Command.** The LOCATE command is used to control both the shape and the position of the cursor. Its full syntax is

LOCATE [row][,[column][,[cursor][,[start][,stop]]]]

where the parameters *row* and *column* act the same as with

**Figure 9-4**

Example 2-2 on the Monochrome Unit

the Color/Graphics Adapter. The *cursor* parameter specifies whether or not the cursor is visible or invisible (0=invisible and 1=visible). The fourth and fifth parameters, *start* and *stop*, specify the size and shape of the cursor. Because there are 14 lines in the dot matrix for a character position on the Monochrome Adapter, the values for *start* and *stop* can range from 0 to 13. Within the character position where the cursor is located, the cursor will consist of those rows of the dot matrix starting with the one specified by *start* and ending on the one specified by *stop*. Examples for how this works on the Color/Graphics Adapter can be found in Chapter 6. Why don't you try some of these possibilities on the Monochrome Adapter? Modify them so that the values range from 0 to 13 instead of from 0 to 7. For example, try *start*=0 and *stop*=13.

**WIDTH Command.**  The WIDTH command can be used to control the line length of the display. However, instead of doubling and halving the width of the characters at the same time, it forces the PRINT statement to use either the full width of the screen (with WIDTH 80) or half the screen (with WIDTH 40). Try typing

WIDTH 40

**Figure 9-5**

Monochrome 40-Column Display

**Figure 9-6**

Monochrome 80-Column Display

and then displaying the disk directory. There should be only three entries per line occupying only the left half of the screen, as shown in Figure 9-5. Now type

WIDTH 80

and again display the disk directory. This time there should be six entries per line, occupying the full width of the screen, as shown in Figure 9-6.

These are the only commands you need to do all sorts of

graphics with the Monochrome Adapter. Much of the power of these commands stems from the regular and graphics characters available with IBM's extended ASCII code.

## Special Programming

If you are interested in special programming, you will have to understand how the memory is "mapped" for the Monochrome Adapter and how the internal registers of the 6845 video chip are set up. That is, you will have to add these internal details to your programmer's model of the Monochrome Adapter. Fortunately, there is a tremendous similarity between how these details work on the Monochrome Adapter and on the Color/Graphics Adapter.

**Memory Map.** The only difference between the memory mappings of the two adapters is the base address for the video memory. Otherwise, they are both organized in a linear fashion with bytes for ASCII code alternating with bytes for attributes.

As we saw in earlier chapters, the Color/Graphics Adapter's screen memory is contained in the segment whose address number is B800 (hex). This has a base or starting address of B8000 (hex). The Monochrome Adapter's screen memory is contained in the segment whose address number is B000 (hex). This has a base or starting address of B0000 (hex). For PEEKs and POKEs to work right you must tell BASICA about this. To do this, use the command

DEF SEG=&HB800

in BASIC before directly accessing the Color/Graphics screen, and

DEF SEG=&HB000

before directly accessing the Monochrome screen.

The character positions are mapped from the screen memory, starting with the "home" position (upper-left corner of the screen) and continuing across each row, row by row, until reaching the bottom of the screen, as shown in Figure 9-7. Mapping the characters to the screen is the same as discussed in Chapter 2.

If you know the foreground, background, and blink bit attributes for a character position, you can compute its attributes byte with the following formula:

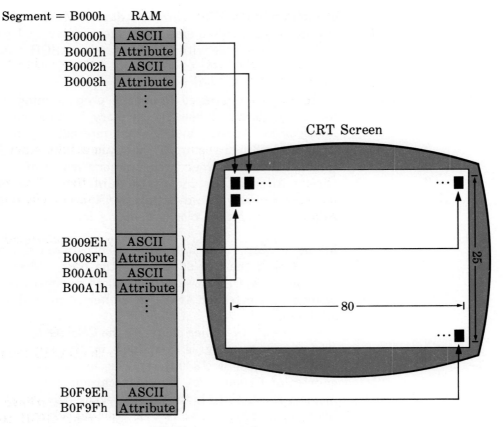

**Figure 9-7**

Memory Map for the Monochrome
Adapter

$$ATTRIBUTES = 128*(blink) + 16*(background) + foreground$$

Notice that the *foreground* is not the *totalforeground;* that is, it does not contain the *blink bit* as before in the COLOR command. The blink bit is handled separately.

We can put each character code and attribute into place with the POKE command and equations in Chapter 2. We can also look at each character code or attributes byte with the PEEK command. Just to make sure that we understand this, let's try the following example: put an "X" in the middle of the second row. We first determine the row and column:

ROW = 2

COLUMN = 40

Now compute the offset:

$$\text{OFFSET} = 160*(2-1) + 2*(40-1) = 238$$

Now look up the ASCII code for "X." It is 88. Put this into memory with the BASIC commands

DEF SEG=&HB000

POKE 238, 88

You should now see the letter "X" on the screen in the middle of the second row.

Now let's change the attributes of the "X" to make it underlined with high intensity and blinking. The attributes are

*foreground* = 9     (High intensity and underlined)

*background* = 0     (Not reversed)

*blink* = 1     (Blinking)

Then compute the attribute byte.

$$\text{ATTRIBUTES} = 128*(1) + 16*(0) + 9 = 137$$

Now put this into the next byte with the BASIC command

POKE 239, 137

You should now see the letter become underlined, more intense, and begin to blink. Try different ASCII codes in location 199 to get different symbols on the screen; and try different attributes bytes in location 200 to get different appearances for the symbols.

Sometimes it is necessary to use this method of POKE commands to put characters on the screen. For example, suppose you want to display the symbols for ASCII codes in the ranges 7 to 13 and 28 to 31. If you merely print these characters (using PRINT with CHR$), the codes will be treated by BASICA as bell, cursor, and carriage control codes and not sent directly to the screen. For example, Table C of the *IBM Technical Reference* manual says that ASCII code 7 corresponds to a circular dot, but if we try to reproduce it by giving the command

PRINT CHR$(7)

we will get a "beep" (the PC's bell). To produce the dot, you must give the command

POKE 238, 7

and a dot symbol will appear on the screen.

**Setting Mode Bits.**   Like the Color/Graphics Adapter, there are certain bits that can be set on the Monochrome Adapter board in addition to the internal registers of the Motorola 6845 video chip on the adapter board. On the Monochrome Adapter, there are only three bits on the board itself that you can set. These are the *high-resolution, video enable*, and *enable blink* bits. All three are accessed through output port 3B8 (hex). The high-resolution bit (bit 0) must always be 1. The video enable bit (bit 3) determines whether or not the video signal is being sent to the display unit. A value of 0 turns off the display and a value of 1 turns on the display. The enable blink bit (bit 5) controls blinking of the text characters in that if this bit is 0, the blink attribute will not cause blinking of the corresponding character. As far as we know, there is no way to prevent the cursor from blinking. The formula for setting this whole port is as follows:

CONTROL = 32*(blink enable) + 8*(video enable) + 1

You use this variable to set the port with the command

OUT &H3B8, CONTROL

If you have cleared the screen since running the TEXT program in Example 2-2, run it again. Try the following. First load and run the TEXT program, and then type

OUT &H3B8, 1

The display should disappear. Both the blink and the video bits are off. This might be useful if you wanted to blank the screen while someone is typing a password, but less extreme methods will also work, such as using the COLOR statement to change attributes temporarily to hide just the characters of the password.
Now type

OUT &H3B8, 9

Unfortunately, you will not be able to see what you are doing because the screen should be entirely blank except for a lonely blinking cursor that moves as you type, but does not show anything. When you press the ENTER key the video enable bit is turned on. The display should reappear, but none of the characters will blink.

Next, type

OUT &H3B8, 41

The characters on the right half of the screen should now blink. These are the character positions which have the blink bit on. Thus we have established control over these few bits. Next, let's take a look at the internal registers of the Motorola 6845 video chip.

**Programming the 6845 Chip.**  The Monochrome Adapter uses the Motorola 6845 video controller chip, the same type as the Color/Graphics Adapter uses. This chip acts as a traffic manager on the Monochrome Adapter in that it generates the address information and the synchronization signals that control the flow of bytes from the screen memory to produce the video signal, which drives the Monochrome Display Unit.

As we saw in Chapter 8, the Motorola 6845 video controller chip has 18 internal registers. The Monochrome Adapter has only one mode, and therefore only one set of values is provided by IBM for programming these registers. Table 9-3 gives the initial values. The Monochrome Adapter uses the same method as the Color/Graphics Adapter to program these registers; that is, one output port (the index port) is used to select an internal register and another output port (the data port) to place data in that register. For the Monochrome Adapter, port 3B4 (hex) is the index port and port 3B5 (hex) is the data port.

Because the Monochrome Adapter uses completely different timing for its video signals, the values for these internal registers are quite different from any of the modes on the Color/Graphics Adapter. The closest is the 80 × 25 high-resolution text mode. In fact, if you were to make a comparison between the values given in Table 9-3 and the values used to program the 80 × 25 high-resolution text mode on the Color/ Graphics Adapter, you would see that register 1 (horizontal displayed) and register 6 (vertical displayed) are the same, but most others are different. In particular, register 0 (horizontal total) and register 5 (vertical total) are set up differently.

Let's experiment with some of these values. In particular, let's see how to make a 50-line display on this adapter as we did on the Color/Graphics Adapter.

**Table 9-3**

6845 Internal Register Values for
Monochrome Adapter

| Register | Value | Register function |
|----------|-------|-------------------|
| 0 | 97 | Horizontal time total |
| 1 | 80 | Horizontal bytes displayed |
| 2 | 82 | Horizontal synchronization position |
| 3 | 15 | Horizontal synchronization width |
| 4 | 25 | Vertical lines total |
| 5 | 6 | Vertical adjust |
| 6 | 25 | Vertical lines displayed |
| 7 | 25 | Vertical synchronization position |
| 8 | 2 | Interlace mode |
| 9 | 13 | Maximum character line |
| 10 | 11 | Cursor start |
| 11 | 12 | Cursor end |
| 12 | 0 | Memory start address (high) |
| 13 | 0 | Memory start address (low) |
| 14 | 0 | Cursor address (high) |
| 15 | 0 | Cursor address (low) |
| 16 | – | Light pen (high) |
| 17 | – | Light pen (low) |

EXAMPLE 9-1

## 50-LINE TEXT DISPLAY

Create a text display mode on the Monochrome Adapter
that has 50 lines and 40 columns. Use the full interlace
mode. To demonstrate this format, fill the screen with the
letter "A." The result is shown in Figures 9-8 and 9-9.

## Solution

```
100 '  INTERLACED TEXT
110 '
120 '  Displays text in interlaced
130 '  mode.
140 '
150    KEY OFF
160    CLS
170    WIDTH 80
180 '
190 '  interlace, 40-column, and center
200    OUT &H3B4,8: OUT &H3B5,3
210    OUT &H3B4,1: OUT &H3B5,40
220    OUT &H3B4,2: OUT &H3B5,65
230 '
240    PRINT TAB(12);"INTERLACED TEXT"
250 '
260    DEF SEG = &HB000
270    FOR I = 3 TO 49
280      FOR J = 0 TO 39
290        POKE 80*I+2*J,65
300      NEXT J
310    NEXT I
320 '
330    LIST
```

## Example 9-1

## Solution, continued.

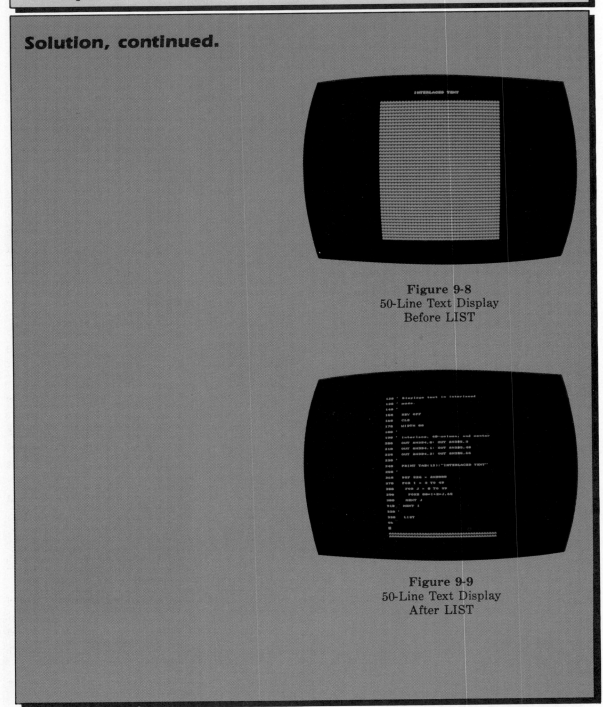

Figure 9-8
50-Line Text Display
Before LIST

Figure 9-9
50-Line Text Display
After LIST

In this example, we first turn off the function key display and clear the screen. We also set the width to 80. Then comes the special programming. We select register 8 (interlace mode) by sending an 8 to the index port for the 6845 video chip, and then we place a 3 in this register by sending a 3 to the data port. This sets up the fully interlaced mode. Next we select register 1 (horizontal displayed) by sending a 1 to the index port, and we send 40 to it via the data port. This specifies that 40 characters will be displayed per line. Next we select register 2 (horizontal synchronization position) by sending 2 to the index port, and we send a value of 65 to it via the data port. This adjusts the picture to be displayed in the middle of the screen.

Next the PRINT statement puts the title on the top row of the screen, and the next section fills rows 3 through 49 with the letter "A" by placing the ASCII code for that letter in every other memory location for the appropriate number of bytes of the video RAM. Recall that it takes two bytes to specify each character position. Notice that the DEF SEG command sets up the Monochrome Adapter's video RAM as the data segment for subsequent POKEs into memory.

On most TVs, a fully interlaced computer display would cause a great deal of flicker. However, on the Monochrome Display, there is no flicker, even when we run this special program. This is because of the long-persistence phosphor.

You might notice that we used only 40 columns and not the full 80 columns. This was done because the Monochrome Adapter has only enough video memory for 2000 character positions. This number is exactly right for the standard 80 × 25 mode, but not enough if we have an 80 × 50 display. If we halve the number of columns, it works out just right. If, however, you want to experiment, try putting 80 instead of 40 in line 210. You will see two copies of everything on the screen, one in the upper half and one in the lower half of the screen. This happens because, when the screen mapping runs out of video memory, it repeats itself, starting at the beginning of its video RAM.

This mode demonstrates that it is possible to achieve very dense, yet readable text displays. If we had twice the amount of memory in the Monochrome Adapter's video RAM (and twice the addressing range for it), we would be able to have text displays with 80 columns *and* 50 rows of characters.

We have seen how to program the Monochrome Adapter

on several levels: first on a high level, by using PRINT, COLOR, LOCATE, and WIDTH commands; then on lower levels using POKE to get directly at the screen memory and the OUT command to get directly at the bits on the board and the internal video chip registers. In the next section, we learn how to arrange special graphics characters to create interesting patterns on the screen.

# WORKING WITH SPECIAL GRAPHICS CHARACTERS

As we saw in Chapter 7, character graphics involves positioning characters on the screen to form pictures. This area of graphics involves an added layer of complexity beyond that of plotting points, because our "points" have shapes, colors, and other attributes of their own. Thus, the programmer or user must understand picture-making in two stages: the selection process and the positioning process. When we studied dot or APA graphics, we learned many commands for stringing dots together to make interesting shapes, and we found many tools for assisting with the positioning process. We had only one command, the COLOR command, for changing the attributes (blinking and colors) of the points. With character graphics, the situation is reversed. Instead, we are given 256 predefined shapes and many possible attributes to choose from. With so many shapes to choose from, selecting just the right shape and attributes now becomes as important as positioning that shape.

We start by looking at a special subset of graphics characters available on the IBM Monochrome Unit. These characters allow us to draw single and double lines, corners, T turns, and crossings. With these characters we can construct rectangular figures, including boxes and borders, particularly suitable for business graphics applications.

These special graphics symbols have been assigned extended ASCII codes in the range from 179 to 218 in a somewhat unusual order. Each row of our chart contains variations of one particular shape. For example, the first row contains the two variations of the vertical and horizontal lines, single and double; and the third row contains all four "left-to-top" corners.

Notice that there are two variations of each line and four

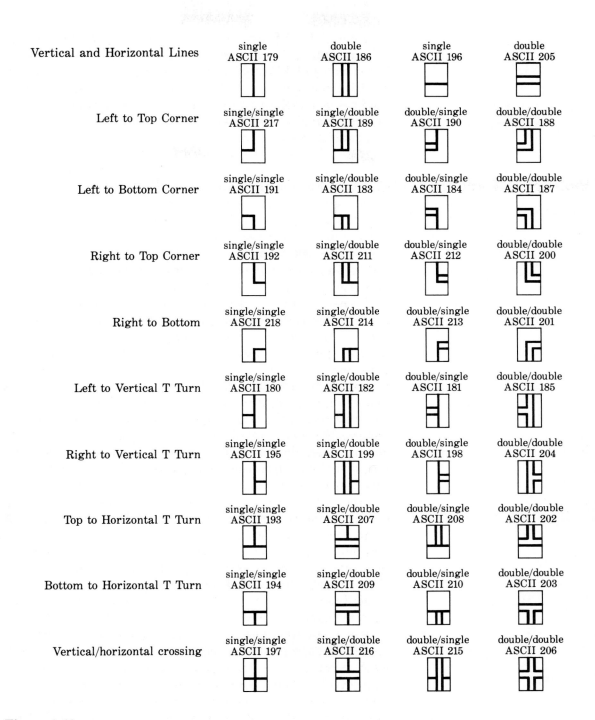

**Figure 9-10**

Chart of Line and Corner Symbols

variations of each corner, T turn, and crossing.

You cannot print these symbols on most printers, but if you have a Color/Graphics Adapter, you can use the font editor to make a set of custom characters in graphics mode that corresponds to these hard-wired characters. Then use the "screen dump" to print displays that you make on the screen in graphics mode.

There is a special way to produce these symbols directly on your screen using the ALT key. Just hold down the ALT key and type the corresponding three-digit ASCII code on the numeric keypad. When you release the ALT key the symbol appears on the screen. You can use the cursor keys to move around to different parts of the screen to place these characters where you want them. In this manner you can design forms. Later we will show a character graphics editor to do this more efficiently.

These symbols are designed to fit neatly together to make larger figures, such as boxes and frames. Try making a small box on your screen using the ALT key with the ASCII codes from Figure 9-10. Start out by using the four single line corners.

For each symbol, you see that the patterns are set up in a consistent manner within their dot matrix and all protruding lines extend all the way to the edges of the dot matrix. This ensures the continuity of lines from one character position to the next. Let's look at this in more detail, starting with single line symbols and then extending to double lines and mixed single and double line symbols.

The symbol for a single vertical line is represented by a column of dots in the center of its $9 \times 14$ dot matrix. Counting from the left (starting with 1 as the first column), this is column number 5. The pattern consists of a full column of 14 dots extending from the bottom to the top of the dot matrix. This ensures continuity if we want to make a long single vertical line by placing a number of these single vertical line symbols together, one on top of another. The dots for one character position just merge into the dots for the next.

Single horizontal lines fit together just as nicely. However, there is not a "center" row on a $9 \times 14$ dot matrix, because the number of rows is even. (In the previous case the number of columns was odd.) The center position for the rows is really between rows 7 and 8, counting from the top. The lower of the two rows (row 8) is used for horizontal single line patterns. For a *single* horizontal line, the full 9 dots of this row are filled in, ensuring continuity in this direction as well.

Single line corners, T turns, and crossing work well too, because any lines extending out from the corners always use column 5 or row 8 and always extend to the edge of the dot matrix.

You can check out these various possibilities by hand, but Example 9-3 will demonstrate how well all these single line shapes fit together.

Now let's look at how character graphics can be used to create graphs. The type of graph that character graphics does best is the bar chart. The next example shows how this can be done. To make this program, we started by designing the actual layout of the axes on the screen. We used the ALT key and the cursor keys to place graphics symbols on the screen as we wanted them to appear when the program ran. We then put line numbers and PRINT statements before each line in our design and enclosed that line in quotes. We used the INSERT key to move the design as we typed in the line numbers and PRINT commands. We then had a program that would produce the axes (including labeling). To this program we added statements to display the data in the form of bars on the bar chart.

**EXAMPLE 9-2**

# BAR CHART WITH CHARACTER GRAPHICS

Use character graphics on the Monochrome Adapter and
Display Unit to draw a bar chart of the monthly sales for a
book for the year 1981. The output is shown in Figure 9-11.

## Solution

```
100 ' BAR CHART WITH CHARACTER GRAPHICS
110 KEY OFF:CLS
120 '
130 COLOR 0,7
140 LOCATE  9,18 : PRINT "1981 SALES DATA"
150 COLOR 7,0
160 LOCATE 10,1
170 PRINT " $        1.0      2.0,     3.0      4.0      5.0 (thousand)"
175 ' Use ALT and keypad to type in graphics characters
180 PRINT " ╔╪╪╪╪╪╪╪╪╪╪╪╪╪╪╪╪╪╪╪╪╪╪╪╪╪╪╪╪╪╪╪╪╪╪╪╪╪╡"
182 ' Left corner is ALT 201, right end is ALT 181
184 ' Bar is ALT 205 three times, tick is ALT 216
190 PRINT "J "
195 ' Vertical bar with tick is ALT 182
200 PRINT "F ╢ "
210 PRINT "M ╢ "
220 PRINT "A ╢ "
230 PRINT "M ╢ "
240 PRINT "J ╢ "
250 PRINT "J ╢ "
260 PRINT "A ╢ "
270 PRINT "S ╢ "
280 PRINT "O ╢ "
290 PRINT "N ╢ "
300 PRINT "D ╨ "
310 PRINT "   ";
315 ' Bottom is ALT 208
320 '
330 ' plot the data in a bar chart
340 '
350  FOR MO=1 TO 12
360    READ DLR
370    SCDLR=DLR/125          'scale to fit in 40 columns, 125 per incr
380    FOR H=1 TO SCDLR
390      LOCATE MO+11,H+3
400      PRINT "█";
```

▶

Example 9-2

## Solution, continued.

```
405 ' Block is ALT 219
410    NEXT H
420   NEXT MO
430 '
440   LOCATE 1,1          ' put the cursor back at home
445 '
450 ' Sales income for Jan - Dec
455 '
460   DATA 478, 958, 2055, 1291, 950, 963, 1049, 787, 1623, 841,
        823, 1718
```

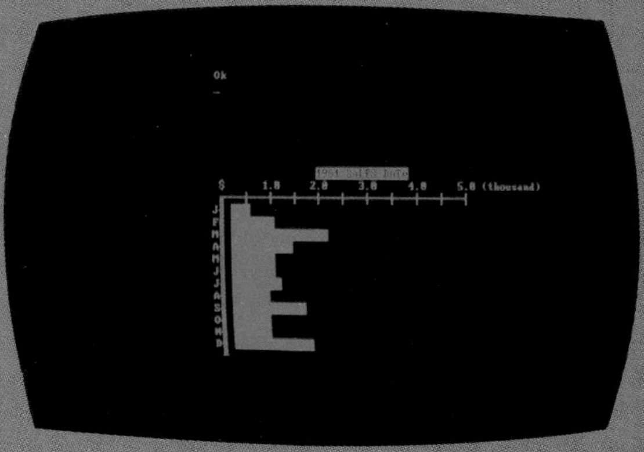

Figure 9-11
Bar Chart with Characters

Looking more carefully at this program, we see that after the function key display and the screen are cleared, the color is changed to give reverse video for a title. If we wanted to, we could have highlighted the title instead.

Immediately after the title is printed, the color is set to normal. Next the axes are drawn. Notice that the graphics characters are included directly in the PRINT statements.

The method for creating these PRINT statements is described previously. We found this took fewer steps and was easier to read than using FOR loops and CHR$ functions. For your convenience we have indicated the ASCII code in REM statements. If you type in the program, you can make these graphics characters by using the ALT key.

In the last part of the program, a nested pair of FOR loops draws the bars on the graph. The block character that is used to produce the bars fills up an entire character position. This gives a "resolution" of 80 × 25. By some very tricky programming you could use block characters that are one-quarter the size of a character position, and thus increase the resolution to 160 × 50.

After the picture is drawn, we return the cursor to home (to prevent scrolling). The data for the chart is found in a DATA statement at the end.

In the next example we show how to use these single line characters to draw a window. Windows are useful for many applications. For example, they can be used to form game boards, signs, and frames for menus and text.

EXAMPLE 9-3

## WINDOW PANES

Use the Monochrome Adapter Display to draw a window
with six window panes arranged in a 2 × 4 pattern. Use
the single line, corner, T turn, and crossings characters.
Write your program so that the number of panes can be
easily changed. The result is shown in Figure 9-12.

## Solution

```
100 ' WINDOW PANES
110 '
120    X=25:Y=3:Z=3        ' window size parameters
130 '
140     S= 32: V=179: H=196:VH=197
150    LT=217:LB=191:RT=192:RB=218
160    LV=180:RV=195:TH=193:BH=194
170 '
180    DEF FNL$(X,A,B,C,D,E) = SPACE$(12)+CHR$(A)+STRING$(X,B)
                               + CHR$(C)+STRING$(X,D)+CHR$(E)
190 '
200    DEF FNT$(X)=FNL$(X,RB,H,BH,H,LB)
210    DEF FNM$(X)=FNL$(X, V,S, V,S, V)
220    DEF FNJ$(X)=FNL$(X,RV,H,VH,H,LV)
230    DEF FNB$(X)=FNL$(X,RT,H,TH,H,LT)
240 '
250    KEY OFF:CLS
260    PRINT FNT$(X):FOR J=1 TO Y:PRINT FNM$(X):NEXT
270    FOR K = 1 TO Z
280       PRINT FNJ$(X):FOR J=1 TO Y:PRINT FNM$(X):NEXT:NEXT
290    PRINT FNB$(X)
300    LOCATE 1,1
```

■

Example 9-3

**Solution, continued.**

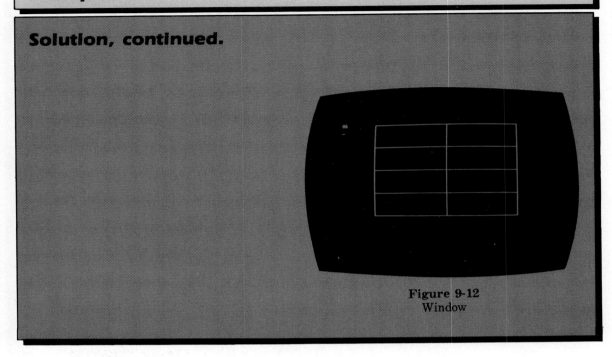

Figure 9-12
Window

Line 120 gives the window size parameters:

X  Width of a window pane
Y  Height of a window pane
Z  Number of panes vertically

These parameters are used in the last part of the program to control the FOR loops that draw the window.

Next we define ASCII codes for each single line, corner, T turn, and crossing. We have used shorthand names for each of these ASCII codes and included the code for a blank. These are shown in Figure 9-13

Next we define a string function FNL$ that makes a generic line of the window. It starts with twelve spaces (to better center the window on the screen), then one character, then a string of X characters, then another character, then another string of X characters, and then a single character. The characters are specified as arguments to this function. Notice that the function occupies two lines of the display, with no line number on the second line. We used the SPACE key to wrap the line around until the second part of the line was aligned underneath the first part.

The next step of the program is to define the various typical lines of the window. This is done via the string functions FNT$, FNM$, FNJ$, and FNB$. FNT$ corresponds to the top of the window, FNM$ corresponds to a midsection, FNJ$ corresponds to a junction where the panes come together, and FNB$ corresponds to the bottom of the window. In each case we use the generic line-making function FNL$, with parameters equal to the codes for the appropriate types of pieces.

First, the top line of the window is printed, then Y midlines of the window are drawn, and then Z copies of a junction line followed by Y midlines are printed. Finally the bottom line of the window is laid down. The X is used as an argument to the line-making functions to control the width of each pane and hence the width of the window. The program can be used to draw windows just about as large as the screen.

This example can easily be modified to demonstrate how well the double line characters fit together with each other. Try changing the ASCII codes in lines 140-160 to the following:

```
140 S=32 : V=186 : H=205 : VH=206
150 LT=188 : LB=187 : RT=212 : RB=201
160 LV=185 : RV=204 : TH=202 : BH=203
```

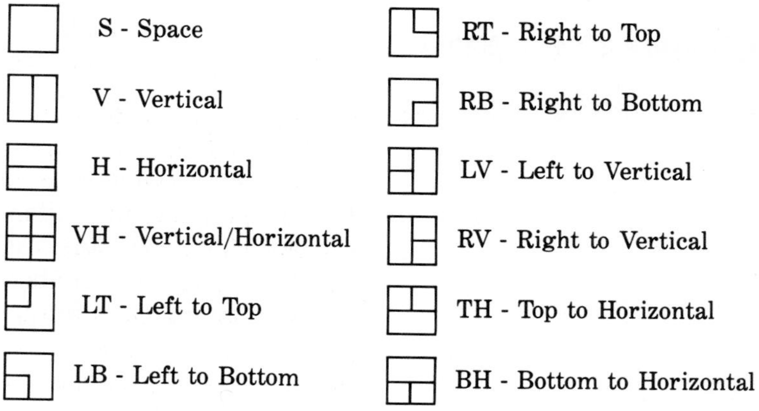

| | | | |
|---|---|---|---|
| ☐ | S - Space | ☐ | RT - Right to Top |
| ☐ | V - Vertical | ☐ | RB - Right to Bottom |
| ☐ | H - Horizontal | ☐ | LV - Left to Vertical |
| ☐ | VH - Vertical/Horizontal | ☐ | RV - Right to Vertical |
| ☐ | LT - Left to Top | ☐ | TH - Top to Horizontal |
| ☐ | LB - Left to Bottom | ☐ | BH - Bottom to Horizontal |

**Figure 9-13**

Single Line Shapes and
Their Abbreviations

When you run the program after making this modification, you will see the window with double lines around all the panes.

You can even change this program so that it uses single lines vertically and double lines horizontally or vice versa. Look up the appropriate codes in Table 9-3 and enter them into your program.

## CHARACTER EDITOR

Our next example shows you how to write a graphics editor. You can use this editor to design axes for Example 9-2, the chart program. Just make the appropriate image on the screen and put line numbers, PRINT commands, and quotation marks around it to turn it into program statements.

EXAMPLE 9-4

## CHARACTER GRAPHICS EDITOR

Write a screen-oriented editor for character graphics on
the Monochrome Adapter and Display Unit. The cursor
keys should allow you to move freely around the screen.
There should be a choice of several character sets,
including one with all the single and double lines, corners,
T turns, and crossings. There should be an adjustable
pointer that determines the direction in which the symbols
will be printed. The result is shown in Figure 9-14.

## Solution

```
100 ' DESIGN
110 '
120    FOR K=1 TO 10:KEY K,"":NEXT
130    CLS
140 '
150 ' set up key at bottom of screen
160    DIM KEYS(3,52)
170 '
180 ' first a row of keys to hit
190    LOCATE 24,1          .
200    FOR K=65 TO 90 :PRINT CHR$(K);:NEXT
210    FOR K=97 TO 122:PRINT CHR$(K);:NEXT
220    FOR K=1 TO 52:KEYS(0,K)=32:NEXT
230 '
240 ' now a row of special symbols
250    FOR K=1 TO 52:READ KEYS(1,K):NEXT
260    DATA  128, 129, 130, 131, 132, 133, 134, 135
270    DATA  136, 137, 138, 139, 140, 141, 142, 143
280    DATA  144, 145, 146, 147, 148, 149, 150, 151
290    DATA  152, 153, 154, 155, 156, 157, 158, 159
300    DATA  160, 161, 162, 163, 164, 165, 166, 167
310    DATA  168, 169, 170, 171, 172, 173, 174, 175
320    DATA  127,  32,  32,  32
330 '
340 ' now another row of special symbols
350    FOR K=1 TO 52:READ KEYS(2,K):NEXT
360    DATA  224, 225, 226, 227, 228, 229, 230, 231
370    DATA  232, 233, 234, 235, 236, 237, 238, 239
380    DATA  240, 241, 242, 243, 244, 245, 246, 247
390    DATA  248, 249, 250, 251, 252, 253, 254,   1
```

►

## Example 9-4

## Solution, continued.

```
400     DATA    2,   3,   4,   5,   6,  14,  15,  18
410     DATA   19,  20,  21,  23,  24,  25,  26,  27
420     DATA   28,  29,  32,  32
430   '
440   ' now a row of line and corner symbols
450     FOR K=1 TO 52:READ KEYS(3,K):NEXT
460     DATA 179, 186
470     DATA 196, 205
480     DATA 217, 189, 190, 188
490     DATA 191, 183, 184, 187
500     DATA 192, 200, 211, 212
510     DATA 218, 214, 213, 201
520     DATA 180, 182, 181, 185
530     DATA 195, 199, 198, 204
540     DATA 193, 207, 208, 202
550     DATA 194, 209, 210, 203
560     DATA 197, 216, 215, 206
570     DATA 176, 177, 178
580     DATA 219, 220, 221, 222, 223
590     DATA 16, 17, 22, 32
600   '
610     X=1:Y=1:CHRSET = 3
620     LOCATE 24,60:PRINT"now graphics";
630     LOCATE 25,1
640     FOR K=1 TO 52:PRINT CHR$(KEYS(CHRSET,K));:NEXT
650   '
660     DELX=1:DELY=0
670     LOCATE  1,71:PRINT"pointer   ";
680     LOCATE  2,74:PRINT CHR$(26);
690     LOCATE  3,71:PRINT"f1=up     ";
700     LOCATE  4,71:PRINT"f3=left   ";
710     LOCATE  5,71:PRINT"f4=right  ";
720     LOCATE  6,71:PRINT"f5=down   ";
730     LOCATE 11,71:PRINT"f9=new key";
740   '
750     ON KEY(1)  GOSUB 1230
760     ON KEY(3)  GOSUB 1280
770     ON KEY(4)  GOSUB 1330
780     ON KEY(5)  GOSUB 1380
790     ON KEY(9)  GOSUB 1140
795     ON KEY(10) GOSUB 1590
800     ON KEY(11) GOSUB 1430
810     ON KEY(12) GOSUB 1470
820     ON KEY(13) GOSUB 1510
830     ON KEY(14) GOSUB 1550
```

►

**Example 9-4**

## Solution, continued.

```
840     KEY(1)  ON
850     KEY(3)  ON
860     KEY(4)  ON
870     KEY(5)  ON
880     KEY(9)  ON
885     KEY(10) ON
890     KEY(11) ON
900     KEY(12) ON
910     KEY(13) ON
920     KEY(14) ON
930  '
940  ' main loop
950     LOCATE Y,X,1
960     A$=INKEY$
970     IF A$="" THEN 940
980     ASCII=ASC(A$)
990     IF CHRSET=0 THEN A=ASCII:GOTO 1050
1000     IF ASCII<65 OR ASCII>122 THEN 940
1010     IF ASCII>90 AND ASCII<97 THEN 940
1020     IF ASCII>90 THEN ASCII=ASCII-6
1030     A=KEYS(CHRSET,ASCII-64)
1040  '
1050     LOCATE Y,X,1
1060     PRINT CHR$(A);
1070     X=X+DELX:Y=Y+DELY
1080     IF X<1   THEN X=1
1090     IF X>70 THEN X=70
1100     IF Y<1   THEN Y=1
1110     IF Y>23 THEN Y=23
1120     GOTO 940
1130  '
1140  ' next character set
1150     CHRSET = (CHRSET+1) MOD 4
1160     LOCATE 24,60
1170     IF CHRSET=0  THEN PRINT "now alpha   ";
1180     IF CHRSET<>0 THEN PRINT "now graphics";
1190     LOCATE 25,1
1200     FOR K=1 TO 52:PRINT CHR$(KEYS(CHRSET,K));:NEXT
1210     RETURN
1220  '
1230  ' turn the turtle up
1240     DELX= 0:DELY=-1
1250     LOCATE  2,74:PRINT CHR$(24);
1260     RETURN
1270  '
```

▶

## Example 9-4

### Solution, continued.

```
1280 ' turn the turtle left
1290    DELX=-1:DELY= 0
1300    LOCATE  2,74:PRINT CHR$(27);
1310    RETURN
1320 '
1330 ' turn the turtle right
1340    DELX= 1:DELY= 0
1350    LOCATE  2,74:PRINT CHR$(26);
1360    RETURN
1370 '
1380 ' turn the turtle down
1390    DELX= 0:DELY= 1
1400    LOCATE  2,74:PRINT CHR$(25);
1410    RETURN
1420 '
1430 ' cursor up
1440    IF Y>1 THEN Y=Y-1
1450    RETURN
1460 '
1470 ' cursor left
1480    IF X>1 THEN X=X-1
1490    RETURN
1500 '
1510 ' cursor right
1520    IF X<70 THEN X=X+1
1530    RETURN
1540 '
1550 ' cursor down
1560    IF Y<23 THEN Y=Y+1
1570    RETURN
1580 '
1590 ' exit program
1600    LOCATE 23,1
1610    END
```

Before looking at this program, we will explain how to operate this program. When the program first comes up, it displays a character set key at the bottom of the screen and a function key display on the right side of the screen. You can control several things in this program, including the character set (by pressing function key 9), the direction that the

**Example 9-4**

**Solution, continued.**

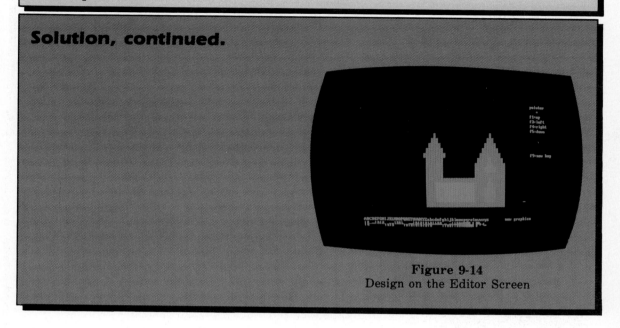

**Figure 9-14**
Design on the Editor Screen

characters will go on the screen (function keys 1, 3, 4, and 5), the cursor position (the cursor keys), and the particular character. To select a particular character, first determine if it is in the normal alpha character set. This includes all characters corresponding to keys on the IBM PC keyboard. If it is one of these, press function key 9 until the alpha character set is indicated. If the desired character is not in the alpha set, press function key 9 until the desired symbol is visible on the bottom line of the display. Then press the key on the keyboard that corresponds to the upper- or lowercase alphabetical character listed on the screen directly above the character you want. To exit the program, press function key 10.

Now for a detailed look at the listing. We first disable all function keys, clear the function key display, and clear the screen. The function keys are disabled to avoid buffer problems if you press a wrong function key while running the program.

The next part of the program sets up the character sets at the bottom of the screen. On line 24 (next to the bottom line) the alphabet in upper- and lowercase is displayed. We will display the various character sets directly underneath (on line 25). There are four character sets. Character set 0 consists of the usual keyboard characters (including numbers and various punctuation marks). Character sets 1 and 2 consist of various miscellaneous symbols, and character set 3 consists of all the single and double lines, corners, T turns, and crossings.

When you use a character set (other than character set 0), you press the key indicated on the upper line and the symbol immediately below appears on the screen.

Next we set up our own function key display along the right side of the screen. We will be using keys 1, 3, 4, 5, and 9. The first four keys are used to set a pointer that will determine the direction in which the character symbols will appear on the screen as we press the keys. Initially, the pointer points right. This is the usual direction for typing text, but we will be able to use these function keys to point the pointer up, down, left, or right. Then after typing each character, the cursor will move one position over in that direction, ready to place the next character on the screen. In this way, we will be able to type forward, backward, upward, or downward. When we use graphics symbols, we will be able to follow the figures around, adding in characters in any of these basic directions.

Function key 9 will allow us to select new character sets. Just press this key and a new character set appears at the bottom of the screen. We can use this key to cycle around and around all four sets.

Lines 750-920 assign and enable the function keys for interactive input.

Lines 940-1120 are the main loop. Here we wait for a character from the keyboard (allowing interrupts from the function and cursor keys). Once we have a character, we check for the alpha character set. If we are using this set, we go right on, skipping the next part, which checks for range, adjusts to make a continuous selection of all upper- and lowercase alphabetical characters, and then looks up the corresponding extended ASCII code in the KEYS array for the selected character of the selected character set. Then the character is printed on the screen in the location (X,Y), and the cursor is moved to the next location, depending upon the direction of the pointer. We then make sure that we will not be running off the screen. Finally, we loop back to look for the next character from the keyboard.

The rest of the program (lines 1140-1580) consists of interrupt service routines to handle the cursor and function keys. They are all short, performing just a few updating functions. The pointer (turtle) routines update DELX and DELY for the pointer and the arrow on the pointer display. The cursor key routines update the position (X,Y). The "next character set" routine updates CHRSET, displays the new character set on line 25, and indicates whether or not we are in the alpha mode (character set 0).

Try using this program to design a few displays. Try making a face, a set of axes, and a ship sailing on the sea (our pictures are shown in Figures 9-15 and 9-16).

This program does not allow you to save your picture directly, but you can put PRINT statements around your picture, turning it into a BASIC program, which you can then save. This process was described earlier.

Another way to save your work is to use the BSAVE (Binary SAVE) command to save your whole screen. To do this, exit the character graphics editor, press **CONTROL-SCROLL LOCK**, and find four free lines on the screen to type

DEF SEG=&HB000

BSAVE filename, 0, 4000

where *filename* is the name *in quotes* of the file in which you

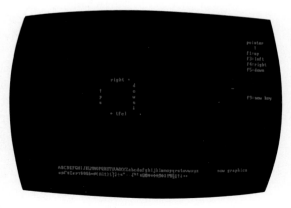

**Figure 9-15**

Playing Card Drawn with the Editor

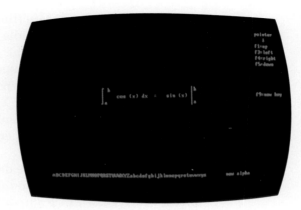

**Figure 9-16**

Equation Drawn with the Editor

want the screen. Then any time you want that screen back again, type

    DEF SEF=&HB000

    BLOAD filename

# CONCLUSION

In this, the final chapter, we have explored the world of character graphics on the IBM PC Monochrome Adapter and Display Unit. We have discussed how the Monochrome Adapter Unit is designed to give a clear, crisp, and dense display of characters useful for applications on the terminal, especially business applications. We then examined some special line, corner, T turn, and crossing characters, showing how they can be used in programs. We showed a graphics example and finally a character graphics editor program that you can use to design your own monochrome graphics screens.

# APPENDIX A: 3-D ROTATIONS

In this appendix we provide the formulas for the principal 3-D rotations and show how to derive formulas for rotations that result when we combine them. Such rotations are used in Chapter 3 as part of the viewing process for both the 3-D function plotting program and the program that displays a 3-D view of a house.

For any 3-D rotation there is a *plane* of rotation, an *axis* of rotation, and an *angle* of rotation, as shown in Figure A-1. The axis of rotation is always perpendicular to the plane of rotation. Thus, to completely specify a rotation, it is necessary to give only its plane of rotation and its angle of rotation.

A *principal* rotation is a rotation whose plane of rotation is one of the principal axis planes. There are three principal types of 3-D rotations corresponding to the three principal

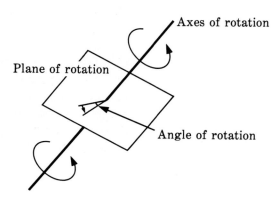

**Figure A-1**

General Rotation

axis planes: the xy-plane, the xz-plane, and the yz-plane. Formulas for these three types are given in Figure A-2. Here (x,y,z) are the 3-D coordinates before the motion and (x′,y′,z′) are the 3-D coordinates after the rotation. These principal rotations can be expressed as $3 \times 3$ matrices, shown in Figure A-3.

Matrices are an easy way to denote and store sets of formulas like these. Matrices can easily be stored in the computer as arrays.

Plane of rotation: **xy-plane**          Axis of rotation: **z-axis**

$$x' = x*\cos(a) - y*\sin(a)$$
$$y' = x*\sin(a) + y*\cos(a)$$
$$z' = z$$

Plane of rotation: **xz-plane**          Axis of rotation: **y-axis**

$$x' = x*\cos(a) - z*\sin(a)$$
$$y' = y$$
$$z' = x*\sin(a) + z*\cos(a)$$

Plane of rotation: **yz-plane**          Axis of rotation: **x-axis**

$$x' = x$$
$$y' = y*\cos(a) - z*\sin(a)$$
$$z' = y*\sin(a) + z*\cos(a)$$

**Figure A-2**

The Principal 3-D Rotations by an Angle $a$

xy-plane of rotation:

$$\begin{pmatrix} \cos(a) & -\sin(a) & 0 \\ \sin(a) & \cos(a) & 0 \\ 0 & 0 & 1 \end{pmatrix}$$

xz-plane of rotation:

$$\begin{pmatrix} \cos(a) & 0 & -\sin(a) \\ 0 & 1 & 0 \\ \sin(a) & 0 & \cos(a) \end{pmatrix}$$

yz-plane of rotation:

$$\begin{pmatrix} 1 & 0 & 0 \\ 0 & \cos(a) & -\sin(a) \\ 0 & \sin(a) & \cos(a) \end{pmatrix}$$

**Figure A-3**

Matrices of the Principal 3-D Rotations

It turns out that any general 3-D rotation can be written as the composite of principal 3-D rotations; that is, you apply a sequence of principal 3-D rotations, one after the other. You will need at most three principal rotations to get any specific rotation. Composites can be computed easily by a process called *matrix multiplication*. If A and B are matrices given by

$$A = \begin{pmatrix} A11 & A12 & A13 \\ A21 & A22 & A23 \\ A31 & A32 & A33 \end{pmatrix} \qquad B = \begin{pmatrix} B11 & B12 & B13 \\ B21 & B22 & B23 \\ B31 & B32 & B33 \end{pmatrix}$$

then their matrix *product* is a matrix C

$$C = \begin{pmatrix} C11 & C12 & C13 \\ C21 & C22 & C23 \\ C31 & C32 & C33 \end{pmatrix}$$

where the $Cij$ are given by the formula

$$Cij = Ai1*B1j + Ai2*B2j + Ai3*B3j$$

More explicitly,

$$C11 = A11*B11 + A12*B21 + A13*B31$$
$$C12 = A11*B12 + A12*B22 + A13*B32$$
$$C13 = A11*B13 + A12*B23 + A13*B33$$
$$C21 = A21*B11 + A22*B21 + A23*B31$$
$$C22 = A21*B12 + A22*B22 + A23*B32$$
$$C23 = A21*B13 + A22*B23 + A23*B33$$
$$C31 = A31*B11 + A32*B21 + A33*B31$$
$$C32 = A31*B12 + A32*B22 + A33*B32$$
$$C33 = A31*B13 + A32*B23 + A33*B33$$

In computer programs that do matrix multiplication, the more general $Cij$ formula is most often used. However, in Chapter 3, we used six of these formulas.

In Chapter 3 we started with two rotations, one for "spin" and one for "tip." The "spin" rotation is a principal rotation whose plane of rotation is the xy-plane and whose angle is called SPIN. The "tip" rotation is a principal rotation whose plane of rotation is the yz-plane and whose angle is TIP. The matrices for these are

$$\begin{pmatrix} 1 & 0 & 0 \\ 0 & \cos(TIP) & -\sin(TIP) \\ 0 & \sin(TIP) & \cos(TIP) \end{pmatrix} \begin{pmatrix} \cos(SPIN) & -\sin(SPIN) & 0 \\ \sin(SPIN) & \cos(SPIN) & 0 \\ 0 & 0 & 1 \end{pmatrix}$$

If you multiply the corresponding matrices together, you should get the following matrix:

$$\begin{pmatrix} \cos(SPIN) & -\sin(SPIN) & 0 \\ \cos(TIP)*\sin(SPIN) & \cos(TIP)*\cos(SPIN) & -\sin(TIP) \\ \sin(TIP)*\sin(SPIN) & \sin(TIP)*\cos(SPIN) & \cos(TIP) \end{pmatrix}$$

You will see formulas similar to these in the programs in Chapter 3.

# APPENDIX B: ASCII CHARACTERS AND SECONDARY CODES

Table B-1 contains the ASCII codes for the 256 characters of the PC. These codes are used with the CHR$ function and with the ALT key to generate characters on the display. They are also returned as values when you use the ASC function.

**Table B-1.**

ASCII Codes for the PC

| Decimal Value | Hexadecimal Value | Character |
|---|---|---|
| 0 | 00 | Null |
| 1 | 01 | ☺ |
| 2 | 02 | ☻ |
| 3 | 03 | ♥ |
| 4 | 04 | ♦ |
| 5 | 05 | ♣ |
| 6 | 06 | ♠ |
| 7 | 07 | Beep |
| 8 | 08 | ◘ |
| 9 | 09 | Tab |
| 10 | 0A | Line-feed |
| 11 | 0B | Cursor home |
| 12 | 0C | Form-feed |
| 13 | 0D | Enter |
| 14 | 0E | ♫ |
| 15 | 0F | ☼ |
| 16 | 10 | ► |
| 17 | 11 | ◄ |
| 18 | 12 | ↕ |

**Table B-1.**

(Continued)

| Decimal Value | Hexadecimal Value | Character |
|:---:|:---:|:---:|
| 19 | 13 | ‼ |
| 20 | 14 | ¶ |
| 21 | 15 | § |
| 22 | 16 | ▬ |
| 23 | 17 | ↨ |
| 24 | 18 | ↑ |
| 25 | 19 | ↓ |
| 26 | 1A | → |
| 27 | 1B | ← |
| 28 | 1C | Cursor right |
| 29 | 1D | Cursor left |
| 30 | 1E | Cursor up |
| 31 | 1F | Cursor down |
| 32 | 20 | Space |
| 33 | 21 | ! |
| 34 | 22 | " |
| 35 | 23 | # |
| 36 | 24 | $ |
| 37 | 25 | % |
| 38 | 26 | & |
| 39 | 27 | ' |
| 40 | 28 | ( |
| 41 | 29 | ) |
| 42 | 2A | * |
| 43 | 2B | + |
| 44 | 2C | , |
| 45 | 2D | - |
| 46 | 2E | . |
| 47 | 2F | / |
| 48 | 30 | 0 |
| 49 | 31 | 1 |
| 50 | 32 | 2 |
| 51 | 33 | 3 |
| 52 | 34 | 4 |
| 53 | 35 | 5 |
| 54 | 36 | 6 |
| 55 | 37 | 7 |

**Table B-1.**

(Continued)

| Decimal Value | Hexadecimal Value | Character |
|:---:|:---:|:---:|
| 56 | 38 | 8 |
| 57 | 39 | 9 |
| 58 | 3A | : |
| 59 | 3B | ; |
| 60 | 3C | < |
| 61 | 3D | = |
| 62 | 3E | > |
| 63 | 3F | ? |
| 64 | 40 | @ |
| 65 | 41 | A |
| 66 | 42 | B |
| 67 | 43 | C |
| 68 | 44 | D |
| 69 | 45 | E |
| 70 | 46 | F |
| 71 | 47 | G |
| 72 | 48 | H |
| 73 | 49 | I |
| 74 | 4A | J |
| 75 | 4B | K |
| 76 | 4C | L |
| 77 | 4D | M |
| 78 | 4E | N |
| 79 | 4F | O |
| 80 | 50 | P |
| 81 | 51 | Q |
| 82 | 52 | R |
| 83 | 53 | S |
| 84 | 54 | T |
| 85 | 55 | U |
| 86 | 56 | V |
| 87 | 57 | W |
| 88 | 58 | X |
| 89 | 59 | Y |
| 90 | 5A | Z |
| 91 | 5B | [ |
| 92 | 5C | \ |

**Table B-1.**

(Continued)

| Decimal Value | Hexadecimal Value | Character |
|---|---|---|
| 93 | 5D | ] |
| 94 | 5E | ^ |
| 95 | 5F | _ |
| 96 | 60 | ' |
| 97 | 61 | a |
| 98 | 62 | b |
| 99 | 63 | c |
| 100 | 64 | d |
| 101 | 65 | e |
| 102 | 66 | f |
| 103 | 67 | g |
| 104 | 68 | h |
| 105 | 69 | i |
| 106 | 6A | j |
| 107 | 6B | k |
| 108 | 6C | l |
| 109 | 6D | m |
| 110 | 6E | n |
| 111 | 6F | o |
| 112 | 70 | p |
| 113 | 71 | q |
| 114 | 72 | r |
| 115 | 73 | s |
| 116 | 74 | t |
| 117 | 75 | u |
| 118 | 76 | v |
| 119 | 77 | w |
| 120 | 78 | x |
| 121 | 79 | y |
| 122 | 7A | z |
| 123 | 7B | { |
| 124 | 7C | ¦ |
| 125 | 7D | } |
| 126 | 7E | ~ |
| 127 | 7F | ⌂ |
| 128 | 80 | Ç |
| 129 | 81 | ü |

**Table B-1.**

(Continued)

| Decimal Value | Hexadecimal Value | Character |
|:---:|:---:|:---:|
| 130 | 82 | é |
| 131 | 83 | â |
| 132 | 84 | ä |
| 133 | 85 | à |
| 134 | 86 | å |
| 135 | 87 | ç |
| 136 | 88 | ê |
| 137 | 89 | ë |
| 138 | 8A | è |
| 139 | 8B | ï |
| 140 | 8C | î |
| 141 | 8D | ì |
| 142 | 8E | Ä |
| 143 | 8F | Å |
| 144 | 90 | É |
| 145 | 91 | ae |
| 146 | 92 | Æ |
| 147 | 93 | ô |
| 148 | 94 | ö |
| 149 | 95 | ò |
| 150 | 96 | û |
| 151 | 97 | ù |
| 152 | 98 | ÿ |
| 153 | 99 | Ö |
| 154 | 9A | Ü |
| 155 | 9B | ¢ |
| 156 | 9C | £ |
| 157 | 9D | ¥ |
| 158 | 9E | Pt |
| 159 | 9F | $f$ |
| 160 | A0 | á |
| 161 | A1 | í |
| 162 | A2 | ó |
| 163 | A3 | ú |
| 164 | A4 | ñ |
| 165 | A5 | Ñ |
| 166 | A6 | a̲ |

**Table B-1.**

(Continued)

| Decimal Value | Hexadecimal Value | Character |
|:---:|:---:|:---:|
| 167 | A7 | o |
| 168 | A8 | ¿ |
| 169 | A9 | ⌐ |
| 170 | AA | ¬ |
| 171 | AB | ½ |
| 172 | AC | ¼ |
| 173 | AD | ¡ |
| 174 | AE | « |
| 175 | AF | » |
| 176 | B0 | ░ |
| 177 | B1 | ▒ |
| 178 | B2 | ▓ |
| 179 | B3 | │ |
| 180 | B4 | ┤ |
| 181 | B5 | ╡ |
| 182 | B6 | ╢ |
| 183 | B7 | ╖ |
| 184 | B8 | ╕ |
| 185 | B9 | ╣ |
| 186 | BA | ║ |
| 187 | BB | ╗ |
| 188 | BC | ╝ |
| 189 | BD | ╜ |
| 190 | BE | ╛ |
| 191 | BF | ┐ |
| 192 | C0 | └ |
| 193 | C1 | ┴ |
| 194 | C2 | ┬ |
| 195 | C3 | ├ |
| 196 | C4 | ─ |
| 197 | C5 | ┼ |
| 198 | C6 | ╞ |
| 199 | C7 | ╟ |
| 200 | C8 | ╚ |
| 201 | C9 | ╔ |
| 202 | CA | ╩ |
| 203 | CB | ╦ |

(Continued)

| Decimal Value | Hexadecimal Value | Character |
|:---:|:---:|:---:|
| 204 | CC | ╟ |
| 205 | CD | ═ |
| 206 | CE | ╬ |
| 207 | CF | ╧ |
| 208 | D0 | ╨ |
| 209 | D1 | ╤ |
| 210 | D2 | ╥ |
| 211 | D3 | ╙ |
| 212 | D4 | ╘ |
| 213 | D5 | ╒ |
| 214 | D6 | ╓ |
| 215 | D7 | ╫ |
| 216 | D8 | ╪ |
| 217 | D9 | ┘ |
| 218 | DA | ┌ |
| 219 | DB | █ |
| 220 | DC | ▄ |
| 221 | DD | ▌ |
| 222 | DE | ▐ |
| 223 | DF | ▀ |
| 224 | E0 | $\alpha$ |
| 225 | E1 | $\beta$ |
| 226 | E2 | $\Gamma$ |
| 227 | E3 | $\pi$ |
| 228 | E4 | $\Sigma$ |
| 229 | E5 | $\sigma$ |
| 230 | E6 | $\mu$ |
| 231 | E7 | $\tau$ |
| 232 | E8 | $\Phi$ |
| 233 | E9 | $\theta$ |
| 234 | EA | $\Omega$ |
| 235 | EB | $\delta$ |
| 236 | EC | $\infty$ |
| 237 | ED | $\emptyset$ |
| 238 | EE | $\epsilon$ |
| 239 | EF | $\cap$ |
| 240 | F0 | $\equiv$ |

**Table B-1.**

(Continued)

| Decimal Value | Hexadecimal Value | Character |
|---|---|---|
| 241 | F1 | $\pm$ |
| 242 | F2 | $\geq$ |
| 243 | F3 | $\leq$ |
| 244 | F4 | $\lceil$ |
| 245 | F5 | J |
| 246 | F6 | $\div$ |
| 247 | F7 | $\approx$ |
| 248 | F8 | $\circ$ |
| 249 | F9 | $\bullet$ |
| 250 | FA | $\cdot$ |
| 251 | FB | $\sqrt{\phantom{x}}$ |
| 252 | FC | n |
| 253 | FD | 2 |
| 254 | FE | ■ |
| 255 | FF | (Blank) |

# APPENDIX C: BIBLIOGRAPHY

J. D. Foley and A. Van Dam. *Fundamentals of Interactive Computer Graphics.* Reading, Mass.: Addison-Wesley, 1982.

David Fox and Mitchell Waite. *Computer Animation Primer.* Peterborough, N.H.: Byte Books, 1982.

Christopher L. Morgan and Mitchell Waite. *8086/8088 16-Bit Microprocessor Primer.* Peterborough, N.H.: Byte Books, 1982.

William Newman and Robert Sproull. *Principles of Interactive Computer Graphics,* second edition. New York, N.Y.: McGraw-Hill, 1979.

David Rodgers and J. Alan Adams. *Mathematical Elements for Computer Graphics.* New York, N.Y.: McGraw-Hill, 1976.

Mitchell Waite. *Computer Graphics Primer.* Indianapolis, Ind.: Howard Sams & Co., Inc., 1979.

Mitchell Waite and Michael Pardee. *Microprocessor Primer.* Indianapolis, Ind.: Howard Sams & Co., Inc., 1980.

*Raster Graphics Handbook.* Conrac Division, 1980.

*BASIC Manual.* Personal Computer Hardware Reference Library. Armonk, N.Y.: IBM, 1981.

*Technical Reference Manual.* Personal Computer Hardware Reference Library. Armonk, N.Y.: IBM, 1981.

# APPENDIX D: GLOSSARY

*Analog.* A type of electronic signal that has a continuous range of meaningful values. Analog signals are often used to represent and simulate continuously ranging quantities. The amplitude of an analog signal is usually proportional to the magnitude of the quantity that it is being used to represent. See also *digital*.

*Animation.* Making artificially constructed images appear to move by rapidly showing a sequence of still views.

*APA Graphics.* All Points Addressable graphics. Computer graphics displays in which every point on the screen can be separately addressed for drawing and thus controlled. See also *pixel*.

*ASCII.* American Standard Code for Interchange of Information. A standard code for representing symbols (letters, numbers, and punctuation) and control functions by numbers.

*Aspect Ratio.* The ratio of a picture's height to its width.

*Attribute.* A modifier such as color or intensity for graphics objects like points, lines, and characters.

*Bandwidth.* The total range of frequencies that can be carried by a communication channel. The bandwidth determines the rate at which information can flow through the channel.

*Bar Chart.* A graph in which the magnitude of each quantity is represented by a bar of proportional length or height.

*Buffer.* An area of memory used to store information temporarily.

*Cartesian Coordinates.* For a two-dimensional space, the usual coordinate system in which the position of each point is specified by its x-coordinate (horizontal position) and its y-coordinate (vertical position). For a three-dimensional space, there are three coordinates x, y, and z to specify the position of any point.

*Character.* An individual symbol such as a letter of the alphabet, a digit of a number, a punctuation mark, or a graphics shape.

*Chrominance.* Having to do with color. The chrominance signal carries the color information.

*Color Burst.* A special color alignment signal at the beginning of each scan line that is part of the standard TV signal.

*Composite.* Combined. In TV, a composite signal is a signal that contains synchronization, intensity, and color information.

*CRT.* Cathode Ray Tube. The picture tube of a TV set or video monitor.

*Cyan.* A blue-green color used in graphics.

*Device Coordinates.* A coordinate system used to locate points on a graphics display device, such as a video display screen or a digital plotter.

*Digital.* Using discrete numbers to represent quantities. On computers, these numbers are combinations of the numbers 1 and 0. See also *analog*.

*Dot.* A very small area on a display that represents a point.

*Editor.* A program to assist the user in entering and modifying information stored in a computer system. Text editors are used with documents like manuscripts, and graphics editors are used with pictures like engineering diagrams.

*Field.* On a raster scan system, one traversal of the screen by the beam. Often it takes two fields to make a complete picture. See also *frame*.

*Flicker.* The scintillating effect caused when a picture is not refreshed often enough, allowing the viewer to perceive the change in light intensity.

*Font.* The specific set of symbols assigned to a named set of characters.

*Frame.* On a raster scan system, one complete traversal by the beam of the entire picture. Often it takes two times through the screen for the beam to hit every part of the picture. See also *field*.

*GDL.* Graphics Definition Language. A concise language for representing graphics commands. IBM has a GDL that is used by the DRAW command.

*Hue.* The color (red, green, blue, and so on) of an object.

*Icon.* A symbol that is used to represent an object. An icon should look something like the object it represents.

*Interlace.* On a raster scan system, two separate but interlocking scans of the picture.

*Interrupt Programming.* A method of programming in which events from outside the program (such as pressing a key) control the flow of the program as they happen.

*Magenta.* A purplish color.

*Mapping.* An assignment of values from one system to another system. For example, there is a mapping from memory to the screen on a raster scan video system.

*Mask.* Something that is used to hide something else. In computer programming, a mask is a bit pattern that is placed against other bit patterns to allow only certain bits to appear (like looking through a picket fence). The binary value of 1 in the mask is used to retain the contents of the bit in the corresponding position, and the value of 0 is used to hide the contents of the corresponding bit.

*Megahertz.* One million cycles per second.

*Menu.* A display of choices for the user on a page or video screen.

*Monochrome.* Having one color.

*Nanosecond.* One billionth of a second.

*Nibble.* Half a byte. A nibble is four bits.

*NTSC.* National Television Standards Committee. A standard for broadcast color television.

*Object Space.* A space in which the objects of a particular application are situated.

*Offset.* A memory address relative to the beginning of a memory segment.

*Overscan.* A situation in which an incoming display is mapped to a region larger than the active display area of the display device.

*P39.* A long-persistence phosphor that is used in some picture tubes to reduce flicker.

*Paint.* To fill a region on the screen with a color or pattern. See also *seed.*

*Palette.* A selection of colors used to draw a picture. For example, in the medium-resolution mode there are two palettes, each of which provides a selection of four colors.

*Phosphor.* A material used to coat the inside face of picture tubes. When the electron beam hits the phosphor, the phosphor emits light in proportion to the voltage of the beam.

*Pie Chart.* A graph in which quantities are represented by sectors of a circle. The angle (and hence the size) of each sector is proportional to the magnitude of the quantity it represents.

*Pixel.* A picture element. A pixel is the smallest element of a picture that can be separately addressed. See also *APA Graphics.*

*Point.* A mathematical object having position, but no size.

*Pointer.* A memory cell that contains the address of another memory cell.

*Port.* An addressable logical cell through which input and output information can be passed. Ports are accessed via special input/output instructions.

*Projection.* A shadow-like image of an object, usually in a lower dimension than the object itself. For example, you can view a 3-D object by drawing its 2-D projection on the viewing screen.

*Radian.* A measure of angles. On a unit circle the radian measure of an angle is the length of its arc. 360 degrees equals 2×PI radians.

*Raster.* A scanning pattern in which a beam moves back and forth and up and down to cover a two-dimensional area.

*Recursion.* A situation in which procedures can call themselves either directly or indirectly.

*Retrace.* On a raster scan system, the time period during which the electron beam is moving without displaying.

*RF Modulator.* Radio Frequency Modulator. A device used to convert direct video signals to broadcast band frequencies higher than a TV is designed to receive.

*RGB.* Red, Green, Blue. RGB is a system for separately sending the three primary colors of a color video picture.

*Rotation.* A circular motion in space that involves turning by an angle.

*Scan Line.* On a raster scan system, one traversal of a beam horizontally across the picture.

*Seed.* The beginning point for painting an object. See also *paint.*

*Segment.* A contiguous section of memory used by the processor to store programs or data.

*SGP.* Simple Graphics Package. A set of routines that helps interface between applications programs and graphics devices.

*Stack.* An area of memory used to store data in a last-in, first-out manner, like the in box on a desk. Associated with a stack are two instructions: PUSH and POP. PUSH is used to store data on the stack and POP is used to retrieve data from the stack.

*Subcarrier.* A frequency relative to the base frequency of a channel used to carry information separately within the channel.

*Synchronization Signals.* Signals used to help align the picture on a raster scan system.

*Topology.* A branch of mathematics that studies the shapes of objects.

*Translation.* A motion in space in which all points move the same distance in the same direction.

*Turtle.* An imaginary graphics cursor used for drawing on paper or on a video screen. As the turtle moves, it leaves a trail of ink or light showing where it has been.

*User Coordinates.* A coordinate system natural for describing objects in the user's application.

*Vector.* A mathematical quantity that has magnitude and direction.

*Vertex.* A corner of a figure made of edges and faces.

*Viewport.* A rectangular region of the active area of a display device. The picture appears within the viewport on the device.

*Window.* A rectangular region of the object or user coordinate space containing the objects that are to appear in the picture.

# INDEX

## A

A command, 181-83
Adapters, video
  connection of, 9
  initialization of, 10
  switching between, 10,
    381-83
Algorithms
  scan conversion, 241
  scan line, 214
ALT key, 400-01
Animation, 196-98
  character, 323-26
  page flipping, 332-35
  with PUT XOR action,
    273-78
Arrays, 259-86
  and GET command, 278-83
  integer, 297
  and PUT PRESET/PSET
    actions, 283-86
  and PUT XOR action,
    266-78
  real and string, 281
  size of, determining, 263-65
ASCII codes
  and custom characters,
    309-23
  extended in IBM PC, 40
  secondary, and characters,
    421-28
  for special graphics
    characters, 398-400
Aspect ratio
  and the A command, 181
  default value for, 113
  defined, 110

## B

Attribute bytes, 40-41, 358-59
  controlled by COLOR
    command, 385-86
  and video mapping, 389-91

B command, 175-77
Background color, 34-35, 41,
51
  use in background scene,
    250-55
  using PRESET to plot a
    point of, 63
  and PUT XOR action, 272
  set by bits in color port,
    360
BLOAD command, 322-23, 416
Border color, 34-36, 41, 360
BSAVE command, 322, 415

## C

C command, 179-81
CALL command, 21
Character graphics, 302-35,
372-416
  and animation, 323-35
  character cells in, 303
  cursor and character
    commands in, 320
  custom characters of,
    309-26
  editor for, 408-16
  graphics characters of,
    304-08, 326-32
  with the Monochrome
    Adapter, 372-416

Character graphics, *continued*
  special graphics characters
    of, 398-408
  vs. APA graphics, 302-04
Character ROM. *See*
Read-only memory (ROM),
  character.
Charts
  bar, 128-30
  bar, with character
    graphics, 401-04
  coloring a pie, 246-47
  pie, 113-16
CHR$ function, 226-29
Chrominance signal
  color burst of, 17, 32
  color subcarrier frequency
    of, 17
  hue and saturation of, 16-17
CIRCLE command, 103-16,
213
  aspect ratio parameter of,
    110-11
  use of commas in, 113
  drawing arcs with, 107-10
  drawing ellipses with,
    110-12
  drawing globes with,
    139-40
  drawing pie charts with,
    113-16
  radius drawing feature of,
    113
  radius parameter of, 107,
    110
CLEAR statement, 240
CLS command, 22, 33, 120

Color clocks, 17-18, 345
Color codes, 41-43
COLOR command, 33-36, 41, 332
  and color bits in Color/ Adapter, 354
  in graphics mode, 46
  use with Monochrome Adapter, 385-86
  in text mode, 326
Color/Graphics Adapter
  basic characteristics of, 11-14
  and character graphics, 302-03
  color bits for, 360-61
  display formats of, 372-76
  graphics mode of, 13-14
  I/O ports of, 340-41
  mode bits for, 354-55
  programming, 354-60
  special graphics mode for, 361-66
  text mode of, 11-12
  and the 6845 video chip, 341-44
Color video
  limitations of, 14-16
Computer graphics
  defined, 5
  examples of, 6
  history of, 6-8
Coordinates, Cartesian
  absolute and relative, 65
  defined, 64
  use of expressions in, 89
  order in graphics commands, 67
  use of STEP keyword with, 65
COS function, 86, 101-02
CSRLIN system variable, 304
Current position
  default value of, 67
  function of, 26
  function with CIRCLE command, 105
  function with LINE command, 72
  function with PSET and PRESET, 65
  returning to its previous position, 177-78
  as seed point, 244
Cursor control keys, 140
  animation and, 196-99
  font editor and, 320

Custom characters, 309-26
  animation with, 323-26
  enlarging, 310-12
  font editor for, 313-23

**D**

D command, 172-75
DEF SEG statement, 40, 322, 382-83
Device coordinate system. See Screen coordinate system.
DIM statement, 260-63
Disk drives, 10
Display, video
  aspect ratio of, 113
  controlling number of scan lines on, 347-50
  coordinate system of, 117
  format of, 372-74
  horizontal and vertical retrace on, 15
  initialization of, 25
  interlaced fields on, 15
  overscan of, 16
  scrolling on, 352-54
  shrinking and stretching of, 345-46
DRAW command, 21, 166-205, 212-13. See also Graphics Definition Language.
  drawing arrows with, 169, 176, 182
  drawing electronic symbols with, 199-204
  drawing polygons with, 180, 188, 190
  drawing space-filling curves with, 193-95
  drawing spirals with, 173, 184, 186
  drawing stars with, 171, 178
  painting with, 241-45

**E**

E command, 172-75

**F**

F command, 172-75
Font editor, 313-23
  explanation of program, 321-23
  operation of, 320-21
  program, 313-19

Foreground color, 34-35, 41, 51
  using PSET to plot a point of, 63
Forgetting transformations, 143, 145-46
Frequencies, video
  character clock, 377
  color subcarrier, 17
  dot clock, 376-77
  horizontal, 377-78
Function keys, 197, 320-21, 413-14

**G**

G command, 172-75
GET command, 259-63, 278-83. See also PUT command.
GOSUB statement, 63, 130
GOTO statement, 58, 127
Graphics characters, 304-08
  coloring of, 326-32
  special, 398-408
Graphics cursor. See current position.
Graphics Definition Language (GDL), 166-205
  calling subroutines in, 189-91
  drawing space-filling curves with, 192-96
  global move command in, 166-71
  interactive input with, 197-205
  local move commands in, 172-75
  moving the current position with, 175-78
  painting in, 241-45
  scaling figures with, 187-89
  setting the angle of a frame with, 181-86
  vs. turtle graphics, 191-92
Graphics devices, 8
Graphics modes
  colors in, 47-49
  custom characters in, 303
  high-resolution mode in, 12-14, 50-53, 270
  medium-resolution mode in, 12-13, 46-49, 270
  programming special, 361-66
  vertical register values in, 348-49

**H**

H command, 172-75

**I**

Icons, 291-98
  using GET and PUT to
    position, 291-92
  program, 293-98
IN command, 342
INKEY$ function, 322
Input/Output (I/O)
  devices, 340
  port addresses on Color/
    Graphics Adapter, 355
  port addresses on Mono-
    chrome Adapter, 393
  ports, 340-41
  space, 339-40
Image arrays. *See* GET
command; *see* PUT
command.

**K**

KEY ON command, 22,
  197-98, 297

**L**

L command, 172-75
LINE command, 20-21, 23,
  68-102
  advanced programming
    uses, 94-102
  Box Fill option of, 47,
    77-78, 219-21, 240-41
  Box option of, 73-74
  color parameter of, 70
  drawing polygons with,
    91-97
  drawing rectangles with,
    71-77
  line style option of, 79-84
  types of coordinates used
    with, 68
LOAD command, 20
LOCATE command, 62, 204,
  305-06, 386-87
Luminance signal, 16

**M**

M command, 166-71
Mapping, video, 38-42
  attribute bytes and, 40-41
  controlling with SCREEN
    command, 119
  in high-resolution graphics
    mode, 52-53

Mapping, video, *continued*
  of line style bits to pixels,
    83-85
  in medium-resolution
    graphics mode, 50
  in the Monochrome
    Adapter, 389-92
  starting position of, 79
  from video RAM to display,
    356-59
Masks, 289-90
Matrix method, 101-02
Memory capacity, IBM PC, 10
Memory offsets, 40, 352, 391
MOD function, 99, 183, 226
MODE command, 10
Monochrome Adapter
  basic function of, 11, 372
  display formats of, 372-76
  examples of graphics with,
    401-08
  graphics editor for, 408-16
  high-level programming of,
    384-89
  lower-level programming
    of, 389-98
  mode bits for, 392-93
  special text mode for,
    395-98
  video memory, size of, 397
  video signals of, 376-80
Monochrome Display Unit
  bandwidth of, 377
  basic function of, 9-11
  display of, 373, 380-81
  raster scan rate of, 11,
    376-79

**N**

N command, 177-78
National Television Standards
  Committee (NTSC), 17
Normals
  face, 152-54
  in three-dimensional
    drawing, 149
Numbers
  binary, 281
  double-precision, 85
  hexadecimal, 290-91

**O**

OUT command, 339, 342,
  345-46, 392-93

**P**

P command, 241-45
PAINT command, 21, 210-41,
  245-55
  applications of, 245-55
  background option of,
    235-37
  boundary option of, 222-25
  function with complex
    regions, 238-40
  paintcolor option of, 219-21
  seed point of, 210-18
  tiling with, 225-37
  vs. LINE BOX Fill option,
    240-41
Palettes, 47, 360
PEEK function, 40, 281,
  308-09
Pixels, 46
  choosing number of bits
    mapped per, 358
  and video mapping, 50, 79
PMAP function, 125-26
POINT function, 125-26, 305
POKE command, 40, 308-09,
  390-91
POS function, 304
Positioner functions, 97
PRESET command, 63-68, 213
  color options of, 64
  default color scheme of, 64
PRINT command, 307-08, 385
Programs
  entering and deleting
    lines, 19
  initialization of, 58-59
  loading, 20
  saving, 19-20
  timing of, 95
PSET command, 23, 63-68
  color options of, 64
  default color scheme of,
    64-65
  range of coordinates
    allowed, 23
PUT command, 259-78, 283-98
  action options of, 265
  AND and OR actions,
    286-91
  and icons, 291-98
  PSET and PRESET
    actions, 283-86
  XOR action, 266-78

**R**

R command, 172

Random-access memory
(RAM), video
determining number of
bytes displayed, 346
divided in graphics mode,
348
how colors are stored in,
283
and PUT command, 265
size of in Monochrome
Adapter, 397
size of in text modes, 38-39
starting address of, 38
and tiling, 225-26
and 6845 video chip, 341,
348
Raster scan pattern
defined, 14, 343
horizontal and vertical
retrace of, 15
scan line of, 15, 343
and synchronization
signals, 16
and video mapping, 38
Read-only memory (ROM),
character, 356-58, 377
Recursion, 192-93
RETURN statement, 198
RF NTSC modulator, 11
RGB transmission, 18, 380
RND function, 75
RUN command, 58

**S**

S command, 187-89
SAVE command, 20
SCREEN command, 22, 32-33,
382-83
and mode bits of Color/
Graphics Adapter, 354
and page flipping, 332-35
Screen coordinate system,
117-18
viewing transformations,
122-24
Screen display. *See* Display,
video.
SCREEN function, 304-05
Signals, video
digital vs. analog, 379-80
RS-232 standard for, 16
SIN function, 86, 101-02
SOUND command, 327
Space-filling curves, 192-96

Stacks, 239-40
STEP keyword, 65
Subroutines
to draw a bug, 261-63
function plotting, 132-34
to initialize and clear
screen, 363-64
interrupt service, 198
outline, 218
pause and title, 61-62
in space-filling curve
program, 196
special point plotting,
362-63, 366
Synchronization signals, 16-18,
346-47

**T**

TA command, 183-86
Text modes
graphics characters in, 303
high-resolution mode of,
12-14, 32
low-resolution mode of,
12-13, 32
page flipping in, 332-35
programming special,
395-98
size of video RAM in, 38-39
vertical register values in,
348
Three-dimensional (3-D)
cubes, drawing, 220-24
defined, 117
function plotting, 147-49
graphics, 141-44
house, drawing a, 149-60
painted house, drawing a,
247-49
parallel projections to 2-D,
143
rotations, 143, 417-20
Tiling, 225-37
creating new NTSC colors
with, 230-32
drawing wallpaper with,
234-35
over a previously tiled
area, 235-37
and video RAM, 225-26
Trigonometric functions, 86,
105
TTL RGB color monitor, 12
Turtle graphics, 191-92
Two-dimensional (2-D), 117

**U**

U command, 172-75
User coordinate system, 97-99,
117-18, 122-24
USR command, 21
Video chip, Motorola 6845,
340-54
and the Color/Graphics
Adapter, 356-57
horizontal registers of,
345-47
interlace mode in, 349-52
I/O ports of, 340-41
and the Monochrome
Adapter, 393-98
using registers of, 341-44
scrolling registers of,
352-54
vertical registers of, 347-52
and video frequencies,
377-78
Video RAM. *See* Random-
access memory (RAM),
video.
VIEW command, 20, 98,
118-25
SCREEN option of, 119
setting up a viewport
with, 124
Viewing transformations,
97-99, 118-25
deriving the constants of,
122-25
and the SCREEN option,
124
viewports and, 118-21
using the WINDOW and
VIEW commands, 118-22
windows and, 120-22
Viewports, 118-21

**W**

WIDTH command, 22, 33,
387-89
WINDOW command, 20, 98,
118-25
SCREEN option of, 121
setting up a window with,
124
Windows, 120-22
panning and zooming, 135
World Coordinate System. *See*
User Coordinate System.

**X**

X command, 189-91, 192

# Other Osborne/McGraw-Hill Publications

An Introduction to Microcomputers: Volume 0—The Beginner's Book, 3rd Edition
An Introduction to Microcomputers: Volume 1—Basic Concepts, 2nd Edition
Osborne 4 & 8-Bit Microprocessor Handbook
Osborne 16-Bit Microprocessor Handbook
8089 I/O Processor Handbook
CRT Controller Handbook
68000 Microprocessor Handbook
8080A/8085 Assembly Language Programming
6800 Assembly Language Programming
Z80® Assembly Language Programming
6502 Assembly Language Programming
Z8000® Assembly Language Programming
6809 Assembly Language Programming
Running Wild—The Next Industrial Revolution
The 8086 Book
PET®/CBM™ and the IEEE 488 Bus (GP1B)
PET® Personal Computer Guide
CBM™ Professional Computer Guide
Business System Buyer's Guide
Osborne CP/M® User Guide, 2nd Edition
Apple II® User's Guide
Microprocessors for Measurement and Control
Some Common BASIC Programs
Some Common BASIC Programs—Atari® Edition
Some Common BASIC Programs—TRS-80™ Level II Edition
Some Common BASIC Programs—Apple II® Edition
Some Common BASIC Programs—IBM® Personal Computer Edition
Some Common Pascal Programs
Practical BASIC Programs
Practical BASIC Programs—TRS-80™ Level II Edition
Practical BASIC Programs—Apple II® Edition
Practical BASIC Programs—IBM® Personal Computer Edition
Practical Pascal Programs
CBASIC
CBASIC™ User Guide
Science and Engineering Programs—Apple II® Edition
Interfacing to S-100/IEEE 696 Microcomputers
A User Guide to the UNIX™ System
PET® Fun and Games
Trade Secrets: How to Protect Your Ideas and Assets
Assembly Language Programming for the Apple II®
VisiCalc®: Home and Office Companion
Discover FORTH
6502 Assembly Language Subroutines
Your ATARI™ Computer
The HP-IL System
Wordstar® Made Easy, 2nd Edition
Armchair BASIC
Data Base Management Systems
The HHC™ User Guide
VIC 20™ User Guide
Z80® Assembly Language Subroutines
8080/8085 Assembly Language Subroutines
The VisiCalc® Program Made Easy
Your IBM® PC: A Guide to the IBM® Personal Computers

# COMPLETE LIST OF DISKETTE PROGRAMS FOR
## GRAPHICS PRIMER FOR THE IBM PC

The following programs are contained on the diskette:

| | | |
|---|---|---|
| HiRes Mandala | Color Boxes | Painted House |
| Character Plot | GDL — Move | Painted Background |
| Text Mode | GDL — Star | Animated Bug |
| Medium Res Color Mode | GDL — Spiral | Background-Foreground Animation |
| Lines Across Screen | GDL — Arrows | Character Font Generation |
| Rectangles — 3 Ways | GDL — Asterisk | Colored Fonts |
| Colored Boxes | GDL — Rectangles | Enlarged Characters |
| Filled Color Boxes | GDL — Arrows Turning | Iconic Operating System |
| Line Styles | GDL — Rounded Spiral | Walking Man Animation |
| Styled Disk | GDL — Spiraling Circles | Animation Strings |
| Right Triangles | GDL — Triangles | 50 Line Text Mode |
| Regular Polygons | GDL — Polygons | Color Text Scroller |
| More Polygons | Fractals — Space Filling Curve | 160 × 80 Hidden Mode |
| Circle the Easy Way | Electronic Symbols | 50 Line Monochrome Mode |
| Arcs the Hard Way | Electronic Painting | Alt Character Set Bar Graph |
| Arcs Using Circle | Colored Patterns | Alt Character Set Windows |
| Family of Ellipses | NTSC Colors | Alt Screen Designer |
| Pie Chart | Wall Paper | 3D Globe Using Windows |
| Bar Chart | Baffles | |
| 2D Function Plot | Bug | |
| 3D Function Plot | Piefill | |

## DISKETTE TIME-SAVER AVAILABLE

A diskette containing more than 70 graphics programs presented in this book is available separately. It will save you hours of time and trouble by eliminating the need for you to type in all of the listings contained in this book. Now you can get right down to what you're really interested in doing—learning all about IBM PC graphics—without having to spend time practicing your typing skills.

The single-sided, double-density diskette, containing more than 110,000 bytes of code, is compatible with DOS 1.0 and up. And, since all of the programs are provided in IBM PC BASICA source code, you can easily modify and extend them to suit your own applications.

The diskette contains programs covering the following areas:

| | | |
|---|---|---|
| Computer Art | Plotting & Line Drawing | Games |
| Computer Aided Design | Character Editing | 3D Transformations |
| Animation | Mathematics | Business Graphics |

To order your copy, write or phone:

Comprehensive Software Support
2316 Artesia Blvd., Suite B
Redondo Beach, CA 90278

213-318-2561

The price of the diskette is $29.95 (*) plus $3.00 shipping and handling charge. California residents please add 6.5% sales tax ($1.95).

MasterCard or Visa accepted.

*Price subject to change without notice.

Magnetic-surface program adaptations described above are solely the work of The Waite Group and are not a publication of Osborne/McGraw-Hill.